US Nuclear Weapons Policy after the Cold War

This book offers an in-depth examination of America's nuclear weapons policy since the end of the Cold War.

Exploring nuclear forces structure, arms control, regional planning and the weapons production complex, the volume identifies competing sets of ideas about nuclear weapons and domestic political constraints on major shifts in policy. It provides a detailed analysis of the complex evolution of policy, the factors affecting policy formulation, competing understandings of the role of nuclear weapons in US national security discourse, and the likely future direction of policy. The book argues that US policy has not proceeded in a linear, rational and internally consistent direction, and that it entered a second post-Cold War phase under President George W. Bush. However, domestic political processes and lack of political and military interest in America's nuclear forces have constrained major shifts in nuclear weapons policy.

This book will be of much interest to students of US foreign policy, nuclear proliferation, strategic studies and IR in general.

Nick Ritchie is a Post-Doctoral Research Fellow at the Department of Peace Studies, University of Bradford. He is co-author of *The Political Road to War with Iraq* (Routledge 2006).

Routledge global security studies

Series editors: Aaron Karp, Regina Karp and Terry Terriff

1 **Nuclear Proliferation and International Security**
Sverre Lodgaard and Morten Bremer Maerli

2 **Global Insurgency and the Future of Armed Conflict**
Debating fourth-generation warfare
Terry Terriff, Aaron Karp and Regina Karp

3 **Terrorism and Weapons of Mass Destruction**
Responding to the challenge
Edited by Ian Bellany

4 **Globalization and WMD Proliferation**
Edited by James A. Russell and Jim J. Wirtz

5 **Power Shifts, Strategy and War**
Declining states and international conflict
Dong Sun Lee

6 **Energy Security and Global Politics**
The militarization of resource management
Edited by Daniel Moran and James A. Russell

7 **US Nuclear Weapons Policy after the Cold War**
Russians, 'rogues' and domestic division
Nick Ritchie

US Nuclear Weapons Policy after the Cold War

Russians, 'rogues' and domestic division

Nick Ritchie

LONDON AND NEW YORK

First published 2009
by Routledge
2 Park Square, Milton Park, Abingdon, Oxfordshire OX14 4RN

Simultaneously published in the USA and Canada
by Routledge
711 Third Avenue, New York, NY 10017

First issued in paperback 2014

Routledge is an imprint of the Taylor & Francis Group, an informa business

Typeset in Times by Wearset Ltd, Boldon, Tyne and Wear

British Library Cataloguing in Publication Data
A catalogue record for this book is available from the British Library

Library of Congress Cataloging in Publication Data
A catalog record for this book has been requested

ISBN13: 978-1-138-87352-0 (pbk)
ISBN13: 978-0-415-46626-4 (hbk)

For Scarlett, a joy.

Contents

Acknowledgements

The author would like to thank his wonderful wife Sally, Professor Paul Rogers for his unswerving support, the Economic and Social Research Council for funding the doctoral research on which this book is based, the many people that facilitated the research, those that took time out of busy schedules to be interviewed, Andrew Humphrys at Taylor & Francis and the extraordinary wealth of knowledge, ideas and support at the Department of Peace Studies at Bradford University.

Acronyms

ABM	Anti-Ballistic Missile
ACDA	Arms Control and Disarmament Agency
ACI	Advanced Concepts Initiative
ACM	Advanced Cruise Missile
ALCM	Air-Launched Cruise Missile
ATSD(NBC)	Assistant to the Secretary of Defense for Nuclear, Chemical and Biological Defense Programs
BMD	Ballistic Missile Defence
C4ISR	Command, Control, Communications, Computers, Intelligence, Surveillance and Reconnaissance
CPI	Counterproliferation Initiative
CTBT	Comprehensive Test Ban Treaty
DNA	Defense Nuclear Agency
DOD	Department of Defense
DOE	Department of Energy
DSB	Defense Science Board
DSWA	Defense Special Weapons Agency
DTRA	Defense Threat Reduction Agency
GAO	General Accounting Office
GLCM	Ground Launched Cruise Missile
GPALS	Global Protection Against Limited Strikes
HDBT	Hard and Deeply Buried Target
ICBM	Intercontinental Ballistic Missile
INF	Intermediate Nuclear Forces
JCS	Joint Chiefs of Staff
LANL	Los Alamos National Laboratory
LLNL	Lawrence Livermore National Laboratory
MIRV	Multiple Independently-targetable Re-entry Vehicle
NAS	National Academy of Sciences
NMD	National Missile Defense
NNSA	National Nuclear Security Administration
NPR	Nuclear Posture Review
NPT	Nuclear Non-Proliferation Treaty

NSA	Negative Security Assurance
NSPD	National Security Presidential Directive
NSS	National Security Strategy
NWC	Nuclear Weapons Council
OSD	Office of the Secretary of Defense
PDD	Presidential Decision Directive
PLYWD	Precision Low Yield Weapon Design
PNET	Peaceful Nuclear Explosions Treaty
PNI	Presidential Nuclear Initiatives
PPBE	Programming Planning Budgeting and Execution system
QDR	Quadrennial Defense Review
RNEP	Robust Nuclear Earth Penetrator
SAC	Strategic Air Command
SALT	Strategic Arms Limitation Talks
SDI	Strategic Defense Initiative
SIOP	Single Integrated Operations Plan
SLBM	Submarine Launched Ballistic Missile
SNDV	Strategic Nuclear Delivery Vehicle
SORT	Strategic Offensive Reductions Treaty
SSBN	Ship Submersible Ballistic Nuclear (nuclear powered ballistic missile submarine)
SSP	Stockpile Stewardship Program
START	Strategic Arms Reduction Treaty
STRATCOM	Strategic Command
SWPS	Strategic Warfare Planning System
TLAM-N	Tomahawk Land Attack Missile-Nuclear
TMD	Theater Missile Defense
TTBT	Threshold Test Ban Treaty
WMD	Weapons of Mass Destruction
XON	Air Force Directorate for Nuclear and Counter-proliferation

Introduction

Deep into the post-Cold War era the perceived threats from nuclear weapons continue to dominate international security. Nuclear-fuelled hostility between India and Pakistan, North Korea's nuclear weapons programme, Iran's suspected nuclear weapons programme, modernisation of nuclear weapons by America, Britain, Russia, France and China, and the potential for acts of catastrophic nuclear terrorism regularly grab the headlines.

In the late 1960s a bargain was struck between the countries that had already acquired nuclear weapons and those that had not and enshrined in the 1968 Nuclear Non-Proliferation Treaty (NPT). At the time the five states that had already developed nuclear weapons (the nuclear weapon states (NWS): the USA, USSR, China, France and Britain), agreed to assist non-nuclear weapon states (NNWS) in exploiting civilian uses of nuclear technology. In exchange each NNWS agreed to conclude a safeguards agreement with the International Atomic Energy Agency (IAEA) to ensure that any nuclear technology acquired would not be diverted to a military programme and agreed never to acquire nuclear weapons. The NWS agreed not to provide any country with military nuclear technology or actual nuclear weapons and agreed to pursue negotiations to end the Cold War nuclear arms race and achieve nuclear disarmament.

The NPT therefore provided a framework to order the nuclear weapons world and prevent a disorderly and destabilising spread of nuclear weapons. The NPT is the only agreement in which the NWS agree to work towards nuclear disarmament and in which the nearly all the other countries agree not to develop or acquire nuclear weapons of their own. Only Israel, India, Pakistan and North Korea remain outside the NPT, all of which possess nuclear weapons. Discussion about nuclear proliferation, nuclear disarmament and the nuclear policies and actions of NWS generally takes place within the context of the NPT and the bargain struck in 1968.

Nuclear weapons in general and America's nuclear weapons policy in particular evoke passionate responses. For some, nuclear weapons are ethically and morally abhorrent. As nuclear weapons proliferate so too do the risks of a crisis escalating into a devastating nuclear conflict through accident or miscalculation. There is a powerful sense that America is the only state with the military, economic and political power to reduce the salience of nuclear weapons in international security and move the international community towards greater control and reduction of nuclear arsenals. Since America played a lead role in developing the NPT and imposing a degree of order on an increasingly fractious nuclear world it is incumbent upon America to lead the international community towards nuclear disarmament.[1] For others, nuclear weapons and nuclear deterrence have brought stability to major power relations by making the costs of large-scale war unthinkably high. They cannot be disinvented and it is essential that America prevent so-called 'rogue' states and terrorist organisations from acquiring nuclear weapons and other weapons of mass destruction (WMD) whilst maintaining its own credible nuclear forces to deter regional 'rogue' aggression.

In the early 1990s the prospect of rapid progress towards very low levels of nuclear armaments seemed a realistic goal, but nearly two decades since the end of the Cold War arms race nuclear weapons remain an enduring feature of American national security strategy. As the House of Representatives Republican Policy Committee stated in 2003, 'nuclear weapons and deterrence remain as relevant today as they were at the height of the Cold War'.[2]

In the late 1990s and early 2000s a series of events made it clear that American nuclear weapons policy was in transition with no easily discernible long-term sense of direction. The post-Cold War nuclear arms reduction process with Russia ground to a halt in Clinton's second term and the Republican-controlled Senate refused to ratify the Comprehensive Test Ban Treaty (CTBT) in 1999 for party political as well as genuine national security reasons. The Bush administration's 2001 Nuclear Posture Review appeared to take nuclear weapons policy in a new and potentially destabilising direction and its withdrawal from the Anti-Ballistic Missile (ABM) treaty in 2002 evoked a chorus of disapproval and dire predictions of a new global nuclear arms race from the arms control community. Important questions began to be asked about the long-term direction of nuclear weapons policy, the role of nuclear weapons in national security strategy, the continuing relevance of the bargain struck in 1968 and the nuclear arms control process with Russia.

The primary aim of this book is to discern that sense of direction through a detailed examination of America's nuclear weapons policy since the end of the Cold War from 1990 to 2007. It aims to provide a thorough understanding of the complex evolution of policy, the factors affecting policy formulation, the role and perception of nuclear weapons in American national security discourse, and the likely medium- to long-term direction of policy.

The book is based on a detailed and systematic analysis of official statements and reports and analysis of the wider discourse on nuclear weapons policy. It employs a broad definition of policy to include declaratory nuclear policy, operational nuclear policy, strategic threat perceptions, force structure, the nuclear weapons production complex, and nuclear arms control. Use of a broad definition of nuclear weapons policy is supported by General George Lee Butler who, as head of US Strategic Command, stated in 1993 that nuclear weapons policy should be informed by 'a rigorous assessment of the complex interaction among force posture, arms control entitlements and constraints, funding requirements and targeting directives'.[3] It is also supported by Leon Sloss who argued in 2001 that the subjects of nuclear deterrence, missile defence, nuclear weapons, the production complex, and arms control could no longer be considered separately but should be addressed within a framework that examines the 'total nuclear posture'.[4]

The research draws on a variety of sources including public statements by a range of senior officials, influential members of Congress and military leaders involved in different aspects of nuclear weapons policy; official reports from a number of government departments and agencies; and academic analysis and opinion from leading journals, books, and reports by independent research organisations. These are complemented by a series of off-the-record interviews conducted in 2005 and 2006 with current or former government officials and independent experts that have been involved in American nuclear weapons policy-making or have studied it in detail for many years. Despite the broad scope of the research it does not examine American policy explicitly covering non-strategic nuclear forces, American nuclear defence commitments to allies, nuclear non-proliferation policy, non-nuclear arms control policies, or missile defence policy and plans. In addition it does not examine in detail the nuclear and WMD policies and programmes of other states.

American nuclear weapons policy has often been explained as a necessary and rational response to the imperatives of an anarchic international political system. This reflects the 'realist' school of international political theory that has dominated American academia and policy-making since the Second World War. This book takes a different approach by adopting a critical analytical framework. It argues that both material factors, such as weapons, and non-material factors, such as identities, interests, collectively held beliefs, the meanings assigned to issues and events, and shared understandings of what constitutes appropriate behaviour, must be examined in order to provide as complete an understanding of an issue as possible. It argues that what constitutes the accepted 'reality' of an issue is generally a social construction. This 'reality' is produced and reproduced through the actions and interpretations of those involved in the issue. In this context the relationship between knowledge and political power is crucial, in particular the power to shape the debate around an issue by including and therefore legitimising particular ideas, concepts, interests, collective understandings and meanings and excluding others.

This approach views 'normal' understandings, meanings, and ways of interpreting events and behaving appropriately as generally a function of the political power of a particular set of ideas that has been institutionalised into political power structures. It argues that a full understanding of an issue requires critical questioning of what is often taken for granted as a natural order. In this context the idea of a 'correct' nuclear weapons policy as an objective, rational response to an external and objectively knowable international environment is rejected. It is instead something that is constructed and reproduced through collective understandings and practices.[5]

When examining American nuclear weapons policy it is therefore important to problematise the dominant interpretations of the concepts on which nuclear weapons policy is founded and the meanings of nuclear weapons for policy-makers. This requires detailed examination of the nuclear weapons policy discourse and the dominant sets of ideas within that discourse. This involves exploring different interpretations of national security interests and identity in the context of nuclear weapons; understandings of nuclear deterrence, arms control and strategic threats; and the meanings assigned to material factors such as Russia's nuclear arsenal and the state of the nuclear weapons production complex. It also requires examination of the domestic political context in which the discourse is located by exploring the bureaucratic practices, procedures, and rules that affect nuclear weapons policy.

This book therefore does not attempt to 'prove' the validity of one particular version of nuclear weapons policy as the single, correct and rational approach. The aim, instead, is to understand how and why nuclear weapons policy has evolved in the manner that it has and its likely future direction.

Three core propositions emerge from this research. First, policy has not proceeded in a linear, rational and internally consistent direction since the end of the Cold War. It has instead been subject to the relative political power of competing and often contradictory sets of ideas about nuclear weapons policy whose effect on policy is a function of domestic political processes. Second, policy has entered a second post-Cold War phase under President George W. Bush. A series of shifts in different aspects of nuclear weapons policy throughout the 1990s were institutionalised and supplemented under George W. Bush to constitute this new phase. Third, domestic political processes have constrained major shifts in nuclear weapons policy since the end of the Cold War. Bureaucratic politics and organisational processes have deeply affected policy outcomes, the institutionalisation of competing sets of ideas about nuclear weapons policy, and the salience of nuclear weapons policy in American national security strategy as a whole.

The book begins with a concise description of the processes and people involved in making nuclear weapons policy in the Department of Defense, Congress and armed services. The second chapter provides a brief analysis of American nuclear weapons policy as the Cold War drew to a close in the late 1980s.

Chapter 3 examines policy under George H. W. Bush, in particular nuclear arms reductions under the START process and Presidential Nuclear Initiatives; scepticism about Soviet/Russian political and economic reforms and nuclear modernisation; confrontation with Congress on nuclear testing and force modernisation; major problems with the nuclear weapons production complex; and the beginning of a reorientation of nuclear weapons policy away from the Soviet Union/Russia and towards the emerging class of WMD-armed 'rogue' states. Chapter 4 examines policy under Bill Clinton, including the considerable problems with the START process, the outcomes of the 1994 Nuclear Posture Review, modernisation and consolidation of strategic nuclear forces, the fierce debate over a comprehensive nuclear test ban, nuclear planning for regional

WMD-armed adversaries and continuing problems with the production complex. Chapter 5 examines policy under George W. Bush, including the 2001 Nuclear Posture Review, a decisive shift towards regional nuclear planning, the 2002 Moscow Treaty and 'new strategic framework' with Russia, and the controversial Reliable Replacement Warhead and Complex-2030 programmes to address enduring concerns about the production complex and the massive nuclear warhead life extension programme.

Chapter 6 identifies the key post-Cold War trends that have defined the evolution of policy. Chapter 7 identifies and examines three competing nuclear weapons 'policies', or idea sets, within the nuclear weapons policy discourse that reflect key decisions, trends and debates. They are described as: *Management* – managing the drawdown of Cold War nuclear forces; *Restraint* – responding to nuclear proliferation through progress in nuclear arms control and steps towards nuclear disarmament; and *War-fighting* – responding to nuclear proliferation by re-orienting Cold War nuclear weapons policy to a post-Cold War regional war-fighting policy. Chapter 8 places this framework of competing sets of ideas in the context of domestic politics, in particular the constraints on policy change that stem from domestic political factors. These include the absence of a broad political consensus on nuclear weapons policy and a major reduction in senior-level political and military interest in American nuclear weapons over the post-Cold War period. The final chapter presents a number of policy conclusions and discusses what the future is likely to hold for America's nuclear weapons.

1 The policy-making process

Before commencing a detailed study of America's nuclear weapons policy it is necessary to outline the agencies and organisations involved. The primary centres of policy-making are the White House, the Department of Defense (DOD), the armed services, the Department of Energy (DOE), and Congress. The national security policy-making process can be usefully conceived as a number of policy rings in which a range of individuals, organisations and agencies are situated.[1] This applies equally to nuclear weapons policy.

Actors involved in nuclear weapons policy

At the centre of the nuclear weapons policy-making process stand the White House, in particular the office of the president, and the National Security Council. The president is the ultimate decision-maker but in practice is rarely involved in nuclear weapons-related issues.[2] The National Security Council is the President's principal forum for considering national security and foreign policy matters with senior national security advisers and cabinet members. It often plays a coordinating role as a broker of interagency agreements through both formal and informal processes.[3] Like the presidency, the National Security Council has no regular role in nuclear weapons policy but it will be involved in major issues such as the START process with Russia, the nuclear test ban, missile defence policy, and requirements stemming from Congressional legislation. The NSC staff may examine issues affecting nuclear weapons policy initiated by an agency or department, the president or the NSC itself.[4]

The next policy ring encompasses executive departments and agencies. The two primary government organisations involved in nuclear weapons policy are DOE and DOD. DOE is responsible for administering the nuclear weapons laboratories and the manufacture of nuclear warheads as well as the production of nuclear materials required for the weapons programme. Within DOE responsibility lies with the semi-autonomous National Nuclear Security Administration established in 2000. NNSA is functionally divided into three areas: Defense Programs, Nuclear Nonproliferation and Naval Reactors. Matters relating to the nuclear stockpile fall under the remit of Defense Programs. It is responsible for the safety, security and reliability of the stockpile through the science-based

Stockpile Stewardship Program established in 1993. DOE's three national nuclear laboratories – Lawrence Livermore National Laboratory, Sandia National Laboratory and Los Alamos National Laboratory – also have an influential voice in nuclear weapons policy.

The Office of the Secretary of Defense (OSD) is responsible with the Joint Chiefs of Staff (JCS) and US Strategic Command (STRATCOM) for policy development, budgetary and programming decisions and implementing policy through detailed nuclear employment, deployment and sustainment plans. Within DOD the Assistant Secretary of Defense for International Security Policy (ASD(ISP)) within OSD oversees nuclear weapons policy, amongst many other areas of responsibility. The Under Secretary of Defense for Acquisitions Technology and Logistics (USD(AT&L)), the Assistant to the Secretary of Defense for Nuclear, Chemical and Biological Defense Programs (ATSD NCB), and the joint DOE-DOD Nuclear Weapons Council (NWC) also have a crucial role.

The Nuclear Weapons Council is responsible for preparing the Nuclear Weapons Stockpile Memorandum (see below); developing nuclear weapons stockpile options costs; coordinating programming and budget matters pertaining to nuclear weapons programmes between DOD and DOE; examining safety, security and control issues for existing weapons and any new weapon programmes; providing broad guidance regarding priorities for research on nuclear weapons; and coordinating and approving activities conducted by the DOE for the study, development, production, and retirement of nuclear warheads.[5] It comprises USD(AT&L) as chair, a senior representative appointed by the Secretary of Energy, and Vice Chairman of the JCS. ATSD NCB (formerly the Assistant to the Secretary of Defense for Atomic Energy) is the Council's staff director and principal staff assistant to the Secretary of Defense for nuclear weapons-related matters.[6]

Within the armed services STRATCOM, the Air Force Directorate for Nuclear and Counter-proliferation (XON), the Navy Strategic Systems Programs (SSP) command and Submarine Warfare Division, and the J5 Strategic Plans and Policy directorate of the Joint Staff are centrally involved in advising civilian policy-makers on nuclear weapons issues, maintaining nuclear forces and preparing operational plans for use of nuclear weapons. STRATCOM coordinates with the supporting Services to monitor the day-to-day status of the stockpile. It sponsors a senior-level Strategic Advisory Group to provide assessments of current and future issues related to the nuclear stockpile and associated systems. Each nuclear weapon type in the stockpile also has a Project Officer Group (POG) to which weapon system specialists are assigned. The POGs are responsible for monitoring the state of the stockpile and submitting recommendations for improving stockpile safety, reliability or security to the NWC Standing and Safety Committee.[7] The Navy's SLBM and non-deployed nuclear-armed Tomahawk Land-Attack Missiles (TLAM/N) are overseen by its SSP command. The Air Force's XON directorate, established in 1997, oversees the Air Force's ICBM and air-launched nuclear forces and represents the Air Force on the NWC Standing and Safety Committee.[8]

The Defense Threat Reduction Agency (DTRA) is also involved in nuclear weapons issues. Its official mission is to reduce the WMD threat to America through a number of programmes that include supporting the nuclear arsenal.[9] Under its 'combat support' mission DTRA reports on the current status of American nuclear weapons, provides independent assessments of nuclear safety, security and reliability to OSD, NNSA, JCS and the armed services and runs DOD's Defense Nuclear Weapons School. The Director of DTRA reports to USD(AT&L) and also serves as Director of STRATCOM's Center to Combat Weapons of Mass Destruction.

On issues of nuclear weapons policy the Secretary and Deputy Secretary will likely consult the Under Secretary of Defense for Policy (USD(Pol)) and the assistant secretaries in that office, and if necessary the Comptroller on budget issues. The Chairman of the JCS and his colleagues, relevant service chiefs of staff, and STRATCOM may also be consulted.[10] Nevertheless, it is the Secretary of Defense who is ultimately responsible for nuclear weapons policy and planning, not the JCS, unified commands or individual services.[11] It is the budget and programming process under the Secretary's direction that sets priorities and resources for competing missions and elements of the armed services (discussed further below).[12]

Within DOD and the services nuclear weapons policy has been guided by what is often referred to as the nuclear weapons policy community. This community generally comprises those civilian and military officials within the Pentagon bureaucracy responsible for nuclear policy, planning and targeting strategy in the policy office of the Office of the Secretary of Defense, STRATCOM and the Joint Staff. It also includes members of Congress and scholars at think-tanks close to government that have involved themselves in nuclear weapons policy issues. A small cadre of civilian and military officials have been extensively involved in crafting operational and declaratory nuclear weapons policy for a number of successive administrations from Reagan onwards. This subset at the heart of the nuclear weapons policy community is often referred to colloquially as the 'nuclear priesthood'.

Four formal processes guide nuclear weapons targeting policy and planning, nuclear weapons stockpile management, nuclear force sustainment and nuclear weapons safety and security. Broad guidance for nuclear weapons targeting policy and planning is issued by the White House to the Secretary of Defense through periodic presidential directives, such as a National Security Decision Directive. OSD staff, the Joint Staff, and STRATCOM staff use this national guidance to develop the targeting requirements and plans which underpin nuclear deterrence policy.[13] The Office of the Secretary of Defense (OSD) issues a policy guidance document for the employment of nuclear weapons (the NUWEP, or Nuclear Weapons Employment Plan) which establishes planning assumptions, attack options and targeting objectives. The Chairman of the JCS develops more detailed guidance that is incorporated into Annex C (Nuclear) of the Joint Strategic Capabilities Plan (now called the Nuclear Supplement) by the Strategic Plans and Policy Directorate (J5) of the Joint Staff. This guidance was used to produce the Single Integrated Operational Plan or SIOP until 2003. Since 2003 the Chairman's guidance has been used by combatant commanders and Service Chiefs to prepare and coordinate a family of operational and contingency strike plans to deploy and employ nuclear weapons. OPLAN 8044 is the successor to the SIOP and still contains its major pre-planned strike options.[14] Civilian oversight of the targeting process lies with OSD's Office for International Security Policy.[15] Civilian reviews focus on the overall consistency of the proposed plan with the basic policy guidance and the responsiveness of military plans to strategy and current conditions. Detailed planning for specific employment plans, including the range of targets, timing, weapon allocation, damage expectancy and so on, is left to military staffs.[16]

The nuclear stockpile is managed according to a formal annual process. Each year a Nuclear Weapons Stockpile Memorandum (NWSM) or Nuclear Weapons Stockpile Plan (NWSP) is produced by the Nuclear Weapons Council. The plan establishes DOD's requirements for the mix and quantities of nuclear weapons and materials and the total number of warheads in the stockpile. It aims to balance military requirements with budgets and limits imposed by the production complex and is broadly consistent with requirements set out in successive Nuclear Posture Reviews and strategic arms control agreements. The plan is jointly developed by OSD, DOE and JCS. The Council oversees its implementation and ensures national policy is being efficiently executed.[17] It is supported by a Standing and Safety Committee for inter-department coordination on sustainment of the stockpile. Policy for the sustainment of nuclear forces is overseen by USD(Pol).[18] Plans for sustaining the nuclear force are developed by DTRA in conjunction with STRATCOM and the armed services. The first Nuclear Mission Management Plan (NMMP) was produced in 2001.[19] Its purpose is to provide a 'comprehensive, integrated DOD roadmap for the sustainment and viability of US nuclear forces, personnel and infrastructure'.[20]

Since the end of nuclear testing and the signing of the Comprehensive Test Ban Treaty (CTBT) by President Clinton in 1996, the Nuclear Weapons Council has also directed annual assessments of the safety and reliability of the nuclear weapons stockpile based on Safeguard F of Clinton's August 1997 CTBT policy statement. STRATCOM also provides an independent assessment covering the same topics to the Secretary of Defense.[21] The Secretaries of Defense and Energy – advised by the NWC, the directors of the nuclear weapons laboratories, and STRATCOM – report annually to the President to certify to a high degree of confidence whether the nuclear stockpile is safe and reliable. This process is embodied in domestic law.[22]

The State Department also exerts influence on nuclear weapons policy since it has primary responsibility for negotiating arms control and disarmament treaties. Nuclear arms control and disarmament issues fall under the remit of the Under Secretary of State for Arms Control and International Security having previously been the responsibility of the Arms Control and Disarmament Agency (ACDA) for most of the 1990s. The intelligence community also has a strong role to play in its assessments of the nuclear capabilities of potential adversaries and other strategic targets against which nuclear weapons could be employed. The intelligence community is made up of many different agencies from a variety of government departments, including DOD. These include the Central Intelligence Agency, the Defence Intelligence Agency, the National Security Agency, the State Department's Bureau of Intelligence and Research, the President's Foreign Intelligence Advisory Board, and the intelligence elements of the military services.

Outside the executive lies Congress in the next policy ring. Congress consists of the Senate, House of Representatives and judiciary. The sharing of constitutional powers to shape national security policy has resulted in 'built-in dynamic tensions' between an increasingly activist Congress and the executive.[23] This can be seen in post-Cold War nuclear weapons policy in which Congress has frequently played an important role. Congress exerts influence over national security policy in a number of ways. The most important constitutional Congressional power is the power of the purse: no money can be spent by an administration unless authorised by Congress. Its committees annually scrutinise the administration's defence spending requests, including those relating to nuclear weapons. Key committees are the House and the Senate Armed Services Committees and Appropriations Committees and the Senate and House committees on energy that also cover DOE's nuclear weapons activities and budgets. These committees can remove funding for a programme or increase funding if a programme becomes a Congressional priority. The main influence of Congress is negative by denying funding for particular programmes as opposed to taking a positive lead on policy development.[24] The Senate Foreign Affairs Committee also has the power to approve, vote down or amend treaties affecting nuclear weapons policy.

Congress can also request policy statements and full-scale reviews on broad national security and specific nuclear weapons issues that can push DOD or DOE in one direction or another and hold administration decisions to account. The Senate and House Armed Services Committees, for example, require annual reporting from the Nuclear Weapons Council as a key tool to enable 'Congress to perform effective oversight of our nation's nuclear weapons'.[25] Congress can also restructure policy-making processes by reorganising executive departments and agencies. It can also mandate that specific agencies and offices be consulted on particular issues and decisions.[26] Individual members of Congress can influence policy through membership of committees that have a direct bearing on nuclear policy, or through amendments on the floor of the House or Senate that can change committee policy with sufficient support when the committees' bills are debated and voted on.[27]

Nevertheless, the impact of Congress is generally limited and it must be regarded as a junior partner in nuclear weapons policy-making. The administration dominates nuclear weapons policy by setting the agenda through its control over information and expertise and relatively few members of Congress have considerable knowledge of and interest in nuclear weapons issues. Consensus has rarely been reached in either the Senate or House on nuclear weapons policy issues. In fact the multiplicity of interests and decentralisation of power in Congress has generally precluded agreement on national security priorities other than through the budget process.[28] Congress' ability to assess and evaluate alternatives for all of the programmes in DOD's massive budget request is limited. The burden rests with Congress to demonstrate that a DOD programme should *not* be funded. DOD can repeatedly bring programmes back to Congress in the next fiscal year if they are denied sufficient funding and try to increase support for a beleaguered programme.[29] Congress' role has therefore been primarily reactive and it tends to only deal with nuclear weapons policy issues when there are significant fiscal, policy or management concerns.[30]

Outside government lie arms contractors and advocacy organisations. The influence of arms contractors such as Boeing and Lockheed Martin on nuclear weapons policy has diminished considerably with the end of the Cold War, with no new nuclear weapons and nuclear delivery systems in production. Nevertheless the power of the defence industry and links between the defence industry and DOD are strong and it is common for executives from the defence industries to take up senior positions in the DOD and vice versa. Think-tanks and NGOs continue to advocate different positions on nuclear weapons policy with the public, military, DOD, White House and Congress. Think-tanks with strong links to government can be an important source of new ideas that can later be brought into government. Members of the advisory boards and boards of directors of conservative think-tanks can often revolve in and out of government.[31]

The annual nuclear policy budgetary process

DOD budgets and its budgetary system, the Planning, Programming and Budgeting Execution system (PPBE), have a major impact on policy by setting mission priorities, planning requirements and resource allocation.[32] PPBE is 'the primary vehicle for identifying mission requirements and translating them into budget and personnel resources required to accomplish that mission'.[33] The budget process for each fiscal year is a complex, two-year major bureaucratic exercise involving competing organisational interests and compromise deals. Budget priorities can shape national security strategy and military posture and have a lasting impact. Nuclear weapons policy is part of this process.

The process formally involves publication of a National Security Strategy (NSS) by the NSC from which the Joint Staff develop a National Military Strategy (NMS) following a Joint Strategy review process. The NSS and NMS and specific recommendations from the Chairman of the JCS are used by OSD to produce the Strategic Planning Guidance (SPG), which serves as the Pentagon's primary planning document and has replaced the strategy and policy sections of the former Defense Planning Guidance. Every four years a Quadrennial Defense Review is also produced. The SPG together with OSD's Joint Programming Guidance (JPG) is used by the services and defence agencies to produce their own programmes through Program Objective Memoranda (POMs) in a 'lengthy, complex and contentious' process in which 'internal organisations force choices between readiness, force structure, personnel, military construction, research and development, and procurement'.[34] POMs are reviewed in OSD and differences resolved by the Defense Resources Board. On final agreement the DOD budget is put together by the OSD Comptroller as the Future Years Defense Program (FYDP) six-year planning document. The services and agencies then repackage their POMs from the FYDP into the appropriations categories used by Congress. OSD submits the final budget (the Budget Estimate Submission, BES) to the Office of Management and Budget (OMB) in the White House. OMB reviews DOD's submission and then the administration's full budget is submitted to Congress.[35]

The 'power of the purse' is employed every year through the congressional budget process. Each fiscal year the Senate and House Budget Committees pass a Budget Resolution that establishes the overall ceiling for spending by DOD and other agencies. After the White House has submitted its annual budget request to Congress, the Senate and House Armed Services Committees and their subcommittees 'mark up' the Defense Authorization Bill based on DOD's budget proposal. Government and non-government witnesses are called to be questioned by the committees and their subcommittees about the substance of the administration's proposals through a number of hearings on a range of issues. These hearings are often used to challenge administration policy, strategy or ongoing initiatives.[36] The authorisation bills establish spending ceilings for individual DOD programmes, including those relating to nuclear weapons. The committee version of the bill will ultimately be voted on by the entire body and then sent to conference with the other legislative chamber. A Conference Committee is subsequently established to work through differences between the House and Senate bills. After the authorisation process the Senate and House Appropriations Committees' subcommittees for defence spending approve and release funding to pay for programmes. The Senate and House Energy and Water Appropriations subcommittees provide funding for DOE's nuclear weapons programmes and activities. Appropriations bills can amend authorisation bills in some circumstances.

Once both houses have marked up their appropriations bills a conference is scheduled to reconcile differences between them. The bills are then passed by Congress and signed into law by the president. If the president objects to either the authorisation or the appropriations bills the bills can be vetoed and returned to Congress until agreement can be reached on contentious issues. Individual members of Congress can submit amendments to the bills on the floor of the House or Senate that can change committee policy with sufficient support when the committees' bills are being debated and voted on.[37] Nuclear weapons policy-making, implementation and oversight is therefore a complex process involving many actors, processes, interests and priorities.

2 American nuclear weapons policy at the end of the Cold War

America's post-Cold War nuclear weapons policy did not evolve from a slate wiped clean with the demise of the Soviet Union. It has instead developed from the particular historical context of 45 years of political, intellectual and technological change during the Cold War.

The history of American nuclear weapons policy is therefore intimately linked to the long confrontation with the Soviet Union. The early Cold War was characterised by acute post-war military insecurity exacerbated by ideological conflict between Washington and Moscow, which President Truman described before Congress as an adversarial struggle between American and Soviet ways of life.[1] Soon after the Second World War Truman abandoned all hope of a cooperative superpower relationship and concluded that confrontation was inevitable. He came to view the Soviet Union as a ruthless, expansionist power that had to be militarily contained.[2] This 'containment' policy ushered in a 'Cold War' and defined America's long-term post-war relationship with Moscow.[3]

America tested the first nuclear weapon in July 1945 and used two nuclear bombs to devastate the Japanese cities of Hiroshima and Nagasaki the following month, ending the war in the Pacific. The new technology of nuclear weapons was seen to offer a solution to America's post-war insecurity and the perceived inevitability of conflict with Moscow based on the emerging concept of nuclear deterrence. Early nuclear deterrence theory argued that nuclear weapons were so uniquely destructive that there could be no defence against them. Nuclear weapons would inevitably proliferate but states could guard against nuclear attack if they had the ability to retaliate in kind. The purpose of nuclear forces was therefore to avert, rather than win, future wars by deterring an adversary from launching a nuclear first-strike. Deterrence theory argued that many hundreds, if not thousands, of nuclear bombs might be needed to ensure that enough could be successfully delivered in a conflict.[4] America saw little choice but to rely on a nuclear defence policy given the imbalance in conventional forces in Moscow's favour, and nuclear weapons were soon ordained as a key component of America's response to the new Cold War confrontation.[5] The deployment of a large nuclear arsenal was advocated in order to maintain decisive military superiority over the Soviet Union and thereby deter a surprise first-strike.

Embracing the theory of nuclear deterrence came at the expense of a competing argument embodied by Secretary of War Henry L. Stimson. Stimson argued that America should negotiate with the Soviet Union and Britain to control and limit nuclear arms because of their destabilising effect on US–Soviet relations and the dangerous possibility of a devastating American or Soviet first-strike.[6] Truman explored the diplomatic approach and a proposal known as the Baruch plan was presented to the United Nations in 1946. This was rejected by the Soviet Union since it allowed America to retain its atomic weapons for the foreseeable future.[7] America locked itself into a nuclear strategy when it responded to the first Soviet nuclear test in 1949 not by reducing reliance on nuclear weapons and seeking control of the technology, but by moving to develop the far more powerful and destructive hydrogen bomb, which was successfully tested in 1952.[8]

Nuclear strategy evolved through a number of permutations during the Cold War and nuclear forces and strategy options expanded rapidly through improvements in accuracy, weight and yield, mass production technologies and growth in potential targets through improved intelligence. New weapons included advanced long-range bombers, nuclear cruise missiles, submarine-launched ballistic missiles (SLBMs), Intercontinental Ballistic Missiles (ICBMs), and a host of tactical nuclear weapons for land, sea and air.

In the 1950s President Eisenhower articulated a strategy of 'massive retaliation' that put nuclear policy on the offensive. The strategy declared that America must be able to inflict enormous retaliatory damage on the Soviet Union in response to Soviet aggression in order to counter any temptation Moscow may have had to launch a surprise nuclear attack. It also required continued nuclear superiority at a time when Moscow seemed intent on building a nuclear missile force to deliver a disarming first-strike.[9] The credibility of the massive retaliation strategy was called into question when the Soviet Union developed the capacity to retaliate in kind. These concerns led to a strategy of 'flexible response'. The concept of 'escalation dominance' was at the heart of the new strategy, which sought to develop the ability to control the escalation of a conflict by signalling intent to move to the next level of destructive warfare if the enemy did not relent.[10] It was also based on the capability to target and destroy Soviet conventional and nuclear forces, rather than cities, based on the concept of 'counter-force' targeting. The concept of 'damage limitation' was also introduced based on the idea that America should be able to quickly destroy Soviet forces and other strategic targets in a retaliatory second-strike after absorbing a surprise Soviet nuclear attack. This in turn required a large, diverse nuclear force and nuclear superiority.[11]

The counter-force/damage limitation strategy provided no inherent limit to the size of the nuclear arsenal because it was proportional to the size of the Soviet nuclear force and other Soviet targets that would inevitably grow in response to America's nuclear expansion. Critics argued that this weakened deterrence and would encourage a perpetual arms race to retain the superiority required by the counter-force rationale. A strategy of 'assured destruction' was therefore developed in the 1960s under President Johnson to set limits on the level of destruction considered necessary to deter a Soviet attack and the number of nuclear weapons needed to achieve it. This evolved into a strategy of mutual assured destruction (MAD) as the inevitability of Soviet nuclear parity was accepted.[12] MAD rested on an acceptance of the necessity of mutual vulnerability to nuclear attack for strategic stability. This led to the SALT treaty (formally known as the Interim Agreement on Certain Measures with Respect to the Limitation of Strategic Offensive Arms) and Anti-Ballistic Missile (ABM) treaty in the early 1970s period of détente. These were designed to place a ceiling (albeit a high one) on the deployment of strategic nuclear delivery vehicles and to keep missile defence systems designed to shoot down incoming enemy nuclear missiles to a minimum. Extensive deployment of ABM systems would, it was argued, threaten strategic stability by undermining mutual vulnerability to nuclear attack.[13] The SALT agreement was quickly superseded by the wide-scale deployment of missiles with multiple warheads known as MIRVs (multiple independently-targetable re-entry vehicles). It was now the number of warheads that counted rather than the number of missiles.

The doctrine of mutual assured destruction was challenged as the détente process faltered in the mid-1970s. Critics were fearful that if countries started to view the Soviet Union as superior to America then the global balance of power would shift in Moscow's favour as it surged ahead with a massive ICBM programme. This led to Nixon's strategy of 'essential equivalence' based on maintaining a counter-force nuclear arsenal at least as capable as the Soviet Union's, as well as a range of pre-planned limited nuclear strike options.[14]

President Carter reverted to a 'countervailing strategy' when his predilection for détente was overwhelmed by external events in the late 1970s. This emphasised a counter-force doctrine to fight a protracted nuclear war to deny the Soviets victory at any stage of a conflict by threatening selective and large nuclear attacks and ensuring that the costs of aggression would always be judged too high in Moscow.[15] The new strategy was supported by a major counter-force arms procurement programme focused on reducing the perceived vulnerability of American ICBMs to a Soviet first-strike and recapturing strategic superiority.[16] This included the MX Peacekeeper MIRVed ICBM and Trident II D5 MIRVed SLBM.

Nuclear strategy shifted under Reagan from 'countervailing' to 'prevailing': a nuanced distinction that based strategy on fighting and winning a long, protracted nuclear war.[17] The credibility of American nuclear deterrent threats required a superior nuclear force capable of responding to a wide range of attacks and able to absorb a Soviet first-strike and then threaten greater losses on the Soviet Union than those inflicted on America. Without the superiority needed for 'escalation dominance' the Soviet Union would be more aggressive and force political concessions. By allowing the Soviet Union to attain nuclear parity, the government argued, America had effectively disarmed itself.[18] Reagan was still prepared to negotiate, but only from a position of military strength. To regain nuclear superiority Reagan planned to accelerate the Trident II programme and B-2 stealth bomber programme, deploy mobile ICBMs, including making the MX mobile, modernise tactical nuclear forces and modernise the nuclear command and control infrastructure.[19]

The counter-force build-up met strong resistance in Congress where funding was curtailed and dependent on progress in arms control with Moscow. Reagan therefore looked to escape the dilemma of nuclear vulnerability and the reality of mutual assured destruction through the 'Star Wars' Strategic Defense Initiative (SDI).[20] The aim of SDI was to both destroy incoming Soviet nuclear warheads and increase economic pressure on the Soviet Union as it struggled to compete in a new defensive technological arms race. As SDI faltered in the mid-1980s Reagan eventually reverted to arms control to escape the nuclear dilemma, facilitated by the emergence of Mikhail Gorbachev as a new, young Soviet leader. This resulted in the 1987 Intermediate Nuclear Forces Treaty (INF) and the foundation of the Strategic Arms Reduction Treaty (START).[21] Gorbachev and Reagan also came remarkably close to agreeing to eliminate all ballistic missiles by 1996 at the 1986 Reykjavik summit following Gorbachev's proposal to eliminate all nuclear forces by 2000.[22]

Cold War nuclear weapons policy was characterised by two broad sets of competing ideas about the role of nuclear weapons, the meaning of nuclear deterrence, the utility of negotiations and arms control, and the intentions of the Soviet leadership. The first maintained that nuclear strategy should be one of deterrence based on the threat of nuclear retaliation in response to a Soviet attack since the *only* role for nuclear weapons was to deter the Soviet Union from using theirs.[23] This required an invulnerable second-strike force, which SLBMs could provide, and assumed that nuclear parity would be an essential fact of the superpower relationship. The credibility of the nuclear threat lay in the fundamental reality of mutual assured destruction based on the impossibility of controlling or winning a nuclear war in any meaningful sense. It was not explicitly assumed that the Soviet Union was preparing to fight and win a nuclear war. Instead Moscow was considered aggressive but cautious. Furthermore, it was increasingly accepted that the arms race operated according to an action-reaction cycle that could only be controlled through mutual restraint. Value was seen in strategic arms control and a certain degree of cooperation based on recognition of a mutual interest in capping the nuclear arms race and stabilising the strategic relationship. This approach was encapsulated by McGeorge Bundy, adviser to Presidents Kennedy and Johnson on national security, who argued that the deterrent effect of nuclear weapons was based on their existence alone and that the nuances of location, capability and strategy were essentially irrelevant.[24]

The second set of ideas maintained that America should not accept or assume nuclear parity but should maintain nuclear superiority. This was based on three assumptions. First, that the Soviet Union was an aggressive, expansionist state actively developing a disarming nuclear first-strike capability to destroy America's nuclear arsenal and coerce Washington during political crises. Second, America's nuclear build-up and efforts to retain superiority were a defensive and necessary response to an overwhelming Soviet threat. Third, that strategic superiority was an essential political tool that enabled more convincing demonstrations of national resolve.[25] Credibility rested not on targeting cities but on targeting the enemy's forces through a counter-force doctrine and preparing to wage limited nuclear wars in response to any form of Soviet aggression. It was argued that the use of nuclear weapons in a conflict with the Soviet Union could be controlled and would not necessarily result in 'mutual assured destruction'. The action-reaction model of the nuclear arms race was rejected and advocacy of missile defences to complement strategic nuclear deterrence was firm. This required a large, diverse nuclear force and nuclear superiority to control the escalation of nuclear conflict, prevail at any level of conflict, and avoid self-deterrence. Only by demonstrating the resolve to fight and win a nuclear war could Soviet aggression be deterred. Less value was seen in arms control negotiations with such a menacing adversary, and rapprochement was firmly aligned with weakness.

The second set of ideas appears to have dominated American Cold War strategic thinking. Nuclear weapons were the currency of Cold War military *and* political power and at the heart of a militarised (and increasingly nuclearised) national security paradigm based on containing the Soviet Union. A powerful link between material nuclear power and broader political power and influence in relations between the two adversaries and other countries was widely accepted.[26] The search for a credible nuclear threat based on nuclear superiority and later missile defences was a vital driver of nuclear strategy and force structure. Policy was dominated by efforts to retain the unique military advantage provided by Washington's initial nuclear monopoly, efforts to design credible options to fight, control and win limited nuclear wars, and a retaliatory nuclear capability requiring a massive, diverse nuclear arsenal. Arms control remained secondary to the arms build-up and there was little trust in Soviet arms control intentions, even with the emergence of Gorbachev. The Soviet Union was consistently portrayed as an aggressive, expansionist enemy capable of launching a devastating surprise nuclear attack and intent on political coercion through strategic military superiority. Periods of détente had little effect on this mindset and suspicion of Soviet motives for engagement remained strong.[27] The opportunities to control the nuclear arms race and reduce nuclear arsenals in the late 1940s, the 1970s détente process and the 1986 Reykjavik summit were not taken.

'Peace through strength' was the dominant mantra: only through nuclear and conventional military superiority could America negotiate successfully with Moscow to reduce the threat posed by the Soviet Union and avoid political coercion. It is in this context that nuclear weapons strategies and force deployments were regularly portrayed as a defensive response to Soviet actions. The end of the Cold War largely on American terms was seen to reinforce and validate this set of ideas and the role of nuclear weapons, nuclear deterrence and arms control it represented. The view that America won the Cold War by successfully pursuing a 'peace through strength' strategy had important implications for nuclear weapons policy after the collapse of the Soviet Union.

3 Nuclear weapons policy under George H. W. Bush

This book employs a broad definition of nuclear weapons policy to encompass nuclear force structure, the nuclear weapons production complex that supports it, operational targeting doctrine, and the political decisions and rationales that have affected and to an extent defined these elements of policy. It is based on a large body of research on the evolution of America's nuclear weapons policy from 1990 to 2007 that has examined statements by leading policy-makers and legislators and official reports from the Department of Defense, Department of Energy, White House, State Department, Strategic Command, and Congress, together with examination of material changes to nuclear forces, the nuclear weapons production complex, and policy decisions.

Key decisions

The first step towards understanding the evolution of America's nuclear weapons policy after the Cold War involves identifying the key decisions that have constituted that evolution. These decisions do not reflect a political consensus or one particular world view. It is therefore important to examine the debates around them in order to fully understand how and why policy has evolved in the manner that it has. Without these specific decisions policy could have been quite different as there are a number of important variables, including nuclear force size and structure, the development of new weapons, the roles assigned to nuclear forces and the scope of operational plans, the pace of nuclear force modernisation and reduction and the state of the nuclear weapons production complex. Fifteen key decisions are identified and the following three chapters examine these decisions and the debates around them under the presidencies of George H. W. Bush, Bill Clinton and George W. Bush. The decisions are:

1. The 1991 ratification of the Strategic Arms Reduction Treaty (START) to cut the number of deployed strategic nuclear warheads to 6,000 over a ten-year period.
2. The 1991 and 1992 Presidential Nuclear Initiatives (PNIs) in which America unilaterally withdrew the majority of its forward-deployed tactical

nuclear weapons and cancelled or curtailed a number of nuclear programmes, actions that were reciprocated by the Soviet Union/Russia.

3 The Establishment of US Strategic Command (STRATCOM) in 1992 that brought the nuclear planning of the individual armed services under one command for the first time and led to the modernisation of nuclear war planning and targeting infrastructure and the development of an adaptive nuclear planning capability through the 1990s.
4 The 1992 congressional testing moratorium and the successful negotiation of a zero-yield Comprehensive Test Ban Treaty (CTBT) in 1996.
5 The formulation of the Complex-21 plan to consolidate the decaying nuclear weapons production complex and sustain it for the long term.
6 The 1993 congressional ban on research and development of new low-yield nuclear weapons.
7 The signing of START II in 1994 to reduce deployed strategic nuclear warheads to 3,500 each by 2007 and end the deployment of missiles with multiple nuclear warheads that were considered strategically destabilising.
8 The establishment of the multi-billion dollar Stockpile Stewardship Program (SSP) in 1993 to maintain the safety and reliability of the nuclear stockpile in an era without nuclear testing and without new weapons development and production.
9 The 'lead but hedge' strategy set out in the 1994 Nuclear Posture Review, asserting leadership in reducing forces whilst hedging against a resurgent Russia and strategic uncertainty by keeping a large reserve (a 'hedge') of nuclear warheads and modernising the strategic triad of ICBMs, SLBMs and long-range bombers.
10 The postural changes set out in the 1997 Presidential Decision Directive 60 (PDD-60) that revised President Reagan's 1981 nuclear planning guidance to facilitate a reduction in deployed force levels to between 2,500–2,000 warheads under the prospective START III framework.
11 The 1997 US-Russian agreements at Helsinki that firmly linked entry into force of START II and negotiation of START III to the continued viability of the ABM treaty.
12 The force structure and targeting decisions set out in the 2001 Nuclear Posture Review that established a new triad of offensive strike systems, defences, and a revitalised defence infrastructure and placed considerable emphasis on targeting regional WMD-armed adversaries.
13 The 2002 Moscow Treaty (SORT) to reduce Russian and American deployed strategic nuclear warheads to between 1,700 and 2,200 within ten years.
14 The formation of a new STRATCOM in 2002 and its development of Global Strike capabilities.
15 The 2005/2006 Reliable Replacement Warhead and Complex-2030 plans to consolidate and modernise the nuclear weapons production complex and the nuclear arsenal.

Nuclear arms control

Nuclear weapons policy underwent important changes following the collapse of the Soviet Union and the end of the Cold War and the nuclear arms race. Six of the key decisions identified were taken under George H. W. Bush: the signing of START I; the signing of START II; the PNIs; the Complex-21 plan; the establishment of STRATCOM; and the imposition of a nuclear testing moratorium by Congress. Nuclear weapons policy also began to shift away from the Soviet Union/Russia and towards perceived threats from Third World states armed with weapons of mass destruction (WMD) and ballistic missiles.

America's nuclear force structure came to be guided by arms control processes and an activist Democratic-controlled Congress as the unifying threat from the Soviet Union receded. The White House did not articulate a new strategic nuclear vision but insisted that America should cautiously reduce but modernise its strategic nuclear triad through the START process.

The first START agreement was signed in July 1991 by Presidents Bush and Gorbachev. Both sides agreed to reduce deployed (rather than total) strategic nuclear weapons to 6,000 'accountable' warheads over a ten-year period with further restrictions on delivery vehicles and intrusive verification measures. This included no more than 1,600 Strategic Nuclear Delivery Vehicles (SNDVs), 4,900 ballistic missile warheads, and 1,540 warheads on 154 'heavy' intercontinental ballistic missiles (ICBMs) for the Soviet Union.[1] Ratification of the treaty was complicated by the collapse of the Soviet Union five months later, which left its nuclear arsenal dispersed amongst Russia, Kazakhstan, Belarus and Ukraine. Both Bush and Russian President Boris Yeltsin were determined to ensure that all Soviet nuclear weapons would be placed under Russian control and transferred to Russian territory so that no new nuclear weapon states emerged from the wreckage of the Soviet empire. This was formalised in the May 1992 Lisbon Protocol to the treaty. START finally entered into force in December 1994 after difficult negotiations with Ukraine.[2] It was successfully completed in December 2001 and is due to expire in 2009.[3]

START enjoyed widespread but not unanimous support from the military and Congress.[4] After the collapse of the Soviet Union there were calls in Congress and from defence intellectuals to renegotiate the treaty in order to lift some restrictions on American nuclear forces whilst further restricting Russia. Distrust of Russia remained strong amongst START's opponents who argued that Russia could not be trusted to comply with arms control agreements, that Russia was still building nuclear weapons, and that START would increase Russia's strategic superiority.[5]

Others argued that the treaty did not go far enough primarily because the administration had refused to agree to deeper cuts and that START had little impact on new weapon developments because it only formalised routine schedules for withdrawing obsolete weapons whilst limiting the introduction of new ones.[6] In 1989 Presidents Reagan and Gorbachev indicated that START would cut strategic nuclear forces by 50 per cent.[7] The figure of 6,000 'accountable' warheads signified a major reduction in deployed nuclear weapons but the *actual* number of permitted warheads was just short of 8,000 with more in reserve. In fact Strategic Air Command (SAC) estimated that 11,700 warheads could be retained under START's accounting rules, though not all deployed. This represented only a 10 per cent reduction in strategic nuclear warheads following the end of the Cold War.[8]

After signing START there was considerable domestic pressure for Bush to go further with a follow-on treaty.[9] In June 1992 the House of Representatives passed the Nuclear Weapons Reduction Act that called for 'immediate agreement with Russia to bilaterally reduce strategic nuclear weapons levels to between 2,500 and 4,700' and eventually reduce to between 1,000 and 2,000.[10] Washington and Moscow had in fact signalled their intention to negotiate a second treaty before START was finalised.[11] START II was finally signed in January 1993 having been delayed by entry into force of START I. It cut the number of deployed strategic nuclear warheads to between 3,000 and 3,500 by 2003. This included a complete ban on MIRVed ICBMs and other limits including a limit of 1,700–1,750 SLBM warheads. It was widely seen as completing the work of START I and enjoyed widespread congressional support.[12]

The START treaties served a number of purposes. The administration's formal rationale was to ensure and enhance deterrence and 'strategic stability' through cooperative management of a nuclear reductions process. Strategic stability was defined as improving the survivability of nuclear forces, reducing incentives for a first-strike, deploying strategic defences to complement offensive forces, parallel reductions in nuclear forces to ensure parity, modernisation of nuclear forces to ensure a 'credible' deterrent, and generally moving away from a relationship of assured destruction to full cooperation, rather than just dampened competition.[13] According to Senator Sam Nunn, chair of the powerful Senate Armed Services Committee, the goal was to achieve stability at lower levels of nuclear weaponry rather than reductions for reductions' sake.[14]

The second purpose was to allow America to maintain as flexible a triad of strategic nuclear forces as possible and limit those weapon programmes in which the USSR enjoyed an advantage, such as mobile and heavy MIRVed ICBMs.[15] Washington argued that the elimination of MIRVed ICBMs on both sides would massively reduce any remaining incentives for a nuclear first-strike during a crisis. It did not, however, want to trade elimination of Soviet/Russian MIRVed ICBMs for elimination of American MIRVed SLBMs. This was criticised by Yeltsin since it would leave America in a far stronger position, with Russia having to dismantle the backbone of its strategic nuclear force (its MIRVed ICBMs) whilst leaving the backbone of America's force (its SLBM arsenal) largely intact.[16] Achieving this long-standing goal of 'de-MIRVing' the Soviet ICBM fleet was portrayed as a sign of a new cooperative relationship with Russia that was also reflected in the 1992 Charter for American-Russian Partnership and Friendship.[17]

The third purpose was to establish a formal, structured, verifiable, transparent and legally binding set of obligations on the Soviet/Russian leadership.[18] The fourth was to cut the cost of the nuclear weapons programme based on an 'urgent requirement to bring Government spending and revenues more nearly into balance', according to Vice Chairman of the JCS, Admiral David Jeremiah.[19] The final purpose was to reinforce the Nuclear Non-Proliferation Treaty (NPT) by encouraging swift accession by Kazakhstan, Ukraine and Belarus.[20]

The START process was complemented by a series of major US–Soviet/Russian unilateral withdrawals, cancellations and reductions of nuclear forces in 1991 and 1992. In the first of these Presidential Nuclear Initiatives in September 1991 the White House announced the withdrawal and planned destruction of all 1,300 nuclear artillery shells and 850 short-range Lance missile warheads deployed abroad; withdrawal of all tactical nuclear weapons from surface ships, submarines and land based naval aircraft; de-alerting of all strategic bombers and ICBMs scheduled for deactivation under the START agreement; cancellation of the MX Peacekeeper ICBM rail garrison programme, the programme to make the planned Midgetman small ICBM mobile and a new short-range attack missile (SRAM-II); and proposed an agreement to eliminate all MIRVed ICBMs, later reached under START II. The second initiative in January 1992 cancelled the entire small ICBM programme, any further production of the Trident II W-88 warhead, and any further production of the Advanced Cruise Missile; stated that America would eliminate all MX ICBMs in exchange for the elimination of all Russian MIRVed ICBMs; reduced the number of deployed SLBM warheads by a third below planned START levels to balance Russian ICBM cuts; and reoriented most heavy bombers to conventional roles.[21]

The PNIs were influenced by a number of factors. The reduced risk of conflict in Europe and Asia with the end of the Cold War led to a major 'clean sheet' defence review to reassess American and NATO nuclear requirements.[22] Some of these systems, such as the SRAM-II, were also experiencing technical difficulties that undermined their continuation.[23] Major financial pressure from Congress to reduce defence spending, reduce the federal budget deficit and divert resources to domestic programmes also undermined the scope and necessity of some of the planned new strategic nuclear weapon programmes.[24] Senator Al Gore, for example, stated that the PNIs were a 'race to beat Congress to the punch, since some of the President's key concessions to the Soviets – such as cancellation of the rail garrison MX and the SRAM-T – were virtually assured already for budgetary reasons'.[25] From a strategic perspective the administration judged that the PNIs would be matched by withdrawal and subsequently centralised control of Soviet tactical and strategic weapons as the Soviet Union began to unravel following the failed coup in August 1991.[26] Finally, a number of the strategic and tactical systems that were withdrawn, such as the Polaris C3 SLBM, were redundant and had either been scheduled for destruction or had been superseded by more advanced systems.[27]

The PNIs were therefore a pragmatic response to geo-political, financial and technical realities rather than a sweeping away of Cold War doctrine as some argued.[28] America took advantage of the dramatic changes in the Soviet Union and Europe to reduce the threat of nuclear conflict, enhance strategic stability, significantly reduce the cost of nuclear forces and the size of the defence budget, address technical challenges affecting some nuclear systems, facilitate political and military change in the USSR, and accommodate international and domestic agitation for nuclear force reductions.[29]

Nuclear forces

Nuclear force structure was guided by two primary issues: scepticism in government and Congress about Soviet/Russian nuclear weapons policy during the early 1990s, and the emergence of a consensus in DOD on a post-Cold War nuclear force structure immediately after fall of the Soviet Union.

Scepticism over Soviet/Russian nuclear weapons policy was powerful as Soviet modernisation of its silo-based and rail-mobile ICBMs, Blackjack and Bear-H bombers, Delta IV and Typhoon SSBNs continued with follow-on systems in development.[30] Critics such as Senator Strom Thurmond argued in 1990 that America was struggling to keep pace with this vigorous nuclear modernisation programme.[31] Sceptics also claimed that Moscow could not be trusted to comply with arms control agreements, that it was still intent on gaining missile superiority, that Soviet nuclear modernisation programmes were insulated from the Soviet economic crisis and that Soviet nuclear policy had not changed at all since the end of the Cold War.[32] As the head of SAC, George Lee Butler, stated: '...the Soviet military establishment has yet to remove its overcoat. It remains largely insulated from the harsh economic climate affecting all other segments of Soviet life, in that modernization programs for strategic nuclear forces appear to continue unabated.'[33] As a result of Moscow's 'unabated modernisation of all components of their strategic offensive forces' Washington should, according to Secretary of the Air Force Donald Rice, base its own nuclear posture on new Soviet capabilities rather than Gorbachev's stated intentions.[34]

This induced considerable caution into the Bush administration's nuclear weapons policy amid concerns that Gorbachev's peace offensive might be a calculated strategy to disarm the West.[35] The administration argued vociferously that there would be no deep cuts and that strategic nuclear parity was vital to national security and a key component of strategic stability that underpinned the START process. According to Chairman of the JCS General Colin Powell 'our strategic forces must be modernised. They must be modernised to continue to deter a modernised Soviet force that is getting better with each passing day'.[36] Nuclear weapons would also continue to play a vital role in national security well into the future based on the belief that 'peace through strength' had won the Cold War. This was reflected in the official rationales for the START treaties and statements by a number of policy-makers. John Tuck, head of Defense Programs at DOE, for example, stated in 1990 that America must 'maintain a credible nuclear deterrent for the foreseeable future. This lesson has been realized from 45 years of peace through strength, and we must not lose sight of it'.[37]

Immediately after the Cold War it is reported that radical arms control measures were discussed at senior levels within SAC, and serious consideration was given to eliminating the ICBM force, de-mating warheads from ballistic missiles and keeping SSBNs in port.[38] Nevertheless, in 1991, shortly after the signing of the START treaty, SAC completed a review of nuclear force levels called the Phoenix Study. This was followed by a second review in November 1992 on force structure options through to the year 2000 under START II by the new Strategic Command. STRATCOM was established in June 1992 to replace SAC and it brought the nuclear planning of the individual armed services under one command for the first time and provided a single point of authority for strategic forces.[39] Both studies accepted that nuclear forces had to be reduced but recommended maintaining a modernised, flexible, diverse and survivable strategic nuclear triad, retaining a large reserve force of nuclear weapons as a hedge against future Soviet/Russian intentions, and maintaining a nuclear umbrella for allies, including nuclear weapons in Europe.[40] This was 'the first unanimously agreed to position on strategic nuclear force projections in American defense history' according to STRATCOM.[41]

Calls to eliminate the ICBM capability and move to a dyad of nuclear forces were dismissed because the triad had 'proven' its worth in the Cold War.[42] Its 'synergism' and the degree to which it complicated Soviet nuclear attack plans was highly valued and, according to Gottemoeller, a dyad was not politically viable since neither the Air Force nor the Navy were willing to reduce their share of the nuclear mission.[43] Modernisation of strategic counter-force capabilities would still enable America to cover the full set of Soviet targets even if Cold War levels of nuclear forces were cut in half and fulfil Reagan's countervailing nuclear doctrine that was still in place.[44]

Strategic modernisation for a 'credible' post-Cold War nuclear deterrent initially included procuring 75 B-2 bombers, a rail-mobile MX Peacekeeper ICBM programme, a mobile small 'Midgetman' ICBM programme, a full complement of Trident II (D5) SLBMs for 24 Ohio-class SSBNs, and 1,000 Advanced Cruise Missiles (ACMs).[45] Maintaining the capability to reconstitute nuclear forces should Soviet/Russian reforms fail and the Cold War return was also pivotal to the new defence strategy set out by the JCS and DOD in 1990–1991.[46] This would eventually be formalised as a policy of 'hedging' in the 1994 Nuclear Posture Review under President Clinton.

Modernisation had many supporters in Congress where suspicion of Soviet nuclear force modernisation was strong and American strategic modernisation was deemed an essential part of the START process and crucial to national security.[47] There was also fierce criticism and significant pressure to cut defence spending and terminate the nuclear arms race. Congressional critics were no longer willing to support major nuclear force modernisation in exchange for arms control goals as they had in the past. They considered major modernisation unnecessary and lambasted the administration's initial reluctance to terminate any nuclear modernisation programmes in its fiscal year 1991 budget request.[48] They were supported by CIA Director Robert Gates who argued that most or all

Soviet plans for Soviet strategic offensive force modernisation would probably be abandoned given internal difficulties and 'rapid dissipation of tensions with the West'.[49] A 1991 National Academy of Sciences report also found that even if the Soviet Union reverted to a confrontational authoritarian regime it would likely be too preoccupied with internal problems to engage in external aggression.[50]

Congressional pressure was reflected in the two PNIs; in limiting the B-2 bomber programme to 20 planes from the 132 originally envisaged; eliminating funding to make the MX Peacekeeper ICBM rail-mobile, later followed by termination of the small ICBM programme and a decision to extend the service life of the Minuteman III ICBM instead; a reduced order of only 460 ACMs; and termination of the Ohio-class SSBN programme at 18 rather than 24 submarines.[51] The administration was therefore forced to adjust its definition of force requirements necessary for 'strategic stability' and a 'credible' nuclear deterrent that had previously required new mobile ICBMs and a large B-2 fleet.[52]

After START I and II, the PNIs, the force structure consensus that emerged through SAC and STRATCOM studies, and the effect of congressional budgetary pressure the Bush administration continued with only two nuclear weapons systems and two delivery platforms: the Trident II (D5) SLBM (deployed in 1990) and its delivery platform the Ohio-class SSBN (13 were deployed by 1992), the Advanced Cruise Missile, and the B-2 stealth bomber.[53] Towards the end of the Bush presidency America deployed an estimated 7,900 strategic nuclear warheads with a total stockpile of 16,750. This was down from approximately 21,000 warheads at the end of the Cold War in 1989–1990, of which almost 13,000 were deployed strategic warheads.[54]

As part of the modernisation effort STRATCOM also initiated a long-term programme in 1992 to modernise strategic nuclear planning by developing a flexible, global Strategic War Planning System (SWPS). This would establish so-called adaptive planning capabilities to enable future planning systems to respond in real time to changes in policy, threat and force structure.[55] It envisaged rapid nuclear targeting for a range of potential adversaries and much quicker wholesale revision of attack plans.[56] The process was initiated to streamline the bloated Single Integrated Operational Plan (SIOP) that had seen the number of targets cut from 12,500 in 1990 to 2,500 in 1992.[57]

'Rogue' states and nuclear planning

Immediately after the Cold War DOD and JCS began to examine the role of nuclear forces in the context of the proliferation of nuclear, biological and chemical weapons to the Third World, particularly to despotic or 'rogue' states. In 1995 Mandelbaum defined 'rogue' states as Iraq, North Korea, Iran and perhaps Syria, Libya and Algeria:

> Each is influenced by an ideology – Marxism, Leninism, Islamic fundamentalism or Arab socialism – with anti-Western and anti-American features. All suffered politically and militarily from the collapse of the

> Soviet Union, which, by depriving them of a patron and protector … gave added impetus to their nuclear ambitions. None is a fully fledged democracy.[58]

It was argued that this new breed of 'rogue' states would attempt to use WMD to deter America from taking action against them on issues affecting its vital interests.[59] The defence establishment accepted in the very early 1990s that whilst the Soviet/Russian nuclear threat would continue to drive nuclear policy, the threat from WMD-armed 'rogue' states would have a growing impact.[60] In fact these states were soon considered the primary strategic threat to national security.[61] The Bush administration and many outside the government argued that America needed to respond by reorienting its Cold War military forces designed to fight the USSR to regional missions, an argument that was reinforced by Iraq's invasion of Kuwait in August 1990.[62] As President Bush said after the Gulf War:

> The Soviet bear may be dead, but there are a lot of wolves in the woods … you've got all kinds of people trying to acquire nuclear weapons. And who knows where the next challenge will come to the security of the United States.[63]

Prominent members of Congress also characterised these WMD-armed 'rogue' states as *the* new strategic threat. Senator John Kerry, for example, argued in 1992 that a new containment policy was needed, 'directed not against a particular nation or ideology, but against a more diffuse and intensifying danger – the danger that nuclear, chemical and biological weapons, and ballistic missiles to propel them, could pass into the hands of rogue-states or terrorists'.[64] Senator Carl Levin, later chair of the Senate Armed Services Committee, dramatically insisted that 'a few nuclear weapons in the hands of a Khaddafi or a terrorist group would pose a greater danger to us than the 30,000 nuclear weapons in Gorbachev's arsenal did'.[65]

The discovery of the advanced and clandestine nature of Iraq's nuclear, chemical and biological weapons programmes after the 1991 Gulf War reinforced calls for a reorientation of nuclear forces against the kind of threat posed by Saddam Hussein in Iraq and Kim Il Sung in North Korea, where a hostile and clandestine nuclear weapons programme was also suspected. In 1990 SAC established the Deterrence Study Group to examine options for nuclear operations against such states. The subsequent Reed Report, after chair and former Secretary of the Air Force Thomas C. Reed, recommended that nuclear weapons be retargeted at any potential adversary and that a nuclear expeditionary force be established to counter emerging nuclear arsenals in 'rogue' states. Prior to this, WMD proliferation rarely featured in nuclear doctrine.[66] The report also argued that the current nuclear arsenal of high-yield, multiple warhead strategic nuclear weapons was unsuited to deterring such states, that new low-yield nuclear weapons may be required and that policy on the use of nuclear weapons in response to a chemical, biological or conventional attack should remain ambiguous.[67]

In June 1990 Secretary of Defense Dick Cheney reportedly stated that the proliferation of WMD was sufficient reason for maintaining a large nuclear arsenal.[68] After the Gulf War he issued a new and classified Nuclear Weapons Employment Policy (NUWEP) that formally tasked the military with planning nuclear operations against potential nuclear proliferators.[69] The 1991 National Military Strategy of the United States, 1991 JCS Military Net Assessment report, the 1992 DOD Annual Report, and the 1992 JCS Joint Strategic Capabilities Plan all reportedly highlighted the growing threat from WMD-armed Third World states and the need to retarget nuclear weapons to these countries.[70] By 1993 the role of nuclear forces in deterring and if necessary destroying 'rogue' WMD arsenals was formally established in the 1993 JCS Doctrine for Joint Nuclear Operations.[71] Kristensen argues that the absence of new White House nuclear policy guidance after the Cold War allowed nuclear contingency planning against emerging WMD threats to become policy by default.[72]

Critics in Congress objected to the expansion of the role of nuclear weapons to target Third World states, with some arguing that the Gulf War had demonstrated the irrelevance of America's nuclear weapons.[73] This was supported by Chairman of the JCS General Colin Powell and National Security Advisor General Brent Scowcroft who state in their memoirs that use of nuclear weapons against Iraq was ruled out from the very beginning, despite veiled threats delivered by Secretary of State James Baker to use them in response to Iraqi use of WMD.[74] Senator Biden, chair of the Senate Judiciary Committee and later chair of the Senate Foreign Relations Committee, was 'troubled that our defense intellectuals are now feverishly searching for new rationales for nuclear weapons' and argued that preservation of a large nuclear force directed against 'newly inflated Third World threats for which nuclear weapons are totally irrelevant' would undermine the nuclear reduction processes with Russia.[75] Representative Stark also argued that expanding nuclear deterrent threats to 'terrorist regimes like Iraq and North Korea' was not credible and would only increase incentives to acquire nuclear weapons.[76]

The issue of missile defence was closely linked to post-Cold War strategic nuclear force reductions, the perceived threat from WMD-armed 'rogue' states, and the credibility of American nuclear deterrent threats. CIA director William Webster warned in 1990 that between 15 and 20 developing nations would possess ballistic missile capabilities by 2000 and that at least three of them would have long-range ballistic missiles.[77] Following the Gulf War it was argued that missile defences would not only offer protection against the Soviet Union, but against the likes of Iraq, Iran and Libya who might not be deterred by America's massive nuclear force.[78] Some went further and argued that deployment of the Global Protection Against Limited Strikes (GPALS) system would deter Third World hostile regimes from developing ballistic missile programmes altogether.[79]

Reagan's SDI programme was scaled down with the end of the Cold War and major constraints on the defence budget and re-branded GPALS.[80] It still envisaged thousands of interceptor missiles at multiple sites to provide a nationwide defence against ballistic missiles together with a global space-based element.[81] Deployment of ballistic missile defences was seen as part of the START arms reduction process and a decisive move away from a nuclear strategy of mutual assured destruction and towards a more defensive posture. The principal barrier to this was the 1972 ABM treaty that prohibited nationwide defences.[82] The administration wanted to modify the treaty and work with the Soviet Union/Russia to deploy an extensive missile defence system and both Gorbachev and Yeltsin appeared receptive.[83]

Many in Congress insisted that America should only proceed with further nuclear reductions if extensive missile defences were deployed to enhance deterrence and the ABM treaty was renegotiated or abrogated.[84] Others argued for limited ground-based and theatre missile defences and continued adherence to the ABM treaty and took steps to limit GPALS.[85] Consensus was reached in the 1991 Missile Defense Act that directed the White House to deploy a treaty-compliant system by 1996 whilst continuing research into a non-treaty compliant missile defence system and negotiating an amended ABM treaty with Moscow.[86] Nevertheless, early cooperative endeavours to negotiate a new treaty regime evaporated following the dissolution of the Soviet Union.[87]

The nuclear weapons production complex

Three issues had a major impact on the nuclear weapons production complex following the end of the Cold War: the deterioration of the complex infrastructure; efforts to develop a new range of low-yield nuclear weapons; and the divisive issue of nuclear testing.

At the end of the Cold War the nuclear weapons production complex was crumbling. Many sites were heavily polluted with radioactive contamination, many buildings dated back to the 1940s and 1950s and major parts of the complex were simply worn out after manufacturing some 60,000 nuclear weapons and retiring some 40,000.[88] Under legal, budgetary and congressional pressure the complex was forced to shift its focus from large scale nuclear weapons production to clean-up and downsizing as safety, security and environmental problems caught up with it.[89]

A number of sites had to be closed, new projects abandoned, and some key capabilities lost. These included the Rocky Flats plutonium production plant shut down in 1989 for severe breach of health and environmental laws terminating the ability to produce plutonium pits for nuclear warheads; the Savannah River Site that produced tritium gas for nuclear warheads; and the plutonium separation plants at the Hanford Reservation site. Plans to build a new plutonium refining facility and a Special Nuclear Materials Laboratory were also abandoned.[90]

DOE subsequently conducted a major study to reconfigure the complex. It was submitted to Congress in February 1991 and became known as Complex-

21. It recommended significant downsizing to make the future complex smaller, less diverse and less expensive to operate in order to sustain the nuclear arsenal until the middle of the twenty-first century.[91] Implementing the Complex-21 plan would be long and difficult. It was estimated that it would take at least 12 years to relocate the capabilities performed at the Rocky Flats Plant.[92] The START treaties and PNIs also placed additional emphasis on weapons dismantlement on top of the consolidation and clean-up of the complex.[93]

The problems affecting the complex, particularly the closure of Rocky Flats, severely limited ongoing nuclear weapon programme requirements that still required thousands of new warheads even as the Cold War ended.[94] In fact DOE had planned to produce a total of 3,500 warheads through to 1995, including the high-yield W88 warhead for the Trident II (D5) SLBM, the W80-1 Advanced Cruise Missile warhead and the B61 gravity bomb.[95]

To some this represented a real threat to American national security since a renovated and fully functioning production complex was needed to respond to current and emerging nuclear threats.[96] If the complex deteriorated further America would effectively be disarming itself if it could no longer produce nuclear weapons or nuclear weapons materials, particularly since the Soviet Union/Russia retained a full range of nuclear weapons production capabilities.[97] Others argued that a comprehensive nuclear weapons complex was no longer required since old weapons could be recycled, no more plutonium was required and the START process would bring nuclear stockpiles to much lower levels.[98]

As the new doctrine of nuclear deterrence against WMD-armed 'rogue' states evolved, so too did arguments for new types of nuclear weapons to fulfil its requirements. In late 1991 two senior weapons analysts at the Los Alamos National Laboratory argued that current nuclear forces were too powerful for the threat to use them against the likes of Saddam Hussein to be taken seriously. They argued that a series of new low-yield nuclear weapons should be developed. These included a 'micronuke' with a yield of ten tons for destroying airfields and underground targets with an earth-penetrating capability; a 100 ton 'mini-nuke' for anti-ballistic missiles to destroy enemy missiles that might be armed with a nuclear, chemical or biological warhead, a 1,000 ton (1 kt) 'tiny nuke' for enemy forces and tank formations; and exotic technology warheads, such as directed-energy warheads.[99] These arguments reflected the conclusions of the Reed Report that argued for a similar 'mini-nuke' capability. In 1991 the Air Force established a project to explore a Precision Low-Yield Weapons Design (PLYWD) to target WMD-armed 'rogue' states. The PLYWD project was never fully developed, but the idea of new low-yield warheads and earth-penetrating weapons to target 'rogue' states remained, in part because of the difficulty experienced in destroying hardened and deeply buried targets and mobile Scud missile launchers in the Gulf War.[100] New nuclear weapon programmes would also retain expertise at and funding for the weapons laboratories.[101]

The issue of nuclear testing was particularly contentious. The Bush administration and its supporters in Congress were adamant that full nuclear testing was essential and that as long as America deployed nuclear weapons it would need to test them.[102] Ending testing would undermine confidence in the reliability of the stockpile as warheads aged and forces were reduced, and reduce the credibility of America's nuclear commitment to its allies.[103] Testing was needed to incorporate the latest safety and security features into new weapons and to avoid future technological surprise by retaining the capability and expertise to design, develop, test and deploy new warheads.[104] Computing capabilities were also judged insufficient to replace physical testing.[105] The end of the Cold War had also facilitated the ratification of two Cold War treaties to limit nuclear testing: the 1974 Threshold Test Ban Treaty (TTBT) and the 1976 Peaceful Nuclear Explosions Treaty (PNET). The Bush administration argued that it would be prudent to wait ten years to assess the verification of these two treaties before eventually negotiating a Comprehensive Test Ban Treaty (CTBT) to ban all further tests.[106]

Many in Congress disagreed with the administration and argued that a CTBT was required immediately in order to stabilise the nuclear arms race, support the arms reduction process, and reinforce the NPT.[107] Nuclear testing should cease for a year and be followed by a limited programme of tests solely to ensure the reliability and safety of nuclear weapons rather than the development of new warheads. A test moratorium would support those of France and the Soviet Union and lead to a global moratorium.[108] By the end of 1990 both houses of Congress expressed clear support for a CTBT.[109]

Congressional pressure mounted despite a new, much more limited testing policy announced by the administration in July 1992.[110] As Senator George Mitchell insisted:

> It is time to face the facts: This administration will not willingly pursue further limits on testing. It must be required to take a pause, reassess its testing program, and understand how serious Congress – and the rest of the world – is about ending nuclear testing ... a U.S. commitment to ending testing is a critical tool in the effort against nuclear proliferation.[111]

The debate culminated in the passage of the Nuclear Testing Moratorium Act in August 1992 despite major opposition from the White House. The Act imposed a nine-month nuclear testing moratorium, limited testing of no more than six per year after the moratorium with a view to negotiating a CTBT by September 1996.[112]

With the production complex focused on downsizing and major opposition to testing and designing new nuclear weapons, the problem of retaining nuclear weapons expertise in an era with little or no new nuclear weapons developments and no nuclear testing was set to become a major issue.[113]

Conclusion

President George H. W. Bush took a number of steps to alter nuclear weapons policy to reflect the geo-political changes ushered in by the end of the Cold War.

These changes represented a pragmatic adjustment of Cold War nuclear policy, rather than a wholesale revision of the principles of nuclear deterrence and the role and composition of nuclear forces. The administration's approach was largely based on a continuation of Cold War practices founded on a belief in 'peace through strength', suspicion of Soviet/Russian nuclear weapons modernisation programmes, uncertainty about the future success of Soviet/Russian reforms despite proclamations of a new strategic relationship, and retention of Reagan's 'countervailing' nuclear doctrine. Policy remained committed to a Cold War definition of strategic stability based on strategic parity with the Soviet Union/Russia, arms control to limit or ban strategic weapon systems that could be used for a surprise first-strike ('destabilising' weapons) and force structures, operational plans, and targeting options that allowed prompt, flexible launch on warning against a massive target base of Soviet/Russian strategic assets.

This induced significant caution into nuclear policy and the nuclear arms reduction process. The START treaties and PNIs were designed to enhance strategic stability, reduce the costs of nuclear defence and manage the drawdown of nuclear forces in a predictable and verifiable manner. Reductions for reductions' sake were never part of the administration's stated objectives. The risks associated with reductions envisaged through the START process were countered through strategic force modernisation, retention of a strategic triad, a nuclear 'hedge' force, continued nuclear testing, modernisation of the nuclear targeting infrastructure, and extensive but perhaps cooperative missile defence deployments to move away from a strategic relationship with the Soviet Union/Russia characterised by mutual assured destruction. The consensus that emerged very soon after the Cold War through SAC's and the new STRATCOM's force structure studies laid the path for nuclear force structure and supporting rationales for much of the 1990s. STRATCOM also initiated an adaptive planning targeting process to increase the flexibility of targeting plans and their rate of production.

Nuclear doctrine also began to shift inexorably towards targeting the new threat from WMD-armed 'rogue' states. The shift began almost simultaneously with the end of the Cold War and the Reed Report, which focused in particular on Iraq, Iran and North Korea. The 1991 Gulf War reinforced the new orientation, although no new presidential guidance for nuclear weapons policy was issued to formally sanction the shift. This new focus also required missile defences, new types of nuclear weapons to ensure a 'credible' nuclear deterrent threat, and new targeting plans. In August 1990 President Bush made a speech in Aspen that encapsulated his strategic security strategy. His administration would improve stability through arms control, modernised nuclear weapon systems, limited missile defences and enhanced conventional capabilities; promote democratic change in the Soviet Union whilst discouraging any attempt to secure military advantage; and prevent the proliferation of WMD to hostile countries or groups and deter states seeking regional dominance.[114]

An activist Democratic-controlled Congress clamouring for a reduced defence budget and an end to the nuclear arms race took a number of steps to reorient nuclear policy and forced the administration to adjust its concept of strategic stability. Tactical and strategic nuclear weapon modernisation programmes were severely limited, nuclear testing was halted, GPALS was curtailed, and the administration was forced to clean up the deteriorating nuclear weapons production complex and end the production of fissile materials and tritium. Nevertheless, the White House successfully resisted pressure to make very deep cuts in nuclear forces.[115]

The production complex was in severe trouble at the end of the Cold War. New facilities were cancelled, and existing ones closed. The financial squeeze on defence spending and nuclear weapons and support infrastructure compounded the problems of sustaining the ageing and contaminated complex. Cancellation of new facilities and closure of existing sites with the loss of key production capabilities led to fears of 'structural disarmament' that DOE's Complex-21 plan was designed to address.

Nuclear weapons policy in its broadest sense therefore shifted immediately after the end of the Cold War based on a number of drivers: a combination of White House and congressional desire to reduce the salience of nuclear weapons and reduce the threat of global nuclear conflict in response to the dramatic geopolitical changes in Europe; congressional pressure to reduce defence budgets; a commitment to bilateral nuclear arms control; continuation of Cold War practices; wariness of Soviet/Russian nuclear and political intentions; nuclear non-proliferation concerns and the emergence of the WMD-armed 'rogue' state exemplified by Saddam Hussein's Iraq; and, finally, a nuclear weapons complex that was becoming increasingly incapable of supporting a vast, diverse nuclear weapons enterprise.

4 Nuclear weapons policy under Bill Clinton

President Clinton entered office in 1993 committed to nuclear arms control, including the two START treaties and negotiation of a Comprehensive Test Ban Treaty (CTBT) to end global nuclear weapons testing.[1] His administration was also required by Congress to undertake a full review of nuclear weapons policy in all its aspects by conducting a Nuclear Posture Review (NPR) on entering office. Policy under Clinton was underpinned by four considerations. First, it was accepted that America had to retain a robust, survivable and reliable nuclear arsenal to perform a number of roles. Second, this must include a triad of ICBMs, SLBMs and long-range bombers that could be rapidly expanded from reserve forces. Third, the nuclear arsenal must be cut back along with the rest of the armed forces to reduce defence spending. Fourth, arms control agreements must be pursued to enhance strategic stability with Russia and reduce incentives for nuclear proliferation.[2]

The domestic political context of nuclear weapons policy underwent two important changes. On entering office the new administration brought in a number of experts from Washington's arms control community that had a more favourable outlook on the utility of arms control and non-proliferation initiatives. A second major shift occurred when the Republican Party gained control of both houses of Congress following the 1994 congressional elections. This allowed the Republicans to impose their own framework and preferences on nuclear policy that was often at odds with the administration.

Eight of the key decisions previously identified occurred under Clinton: the decisions set out in the 1994 NPR; the extension of the congressional testing moratorium and the signing of the CTBT in 1996; the establishment of the Stockpile Stewardship Program (SSP) in 1993; the development and deployment of the B61-11 earth-penetrating nuclear weapon; the change in nuclear weapons guidance in 1997 to facilitate a START III agreement; congressional action to ban the development of new low-yield nuclear weapons; the decision by Congress to vote down the CTBT in 1999; and failure of the entry into force of START II.

Nuclear forces

The new administration accepted that new nuclear weapon production programmes were politically unacceptable and that the long-term future of the nuclear arsenal lay in modernisation and life-extension of existing weapons, and judged this sufficient to meet nuclear mission requirements.[3] This was confirmed in the 1993 Bottom-Up Review of the armed services, 1994 Nuclear Posture Review and the 1995 Heavy Bomber Study.[4]

The administration also confirmed the need to retain a specific strategic triad together with a stockpile of tactical nuclear weapons. This was set out in the 1993 JCS Doctrine for Joint Nuclear Operations,[5] a number of STRATCOM force structure studies for START II and the prospective START III, and endorsed in the 1994 Nuclear Posture Review.[6] The enduring triad would comprise 500 Minuteman III ICBMs (the MX would be retired), 18 Ohio-class SSBNs armed with Trident II (D5) SLBMs, 76 B-52 and 21 B-2 bombers armed with ACMs, Air-Launched Cruise Missiles (ALCMs) and gravity bombs. The remaining five Ohio submarines were deployed by the end of 1997, ten of which were equipped with the Trident II (D5) SLBM and eight with the older Trident I (C4) version.[7] All 21 B-2s were also deployed by the end of 1997.[8] The Republican-controlled Congress pushed hard for more B-2s but the administration repeatedly stated that it did not require any more of the expensive bombers.[9] This force structure would provide a flexible, sophisticated arsenal to address a range of threats and ensure deterrence and a diversity of warheads to guarantee a level of redundancy should one system or one type of warhead fail as force levels were reduced.

STRATCOM studies included the 1993 Sun City Study to examine different force structure options to counter the Russian nuclear arsenal under a START II agreement; the 1994 Sun City Extended Study to examine force structures vis-à-vis China and 'rogue states'; the 1996 White Paper on post-START II force structures based on a number of principles for post-START II arms control set out in Presidential Decision Directive 37 (PDD-37); and the 1996 Warfighter's Assessment study of force structures under the proposed START III agreement to reduce deployed strategic forces to between 2,500 and 2,000 warheads.[10]

A number of modernisation and life extension programmes were initiated to sustain this triad over the long term.[11] SLBM modernisation programmes involved replacing all Trident I (C4) SLBMs with the Trident II (D5) for its improved accuracy, range and yield and a project to provide two new warhead options to enhance the Trident II W88 warhead stockpile by 2015.[12] It also included a Submarine Warhead Protection Plan initiated in 1995 to upgrade the older W76 Trident II warheads from air-burst to ground-burst to give them the capability to destroy hard targets. By 1998 the Navy was also planning to extend the life of the Ohio submarines and Trident II (D5) SLBMs from 30 to 42 years.[13]

The Air Force established Nuclear Weapon Capabilities Assessment teams to ensure the longevity of the Minuteman III, MX and Advanced Cruise Missile fleets. The Minuteman III fleet would be sustained until 2017 when deployment of a new land-based ICBM was planned. Sustainment and modernisation included guidance and propulsion replacement programmes to allow more accurate targeting and correct age-related defects. The first remanufactured Minuteman III was successfully launched in November 1999.[14]

The arguments presented by the administration for retaining a strategic triad were challenged in 1993 in a major study by the General Accounting Office (GAO). The study concluded that no effort had been made to evaluate the relative effectiveness of similar weapon systems in the triad as a whole and that the capabilities of the new modernised systems for each leg had been overstated. The GAO report recommended ending procurement of the B-2 at 15, no further ICBM modernisation including no life extension for the Minuteman III fleet, no further procurement of the Advanced Cruise Missile, but full deployment of the Trident II (D5) SLBM.[15] Secretary of Defense William Perry refuted these findings.[16] Questions were also asked about the need for a 500-strong ICBM fleet and the virtue of moving to a strategic dyad. These were dismissed by STRATCOM based on the argument that ending ICBM deployments would increase the incentive for a possible first-strike by a potential adversary, however unlikely a first-strike may be.[17]

1994 Nuclear Posture Review

One of the most important reviews of nuclear weapons policy occurred in 1994 through the congressionally-mandated Nuclear Posture Review, which examined the purpose and nature of America's nuclear forces after the Cold War. It was the first major nuclear strategy review in 15 years and it examined six areas of policy: the role of nuclear weapons in national security strategy; nuclear force structure and infrastructure; nuclear force operations and command and control; nuclear safety, security and use control; the relationship between alternative nuclear postures and counterproliferation policy; and the relationship between alternative nuclear postures and threat reduction with the former Soviet Union.[18] The review took ten months and was reviewed and directed by Deputy Secretary of Defense John Deutch and JCS Vice Chairman William Owens.[19]

The policy that emerged from the review was described as 'lead but hedge'. America would assert leadership in reducing forces whilst hedging against a reversal of Russian reforms and future strategic uncertainty.[20] The basic premise of the NPR was that nuclear weapons should play a reduced role in American national security, but it did not examine options beyond START II and concluded that any further reduction of nuclear forces would not facilitate deeper reductions in Russia.[21] It argued instead that with the former Soviet Union countries only in the early stages of making the reductions agreed in START I, and with START II not yet ratified, America should retain the capability to redeploy a large nuclear force in case Russia reverted to a hostile foreign policy.[22] It was therefore considered unsafe to reduce nuclear forces too quickly until relations with Russia further improved and the risks of future strategic confrontation diminished.[23]

The review revalidated the START II-compliant force structure established in SAC and STRATCOM studies based on maintaining and modernising the strategic nuclear triad together with a range of tactical nuclear weapon systems and a large warhead reserve. The 'hedge' would allow relatively rapid reconstitution of a larger nuclear force with timelines for reconstitution that could be extended as Russia stabilised and relations with the former Soviet Union improved.[24] In practice, the policy meant retention of around 2,500 warheads for rapid redeployment on ICBMs, SLBMs and aircraft.[25]

Specific recommendations included retiring the MX Peacekeeper ICBM and reducing Minuteman III missiles from three warheads to one; reducing the number of SSBNs to 14 and replacing all Trident I SLBMs with the Trident II; cutting the number of B-52 bombers from 94 to 66; and switching all 95 B1-B bombers to conventional roles.[26] The review also eliminated the ability to return tactical nuclear weapons to surface ships, including carrier-based dual-capable strike aircraft that were removed under the 1991 PNI but retained the ability to restore Tomahawk nuclear cruise missiles to attack submarines.[27] STRATCOM was unhappy with this force structure, regarding it as the minimum acceptable, with fewer bombers and SSBNs than it wanted.[28] The NPR also required DOE to retain the capability to rebuild warheads in the operational stockpile, design, fabricate and certify new warheads, and maintain a science and technology base to support the nuclear arsenal through the Stockpile Stewardship Program (SSP).[29] The nuclear force sustainment and modernisation programmes underway were endorsed and it was recommended that a ballistic missile industrial production base be maintained.[30] These recommendations were passed by Clinton in Presidential Decision Directive 30 (PDD-30) in September 1994.[31]

The force structure and rationales set out in the NPR were subsequently reflected in the administration's National Security Strategies. The 1995 National Security Strategy reinforced Clinton's dual track approach of pursuing arms control to reduce the dangers of nuclear conflict whilst maintaining robust strategic nuclear forces in case efforts to prevent the spread of nuclear, chemical and biological weapons failed, together with the flexibility to reconstitute or reduce forces as required.[32] This formulation was repeated in National Security Strategies from 1996–2000 and reaffirmed in the 1997 Quadrennial Defense Review that insisted on 'a reliable and flexible nuclear deterrent' for the foreseeable future.[33] The 1997 National Security Strategy also introduced the concept of nuclear dissuasion in which American nuclear forces would serve as 'a disincentive to those who would contemplate developing or otherwise acquiring their own nuclear weapons' and convince adversaries that 'seeking a nuclear advantage would be futile'.[34] The 1998 version also highlighted a continuing need to defend against a surprise nuclear first-strike and still respond at overwhelming levels, however unlikely that may seem.[35]

Some argued that the NPR did not go far enough. It was criticised for not constituting the fundamental reappraisal many had hoped for and that the administration had seemingly promised, and for only exploring force structure options within the framework of START II. Clinton's first Defense Secretary Les Aspin had conducted a major review of nuclear weapons policy in 1992 as chair of the House Armed Services Committee. He had concluded that major changes were needed and perhaps even the elimination of nuclear weapons.[36] Deputy Secretary of Defense John Deutch had also stated that 'the questions and answers posed by the review will reassess our fundamental assumptions and beliefs regarding nuclear issues … a vast variety of alternatives and options are being considered'.[37] But instead of an opportunity for sweeping change, the NPR was seen by the nuclear policy community as a means of placing nuclear strategy and force structure on a stable footing after the upheaval of the first few post-Cold War years.[38] Despite Deutch's stated intention, he believed firmly in the continuity of nuclear weapons policy and was seeking adaptation rather than major change.[39]

Critics therefore argued that the NPR essentially halted the reductions process initiated by President Bush and codified the status quo. Members of Congress and influential voices outside government questioned the continuing need for a large nuclear force or even for a nuclear arsenal at all. They argued that the review failed to question whether the ability to deliver a fast and disarming strike was still required in order to deter a surprise nuclear attack, and whether high levels of strategic forces on high alert configured for counter-force attacks, a strategic nuclear triad, pre-planned massive attack options, and nuclear parity with Russia were still necessary.[40] Blame was cast on the absence of senior oversight or involvement, particularly from the White House, which allowed the Pentagon bureaucracy to dominate proceedings and militated against a truly wide-ranging review as originally envisaged.[41]

This criticism came in the context of growing pressure in the mid-1990s for nuclear disarmament with powerful statements on the danger and irrelevance of nuclear deterrence by the former head of Strategic Command, General George Lee Butler, and head of North American Aerospace Defense Command and U.S. Space Command, General Charles Horner, who stated that 'The nuclear weapon is obsolete. I want to get rid of them all'.[42] This coincided with the report of the Canberra Commission on the Elimination of Nuclear Weapons that called for 'immediate and determined efforts … to rid the world of nuclear weapons and the threat they pose to it'[43] and the Advisory Opinion of the International Court of Justice on the use of nuclear weapons, which declared that 'the threat or use of nuclear weapons would generally be contrary to the rules of international law applicable in armed conflict, and in particular the principles and rules of humanitarian law'.[44] This 'new abolitionist' argument stated that the only rational purpose for nuclear weapons was to deter nuclear attack, that nuclear weapons would not deter WMD-armed 'rogue' states, that the elimination of nuclear weapons would produce a safer world, and that non-nuclear weapons offered a viable alternative to nuclear weapons.[45] The NPR was criticised for failing to address these issues.[46] Others, such as Keith Payne, head of the National Institute for Public Policy, and Senator Strom Thurmond argued that Clinton's nuclear cuts went too far and that the administration had de-emphasised nuclear weapons too much.[47]

Nuclear arms control

Clinton placed considerable emphasis on the importance of nuclear arms control for American national security and came to office with a number of people from Washington's arms control community committed to further nuclear force reductions with Russia. In their 1992 book, *A New Concept of Cooperative Security*, William Perry and Ashton Carter (later Secretary of Defense and Assistant Secretary of Defense for International Security Policy) stated that bold demobilisation of strategic nuclear forces was required through deep, rapid and irreversible arms control reductions.[48]

The START II treaty enjoyed widespread support in the Clinton administration and Congress. Ukraine, Belarus and Kazakhstan acceded to the NPT as non-nuclear weapon states in 1994, allowing entry into force of START I and the START II ratification process to begin. Ratification of the treaty by the Senate was delayed, however, by fierce dispute in Congress over the deployment of national missile defences. In 1995 the White House insisted on progress towards ratification and 35 Senators signed a letter to the Senate Republican Majority Leader urging the Senate to complete action on the treaty.[49]

Congress eventually ratified START II in December 1996 but it took another four years to secure ratification by the Russian Duma in May 2000. Russian officials and parliamentarians delayed ratification for a number of reasons, including concerns over the cost of implementation,[50] NATO expansion,[51] perceived American strategic superiority under START II[52] and American military action in Iraq, particularly the 1998 Desert Fox bombing campaign.[53] The Russian Duma also placed considerable emphasis on continued American adherence to the ABM treaty in exchange for START II ratification.[54] This was unacceptable to the post-1994 Republican congressional leadership, and it was already clear by 1995 that the START process was in real difficulty.[55] This took place in the wider context of a growing distrust of America within Russia's conservative political elite. Critics argued that Clinton's declaratory policy of conciliation and cooperation provided cover for a reckless policy of relentless exploitation of Russia's post-Cold War weakness through broken promises and demands for unilateral concessions.[56] There was increasing disillusionment with the benefits of a pro-Western political strategy amid suspicions that America wanted to establish permanent military superiority over Russia.[57]

Nevertheless, by the end of 1997 the Clinton administration was confident that it had addressed all of Moscow's concerns. At a summit between Presidents Clinton and Yeltsin in Helsinki in March 1997 the administration agreed to quickly move to a START III of 2,000–2,500 warheads once START II had entered into force and extended the timeline for START II to reduce financial pressure on Russian nuclear force reductions. This was formalised in the summit's Joint Statement on Parameters on Future Reductions in Nuclear Forces.[58] The summit also addressed missile defence concerns and the ABM treaty. The administration also signed the NATO-Russia Founding Act in May 1997 to ease Russian concerns about NATO expansion.[59]

The Duma, however, attached a series of conditions to its ratification of START II in 2000, including continued adherence to the ABM treaty and Senate ratification of the nuclear and missile defence agreements reached at Helsinki. The Senate still had no intention of limiting missile defence research, development and deployment. Senator Jesse Helms was categorical when he said 'Any modified ABM Treaty negotiated by this administration will be DOA – dead on arrival – at the Senate Foreign Relations Committee', of which he was the chairman.[60] From 1995–2000 the US–Russian arms reduction process slid towards stalemate and by 2000 it was stuck in limbo with little hope of recovery.[61] As Krepon argues, the administration hoped in vain that Russia would eventually accept START II with all the problems it posed for Moscow in order to secure rapid progression to START III, but differences over missile defence and the ABM treaty proved insurmountable.[62]

START II, indeed the entire START process, had a number of meanings for the Clinton administration and Congress. The majority view in government was that the purpose of START II was to enhance strategic stability rather than to reduce nuclear numbers for the sake of reductions, as under Bush.[63] This had two core components: ending the deployment of MIRVed heavy Russian ICBMs thereby eliminating incentives for a nuclear first-strike according to prevailing understandings of nuclear deterrence; and reducing forces in a deliberate coordinated manner to lock in post-Cold War changes in the US–Russian nuclear relationship through a formal process, particularly given uncertainties over Russia's long-term political direction.[64] As Arms Control and Disarmament Agency (ACDA) director John Holum said, 'the bi-polar standoff is largely over, but we still have to extract its sharpest teeth'.[65] It was also viewed as a positive nuclear non-proliferation and disarmament measure by an administration committed to reducing nuclear weapons globally with the ultimate declaratory goal of elimination.[66] Secretary of State Warren Christopher and members of Congress such as Senator Dorgan, later chair of the Senate Democratic Policy Committee, argued that ratification of START II would reinforce the NPT, demonstrate that America was meeting its disarmament obligations, and encourage further nuclear reductions.[67] Finally, it was seen as a concrete sign of a new, cooperative relationship with Moscow.[68] Secretary of Defense William Perry claimed in 1995, for example, that START II represented the culmination of the Cold War arms control process and a turning point for a new era of US–Russian relations.[69]

START III

Clinton expressed his desire to negotiate further reductions beyond START II early in his presidency.[70] In 1996 STRATCOM was formally requested to produce a study on START III force structure options.[71] The figure of 2,000–2,500 warheads that emerged from these studies was approved for the 1997 Helsinki summit, allowing Clinton to signal his intention to move quickly to a START III treaty with Russia once START II entered into force.[72] The study concluded that President Reagan's 1981 nuclear planning guidance that required the JCS to be able to prevail in a protracted nuclear war needed to be changed to enable further reductions to take place. In 1997 Clinton replaced this guidance with the classified Presidential Decision Directive 60 (PDD-60). This instructed the JCS to be able to absorb a Russian first-strike and retaliate with an overwhelming and devastating response whilst removing language related to waging a protracted nuclear war. This allowed a reduction in the number of Russian targets in the SIOP and a reduction in the number of nuclear weapons needed to hold Russian targets at risk.[73] The directive also reportedly endorsed wider nuclear targeting of China and targeting of specific regions such as the Persian Gulf and Korean peninsula.[74] Kristensen argues that the seven years it took to formally adjust nuclear weapons policy following the end of the Cold War and the fact the DOD had in the meantime 'issued new nuclear weapons employment policy twice and had completed a Nuclear Posture Review; JCS had updated the nuclear appendix to the Joint Strategic Capabilities Plan half a dozen times and published new nuclear doctrine twice', demonstrated how much influence military planners rather than political leaders had in shaping nuclear posture after the Cold War.[75]

By 1998 Clinton was 'anxious to get to work on START III' and in a joint statement on the US–Russian Strategic Stability Cooperation Initiative in September 2000 Clinton and Russian President Vladimir Putin stated that discussions on START III and the future of the ABM treaty had intensified with a view to swift negotiations.[76] Administration officials also raised the prospect of a START IV involving all the declared nuclear weapon states.[77] Nevertheless, START II never entered into force and negotiations on START III never began. Even if negotiations had commenced it is likely they would have been extremely problematic.[78] Official statements suggested that START III should involve increased transparency of warhead inventories and verifiable destruction of warheads; negotiations on tactical nuclear systems and long-range sea-launched nuclear cruise missiles omitted from previous START treaties; relaxation of multiple warhead ICBM restrictions for Russia; and limitations on nuclear weapons production infrastructures given the perceived Russian advantage in this area.[79] The nuclear policy community was also adamant that START III should not require destruction of any nuclear delivery vehicles, particularly SSBNs and long-range bombers. It was suggested that the START warhead accounting rules would have to be changed to exclude nuclear delivery platforms incapable of being employed, such as SSBNs in overhaul.[80] Most of these issues had been excluded from previous START negotiations.

It was also clear that nuclear weapons policy under START III would remain committed to a number of Cold War nuclear planning precepts. Any reduced force would still be based on a strategic nuclear triad.[81] Many forces would remain on high alert with force requirements driven by a Cold War nuclear targeting process according to Senator Bob Kerrey, vice-chair of the Senate Committee on Intelligence.[82] His argument was backed in 2000 by Stephen Younger, Associate Laboratory Director for Nuclear Weapons at Los Alamos National Laboratory (LANL), who stated that:

> Even with the dramatic changes that have occurred in the world during the past decade, nuclear war planning today is similar in many respects to what it was during the Cold War. The Single Integrated Operational Plan (SIOP) is focused on a massive counterattack strategy that aims to eliminate the ability of an adversary to inflict further damage to American interests.[83]

As the START process dragged out through the 1990s pressure increased to unilaterally reduce forces to START II levels regardless of the whether the treaty had entered into force and to then quickly negotiate a START III.[84] In May 1995, for example, Representative Elizabeth Furse and 24 colleagues wrote to President Clinton urging the White House to begin immediate negotiations on a START III.[85] This was based on the growing cost of remaining at START I force levels, Russia's aspiration to move quickly to lower levels, and a desire to unblock the arms control process. Congressional pressure for unilateral reductions and delinking American nuclear force structure from Russia's was supported by the National Academy of Sciences' 1997 report *The Future of US Nuclear Weapons Policy* that urged the administration to move quickly to START III to overcome the START II stalemate;[86] the 1997 National Defense Panel's report *Transforming Defense: National Security in the 21st Century* that stated that America should move to START II levels even if Russia failed to ratify START II;[87] and statements by STRATCOM commander Richard Mies and former STRATCOM commander Eugene Habiger.[88]

Opponents of unilateral cuts insisted that uncertainty in the US–Russian relationship still required caution in the nuclear drawdown process and formal reciprocal actions.[89] They insisted that the promise of American reductions under START II was a major incentive for Russian ratification whereas unilateral reductions based on the hope of reciprocation would undermine the START process, despite the fact that the process was clearly stuck.[90] It was also argued that 'strategic stability' required nuclear parity at all times so that the Russian leadership could never hold a strategic advantage over America.[91] When the Senate ratified START II in 1996 it insisted on maintenance of strategic parity as reductions under the treaty took place and legislation was passed prohibiting the retirement of B-52 bombers, Minuteman III and Peacekeeper ICBMs and Trident SLBMs in order to maintain nuclear forces at the START I level until START II entered into force.[92]

The administration maintained that no tangible arms control benefit would be gained from further unilateral reductions and this remained official policy until the late 1990s.[93] As the cost of maintaining forces at START I levels increased the administration began to lobby against the restriction to stay at START I and Senator Warner, chair of the Armed Services Committee, finally proposed that the next president could reduce nuclear force levels after another Nuclear Posture Review in conjunction with the forthcoming 2001 Quadrennial Defense Review.[94]

Russia, 'rogues' and nuclear planning

The Clinton administration sought to both engage Russia as a national security priority and hedge against the reversal of post-Soviet reforms and the re-emergence of a belligerent nuclear-armed superpower adversary. For Clinton it was imperative America engage Russia and forge a new relationship by supporting the development of democracy, a market economy and the reduction of nuclear weapons.[95] The establishment of a new relationship with Moscow based on partnership rather than competition was declared by the new administration in March 1993.[96] It was formally articulated in the January 1994 Moscow Declaration signed by Clinton and Yeltsin;[97] the 1998 Joint Statement on Common Security Challenges;[98] and the September 2000 Strategic Stability Cooperation Initiative that built on the Joint Statement on Principles of Strategic Stability, adopted in Moscow in June 2000, and the Joint Statement on Cooperation on Strategic Stability, adopted in Okinawa in July 2000.[99]

These declarations were part of a gradual process of reorienting the relationship away from traditional military security issues dominated by mutual assured nuclear destruction and towards cooperation, mutual trust, and recognition of common security interests. This was symbolised in 1994 when Defense Secretary Perry announced that America was formally ready to reject the strategy of mutual assured destruction with Russia and adopt one he labelled mutual assured safety and in a 1994 US–Russian agreement to no longer target strategic nuclear missiles at each other on a day-to-day basis 'in a manner that presumes they are adversaries' (this was largely symbolic, however, since the missiles could be re-targeted in a matter of minutes).[100] It was also reflected at a more sustained level in STRATCOM Commander General Eugene Habiger's initiative to significantly expand the military-to-military exchange and trust-building programme between STRATCOM and its counterparts in Russia in the mid-1990s.[101]

Nevertheless, prevailing nuclear strategy still required retention of a large nuclear hedge force for the foreseeable future to counter the existential threat from the continued existence of Russia's massive nuclear arsenal. It was argued that although Russia was no longer an enemy, relations were not yet warm enough to permit a decisive move away from mutual assured destruction given Russia's capability to destroy America.[102] As JCS chairman John Shalikashvili stated in September 1994, 'the mere existence of this arsenal will remain a most profound danger to our future security'.[103] This hedge concept that emerged under Bush and was formalised in the 1994 NPR was reiterated throughout the 1990s in administration documents such as DOD's 1995 Annual Report to Congress,[104] and in the 1998 Defense Science Board's *Task Force on Nuclear Deterrence* report, which stated that

> While Russia continues to maintain the capability for a massive nuclear attack on the U.S., there is little concern, at present, over the possibility of their doing so. Still, there is an unquestioned need to hedge against Russian capability whilst it exists.[105]

Changes in Russia's nuclear doctrine in 1993, 1997 and its 2000 revised Concept on National Security, as well as ongoing Russian nuclear force modernisation, suggested that Moscow had increased reliance on nuclear weapons for national defense and claimed the right to use nuclear weapons first in a conflict. This reinforced American perceptions of the need for a nuclear hedge. Russia's 2000 strategy document also expanded scenarios for possible nuclear use.[106]

Russia's nuclear arsenal therefore continued to feature heavily in American nuclear weapons policy and planning, but this was primarily as an insurance against a return to an overtly adversarial relationship. The primary strategic threat and the new focus of nuclear weapons policy was the proliferation of WMD, particularly nuclear weapons, to 'rogue' states. The Clinton administration quickly adopted the 'rogue' doctrine formulated under Bush and validated by the Gulf War and argued that these 'rogues' represented a greater threat than the Soviet Union during the Cold War that could have annihilated Western society.[107] 'The old danger we faced was thousands of warheads in the Soviet Union. The new nuclear danger we face,' Defense Secretary Aspin warned in 1993, 'is perhaps a handful of devices in the hands of rogue states or even terrorist groups'.[108] It was argued that these 'rogues', primarily Iran, Iraq and North Korea, were developing WMD to threaten neighbours, exert regional influence and deter American intervention and could 'throw their regions into instability, turmoil, and war'.[109]

The administration responded with a new focus on counter-proliferation that was fully articulated in DOD's 1996 Proliferation: Threat and Response report. It outlined a three point strategy to reduce the threat through diplomatic non-proliferation activities, deter the threat with conventional and nuclear forces and defend against the threat through the Counterproliferation Initiative (CPI) and theatre missile defences.[110] The CPI was established in 1993 to counter the threat of WMD use through better intelligence, new conventional weaponry, and WMD detection and troop protection equipment to reduce the need to resort to nuclear weapons.[111]

Nuclear posture followed suit and continued its reorientation away from Russia to deterrence and, if necessary, defeat of WMD-armed 'rogues'. By the mid-1990s the Russian nuclear threat and planning for a short-notice global nuclear exchange had been firmly replaced by counter-proliferation missions against WMD-armed 'rogue' states. This was articulated in the 1993 JCS Joint Doctrine for Nuclear Operations, its 1996 Joint Doctrine for Theater Nuclear Operations, reportedly in Clinton's 1997 PDD-60 nuclear targeting guidance, and confirmed in STRATCOM's official history published in 2004.[112] The Air Force's 1998 Nuclear Operations doctrine document, for example, states that 'Department of Defense Directive 2060.2 directs the Services to develop doctrine for counterproliferation efforts. Air Force doctrine for nuclear operations is one important component of that requirement'.[113]

STRATCOM began drawing up plans for use of nuclear weapons against regional WMD-armed adversaries in the mid-1990s. These plans took the form of 'SILVER books' (Strategic Installation List of Vulnerability Effects and

Results) comprising 'silver bullet' nuclear counter-proliferation missions against WMD weapons and infrastructure and enemy command and control facilities. A SILVER book was produced on Iran, but in 1995 the JCS ordered a halt to the programme when regional commanders saw it as an incursion into their planning processes. Nevertheless, regional nuclear war planning continued and by 1995 it was reported that targets in the SIOP had risen from 2,500 in 1992 to 3,000 to reflect this development.[114]

The focus on WMD-armed 'rogue' states in nuclear targeting doctrine was facilitated by the adaptive planning nuclear targeting apparatus under development at STRATCOM.[115] The thorough revision of the Strategic War Planning System (SWPS) continued under Clinton to permit rapid re-targeting of nuclear forces, multiple options and halve the time required to fully revise the SIOP. The review was approved in October 1993 with a full upgrade to be completed by 1999 to establish a so-called 'living SIOP'.[116] Part of the modernisation of the Trident II (D5) and Minuteman III missiles involved upgrading their targeting systems to allow rapid re-targeting. For example the Navy began implementing an SLBM Retargeting System (SRS) in 1992 to 'provide increased SLBM retargeting capability'.[117]

The gradual institutionalisation of counter-proliferation missions for nuclear forces reinforced calls for a new range of smaller, low-yield nuclear weapons to target mobile or relocatable targets and hardened underground bunkers.[118] DOE continued to study new 'mini-nukes' for counter-proliferation missions, the 1993 JCS Doctrine for Joint Nuclear Operations argued that low-yield nuclear weapons would be a useful capability for regional contingencies against WMD-armed adversaries, and Clinton's first defence budget proposal included funding for research on such weapons.[119] In response the Democratic-controlled Congress passed legislation in 1993 to ban further research and development that could lead to the production of nuclear weapons with a yield less than five kilotons that had not yet entered production.[120] It was argued that the development of low-yield nuclear weapons would undermine efforts to extend the NPT in 1995 and negotiate a Comprehensive Test Ban Treaty and could lead to greater risk of nuclear use by blurring the distinction between conventional and nuclear conflict.[121]

Research and development on existing weapons was still permitted and work continued on modifying one particular warhead, the B61-7, to give it an earth-penetrating, or 'bunker busting', capability. In 1993 DOD requested that alternatives be found for the ageing high-yield B53 bomb that was currently assigned 'bunker-buster' missions.[122] The 1994 NPR recommended that all 50 B53s be replaced and the Nuclear Weapons Council (NWC) endorsed a modified B61-7 as its replacement to be delivered by the B-2 bomber.[123] The research, design and construction of the new weapon, labelled the B61-11, was controversial. The modified weapon was placed in the stockpile without full explosive nuclear testing in December 1996 with full operational deployment in 1999.[124] Critics argued that it represented a new nuclear weapon and undermined nuclear non-proliferation efforts.[125] DOE insisted that no new nuclear weapons were being built, arguing that the B61-11 was only a modification of an existing design. No changes had been made to the nuclear package and no new mission was being developed.[126]

After the deployment of the B61-11 the nuclear weapons laboratories continued to make the case for the development of new nuclear capabilities more suited to post-Cold War targeting requirements, including low-yield weapons.[127] This gathered support in Congress towards the end of the Clinton administration when the Senate authorised a study of the destruction of hardened and deeply buried targets (HDBTs) possibly using a low-yield nuclear weapon. This met opposition from members of Congress, such as Representatives Edward Markey and Ellen Tauscher, who adopted similar arguments to those used in 1993. They argued that such weapons would make nuclear weapons more 'usable', would lead to renewed nuclear testing in violation of the CTBT, and would undermine nuclear non-proliferation efforts.[128]

Planning for the potential use of nuclear weapons in response to a chemical, biological or massive conventional attack was contentious and declaratory policy remained ambiguous. America reiterated its 1978 Negative Security Assurance (NSA) at the 1995 NPT Review and Extension Conference. This stipulated that it would not attack a non-nuclear weapon state with nuclear weapons unless attacked by a non-nuclear weapon state allied to a nuclear weapon state.[129] This was clarified further in 1997 by Robert Bell, Senior Director for Defense Policy and Arms Control at the National Security Council, who said that America may use nuclear weapons against a nuclear-capable state, against a state that is not in good standing under the Non-Proliferation Treaty or an equivalent international convention, or if a state attacks the United States, its allies or its forces in alliance with a nuclear-capable state.[130] This relatively clear declaratory policy has often been clouded by STRATCOM doctrine that preferred a posture of 'measured ambiguity' over conditions for use of nuclear weapons, particularly in response to a chemical or biological attack.[131]

Missile defence and START II

The rise to prominence of the threat from WMD-armed regional 'rogue' states led to renewed enthusiasm for a missile defence system to protect America from ballistic missile attack. This became a source of bitter disagreement between the administration, Congress and Russia. Calls to abrogate the ABM treaty from the Republican-controlled Congress after 1994 and administration efforts to modify the treaty to allow limited theatre and national missile defences (TMD and NMD) had a major impact on the START process, particularly the ratification of START II.[132]

From the very beginning Clinton declared that any missile defence deployments would remain compliant with the ABM treaty.[133] Nevertheless, the rise of WMD and ballistic missile-armed 'rogue' states necessitated clarification of the type of theatre missile defence systems that could be deployed and talks were initiated with Russia on a 'demarcation' agreement on allowable theatre missile defence characteristics.[134] A long negotiation process finally produced agreement in 1997 at Helsinki.[135]

Nevertheless, the Helsinki agreements needed to be ratified by an increasingly hostile Congress where support for abolishing the ABM treaty was strong.[136] Critics argued that nuclear deterrence could no longer be relied upon to successfully deter the threat or use of WMD by 'rogue' states and that the ballistic missile threat from these 'rogues' was so serious that the ABM treaty was now an obstacle to the deployment of necessary defences. They pointed to the confrontation with North Korea in 1994 over its nuclear weapons and ballistic missile programmes, North Korea's unannounced long-range ballistic missile test over the Pacific in 1998, Iraq and Iran's suspected nuclear weapons and ballistic missile programmes, and the nuclear and missile tests by India and Pakistan in 1998 as further evidence of the need for a missile defence system to protect the entire United States from the growing missile threat.[137] This was bolstered by the 1998 report of the bipartisan Commission to Assess the Ballistic Missile Threat to the United States, also known as the Rumsfeld Commission. It concluded that America faced an imminent 'rogue' ICBM threat that could emerge within the next five years with little or no warning.[138]

Critics considered the ABM treaty an obsolete agreement that perpetuated a relationship of mutual assured destruction with Russia based on mutual vulnerability to nuclear annihilation.[139] America needed to move beyond such a relationship by reducing nuclear weapons whilst deploying missile defences, as President Bush had proposed in the early 1990s.[140] Clinton's resuscitation of the 'sacred text' of the ABM treaty as the 'cornerstone of strategic stability' undermined national security and prevented the emergence of a more cooperative relationship with Russia.[141]

Russia, however, insisted that maintenance of the ABM treaty was a prerequisite for further nuclear reductions and linked entry into force of START II to ratification of the 1997 agreements, as discussed above. Moscow remained suspicious of America's NMD plans that were widely regarded as a long-term strategy to weaken Russia and undermine its strategic nuclear retaliatory capability.[142] The administration and its supporters in Congress argued that deployment of a national missile defence system that abrogated the ABM treaty would end all hope of Russian ratification of START II and terminate the mutual nuclear drawdown process. Russian linkage meant that a choice had to be made between START II and breaking the ABM treaty, which might also prompt Russia to withdraw from START I.[143] Forceful statements were made by a number of Senators and Representatives arguing that continued observance of the ABM treaty was vital to the success of START II and further reductions.[144] Critics chastised the Clinton administration for effectively giving Russia a veto on missile defence deployments, allowing Moscow to extort concessions from America and strongly refuted any link between the ABM treaty and START II.[145]

The two sides in the debate had fundamentally different interpretations of the primary strategic threat to American national security. One side viewed 'rogue' states as the primary threat and prioritised unilateral actions and deployment of missile defences as the appropriate solution. Others regarded Russia's nuclear arsenal as the primary threat and considered cooperative nuclear arms control and non-proliferation as the most important response. This reflected a much longer historical debate between advocates of missile defence and advocates of arms control.[146]

After the Republican Party won control of Congress in 1994 it attempted to compel the administration to deploy national missile defences through legislation. After years of Republican pressure Congress overwhelmingly passed the 1999 National Missile Defense Act. The act legally obliged the administration to field an NMD system when technologically feasible. Clinton reluctantly signed the bill partly to try and diffuse a potent political issue for the Republicans in the upcoming presidential election campaign and partly because congressional pressure could no longer be resisted.[147] Clinton continued to work with Russia to renegotiate the ABM treaty and persuade Putin that a NMD system would not undermine Russia's nuclear arsenal.[148] But Moscow refused to modify the treaty to deal with the growing 'rogue' state threat and no agreement was reached.[149] Congressional proponents of missile defence eventually carried their argument through after battling with the Clinton White House for seven years.

The nuclear weapons production complex

The future of the nuclear weapons production complex was fundamental to the future of America's nuclear weapons policy. The Clinton administration entered office committed to a nuclear test ban and accepting that no new nuclear weapons would be built. It was up to the complex to sustain and modernise the consolidated Cold War legacy nuclear force in an era of no nuclear testing and no new weapons development. At the start of the Clinton presidency the nuclear weapons production complex was in a poor state and getting worse, but it was sustained through the 1990s by a science-based Stockpile Stewardship Program (SSP), a major warhead life extension programme and the continued modernisation of strategic nuclear forces.

Nuclear testing was an intensely divisive issue under Clinton and had a significant impact on the fortunes of the production complex. On entering office Clinton quickly extended the testing moratorium instigated by Congress in 1992 and sought to negotiate a multilateral Comprehensive Test Ban Treaty by September 1996. Caveats were attached to the administration's testing policy, however, including the requirement that DOE maintain the capability for testing nuclear weapons should another country resume testing.[150] The administration also stated that in order to ensure the long-term credibility of the nuclear arsenal it would 'explore other means of maintaining our confidence in the safety, the reliability, and the performance of our own weapons' through a science-based Stockpile Stewardship Program.[151] Formal negotiations on a CTBT began in January 1994 and it was finally opened for signature in September 1996.[152]

Clinton opted for a zero-yield test ban despite pressure from DOD, DOE and the national laboratories to allow continued testing of nuclear weapons with an explosive force equivalent to one kiloton.[153]

Administration support for the CTBT rested on the argument that it would reinforce nuclear non-proliferation objectives, stop the development of new generations of nuclear weapons and ensure the indefinite extension of the NPT in 1995, which was a White House priority.[154] Whilst it was recognised that further limited nuclear testing could provide some additional improvements in safety and reliability, any more tests would undermine the administration's non-proliferation goals and cause other nations to resume testing. Non-proliferation costs were judged to outweigh the benefits of further limited tests.[155] The CTBT was never viewed as a nuclear disarmament measure, however, and the administration was adamant that the treaty should not be designed to impede maintenance of America's nuclear stockpile.[156] Advocates of the test ban in Congress supported these arguments.[157] In 1993, for example, 23 Senators wrote to Clinton urging him to end all nuclear testing or risk jeopardising the extension of the NPT in 1995.[158] They rejected the argument that nuclear tests were essential for ensuring the safety, security and reliability of the nuclear arsenal, pointing to the 1995 report by the JASON group of nuclear scientists that concluded that confidence in the nuclear stockpile was high and no further nuclear testing was needed.[159] They also argued that the CTBT would lock in America's technological advantage[160] and that it was essential that America demonstrate international leadership by ratifying the treaty.[161]

The administration faced severe difficulties in persuading the Senate to ratify it.[162] Senate Foreign Relations Committee chair Jesse Helms remained totally opposed to the treaty and refused to place the CTBT on the committee's agenda: 'I am confident that the Senate will vote to reject this dangerous arms control pact', he said, 'The effect of this treaty would be to forever forbid the United States from testing its nuclear arsenal, while allowing the rogue nations of the world to proceed with their nuclear plans'.[163] Critics also argued that nuclear proliferation was a major threat to national security but that the CTBT would do little to stem the further spread of nuclear weapons and that the administration had overstated the treaty's effectiveness in reducing nuclear proliferation.[164] They insisted that a credible and reliable nuclear arsenal was more important than a test ban in responding to that threat and that this required ongoing nuclear tests to ensure warhead safety, reliability and security.[165] The nuclear weapons laboratories reportedly favoured a 15-year plan based on 15 tests for safety and reliability up to 1996, five years of testing below one kiloton, five years of no testing and then a review.[166]

Doubt was also cast on the ability to adequately and confidently verify compliance with the treaty and the ability of a science-based nuclear stockpile stewardship programme to provide a reliable substitute for nuclear testing.[167] Proponents of continued nuclear testing were backed by five former Secretaries of Defense, two past JCS chairmen, five previous directors of the Central Intelligence Agency, former Secretary of State Henry Kissinger, former National

Security Advisor Brent Scowcroft, former Ambassador to the United Nations Jeanne Kirkpatrick, and former Assistant to the Secretary of Defense for Atomic Energy Robert Barker.[168]

Clinton accepted that the Senate would not ratify the CTBT unless it was convinced that the science-based Stockpile Stewardship Program would work and sought to address Republican concerns by attaching a number of conditions, or 'safeguards', to ratification of the treaty.[169] This involved directing the Nuclear Weapons Council to provide an annual assessment of the safety and reliability of the nuclear weapons stockpile and required the Secretaries of Defense and Energy – advised by the Council, the directors of the nuclear weapons laboratories, and STRATCOM – to certify to a high degree of confidence whether the stockpile was safe and reliable.[170]

In 1999 the treaty was finally subjected to a ratification vote in the Senate after Senator Biden, senior Democrat on the Senate Foreign Relations Committee, along with 34 other Senators introduced a resolution calling for its consideration and all 45 Democrat Senators wrote to Senator Helms urging him to hold hearings and a vote on the treaty.[171] Hearings were eventually held with a vote in October 1999. Despite his administration's efforts and reassurances Clinton was unable to secure the two-thirds vote in the Senate required for ratification and a group of Republican Senators determined to discredit the CTBT successfully led the Senate in its rejection of the treaty.[172] Following the vote there was bitter acrimony and the President was subject to widespread criticism for his handling of the issue.[173] Clinton himself denounced the Republicans' 'reckless partisanship' and Senator John Kerry commented that he had never seen the Senate as personally, ideologically and politically divided as it was over the CTBT vote.[174]

The Stockpile Stewardship Program and warhead life extension programme

The Stockpile Stewardship Program was initiated by Clinton to ensure the safety and reliability of the nuclear stockpile under a CTBT and neutralise opposition to the treaty.[175] The nuclear weapons laboratories were given authorisation to pursue the SSP in a classified November 1993 Presidential Decision Directive (PDD) and the National Defense Authorization Act of 1994 that directed DOE, 'to establish a stewardship program to ensure the preservation of the core intellectual and technical competence of the U.S. in nuclear weapons'.[176] A detailed SSP was set out in DOE's 1995 report *The Stockpile Stewardship and Management Program: Maintaining Confidence in the Safety and Reliability of the Enduring U.S. Nuclear Weapon Stockpile* and later reorganised in DOE's 1999 *Stockpile Stewardship Program: 30-Day Review* report.[177]

The SSP was designed to bring together and coordinate nuclear weapons production, testing and oversight capabilities to sustain the consolidated Cold War legacy nuclear force under START II well into the future.[178] This meant the programme had to develop an understanding of the functioning of all aspects of nuclear weapons and the behaviour of the materials involved as they aged. With no new nuclear weapons programmes current warheads were destined to remain in the stockpile well beyond their original design lifetimes, undergoing subtle age-related changes that would be difficult to detect. It had to maintain the capability to identify problems in nuclear warheads, repair any problems and certify the repairs or replace warheads that could not be repaired all without nuclear testing. This was particularly important as the nuclear stockpile was reduced since there would be fewer types of nuclear weapons, so that a problem with one type could have serious implications.[179] The SSP would also allow the nuclear weapons complex to maintain a cutting edge technological capability and train and retain a highly capable nuclear weapons workforce.[180] These last two objectives were considered crucial to the nuclear arsenal by the defence establishment.

Some critics of SSP, such as Caldicott, argued that the real agenda of the SSP was the development of new nuclear weapons.[181] Others argued that it was a high risk strategy with no guarantee that the new technologies would work well enough to replace knowledge previously gained though nuclear testing and that confidence in the reliability and safety of the nuclear stockpile would inevitably decline. Only nuclear testing could assure the safety, security and reliability of nuclear weapons.[182] In 1998 the Defense Science Board took a more circumspect view, arguing that 'there is no practical alternative for success in Stockpile Stewardship'. Abandonment of SSP would not only require a return to limited nuclear testing but also 'a massive expansion of the planned plutonium and uranium processing (primary and secondary production) capability that went with limited, underground nuclear testing'.[183] Failure was not an option.

The programme was to be implemented through the construction of a host of sophisticated and expensive facilities at a cost of $40 billion over ten years. These included the National Ignition Facility designed to create very brief, contained thermonuclear reactions; a Dual Axis Radiographic Hydrotest Facility (DARHT) to allow nuclear scientists to 'see' inside the explosion of the first stage of a thermonuclear weapon; a more sophisticated facility, the Advanced Hydrotest Facility; the Jupiter Facility for testing weapons' effects; the Atlas Facility for simulating weapon environments; a Contained Firing Facility; a Process and Environmental Technology Laboratory; a High-Explosive Pulsed-Power Facility; and an Accelerated Strategic Computing Initiative to build the most powerful computers in the world at the national laboratories to simulate nuclear explosions.[184] Progress would be monitored through the new annual certification process for validating the safety and security of the nuclear arsenal and a dual revalidation process that required a detailed technical analysis of individual warhead types over a two-to-three year period for the joint DOD-DOE Nuclear Weapons Council.[185]

DOE also began the modification and refurbishment of several types of nuclear warheads through extensive modernisation and life extension programmes (LEPs) that would eventually be applied to the entire deployed and reserve START I stockpile. The nuclear stockpile in 1999 comprised 13 systems with nine weapon classes: the B61-2/4/10 non-strategic bomb for the F-15, F-16 and NATO Tornado fighter aircraft; B61-7/11 strategic bomb for the B-52 and B-2 bombers; W62 Minuteman III ICBM warhead; W76 Trident I (C4) and Trident II (D5) SLBM warhead; W78 Minuteman III ICBM warhead; W80-0/1 ALCM, ACM for the B-52 bomber and Tomahawk Land Attack Missile (TLAM-N) warhead for SSN attack submarines; B83 strategic bomb for the B-52 and B-2; W87 Peacekeeper ICBM warhead; W88 Trident II (D5) SLBM warhead; and the W84 (inactive stockpile) Ground Launched Cruise Missile warhead that had no current carrier.[186] These warhead LEPs would eventually dominate the SSP in addition to the annual certification and dual validation processes. The first LEP began in 1994 to extend the life of the W87 MX Peacekeeper ICBM warhead by 30 years. Although the MX was to be retired its warheads were due to replace some of the older W78 warheads on Minuteman III ICBMs.[187] The next three major LEPs were for the W76, B61 and W80 warheads over the 2010s and studies by DOE and DOD to assess life extension options began in the late 1990s.[188]

Infrastructure

Successful implementation of the SSP and warhead LEPs required a fully functioning, modernised and consolidated production complex. A fully functioning complex was closely tied to arguments for a large reserve force. It was argued that without the ability to produce new nuclear warheads and warhead components America would have to keep many thousands of warheads in reserve in case a particular deployed warhead type malfunctioned catastrophically and had to be withdrawn from service. Clinton's blueprint for change was the Complex-21 plan that was formally approved in 1996 in the Stockpile Management Restructuring Initiative.[189]

The complex had to be able to maintain the enduring stockpile and core research, development and testing capabilities; dismantle nuclear weapons in accordance with DOD planning and arms control; supply warhead components and weapon replacements when required; and provide the ability to reconstitute nuclear testing and weapon production capacities if needed.[190] It envisaged consolidating nuclear weapons manufacturing and surveillance operations at four plants plus the three national laboratories and the Nevada Test Site. The four plants were the Kansas City Plant (production, procurement and dismantlement of non-nuclear warhead components), the Y-12 Plant in Tennessee (uranium component fabrication, modification and evaluation), the Savannah River Site (tritium production and tritium operations) and the Pantex Plant (warhead repair, modification, evaluation, and dismantlement).[191]

This required refurbishing ageing parts of the complex and re-establishing a number of key capabilities. Refurbishment continued throughout the 1990s but by 1999 70 per cent of facilities at the Y-12 plant, 80 per cent of facilities at the Kansas City Plant, 50 per cent of the facilities at LANL, 40 per cent of facilities at Pantex and 40 per cent of those at the Savannah River Site were more than 40 years old and in need of significant maintenance.[192] Key capabilities required included a limited capability to produce plutonium pits in order to remanufacture warheads in the existing stockpile, an assured source of tritium gas for nuclear warheads and the ability to produce uranium components for warheads.[193] A further crucial issue remained the retention of nuclear weapons expertise.

Tritium operations were to be consolidated at the Savannah River Site. DOE estimated in 1994 that it had enough tritium to supply a START II stockpile and maintain a reserve for several years beyond 2009. This was brought forward to 2005 to reflect the delay in entry into force of START II.[194] Congress continually pushed DOE to reach a decision on a new source of tritium throughout the 1990s and in December 1998 DOE announced its decision to use the Tennessee Valley Authority's (TVA) Watts Bar 1 Nuclear Plant as the primary source and to build a new Tritium Extraction Facility at the Savannah River Site to begin construction in 2000 and operation in 2006.[195] Processing operations at the Oak Ridge Y-12 plant for producing uranium components for nuclear warheads were shut down in 1994 due to violations of safety controls. By 1998 the plant had restarted operations in four out of five major areas, but full operation did not materialise under Clinton.[196]

The closure of the Rocky Flats Plant in 1989 ended the capability to produce plutonium pits for nuclear weapons on a large scale. With only tentative plans for a new pit production facility, critics argued that America would only be able to fabricate a small number of plutonium pits for new, redesigned, or remanufactured warheads each year.[197] In 1996 the pit production mission was formally transferred from Rocky Flats to the Los Alamos National Laboratory where a major programme was initiated to produce and certify new plutonium pits for the W88 warhead for Trident II missiles.[198] In 1998 the first prototype pit was produced with plans to develop the capacity to produce 20 pits per years by 2007, down from an original goal of 50 per year by 2005.[199] In 1998 the Defense Science Board's Task Force on Nuclear Deterrence report stated that this was not sustainable and that even at START III levels a production capacity of at least 100 pits per year would be needed to refurbish and sustain the nuclear stockpile. A major new pit production facility was needed.[200] Others disagreed and stated that current capacity at LANL was sufficient to maintain the stockpile.[201]

At the heart of the consolidation and modernisation of the nuclear weapons production complex lay the issue of nuclear weapons expertise and how to sustain it in an era of no nuclear testing and no new weapons development. Expertise was essential for stockpile surveillance, evaluation and maintenance, nuclear weapons repairs, to guard against technological surprise, and to resume production of nuclear weapons if needed.[202] Concern over the loss of nuclear weapons expertise mounted in Congress throughout the 1990s.[203] In 1994 Siegfried Hecker, director of Los Alamos National Laboratory, stated that 'a free falling weapons R&D budget is sapping talent and leaving us dangerously thin in some vital skills needed for nuclear weapons stewardship' and lamented continued budget cuts and the perceived lack of national support under the Clinton administration.[204] DOE's 1999 30-day review, for example, confirmed that it faced challenges in maintaining the proper skill mix and attracting and retaining a first class workforce and reported that the LANL and LLNL were experiencing significant difficulties in attracting and retaining staff for senior positions.[205]

Problems at the DOE

The Clinton administration's tending of the production complex was heavily criticised by Congress. Critics accused the administration of 'erosion by design' by ending testing, under funding the SSP, delaying resumption of tritium and plutonium pit production, and allowing nuclear weapons expertise to wither, leaving America with only a minimal capability to maintain the nuclear stockpile.[206] At the time of the 1994 NPR members of the Senate Armed Services Committee urged the administration to 'revive our nuclear weapons complex' or face an unsafe stockpile leading to unilateral disarmament.[207] Energy Secretary Hazel O'Leary's 1993 Openness Initiative to systematically declassify and reclassify whole areas of information on nuclear testing, the production of nuclear materials and other subjects also drew criticism.[208] The aim was to open up nuclear weapons policy, engage the public on the state of the production complex, and 'lift the veil of Cold War secrecy and move the Department of Energy into a new era of government openness'.[209] This sparked opposition from Congress and led to accusations that DOE was taking 'a strong anti-nuclear weapons stance' from outside and inside the administration.[210] In 1994, for example, O'Leary came under fire from Deputy Secretary of Defense John Deutch for not providing sufficient funds for nuclear weapons activities.[211]

These criticisms were reflected in a number of important reports that lambasted the management, purpose and direction of the SSP, the warhead LEPs and the consolidation and modernisation of the complex under DOE. The 1994 *Task Force on Alternative Futures for the National Laboratories* examined options for change within DOE's national laboratories, particularly the Department's three nuclear weapons laboratories and produced the Galvin Report;[212] the 1996 *Commission on Maintaining United States Nuclear Weapons Expertise* developed a plan for recruiting and retaining nuclear weapons expertise within DOE and led to the Chiles Commission report in 1999;[213] and a study of DOE's management of the nuclear weapons programme was commissioned from the Institute for Defense Analysis in 1997, also known as the 120-day study.[214] All three reports criticised DOE and highlighted poor management and the importance of retaining nuclear weapons expertise. The 1998 Defense Science Board's *Task Force on Nuclear Deterrence* also criticised the administration for having no long-term plan for the nuclear arsenal and a 1999 study by the JASON group of nuclear scientists concluded that there was little evidence of an overall plan for long-term production needs under the SSP.[215]

At the end of the 1990s Congress concluded that DOE's handling of the nuclear mission was not improving and that change required Congressional intervention. Representative Thornberry, for example, stated in 1999 that

> One of the things that is broken is the organizational structure and management of the nuclear weapons complex in the Department of Energy. Study after study, report after report, commission after commission have found that DOE's management of our nuclear weapons program has been a mess.[216]

In 1999 Congress directed DOD and DOE to produce a comprehensive Nuclear Mission Management Plan to ensure 'the long-term viability of the R&D and manufacturing infrastructure for strategic nuclear systems' and a plan to retain core nuclear weapons expertise.[217] Congress also established a Panel to Assess the Reliability, Safety, and Security of the United States Nuclear Stockpile, known as the Foster Panel, to review the SSP and annual stockpile certification process. Its first report in November 1999 recommended, amongst other things, immediate conceptual design work on a new pit production facility, research into alternative robust nuclear weapons designs, and strengthening the annual certification process to more aggressively explore potential problems.[218]

In 2000 Congress took a decisive step and established the National Nuclear Security Administration (NNSA) as a semi-autonomous body within DOE to address enduring concern about the lack of focus and attention in DOE on the nuclear mission since the end of the Cold War and persistent problems with management, the SSP, the consolidation of the complex and security.[219] Security concerns were particularly salient following the discovery of Chinese state espionage at the nuclear weapons laboratories in the late 1990s.[220] A 1999 report by the President's Foreign Intelligence Advisory Board in response to security lapses was fierce in its criticism of DOE's institutional resistance to change, particularly to improvements in security. It stated that, 'The Department of Energy is a dysfunctional bureaucracy that has proven it is incapable of reforming itself' and recommended that DOE's weapon research and stockpile management functions should be placed wholly within a new semi-autonomous agency within the Department of Energy.[221] NNSA's mission was vast, and included maintaining a safe, secure, and reliable nuclear weapons stockpile; promoting international nuclear safety and non-proliferation; reducing the nuclear danger from weapons of mass destruction; providing the Navy with safe and effective nuclear propulsion systems; and supporting American leadership in science and technology.[222]

Nevertheless, change was not immediately forthcoming and in 2000 and 2001 the first head of the NNSA, General John Gordon, gave a damning critique before Congress of the lack of support for the nuclear deterrence mission, problems with the SSP, lack of management cohesion and direction, the absence of confidence from Congress and from DOE's own employees, the problems of an ageing and failing infrastructure and major difficulties in meeting the massive warhead LEP schedule.[223]

Conclusion

The rate of change in nuclear weapons policy slowed considerably under Clinton. With a Democratic president and a Democratic-controlled Congress many people from the arms control and disarmament community expected a significant change of direction in nuclear policy towards a minimum deterrent posture. In fact there was significant continuation but with two important differences: a much greater emphasis on non-proliferation goals in the context of nuclear arms control, nuclear weapons policy and missile defence; and the increasingly central importance of the state of the nuclear weapons production complex and its ability to sustain the nuclear arsenal in an era of zero nuclear testing and no new weapons development.

Despite initial indications of a major shift in nuclear weapons policy the administration remained committed to a Cold War conception of strategic stability based on nuclear parity with Russia, a large nuclear force on high alert able to launch on warning of attack, a strategic triad to deter a Russian first-strike, the ability to deliver a prompt and massive retaliatory strike against many thousands of counter-force and counter-value targets, and a nuclear hedge to reduce the perceived risk of a resurgent adversarial regime in Moscow. The dominant view insisted that as long as Russia's nuclear arsenal existed it had to be deterred with a force structure and planning process rooted in the Cold War. Proposals for moving to a smaller dyad of SLBMs and bombers and de-alerting portions of the deployed force were rejected. This was formalised in the 1994 NPR that largely reinforced the status quo inherited from George H. W. Bush and was only modified in 1997 through new nuclear guidance seven years after the end of the Cold War in PDD-60.

Clinton and Yeltsin and later Putin regularly proclaimed a new relationship based on cooperation, common security and partnership. Some saw incongruence between these statements and actions and an American nuclear weapons policy based on Cold War precepts. Others saw stability in the Cold War-era nuclear relationship and considered it the foundation of a new cooperative partnership. Clinton placed considerable emphasis on the Cold War-era bilateral nuclear arms control process with Russia, particularly START II and III and preservation of the ABM treaty. It is clear, as Avis Bohlen former Assistant Secretary of State for Arms Control under Clinton argues, that the administration did not question the relevance of this structure to the post-Cold War world, particularly the relevance of the ABM treaty, and made no effort to rethink the Cold War conception of strategic stability and the mutual assured destruction paradigm that governed nuclear weapons, arms control, missile defences and relations with Russia.[224]

The administration believed strongly that multilateral arms control in the context of the NPT, particularly the CTBT and indefinite extension of the NPT at the 1995 Review and Extension Conference, was the most appropriate means of addressing the growing perceived threat from nuclear proliferation and 'rogue' states. This led to a major disagreement with the post-1994 Republican-controlled Congress over the relationship between missile defence, nuclear weapons policy, nuclear arms control and nuclear deterrence. This disagreement, vehement at times, prevented Clinton from reducing nuclear forces below START I levels until START II entered into force, led to the voting down of the CTBT and pitched firm support for the development and deployment of missile defence systems and abrogation of the ABM treaty against entry into force of START II.[225] By 1996 it was clear that the START process was in jeopardy and START III was effectively stillborn at Helsinki in 1997. This was compounded by growing Russian distrust of American national security policy through the 1990s with deep suspicion over the long-term implications of America's missile defence plans, NATO expansion and American policy in Iraq and the Balkans. Russian concerns over the cost of implementing START II were further complicating factors. Under Clinton the deployed strategic warhead arsenal remained at roughly 8,500 with a total warhead stockpile of deployed strategic, tactical and reserve warheads of approximately 20,000.[226]

The post-Cold War shift in nuclear weapons policy towards WMD-armed 'rogue' states accelerated under Clinton. STRATCOM and the JCS explored nuclear options for countering WMD-armed dictators in regional conflicts. This was institutionalised in DOD policy and JCS doctrine and facilitated by continued improvements to STRATCOM's adaptive planning capabilities. It was increasingly argued that Cold War deterrence assumptions and planning processes could not be applied to these unpredictable and perhaps irrational 'rogue' state leaders. Pressure increased for new or modified nuclear weapons for specific counter-proliferation missions, in particular to destroy mobile strategic targets and hardened and deeply buried targets (HDBTs). The B61-11 was deployed in Clinton's second term to target HDBTs but research and development on new low-yield 'mini-nukes' was banned by Congress.

It was accepted early in the administration that there would be no nuclear testing and no new nuclear weapons and that the Cold War legacy force had to be sustained for the long term. The long-term credibility and surety of the nuclear arsenal and nuclear deterrent threats were therefore increasingly dependent on the long-term health of a consolidated and revitalised nuclear weapons production complex. Retention or re-establishment of key capabilities and expertise was considered crucial and the slow pace of implementing the Complex-21 plan and inadequate management of the nuclear weapons mission at both DOD and DOE became a growing cause of concern in Congress and the nuclear weapons policy community leading eventually to the establishment of NNSA. The massive warhead life extension programme was a source of significant unease, with DOE already falling behind with a refurbishment schedule that was going to increase dramatically over the next 10–20 years.

Nuclear testing was a major issue for the administration. Clinton was committed to the test moratorium, which he extended and made permanent by signing the CTBT in 1996. The Republican-controlled Congress and many in the nuclear weapons policy community were opposed. Where Clinton saw the CTBT as a key non-proliferation tool and a crucial part of the indefinite extension of the NPT, critics argued that it had little non-proliferation value and would undermine the credibility of American nuclear deterrent threats. There was no substitute for nuclear testing despite the administration's major financial commitment to the Stockpile Stewardship Program. The divisive vote on the CTBT in 1999 highlighted competing views on nuclear weapons policy that were also reflected in debates and disagreements on START II, missile defence and the ABM treaty, the SSP, the value of the NPT, and the extent of the 'rogue' state threat.

Clinton's successor was therefore faced with a number of difficult policy issues: the future of the START process with Russia including ratification of START II and a host of issues around START III; the future of the ABM treaty, missile defence plans and links to further nuclear reductions; the overall relevance of the Cold War concept of strategic stability to American national security and nuclear weapons policy; growing concerns over the state of the nuclear weapons production complex; and the deterrence of WMD-armed 'rogue' states and the long-term role, if any, nuclear weapons might play. George W. Bush would address these issues but in a deeply divisive fashion.

5 Nuclear weapons policy under George W. Bush

As the Clinton presidency drew to a close the nuclear weapons policy community expressed significant concern at the lack of senior-level political and military attention paid to American nuclear weapons under Clinton. Nuclear weapons policy was characterised as drifting with no long-term sense of direction and with insufficient resources.[1] A number of reports recommended a much greater reorientation of nuclear weapons policy towards WMD-armed 'rogue' states, including new types of nuclear weapons, a reduction in nuclear force levels whilst maintaining a robust, modern and survivable counter-force nuclear arsenal, deployment of missile defences and strategic conventional capabilities to bolster deterrence and a renewed commitment to revitalising the nuclear weapons production complex. America was going to remain the pre-eminent global military power and this required superior nuclear forces postured to deter and defeat any WMD-armed adversary.[2]

These views came to dominate nuclear weapons policy under George W. Bush, which was defined by four of the 15 key decisions identified: the 2001 Nuclear Posture Review (NPR), the 2002 Moscow Treaty, the establishment of a new Strategic Command (STRATCOM) in 2002 and the 2005/2006 Reliable Replacement Warhead (RRW) and Complex-2030 plans. The Cold War legacy nuclear arsenal and production complex continued to undergo modernisation and refurbishment but extensive plans for new capabilities were also developed. The NPR established a more explicit focus for nuclear weapons policy on WMD-armed 'rogue' states, presenting a 'new triad' of nuclear capabilities and reconceptualising prevailing understandings of nuclear deterrence. The Moscow Treaty was presented as the foundation of a new cooperative strategic framework with Russia. It resolved the long debate on the future of the START process and missile defence deployments by terminating START II and the ABM treaty. The Complex-2030 plan presented a long-term plan for modernising and consolidating the nuclear production complex through to 2030, with production of controversial Reliable Replacement Warheads at its heart. Despite considerable continuities with Clinton, the Bush administration's nuclear weapons policy initiatives represented a significant break from the past. Some welcomed the new initiatives whilst others considered them deeply destabilising.

Nuclear policy and the 2001 Nuclear Posture Review

During his election campaign George W. Bush pledged to dramatically reduce deployed numbers of strategic nuclear weapons that were lingering at START I levels and to redefine America's strategic relationship with Russia.[3] In May 2001 he declared:

> We can, and will, change the size, the composition, the character of our nuclear forces in a way that reflects the reality that the Cold War is over. I am committed to achieving a credible deterrent with the lowest-possible number of nuclear weapons consistent with our national security needs, including our obligations to our allies. My goal is to move quickly to reduce nuclear forces.[4]

On entering office the administration initiated a number of major defence reviews to restructure the armed forces for the twenty-first century, including reviews of missile defence, space-based capabilities and strategic forces. These flowed into the congressionally-mandated 2001 Quadrennial Defense Review (QDR) and Nuclear Posture Review.[5] President Bush subsequently announced in November 2001 that he would reduce deployed strategic nuclear forces to between 2,200 and 1,700 warheads.[6] The classified NPR was presented to Congress in December 2001, although substantial parts of it were leaked.[7] The administration characterised the NPR as a major change in nuclear weapons policy, with Linton Brooks, head of the National Nuclear Security Administration (NNSA), describing it in 2004 as 'the most sweeping conceptual change in nuclear thinking since the Sloss study in the late 1970s'.[8]

The new approach set out in the NPR was based on a strong presidential desire to significantly reduce deployed nuclear forces and establish a new strategic security relationship with Russia, a powerful conviction that the nature of nuclear deterrence in the post-Cold War era had fundamentally changed because of the growing threat of WMD-armed 'rogue' states and a more general desire to reduce reliance on the Cold War legacy nuclear arsenal in defence planning by developing new conventional and nuclear strategic capabilities.

The NPR recommended a series of changes to nuclear weapons policy and formalised a number of ongoing practices. The traditional strategic nuclear triad of SLBMs, ICBMs and long-range nuclear bombers was replaced by a new triad. The first leg of the new triad consisted of offensive strike systems, including advanced conventional weapons, the traditional nuclear triad and enhanced command and control capabilities. The second leg comprised defences, both active, such as missile defence, and passive, such as WMD troop protection. The third leg constituted a revitalised defence infrastructure for developing, building, and maintaining offensive forces and defensive systems, including a revived nuclear weapons production complex that the review considered to have atrophied since the end of the Cold War.[9] The administration linked further nuclear force reductions to successful deployment of other aspects of the new triad, including advanced conventional capabilities, a more robust infrastructure, and integrated intelligence, planning and reconnaissance capabilities.[10]

Specific recommendations included retaining the traditional strategic nuclear triad with substantial reductions in deployed nuclear forces; deployment of non-nuclear strike forces and defence systems such as ballistic and cruise missile defences, space defences and cyber defences; sustained improvement in the nuclear weapons complex to allow a quick and flexible response to future strategic nuclear threats; a reduction in the time required to test nuclear weapons; establishment of an Advanced Concepts Initiative (ACI) to study new or modified warhead designs at the weapons laboratories; development of new, or enhanced, nuclear weapons capabilities to threaten specific targets, particularly hard and deeply buried targets (HDBTs); a more sophisticated strategic command and control system for rapid response to emerging strategic threats and targets of opportunity; and finally a modified approach to deterring WMD-armed 'rogue' states to reduce the risk of the threat of use or actual use of WMD against American forces, allies or territory.

Following the submission of the NPR to Congress a DOD Nuclear Posture Implementation Plan was signed in March 2002 and the NNSA equivalent in April 2002.[11] The plan led to successive budget requests to Congress to fund programmes to advance the NPR agenda. These included funding for a Robust Nuclear Earth Penetrator (RNEP) weapon, a request to repeal the congressional ban on research and development of new low-yield nuclear warheads, establishment of an Advanced Concepts Initiative with advanced concepts teams to study new warhead designs at the nuclear laboratories and a new Modern Pit Facility.[12]

The NPR established four roles for the new triad: assure, dissuade, deter and defeat. These reflected roles applied to the entire armed forces in the 2001 QDR. The new triad would assure allies and friends through credible non-nuclear and nuclear response options; dissuade competitors by maintaining and developing a range of strategic capabilities to reduce any benefits from competing with America; deter aggressors with nuclear and non-nuclear options and defences; and defeat an enemy if deterrence failed through overwhelming force against a range of targets based on robust war plans and adaptive planning capabilities.[13] These roles were reiterated in the JCS 2005 draft Joint Doctrine for Nuclear Operations, the administration's first formal update of nuclear doctrine.[14] These roles suggested that America's nuclear and conventional superiority would actively counter proliferation of WMD and ballistic missiles by underscoring for potential or would-be peer competitors 'the futility of trying to sprint toward parity with us or superiority'.[15] The assurance role, according to STRATCOM and DOD, would reduce incentives for allies to develop their own nuclear capabilities, and strategic defences and non-nuclear strategic forces would reduce proliferation by reducing incentives for heavy investment in WMD-armed ballistic missiles by potential adversaries.[16]

'Rogue' states and deterrence by denial

The administration argued that the proliferation of nuclear weapons and ballistic missiles to 'rogue' states had created new challenges for deterrence. The international security environment was now characterised by strategic uncertainty where the source of threats would be unpredictable. The NPR therefore restructured nuclear contingency planning into three categories under the headings immediate, potential and unexpected contingencies. Immediate contingencies involved well-recognised current dangers such as an attack using WMD against American forces or allies in the Middle East or Asia. Leaked excerpts of the NPR referred to the risks of an Iraqi attack on Israel or its neighbours, a North Korean attack on South Korea, or a military confrontation with China over the status of Taiwan.[17] Potential contingencies were plausible, but not immediate, dangers that could be prepared for, such as the emergence of a new, hostile WMD-armed military coalition against America or its allies, or the re-emergence of a hostile peer competitor such as Russia. Unexpected contingencies were sudden and unpredictable security challenges such as sudden regime change that could place an existing nuclear arsenal into the hands of a new, hostile leadership, or an adversary's surprise acquisition of WMD.[18]

Contingencies involving WMD-armed regional adversaries (including China)[19] completely replaced Russia as the priority in nuclear weapons policy and planning – a near total reversal from the 1994 NPR according to STRATCOM.[20] This formalised and further institutionalised the process of regional nuclear targeting initiated under Clinton and was not a wholesale shift in direction.[21] It involved planning for contingencies involving North Korea, Iraq, Syria, Iran, Libya and perhaps terrorist groups. These five countries were those that could be involved at all three of the NPR's contingency levels. All were judged to have long-standing hostility toward America, to sponsor or harbour terrorist groups, and have active WMD and missile programmes.[22]

This approach was cemented by the attacks of 11 September 2001 that reinforced the perception of a dangerous and uncertain environment, described by Rumsfeld as 'possibly the most dangerous security environment the world has known'.[23] Deputy Secretary of Defense Paul Wolfowitz argued that, 'The element of surprise – and the reality of little or no warning – must be understood as a critical feature of the security environment America faces – and one we must factor into our defense planning for the decades ahead'.[24] The administration argued that the world changed irrevocably after 9/11, necessitating a new focus on the potential nexus of terrorist networks, WMD and 'rogue' states.[25] This constituted a new national security paradigm and the administration went on to place Iraq at the centre of that nexus.[26] The new paradigm was formalised in the September 2002 National Security Strategy that highlighted the need for counter-proliferation actions against WMD threats with pre-emptive strikes if necessary since containment and deterrence of 'rogue' states, notably Iraq, was no longer acceptable. President Bush stated:

> We must be prepared to stop rogue states and their terrorist clients before they are able to threaten or use weapons of mass destruction against the United States and our allies and friends ... The overlap between states that sponsor terror and those that pursue WMD compels us to action.[27]

The counter-proliferation theme was extended in the December 2002 National Strategy to Combat Weapons of Mass Destruction.[28]

The new paradigm and the NPR reflected a major loss of confidence in America's ability to deter 'rogue' states with existing Cold War-era nuclear forces and practices. The administration argued that 'rogue' states would not be constrained or deterred through diplomatic efforts, international norms and traditional arms control, or deterrence by the threat of nuclear retaliation.[29] Traditional nuclear deterrent threats would have little effect against unpredictable 'rogues' that might collaborate with terrorist groups to inflict massive damage through the use of WMD and could no longer be relied upon to prevent 'rogue' state aggression.[30] As Vice President Cheney stated in 2003:

> In a post-September 11 world.... we cannot continue to rely upon these old, Cold War doctrines in the future. How do you contain 'rogue' states willing to provide terrorists with weapons of mass destruction? How do you deter terrorists who have no nation to defend.... These problems will define the new era in American foreign policy.[31]

The NPR therefore advocated a posture of 'deterrence by denial' for WMD-armed 'rogues' rather than 'deterrence by punishment' in order to deny an adversary any opportunities and benefits that might come from using WMD.[32] During the Cold War deterrence was understood primarily as deterrence by punishment – a retaliatory threat to inflict unacceptable damage upon an adversary if it attacked America, defined by the doctrine of mutual assured destruction. Parts of the nuclear weapons policy community were dissatisfied with this approach and articulated an alternative interpretation of nuclear deterrence. They did not believe the Soviet Union could be deterred by sole reliance on a strategy of deterrence by punishment and attempted to shift deterrence strategy towards one of deterrence by denial. This was based on a counter-force nuclear arsenal and doctrine configured to try and deny the Soviet Union as little advantage as possible from initiating conflict at any level. This was reflected in the development of limited nuclear options, Carter's countervailing and Reagan's prevailing nuclear doctrines explored in chapter two.[33] Nevertheless, during the Cold War a doctrine of deterrence by denial still relied on punitive threats and was only of marginal relevance against a superpower adversary.[34] In the post-Cold War period, however, an explicit strategy of deterrence by denial could more credibly be applied to 'rogue' states that lacked a secure second strike nuclear capability and that were not in an assured societal destruction relationship with America: 'with regional challengers, or even a regional peer adversary, the United States can indeed aspire to meaningful military victory, even if the adversary has or uses WMD'.[35] The administration's approach to countering the WMD assets of 'rogue' adversaries was to develop and deploy credible strategic capabilities for war-fighting to achieve military victory.

The distinction between deterrence by punishment and deterrence by denial was further clarified in the Defence Science Board's 2004 report on *Future Strategic Strike Forces*. The report described a dual role for 'strategic strike forces' in the post-9/11 security environment. In the context of 'rogue' states and terrorist groups their role was to disarm and defeat aggressive non-WMD-armed states, WMD-armed non-state actors, and 'rogues' with modest or robust WMD. In the context of major powers, their role was to control escalation and limit damage in conflicts with major powers armed with WMD and with peer adversaries.[36] This, in fact, represented a significant continuation of the roles assigned to nuclear weapons by the Clinton administration.[37] It is important to note that a 2003 report by RAND on *Future Roles of U.S. Nuclear Weapons* stated that deterrence by denial was 'logically indistinguishable from actual war-fighting capability'.[38]

Deterrence by denial required a new set of offensive and defensive strategic capabilities to respond to a range of enemy capabilities and potential contingencies, rather than a specific single, long-term threat as in the Cold War. These would enhance traditional nuclear deterrent threats and reduce the risks associated with future strategic uncertainty.[39] This was described as a shift to a capabilities-based approach to strategic deterrence based on *how* America might employ its strategic forces, rather against *whom* and *where*. This required the flexibility to tailor strategic deterrence posture to different adversaries and changing circumstances and the integration of nuclear forces into overall military planning, rather than treating them in isolation.[40] Understandings of strategic deterrence therefore shifted to a capabilities-based deterrence by denial posture that expanded that concept of strategic deterrence beyond simply nuclear deterrence.[41]

This approach was integrated into defence planning in 2002 when the administration released its National Strategy to Combat Weapons of Mass Destruction. It was reported that a classified version of the document, National Security Presidential Directive 17 (NSPD-17), signed in September 2002, specifically named Libya, Syria, Iran and North Korea as the focus of the new strategy, which included the potential use of American nuclear weapons.[42] It was reinforced in the 2004 National Military Strategy of the United States.[43] In fact the shift to a capabilities-based approach in response to strategic uncertainty was part of a much broader wholesale transformation of the armed forces initiated by Secretary of Defense Donald Rumsfeld in 2001. He argued that contending with uncertainty was now at the centre of defence planning and that this required much more emphasis on capabilities in addition to threat-based planning to address near-term threats.[44]

This reconceptualisation of strategic deterrence reflected a particular view that had been articulated throughout the post-Cold War period by conservative national security think-tanks. Two individuals were particularly prominent –

Robert Joseph (later Special Assistant to the President and Senior Director for Proliferation Strategy, Counter-proliferation & Homeland Defense in the National Security Council under George W. Bush) and Keith Payne (later brought into DOD for a year to oversee the 2001 NPR). Payne and Joseph published a number of articles in the 1990s that argued that Cold War-style deterrence could not be applied to WMD-armed regional adversaries, that new capabilities, particularly missile defences, were needed to counter this threat, and that nuclear posture had to be more adaptable, responsive and based on deterrence by denial.[45] This culminated in the January 2001 report *Rationale and Requirements for U.S. Nuclear Forces and Arms Control* published by the National Institute for Public Policy. Many of its recommendations and conclusions were reflected in the 2001 NPR.[46] Several participants in the study behind the report went on to serve in the Bush administration in roles affecting nuclear weapons policy.[47] The study was directed by Keith Payne and the final report was fully endorsed in 2001 by STRATCOM Commander Richard Mies.[48]

Pre-emptive planning and 'global strike'

The shift to a capabilities-based deterrence by denial strategy and the administration's emphasis on future uncertainty and unexpected contingencies involving WMD-armed 'rogue' states led to the development of pre-emptive military planning and rapid reaction strategic forces for a new 'global strike' mission.[49] The right to engage in pre-emptive counter-proliferation missions was asserted by the administration in its 2002 National Strategy to Combat WMD.[50]

This was reflected in the establishment of a new Strategic Command. In the first of two changes to the Unified Command Plan in October 2002 United States Space Command was disestablished and its missions incorporated into STRATCOM.[51] STRATCOM was now responsible for nuclear deterrence, space, and computer network operations. The second change in January 2003 gave STRATCOM four previously unassigned responsibilities: global strike, missile defence integration, global integrated information operations, and global command, control, communications, computers, intelligence, surveillance and reconnaissance – collectively labelled C4ISR.[52] STRATCOM's new mission was now to 'provide a global warfighting capability … to deter and defeat those who desire to attack the United States and its allies' with a host of strategic conventional as well as nuclear capabilities.[53] To facilitate the new mission STRATCOM initiated a comprehensive Strategic Warfare Planning System Transformation Study to increase its responsiveness to unexpected emerging strategic threats.[54] The SWPS modernisation (SWPS-M), renamed the Integrated Strategic Planning and Analysis Network, will allow war planners to dramatically shorten the time between developing a strike plan and its execution. It will provide political and military leaders 'with a nuclear war planning and execution tool that vastly surpasses the capabilities in place during the final phases of the Cold War to fight a global war with the Soviet Union'.[55]

The administration repeatedly denied that it was developing any plans for the pre-emptive use of nuclear weapons, but the 2005 JCS draft Joint Doctrine for Nuclear Operations suggested otherwise. It stated that American nuclear forces could be used to counter 'an adversary using or intending to use WMD against US, multinational, or alliance forces or civilian populations' and to counter 'imminent attack from adversary biological weapons that only effects from nuclear weapons can safely destroy', strongly suggesting a pre-emptive nuclear doctrine.[56]

The administration was far more explicit about the possibility of a nuclear response to a chemical or biological weapons attack and considered the NPT's Negative Security Guarantees outdated (see chapter five).[57] In March 2002 State Department spokesman Richard Boucher reaffirmed the 1995 reiteration of the Negative Security Assurance but qualified it by stating that, 'If a weapon of mass destruction is used against the United States or its allies, we will not rule out any specific type of military response'.[58] It was also reported that NSPD-17 emphasised the use of nuclear weapons in response to a biological or chemical weapons attack.[59]

The objective of STRATCOM's new global strike mission was to 'provide future Presidents an integrated, flexible, and highly reliable set of strike options with today's tactical-level flexibility but on a global scale'. It is defined as 'the ability to engage priority targets by moving rapidly from actionable intelligence, through adaptive planning, to senior-level decision-making and the delivery of kinetic or non-kinetic effects across thousands of miles'.[60] The global strike mission would require strategic delivery systems that could 'hit time-urgent targets promptly from long-ranges' and accurately and reliably destroy hard and deeply buried targets.[61]

The focus of the conventional global strike mission has been the conversion of strategic nuclear delivery vehicles to conventional missions. The idea of converting Trident, Minuteman or Peacekeeper missiles to conventional missions was discussed throughout the 1990s.[62] In 2002 the administration announced that it was exploring two advanced conventional strike applications: a 'fast-response, precision-impact, conventional penetrator for hard and deeply buried targets' and 'modification of a strategic ballistic missile system to enable the deployment of a non-nuclear payload'. A prime candidate was the Trident II (D5) SLBM.[63] The 2004 Defense Science Board report *Future Strategic Strike Forces* also recommended development and deployment of a conventional intermediate-range ballistic missile and conversion of the retired Peacekeeper ICBM for conventional delivery to provide 'an affordable, near-term, and prompt strike capability'.[64] A 2007 report *Conventional Prompt Global Strike Capability* by the National Academy of Sciences recommended funding the Navy's Conventional Trident Modification (CTM) programme. The CTM programme planned to install 96 GPS-guided non-nuclear warheads on 24 Trident II missiles throughout the SSBN fleet with total time from decision to 'weapon-on-target' of about one hour. Funding was sought for FY2008 to allow full operational capability by the end of 2012.[65] One of the major problems was that other countries' early-warning systems would not be able to distinguish between a nuclear-armed and a conventionally-armed SLBM or ICBM, leading to potentially disastrous escalation in a crisis.[66] In 2007 Congress refused to fund the CTM programme for this reason, but it did provide funds for work on next-generation conventional strategic systems, such as the Army's Advanced Hypersonic Weapon.[67]

The emphasis on global strike and pre-emptive conventional and nuclear planning was reflected in the demise of the SIOP nuclear war plan and its replacement with a family of strategic strike plans. In 2003 the SIOP was eliminated and replaced with an operations plan, OPLAN 8044, which still contained the major pre-planned strike options from the SIOP. The shift to regional targeting of WMD-armed 'rogues' was reflected in 'OPLAN 8044 Revision 03' – a revision of the nuclear war plan that came into effect in March 2003. It appeared to be based on National Security Presidential Directive-14 signed by the President in June 2002. The new directive reportedly provided guidance to incorporate strike options against regional adversaries into the strategic nuclear war plan and probably replaced Clinton's PDD-60 issued in 1997. By 2005 it had incorporated conventional strike options. It was also reported that a companion contingency plan, CONPLAN 8022, for the global strike mission was developed to enable a prompt response to a number of contingencies with nations other than Russia. It was activated in 2004 and reportedly provides the President with a day-to-day pre-emptive strike option.[68]

The administration argued that these developments would reduce dependence on nuclear forces by expanding the concept of strategic deterrence beyond just nuclear deterrence, integrating nuclear capabilities into conventional force planning and fielding conventional strategic offensive and defensive systems.[69] New capabilities would allow nuclear missions to be reassigned to strategic conventional forces and a posture of deterrence by denial would make deterrent threats more credible and reduce the likelihood of war.[70] According to Deputy Secretary of Defense Paul Wolfowitz this would 'reduce to the absolute minimum the possibility that we would ever need to use those terrible [nuclear] weapons'.[71] With the new STRATCOM now dealing with six strategic missions the role of nuclear deterrence in STRATCOM planning and military planning in general would be further diluted. As STRATCOM commander Admiral James Ellis stated in 2003:

> We will incorporate conventional, non-kinetic, and special operations capabilities into a full-spectrum contingency arsenal and into the nation's strategic war plan to further reduce our reliance on nuclear weapons.... Our intent is to provide a wide range of advanced options to the President in responding to time-critical, high-threat, global challenges and, thereby, raise even higher the nuclear threshold.[72]

Nuclear weapons and flexible nuclear targeting capabilities were still deemed vital to strategic deterrence. They were, however, less central to the active deterrence of WMD-armed 'rogue' states than they were to deterring the Soviet Union.

Criticism of the NPR and the new deterrence strategy

Critics argued that the NPR would increase, not decrease, reliance on nuclear weapons, spur further nuclear proliferation, undermine the Nuclear Non-Proliferation Treaty (NPT) and take nuclear weapons policy in a radically new and possibly destabilising direction. Cirincione, for example, described the NPR as a 'deeply flawed document'.[73] The NPR did not represent a break from Cold War nuclear doctrine because it envisaged maintenance of a substantial force of nuclear weapons on high-alert capable of launching on warning of attack for the indefinite future.[74] The administration had not changed nuclear planning and force structure since it 'remains configured for large-scale counter-force attacks against a broad array of targets in Russia'.[75] It failed to explain why America still needed to deploy thousands of nuclear weapons backed by thousands in reserve if Russia was no longer the primary target of American nuclear forces. The proposed integration of nuclear forces into mainstream military planning would lower the so-called nuclear threshold at which the use of nuclear weapons might be considered in a conflict, thereby increasing the risk that nuclear weapons would be used.[76] The roles assigned to nuclear weapons by the NPR reaffirmed the military utility and necessity of nuclear weapons and sent 'a dangerous message to other nations contemplating development of nuclear weapons'.[77] Critics refuted the notion that American nuclear weapons had a major role to play in the counter-proliferation missions identified in the NPR and argued that emphasising a counter-proliferation role for nuclear weapons could spur some states to develop and deploy nuclear weapons in response.[78] Cirincione also took issue with the new capabilities-based approach, arguing that it simply provided cover to justify a nuclear force of any size or any new weapon system 'that is politically attractive whether or not the threat justifies such capabilities'. The lack of any concrete threat assessment was deemed 'a glaring weakness in the review'.[79]

Cirincione's criticisms were shared by former JCS Vice Chairman Admiral William Owens, former Secretary of Defense William Perry, former Senator Sam Nunn and former STRATCOM commander Eugene Habiger. They argued that the nuclear policy actions set out in the NPR would: increase the salience of nuclear weapons; foster a continuing arms race; expand options for nuclear attacks; and increase the number of targeted nations. Perry, Habiger and Nunn argued that while these ideas 'may have a plausible military rationale, their collective effect is to suggest that the nation with the world's most powerful conventional forces is actually increasing its reliance on nuclear forces' and that others would follow suit.[80] In Congress Representative Frank, for example, concluded that 'this policy review urging more use of nuclear weapons in more situations against more countries is really quite frightening'.[81] Press coverage was equally damning, describing the NPR as a 'menacing' document and increasing 'the risk that nuclear weapons will be used in war'.[82] Others took a moderate line arguing that the NPR was neither the transformational doctrinal innovation its architects claimed it to be nor a dangerous new path to nuclear use as a number of critics argued.[83]

Nuclear forces

The Bush administration remained committed to a triad of strategic nuclear forces and their consolidation and modernisation. This was reaffirmed in the NPR and the Moscow Treaty. At the start of Bush's first term the ICBM fleet consisted of 500 Minuteman III and 50 MX Peacekeeper missiles. The SLBM force stood at 192 Trident I (C4) and 240 Trident II (D5) missiles. The total nuclear bomber fleet consisted of 21 B-2 Spirit bombers and 94 B-52H Stratofortress bombers.[84] The total operational stockpile of nuclear forces was estimated at 11,200 with around 8,700 operationally deployed strategic and tactical warheads.[85]

The administration immediately reduced deployed nuclear forces on entering office by retiring the MX Peacekeeper ICBM, withdrawing four Ohio-class SSBNs from nuclear missions and converting them to conventional roles and permanently ending the ability to return the B-1 bomber fleet to nuclear missions. By 2005 the Peacekeeper fleet had been fully deactivated and retired and the four oldest SSBNs had been withdrawn from nuclear service.[86] All three of these measures had been previously agreed in the 1994 NPR but delayed by the failure of START II to enter into force.

The Navy continued to extend the service life of the remaining 14 SSBNs and the Trident II (D5) missile fleet to 2042 and to replace the remaining Trident I (C4) missiles with the Trident II (D5), a process that was completed in 2005. The Submarine Warhead Protection Program was carried forward, and a new SLBM retargeting system was developed and deployed to allow quick retargeting and enhanced accuracy. The programme to modify the re-entry vehicle for around two-thirds of the W76 stockpile (roughly 2,000 warheads) to give the warheads a groundburst capability to destroy HDBTs also continued. The first of these W76-1 warheads were due to be deployed in late 2007.[87] In 2007 the Navy awarded a procurement contract to Lockheed Martin for the Trident II (D5) life extension programme. 108 D5 Life Extension (D5LE) missiles are scheduled for delivery between 2011 and 2017.[88]

Modernisation programmes for the Minuteman III ICBM fleet also continued. These included the guidance and propulsion replacement programmes to extend the life of the guidance system and improve accuracy to near that of the MX Peacekeeper, a Rapid Execution and Combat Targeting (REACT) programme and a Safety Enhanced Re-entry Vehicle (SERV) programme to reconfigure the missiles to carry the newer and more sophisticated W87 warheads from the retired Peacekeeper missiles.[89] The Air Force continued to examine alternative options for a new ICBM for deployment in 2018 to retain a land-based ICBM force for the next 20–40 years.[90] In 2002 150 Minuteman III missiles were reduced from three warheads per missile to a single warhead and a 'Mission Needs Statement' was issued for a new ICBM.[91] The 2006 Quadrennial Defense Review also announced plans to retire 50 MMIII ICBMs. Current plans envisage a 450-missile force carrying 500 warheads with several hundred warheads in reserve. START II plans to entirely de-MIRV the ICBM fleet were scrapped.[92]

The Navy and the Air Force also continued their joint programme to ensure the long-term viability of the research, development and manufacturing infrastructure for strategic nuclear missile systems.[93]

In 2003 a five-year modernisation programme for the B-2 bomber was completed enabling the aircraft to carry a greater variety of nuclear warheads as well as various conventional weapons. Both aircraft can deliver the variable yield B61-7 strategic bomb, the B61-11 'bunker buster' bomb deployed under Clinton plus the high-yield B83 strategic bomb. The B-52s also carry the Advanced Cruise Missile and the Air-Launched Cruise Missile. Plans to extend the service life of the missiles to 2030 were cancelled in 2007 with a decision to retire the ACM fleet and suspend the life extension programme of the missiles' W80 warhead. Kristensen notes that although the ALCM fleet had just completed a life-extension programme it will likely be reduced by two-thirds over the next five years.[94] The 2006 Quadrennial Defense Review also announced plans to reduce the number of B-52s to 56 to meet Moscow Treaty deployed warhead levels.[95]

The 2001 NPR divided the nuclear stockpile into two new categories: an active stockpile and an inactive stockpile. The active stockpile comprises operationally deployed forces for immediate contingencies and a responsive force of active warheads to augment nuclear deployments should new threats emerge over a period of time. Active warheads are maintained in a ready-for-use configuration with tritium and other limited-life components installed. Inactive warheads do not have limited-life components installed and may not have the latest warhead modifications.[96] The administration stated that nuclear forces needed to address potential contingencies involving Russia were now part of the responsive force, not the operationally deployed force.[97] Douglas Feith, Under Secretary of Defense for Policy, argued that the downgrading of contingencies involving a Russian nuclear attack from 'expected' to 'potential' and exclusion of long-standing requirements focused on the USSR and later Russia from calculations of nuclear requirements for immediate contingencies was a dramatic departure from previous policy.[98]

The NPR called for the destruction of some of the warheads removed from operational status, but not all. Many thousands of warheads would remain in the active and inactive reserves. The size of the active and inactive reserves was not addressed by the NPR but Feith and NNSA head Linton Brooks later stated that it would be substantially reduced from current levels.[99] The administration's primary reason for retaining an 'inactive reserve' was to guard against the emergence of serious safety or reliability problems in the active stockpile. A large reserve was needed because America lacked the capability to produce large numbers of warheads relatively quickly in the event of the catastrophic failure of a warhead type in the active stockpile. A sudden and dramatic change in the global security environment that could require augmentation of the operationally deployed arsenal with warheads from the responsive force and inactive reserve remained a secondary rationale.[100] Nevertheless, administration officials argued that future re-deployment of warheads withdrawn from operational service was very unlikely and that the reductions declared by Bush and formalised in the Moscow Treaty were essentially permanent.[101]

In May 2004 Bush announced a major reduction in the total nuclear stockpile, stating that it would be cut almost in half by 2012 as a result of the Strategic Capabilities Assessment follow-on from the 2001 NPR completed in 2005 in preparation for the 2006 QDR.[102] In December 2007 the White House approved a new stockpile plan to reduce the arsenal by a further 15 per cent.[103] Norris and Kristensen calculate that this will involve a reduction from approximately 10,500 in 2001 to around 4,600 warheads. With 2,200 warheads deployed under the Moscow Treaty this will leave a reserve arsenal of approximately 2,000 warheads and 400 non-strategic warheads.[104]

Serious questions have been asked about the need for such a large reserve given declarations of a new strategic relationship with Russia and confidence in the health of the stockpile through the Stockpile Stewardship Program. In 2002 former STRATCOM Commander Eugene Habiger argued:

> The view is just anachronistic that we have to keep thousands of weapons in reserve as a hedge against a downturn in US–Russia relations … if I were able to present in an open forum the facts on how many warheads we already have in reserve – that logic would not survive the light of day. We have more than enough warheads in our active reserve to guard against all contingencies.[105]

At the end of 2007 America deployed 10 types of nuclear warhead for six delivery platforms. These included tactical nuclear bombs delivered by fighter aircraft and non-deployed TLAM-N cruise missiles capable of being redeployed aboard attack submarines in addition to Trident II SLBMs, Minuteman III ICBMs and B-52 and B-2 bombers.

New nuclear weapons

The drive for new or modified nuclear weapons was reinforced by the administration's focus on WMD-armed 'rogue' states, a capabilities-based approach, strategies for pre-emptive military action for immediate WMD threats and regional deterrence by denial strategies. Deterrence by denial was judged to require warheads with special effects for tailored deterrence to provide the President with as many options as possible for a credible nuclear deterrent threat.[106] This required new or modified precision low-yield, earth-penetrating, and enhanced radiation warheads rather than the high-yield weapons of the Cold War.[107] This was supported by a number of prominent reports published in 2000 and 2001 by influential nuclear weapons experts, many of whom were brought into the Bush administration.[108] These reports all recommended development of new low-yield and earth-penetrating nuclear warheads on precision missiles to target the mobile WMD and HDBTs of 'rogue' states. The focus on new and modified 'bunker buster' earth-penetrating nuclear warheads and low-yield nuclear warheads was often conflated as a drive for a new low-yield 'bunker buster' weapon. In fact the two issues were separate since an earth-penetrating weapon would have to be of relatively high yield to destroy HDBTs.[109] An important secondary rationale was the retention and exercise of nuclear warhead design knowledge and skills.[110]

The NPR reportedly stated that 'Nuclear weapons could be employed against targets able to withstand non-nuclear attack, (for example, deep underground bunkers or bio-weapon facilities)'.[111] It also argued that the B61-11 earth-penetrating nuclear gravity bomb for destroying HDBTs was inadequate and that its limitations significantly reduced the probability of the successful destruction of such important targets. The NPR therefore argued for a more effective earth penetrator weapon to destroy a wider range of buried targets with a much lower yield, although it accepted that defeat of very deep or larger underground facilities, would still require high-yield weapons.[112]

The Robust Nuclear Earth Penetrator (RNEP) programme envisaged a three-year study to assess the feasibility of modifying either the B83 or the B61 bomb to vastly improve the capability to defeat HDBTs followed by a decision on weapon development by the Nuclear Weapons Council. The initial focus of the Advanced Concepts Initiative was to be the RNEP programme.[113] RNEP was controversial and critics, including many in Congress, argued that new or modified 'bunker buster' and low-yield warheads would increase the usability of nuclear weapons and lower the threshold for nuclear use in a conflict. Following the Bush administration's articulation of a doctrine of pre-emptive military attacks against WMD-armed 'rogue' states and its plan to reduce the time required to resume nuclear testing, a number of critics argued that the administration was intent on designing, testing and then using pre-emptively a new suite of 'usable' nuclear weapons.[114] The RNEP programme was therefore regarded as a slippery slope towards a resumption of nuclear testing and deployment of new nuclear weapons for regional war-fighting purposes.

Critics also argued that development of new or modified nuclear weapons would encourage other countries to develop similar weapons. Representative Mark Udall, for example, stated that 'By continuing the development of new U.S. nuclear weapons at the same time that we are trying to convince other nations to forego obtaining such weapons, we undermine our credibility in the fight to stop nuclear proliferation'.[115] Senator Feinstein argued in 2005 that:

> A study on the development of new nuclear weapons will still greatly undermine our nuclear nonproliferation efforts by telling the rest of the world that when it comes to nuclear weapons, do as we say and not as we do. This is hypocrisy, pure and simple.[116]

A study by the National Academy of Sciences in April 2005 also confirmed that an RNEP weapon would produce major radioactive fallout that could not be contained by burrowing the warhead deep into the ground prior to detonation as some proponents claimed.[117]

To exert further control over the process Congress withheld funding for the RNEP programme in 2002 until DOD and DOE had submitted a detailed report describing RNEP's military requirements, the employment policy for the weapon and a full description of the categories or types of targets that the RNEP was designed to hold at risk.[118] In 2003 Congress barred DOE from entering engineering development, or subsequent development phases, of RNEP 'unless specifically authorised by Congress' but it did authorise continuation of the study.[119] Congress did, however, repeal the 1993 ban against research into new low-yield nuclear warheads below five kilotons in 2003 to allow the administration to proceed with the Advanced Concepts Initiative.[120]

The administration and its supporters in Congress insisted that American nuclear weapons research would not have any effect on nuclear proliferation.[121] They argued that the ACI, RNEP, the plan to reduce test readiness and the administration's pre-emptive doctrine were separate developments and should not be linked together. NNSA head Linton Brooks remarked in 2004 to the Heritage Foundation:

> It became part of the conventional wisdom that there were Administration plans to develop new, low-yield weapons. There are no such plans. Second, people saw these separate things as part of an overall strategy; that we were emphasizing 'nuclear preemption' in U.S. military doctrine. I have had a Committee chairman tell me we were planning on developing low-yield weapons to use preemptively against terrorists in places like Afghanistan. I assume you all understand this is nonsense.[122]

The administration was adamant that it did not intend to develop and deploy any *new* nuclear weapons and insisted that the RNEP programme was just a study.[123] In 2003 the Air Force and Navy both stated that they had no requirements for a *new* nuclear weapon and STRATCOM commander James Ellis stated in 2003 that 'to date, the Department of Defense has not identified a specific requirement for a new low-yield nuclear weapon'.[124] Furthermore, nuclear weapons were only one option under consideration for targeting HDBTs.[125] Ellis noted that the need for a nuclear capability to defeat HDBTs had been validated by the military and the Nuclear Weapons Council on a number of occasions under Clinton and George W. Bush.[126] Nevertheless, the administration continued to work on modifying a range of nuclear warheads beyond the RNEP study. These were listed by Brooks in 2003 as a concept study by the Air Force on an Enhanced Cruise Missile; a study by Air Force Space Command on alternate yield options for a small quantity of Minuteman III ICBM warheads; and interest from the Navy in examining alternate yields for the W76 Trident warhead. Brooks also stated that the military may initiate studies into warhead designs with reduced fission or low-yield.[127]

In 2004 Congress cut funding for RNEP and ACI. As feasibility study costs for the programme rose from $45 million to $145 million the House Armed Services Committee eliminated all RNEP funding in 2005 and transferred it to work on a conventional non-nuclear version leading to the termination of the RNEP programme.[128]

Nuclear arms control

A new relationship with Russia

On entering office the Bush administration declared its intention to transform relations with Russia through 'a new strategic framework' and consign to history the doctrine of mutual assured destruction as a feature of their relations. The Clinton administration previously attempted to transform the US–Russia strategic relationship into a fully cooperative relationship through the START arms control process, an ABM treaty demarcation agreement and confidence building measures, such as the Cooperative Threat Reduction programme and NATO-Russia Founding Act. In September 2000 Clinton had argued:

> Strategic stability, based on mutual deterrence, is still important, despite the end of the Cold War. Why? Because the United States and Russia still have nuclear arsenals that can devastate each other. And this is still a period of transition in our relationship.... But while we are no longer adversaries, we are not yet real allies. Therefore, for them as well as for us, maintaining strategic stability increases trust and confidence on both sides. It reduces the risk of confrontation. It makes it possible to build an even better partnership and an even safer world.[129]

Deploying national missile defences, breaking the ABM treaty, and abandoning the START process would undermine this concept of strategic stability.

The Bush administration wholly disagreed and sought to resolve the deadlock over the START process and the ABM treaty by transforming the concept of strategic stability. It looked to shift the meaning of the concept from one focused on an adversarial relationship to one based on cooperation to meet the new strategic threats faced from 'rogue' states armed with WMD and ballistic missiles. As Bush argued in June 2001:

> The Cold War is forever over, and the vestiges of the Cold War that locked us both into a hostile situation are over. And we're exploring the opportunity to redefine the strategic framework for keeping the peace not that as existed in the past but a strategic framework as we go out in the 21st century.[130]

Douglas Feith also stated that 'We are intent on creating a cooperative, non-hostile, one hopes, eventually, even quite thoroughly friendly relationship with Russia ... our goal is to transform the relationship'.[131]

The White House argued that America's relationship with Russia was still locked into a Cold War adversarial framework by Cold War arms control agreements and processes were no longer relevant to the contemporary strategic threat environment and in fact hindered a cooperative relationship with Russia required to address current threats. A 'new strategic framework' was required for a decisive shift away from nuclear planning and force structure based almost exclusively on targeting Russia and away from a relationship of deliberate mutual vulnerability in which the deployment of missile defences was deemed inherently destabilising. 'I want to complete the work of changing our relationship from one based on a nuclear balance of terror to one based on common responsibilities and common interests', Bush stated in May 2001, 'We may have areas of difference with Russia, but we are not and must not be strategic adversaries'.[132]

The development of a 'new strategic framework' was facilitated by the 9/11 attacks that reinforced the administration's desire to shift its strategic focus away from Russia and towards a cooperative relationship to address the challenges of WMD proliferation, international terrorism, and regional instability.[133] In May 2002 Presidents Bush and Putin signed a Joint Declaration on a New Strategic Relationship between Russia and the United States that formally marked the end of 'the era in which the United States and Russia saw each other as an enemy or strategic threat'. Russia and America were now officially cooperative partners 'to advance stability, security, and economic integration, and to jointly counter global challenges and to help resolve regional conflicts'. This was to be facilitated through a new Consultative Group for Strategic Security to be chaired by Foreign Ministers and Defence Ministers with the participation of other senior officials.[134] The new strategic framework was formalised in the 2001 NPR, the 2002 Moscow Treaty, a range of declarations and confidence building measures, and reinforced in the 2002 National Security Strategy (NSS). The NSS stated:

> With Russia, we are already building a new strategic relationship based on a central reality of the twenty-first century: the United States and Russia are no longer strategic adversaries. The Moscow Treaty on Strategic Reductions is emblematic of this new reality.[135]

The administration was keen to reduce nuclear forces as part of the new strategic framework through mutual unilateral reductions and confidence-building measures, an approach prohibited by Congress under Clinton. It also wanted maximum flexibility to structure its nuclear forces without strict reference to Russia's nuclear posture in the new, uncertain post-9/11 security environment.[136] Large nuclear arsenals were, according to Secretary of Defense Rumsfeld 'the physical manifestation of that adversarial relationship' to which both sides had grown accustomed.[137] Nuclear weapons would play a much reduced role in the 'new strategic framework' since Russia was no longer considered a strategic nuclear threat.[138] As Rumsfeld noted in 2001:

> We do not consider Russia a threat to the United States of America. We do not plan to arrange our forces to prevent a tank attack across the North

> German Plain. We do not intend to get up in the morning and fret over the possibility of a strategic nuclear exchange ... the idea of an arms race between the United States and Russia today is ludicrous.[139]

Feith also argued that 'we don't think about annihilating Russia. We don't think that Russia thinks about annihilating us. We don't think that counting the nuclear weapons that they have and balancing them against the nuclear weapons we have is the basis for international stability'.[140]

Bush insisted that whilst he was prepared to codify nuclear reductions in an agreement with Russia, 'a new relationship based upon trust and cooperation is one that doesn't need endless hours of arms control discussions ... we don't need arms control negotiations to reduce our weaponry in a significant way' or to 'narrowly regulate every step we each take, as did Cold War treaties founded on mutual suspicion and an adversarial relationship'.[141] A decisive break with the START process was needed to 'break through the long impasse in further nuclear weapons reductions caused by the inability to finalize agreements through traditional arms control efforts'.[142] This approach to arms control had been advocated in 1999 by Stephen Hadley, later Deputy National Security Adviser and National Security Adviser to George W. Bush, and Robert Joseph, later Senior Director for Proliferation Strategy, Counterproliferation and Homeland Defense in the National Security Council and Under Secretary of State for Arms Control and International Security.[143]

The administration's reconceptualisation of 'strategic stability' included a notable turnaround on the long-term goal of de-MIRVing the Russian ICBM force. This was no longer considered important since the equation of strategic stability in which MIRVed ICBMs were deemed destabilising in a crisis no longer applied.[144] Rumsfeld, for example, argued that

> Russia's deployment of MIRVs has little impact on US national security under current conditions ... Since neither the US nor its allies nor Russia view our strategic relationship as adversarial we no longer view the deployment of MIRVed ICBMs as destabilising to this new relationship.[145]

This reflected the view expressed by Payne in 1996 that stability was relative and that organising strategic weapons into deterrence/stabilising or war-fighting/destabilising categories was a Cold War construct now devoid of meaning in the post-Cold War world.[146]

The whole emphasis on multiple bilateral constraints, intrusive verification, incorporating tactical nuclear weapons into the START process and ensuring strict parity was dismissed as part of an outdated adversarial approach to arms control and US-Russian relations that had little relevance to the new concept of strategic stability.[147] The purpose of arms control was no longer to constrain Russia and be similarly constrained by treaties involving hundreds of pages of verification procedures and accounting mechanisms but to reassure and inform Russia through trust and openness.[148]

Nevertheless, the administration's critics and the Russian leadership saw continuing value in codifying the planned reductions in a treaty.[149] In Congress Senator Biden argued that the benefits of predictability in nuclear force structures required the proposed nuclear reductions to be set out in a treaty based on specific commitments.[150] The outcome of this approach was the Strategic Offensive Reductions Treaty (SORT), or Moscow Treaty, signed in May 2002, that replaced START II.[151]

The treaty will reduce deployed nuclear warheads to between 1,700 and 2,200 by 2012. Force structure levels will be met by downloading warheads from ICBMs, SLBMs and bombers. The total force structure will fall somewhere between START II and III levels due to different warhead accounting rules.[152] This number of deployed operational warheads was deemed necessary to meet requirements for immediate deterrence contingencies (which no longer include Russia), the goals of reassuring allies and friends, dissuading potential opponents from competing with America and providing a hedge against technological failure or breakdown in strategic political relations. The administration rejected the arguments that the level of 1,700–2,200 was still too high and could only mean that Russia was still the primary target of America's nuclear posture (see criticisms of the NPR above).[153] In fact it was reported that America planned to reduce the 'hard' alert level of its nuclear forces over a ten-year period from around 2,500 warheads to approximately 750. A further 500 warheads would be ready to rapidly move to high alert if needed.[154] As indicated in the discussions around a START III under Clinton, America was not prepared to eliminate any nuclear delivery vehicles such as SSBNs and strategic bombers in any new treaty.[155] In addition the treaty does not stipulate any verification mechanisms or that any warheads need be destroyed.[156]

The administration's 'new strategic framework' rhetoric seemed to gloss over the changes that had taken place in America's relationship with Russia under Clinton. It repeatedly compared the contemporary state of the relationship to the confrontational relationship of the Cold War to justify the changes sought by Bush. It argued that the relationship needed to be transformed beyond a lingering Cold War mentality that still locked the two countries into a profoundly hostile relationship, despite the fact that the relationship had moved some distance beyond such a characterisation under Clinton.[157] Rumsfeld, for example, insisted that 'it's time to put the Cold War behind us. I know it's hard; it involved much of our lives for 50 years, but it's over and we need to get over it'.[158]

This led critics to argue that the 'new strategic framework' rhetoric was simply a means to an end of deploying missile defences with minimum international criticism, developing the capabilities to ensure strategic superiority over Russia for the first time since the 1950s, and developing new nuclear weapons and planning capabilities to target 'rogue' states. It was a vehicle for implementing the long-term policies of a conservative national security strategy based on removing legal treaty-based constraints on American strategic policies and actions. It was these constraints and their perceived effect on Washington's ability to confront new strategic threats with new military capabilities that were associated with outdated Cold War thinking. In essence the administration had used 'profound changes in the real world to rationalize old policies dressed up as new' to attain maximum freedom of action.[159] Krepon notes that the list of nuclear war-fighting and missile defence capabilities set out in the 2001 NPR 'is entirely familiar from the Cold War' with little to distinguish the 'ambitions of anti-Soviet nuclear strategists and those who now profess to want a new, friendly relationship with Russia'.[160] The strategic relationship could have been transformed under Clinton in the manner described by the Bush administration had the Republican-controlled Congress accepted an ABM treaty demarcation agreement and permitted entry into force of START II and rapid progress on START III. The new approach saw a shift from seeking strategic predictability through bilateral arms control with Russia to seeking maximum flexibility unfettered by arms control constraints through unilateral force reductions (albeit codified in a treaty), new initiatives under the NPR and withdrawal from the ABM treaty in 2002.[161]

The Moscow Treaty was criticised for the absence of verification measures and requirements to destroy nuclear warheads or delivery vehicles, the slow pace of reductions and plans to retain a large nuclear reserve force.[162] Senator Dorgan argued that it was not a reductions treaty but a 'marshmallow' agreement to move warheads from deployed status into storage and 'pretend we have reduced the number of nuclear weapons'.[163] Senator Kerry similarly argued that the treaty was 'as flimsy a treaty as the Senate has ever considered' because it let 'the vast stockpiles of nuclear warheads in this country and in Russia remain unchanged'.[164] Critics also argued that declarations of a 'new strategic relationship' could not themselves constitute a new relationship without a concerted effort to build and sustain a high level of trust between Washington and Moscow. Russian suspicion of Washington's missile defence plans and nuclear superiority free of binding bilateral constraints would undermine the trust-building process. The emergence of a truly new relationship would take time, effort and care.[165] Fuerth warns against 'a complacent view of U.S. trustworthiness' based on an assumption that America's declarations that its intentions are benign will be automatically accepted and an assumption that America and Russia have 'attained a durable friendship'. He contends that 'strategic stability' cannot be imposed but must be based on mutual agreement with those with whom stability is sought.[166] This reflected the view of the first Bush administration's response to Gorbachev's declaration of a new US–Soviet relationship, in which Bush senior had argued that 'a new relationship cannot be simply declared by Moscow or bestowed by others; it must be earned. It must be earned because promises are never enough'.[167]

In Bush's second term the 'new strategic framework' suffered a series of setbacks. The administration wanted Russia to take a much harder line with Iran and commit to broad sanctions against the regime in Tehran. Putin argued instead that Iran must not be forced into a corner and that dialogue was the only option for resolving the confrontation over Tehran's uranium enrichment capabilities and suspected nuclear weapons programme. The administration also expressed concern about the retreat of democratic institutions and accountability in Russia. This was apparent in the 2006 National Security Strategy, which stated that:

> Strengthening our relationship will depend on the policies, foreign and domestic, that Russia adopts. Recent trends regrettably point toward a diminishing commitment to democratic freedoms and institutions. We will work to try to persuade the Russian Government to move forward, not backward, along freedom's path.[168]

The administration also forged ahead with plans to deploy ten missile defence interceptor missiles in Poland linked to a new radar in the Czech Republic to address the perceived threat from Iran's long-range ballistic missile programme.[169]

Moscow deeply resented American and wider Western statements about the nature of Russian democracy and is deeply hostile to American missile defence plans in Europe.[170] It regards such deployments as a threat to Russia and responded by suspending its participation in the Conventional Forces in Europe (CFE) treaty, threatening to withdraw from the Intermediate-range Nuclear Forces (INF) treaty and threatening to target European missile defence installations with its nuclear missiles. It has also placed renewed emphasis on rebuilding its nuclear forces after their deterioration through the 1990s.[171] In May 2007 Putin blamed America for Russia's decision to revamp its nuclear arsenal citing Washington's withdrawal from the ABM treaty, missile defence deployments and failure to ratify an updated version of the CFE treaty negotiated in 1999.[172] Russia has also demanded a legally binding agreement to formally replace the verification requirements of the START I treaty when it expires in 2009. The Bush administration only wants to replace some parts of the accord.[173] Critics of the Moscow Treaty have urged the White House to extend START's verification and transparency elements and add verification measures to the Moscow Treaty.[174]

By 2007 it was clear that Moscow did not agree with the Bush administration's insistence that the 'old' thinking of the Cold War embodied in the START process, confidence-building measures such as the CFE treaty and controls on missile defences through the ABM treaty was redundant. It was not reconciled to the vision of strategic flexibility articulated and practiced by America as a unipolar power. Instead it viewed American actions as potential strategic threats in a multipolar world to be mitigated through bilateral agreements to constrain strategic capabilities and enhance predictability and strategic stability, cooperation on missile defence and a modernised Russian strategic nuclear triad.

The Anti-Ballistic Missile Treaty

The Bush administration was determined to deploy extensive ballistic missile defences to protect the entire United States in response to the perceived threat from WMD-armed 'rogue' states. America's lack of defences was considered a policy of deliberate vulnerability and an incentive for missile proliferation, which, when combined with WMD, could 'give future adversaries the incentive to try to hold our populations hostage to terror and blackmail'.[175] Missile defence deployments were integral to further nuclear force reductions and the new triad established in the 2001 NPR.

Under Secretary of Defense Doug Feith noted in June 2001 before Congress:

> The President has established missile defense as a top priority. Our policy is to deploy ballistic missile defenses based on the best available options, at the earliest possible date, that are capable of defending not only the United States but also friends and allies and U.S. forces overseas.[176]

This meant terminating the ABM treaty. The administration framed treaty withdrawal as part of the 'new strategic framework', arguing that like the START process it was outdated and perpetuated an adversarial relationship with Russia that was no longer appropriate. In May 2001 President Bush stated:

> We need a new framework that allows us to build missile defenses to counter the different threats of today's world. To do so, we must move beyond the constraints of the 30-year-old ABM Treaty. This Treaty does not recognize the present or point us to the future; it enshrines the past.[177]

He described it as 'a piece of paper that's codified a relationship that no longer exists, codified a hateful relationship'.[178] Deputy Under Secretary of Defense for Policy Stephen Cambone urged that 'the ABM Treaty should be replaced with a new framework that reflects a break from Cold War thinking and facilitates development of a new, cooperative relationship between the United States and Russia'.[179]

Critics argued that treaty withdrawal would undermine national security and that there was no reason to abandon the treaty in 2001 since missile defence technology was not yet hindered by the treaty's restrictions.[180] Some critics argued that withdrawal would have disastrous consequences for relations with Russia and China and spark a renewed strategic arms race.[181] This logic was disputed by the administration and Republicans in Congress who insisted that America could deploy missile defenses without upsetting its relationship with Russia or undermining strategic stability.[182] Defense Secretary Rumsfeld argued:

> Far from causing a 'deep chill' in relations the U.S. withdrawal from the ABM Treaty was greeted in Russia with something approximating a yawn. Indeed, President Putin declared the decision 'does not pose a threat' to Russia. Far from launching a new arms race, the U.S. and Russia have both decided to move toward historic reductions.[183]

Feith also insisted that 'when the United States withdraws from the ABM Treaty, it will not be the end of the world, and it will not be the end of the relationship with Russia'.[184] Critics suggested that codification of nuclear arms reductions in the formal Moscow Treaty was Putin's pay-off for accepting American withdrawal from the ABM treaty and for securing Russian intelligence sharing and cooperation in the post-9/11 'war on terror'.[185]

In June 2002 America formally withdrew from the treaty and in December 2002, the administration announced its decision to begin fielding an initial national missile defence capability in 2004–2005.[186] The administration's missile defence programme continued to court controversy over the costs of the programme, the difficulties experienced in overcoming major technological barriers, competing interpretations of the scale of the 'rogue' ballistic missile threat, the impact of American missile defences on strategic stability and nuclear proliferation, and the planned deployment of missile interceptors and a missile defence radar in Poland and the Czech Republic.[187]

The nuclear weapons production complex

The nuclear weapons production complex experienced mixed fortunes marked on the one hand by continued revival through the Stockpile Stewardship Program and new initiatives set out in the 2001 NPR and on the other by serious congressional criticism about the state of the nuclear weapons complex and its capacity to successfully execute planned warhead life extension programmes (LEPs). This culminated in congressional insistence that the administration produce long-term plans for both the size and purpose of the nuclear stockpile and consolidation of the weapons complex. New nuclear weapons activities would only be funded when plans had been produced to the satisfaction of Congress.

The National Nuclear Security Administration's (NNSA) response was set out in a 2006 report describing steps that would be taken to further consolidate the complex by 2030.[188] This 'Complex-2030' plan was tied to the development of a new Reliable Replacement Warhead (RRW). NNSA argued that further consolidation of the production complex could only be accomplished if Cold War-era warheads were phased out of the stockpile and replaced with RRWs and that the warhead LEP approach was unsustainable for reasons outlined below. RRWs would be based on existing tested designs but incorporate less exacting design requirements, enhanced safety features and be easier to monitor and maintain than the existing arsenal of Cold War-era warheads. The Complex-2030 plan and its heavy reliance on RRWs was criticised by powerful members of Congress who insisted that the new approach did not constitute the detailed rethink of nuclear weapons policy demanded by Congress but an expensive and contentious programme to rebuild the nuclear arsenal based on existing doctrine.

A responsive infrastructure

The administration insisted that a robust and responsive nuclear weapons production complex was integral to America's long-term deterrence posture and a crucial hedge against future uncertainty and potential problems with the ageing nuclear stockpile.[189] The link was made explicit in the 2001 NPR that established a revitalised weapons complex as a core component of the new triad. The state of the complex would influence the pace of nuclear reductions and the size of the nuclear reserve force with force reductions 'determined in part by the state of our infrastructure and the very real limits of our physical plant and workforce, which has deteriorated significantly'.[190]

Cuts in the active and inactive reserve stockpile were dependent upon progress in re-establishing lost production capabilities and infrastructure, response times to fix problems in the stockpile, carry out planned warhead refurbishments and develop and produce new or modified warheads if needed and a 'desire to retain a sub-population of non-refurbished warheads to hedge potential common mode failures'.[191] John Foster, chair of the Foster Panel, also stated:

> The adequacy of the production complex is a critical factor in determining the appropriate size and state of readiness of the inactive reserve of weapons and the pace of dismantlements. If we had the necessary capacity to repair or produce weapons, the U.S. could relieve our dependence on an inactive reserve.[192]

The criteria for a 'responsive infrastructure' were the same five key capabilities set out in the 1993 Complex-21 plan, the 1995 SSP framework report and the 1999 reorganisation of the SSP: successful annual certification of the health of the stockpile without testing; production of plutonium pits; production of tritium; production of uranium components for nuclear warheads; and refurbishment of operationally deployed warheads through LEPs. NNSA planned to be able to fix relatively minor stockpile problems within one year; adapt existing weapons through modification or repackaging of existing warheads within 18 months; design, develop, and produce a new warhead within three to four years; and be able to produce new warheads in quantity if needed without disrupting ongoing refurbishments.[193]

These plans were supplemented by NNSA's 2003 infrastructure plan and 2004 strategic plan that set out a number of objectives. These included maintenance of an effective, reliable, capable and smaller nuclear arsenal through the Moscow Treaty reductions and annual assessment of the enduring stockpile, and refurbishment of the stockpile.[194] It also included three specific initiatives to enhance the responsiveness of the nuclear weapons complex set out in the NPR: the Advanced Concepts Initiative to re-establish advanced warhead concepts teams disbanded in the 1990s at the three nuclear weapons laboratories to train weapons designers and examine options for earth-penetrating warheads and low-yield warheads; a programme to reduce the time needed to resume nuclear testing at the Nevada Test Site to well below the current two- to three-year time-frame; and the establishment of an interim pit production capability at Los Alamos National Laboratory (LANL) prior to construction of a new Modern Pit Facility (MPF) over the long term. These in turn reflected recommendations from the February 2001 report of the Foster Panel to Assess the Reliability, Safety, and Security of the United States Nuclear Stockpile.[195]

Pit production remained a source of concern within the nuclear policy community. NNSA continued to pursue an interim pit production facility at LANL to produce 20 pits per year by 2007 and later be capable of producing up to 150. New pits were needed to produce W88 warheads for Trident II (D5) missiles and LANL planned to deliver its first fully qualified and certified W88 War Reserve Pit in 2007.[196] In the meantime DOE would initiate plans to construct a MPF capable of producing 250–900 pits per year at a cost of $4 billion.[197] The capability to produce new pits would, it was argued, enable NNSA to replace ageing warheads and thereby reduce reliance on a large reserve as a hedge against the failure of an entire warhead type.[198] In 2003 DOE reported that pit ageing experiments demonstrated that existing plutonium pits would perform adequately for 45–60 years, suggesting the construction of a MPF could be delayed. Most pits in the stockpile were made between 1978 and 1989 and so could last to between 2038 and 2059 when a new MPF would need to be operational to sustain the current nuclear stockpile.[199] Research by the JASON group of nuclear scientists later concluded that pits could last at least 100 years, further undermining the case for a new pit production facility.[200] Congress continued to fund DOE pit production activities and MPF conceptual work in 2001 but later refused funding and NNSA incorporated the MPF concept into the Complex-2030 plan.[201]

Efforts to re-establish tritium and uranium component production capabilities continued. In 2000 Congress ratified DOE's decision to produce tritium in the TVA Watts Bar nuclear reactor over a 40-year period. In October 2003 DOE began the process of producing tritium to be extracted at a new Tritium Extraction Facility (TEF) under construction since 2000 at the Savannah River Site. The TEF began producing new tritium in 2007. Uranium component production capabilities were still not resolved. Leaked excerpts of the 2001 NPR stated that it would take another seven to eight years to restore the capability to produce a complete nuclear weapon secondary and other uranium components at the Y-12 Plant.[202] By 2006 NNSA stated that it had brought some uranium processing capabilities back online and was modernising others to meet the demands of the warhead life extension programmes.[203]

The NPR stated that a responsive infrastructure also required reducing the time needed to conduct any new tests to 18 months by September 2005.[204] This reflected the conclusion of the Foster Panel that two to three years from a decision to a test was too long. The administration stated that if a problem with a weapon system was discovered that needed to be rectified through testing, a much shorter timeline would be required.[205] NNSA settled on a 24-month readiness posture that it achieved in 2007.[206] The administration did not intend to seek ratification of the CTBT. It expressed considerable scepticism about the nuclear testing moratorium in place since 1992, the viability of the treaty and NNSA's ability to sustain and modernise the nuclear arsenal without full nuclear testing.[207] Under Secretary of State for Arms Control and International Security

John Bolton reportedly said that the CTBT was 'profoundly misguided and potentially dangerous' and an 'unenforceable treaty with illusory protections'.[208] The administration did state, however, that it would adhere to the testing moratorium and had no reason or plans to conduct any new nuclear tests.[209] It also remained bound by Clinton's signature to the treaty under Article XVIII of the Vienna Convention on Treaties unless it is removed.[210]

Warhead Life Extension programmes

A joint NNSA-DOD stockpile refurbishment programme planned to refurbish eight warhead types in the stockpile up to 30 years beyond their original minimum lifetime of about 20 years over a 25-year period from 2001 through the SSP.[211] This massive warhead modernisation and refurbishment programme involved substantial and costly upgrades and improvements in the operation of the warheads and presented significant problems.[212]

The 2001 NPR approved three LEPs for the W76 (Trident SLBM), W80 (Air-Launched Cruise Missile, Advanced Cruise Missile, and nuclear Tomahawk-Land Attack Missile) and B61-7/11 (gravity bomb) warhead types, in addition to the ongoing refurbishment of the W87 ICBM warhead planned for completion by 2004.[213] This represented a major escalation of refurbishment activity for a nuclear weapons complex that had, according to John Foster, 'been unable to meet the schedule for today's workload, which is modest compared with the future plans'.[214] This was compounded by the view that the stockpile was showing more signs of ageing and manufacturing defects than previous reliability assessments had suggested.[215]

The refurbishment process is long and complicated. For example the first stage of the W76 refurbishment plan was approved in 2000 for one quarter of the W76 stockpile, later increased to two-thirds in 2005. The aim was to produce a first refurbished unit in 2008 and decide whether to apply the first stage to all W76 warheads. The first stage would be completed by 2012. The second stage of the refurbishment process, if approved, would continue from 2012 to 2022 to fully refurbish all W76 warheads.[216] NNSA planned to deliver first production units (FPUs) for the B61-7 in June 2006, the B61-11 in January 2007 and the W76 in September 2007.[217] It also involves the entire weapons complex (Kansas City Plant, Savannah River Site, Oak Ridge Y-12 Plant, Pantex Plant and all three national laboratories) to disassemble warheads, refurbish, replace and test key components, and reassemble and certify each warhead type.[218] All of these tasks require high levels of expertise.

By the end of Bush's first term there was considerable concern about the ability of NNSA to sustain the Cold War legacy nuclear stockpile through the SSP and planned LEPs. A report by the three weapons laboratories argued that the SSP and the refurbishment programme were unsustainable and that plans to 'merely preserve nuclear weapons with a ponderous and expensive enterprise required to support old technology' should be replaced with plans for a more sustainable complex based on warhead replacement rather than warhead refurbishment by building new Reliable Replacement Warheads without nuclear testing.[219] This reflected the recommendations of the Foster Panel's report in 1999 and the Defense Science Board's 2004 report *Future Strategic Strike Forces*. The latter stated that 'the nuclear weapons program as currently conceived – a program focused primarily on refurbishing the legacy stockpile – will not meet the country's future needs' and recommended significantly scaling back planned life extension programmes and shifting 'toward a new vision: a stockpile based on previously tested nuclear devices/designs to provide weapons more relevant to the future threat environment'.[220]

The weapons laboratories and others argued that it may not be possible to maintain warheads beyond the planned 20–30 year warhead LEPs currently underway and therefore the LEP process *might* not be sustainable over the long term.[221] The performance margins of existing warheads are too tight, they argued, since they were designed during the Cold War to minimise weight and size and maximise yield giving very little room for error as weapons age.[222] Minor but inevitable variations between original and replacement warhead components might also accumulate with successive refurbishments and 'may pose an unacceptable risk to maintaining high confidence' in the safety and effectiveness of LEP warheads.[223] Finally, as time passes it will become much more difficult to maintain warheads that were built with technology, materials, skills and processes that are now anachronistic and less readily available.[224]

Changes in warheads will inevitably occur as they age and parts are replaced and a resumption of nuclear testing will become the only way of credibly certifying warhead safety and reliably. The alternative is to accept a steady reduction in confidence in warhead safety and reliability. These arguments reflect many of those levelled at the SSP in the early 1990s after Clinton announced his intention to permanently end nuclear testing. These concerns were amplified by the state of the production complex infrastructure, which was still in poor shape after years of neglect and massive clean-up problems. In 2001 it was reported that only 26 per cent of the weapons complex's buildings were in excellent or good condition, down from 56 per cent in 1995, with a quarter of buildings dating back to the 1940s.[225] In 2002 NNSA head John Gordon stated that there was a backlog of $800 million in deferred maintenance of facilities and a need for an additional $500 million per year over the next ten years to recapitalise the production complex infrastructure.[226] The 2001 *Hart–Rudman* report *US Commission on National Security* also stated that 'the physical circumstances in which lab professionals work have also deteriorated, in many instances, to unacceptable levels'.[227]

NNSA officials argued that the level of disrepair would hinder the massive warhead LEP process and long-term viability of the nuclear stockpile if not remedied, despite programmes in place to maintain a robust infrastructure and reduce the large backlog of deferred maintenance.[228] 'Past under-investment in the enterprise – in particular, the production complex – has increased risks and will limit future options', warned Gordon in 2002.[229] Without significant refurbishment of engineering, design and production capabilities the life extension programmes for the W76, W80 and B61 would be in doubt.[230] NNSA was also struggling to complete major new SSP facilities on time and to budget such as the National Ignition Facility (NIF) and the Dual Axis Radiographic Hydrodynamic Test Facility (DARHT). These and other facilities would now only become operational a decade later than planned, be considerably less capable than originally envisaged and be available when a great deal of stockpile life extension work had been completed without them.[231]

Complex-2030

Enduring problems with the management of nuclear weapons activities, the SSP and concerns about the major LEP programme made Congress reluctant to fund new initiatives set out in the NPR. The joint NNSA-DOD stockpile plan to refurbish the entire START I arsenal of deployed and reserve warheads was questioned in 2001 by Representative David Hobson, chair of the House Appropriations Committee subcommittee on Energy and Water Development, whose remit covered DOE's nuclear weapons activities.[232] Hobson argued that Congress should not fund any new nuclear weapons initiatives such as RNEP, ACI, increased test readiness and the MPF, until the administration had completed a full review of the nuclear weapons complex that he considered too large and inefficient and presented Congress with a sustainable and affordable long-term plan for the production complex.[233]

Congress instead provided only half the funding requested by the administration in 2003 and 2004 and directed DOE to provide a detailed long-term nuclear stockpile plan that would focus on management of the ageing stockpile before it went forward with new concepts and research.[234] NNSA delivered a stockpile plan as requested, but Hobson remained unconvinced:

> The Congress just received a plan that finally shows major reductions in our nuclear weapons stockpile. However, much of the DOE weapons complex is still sized to support a Cold War stockpile. The NNSA needs to take a 'time-out' on new initiatives until it completes a review of its weapons complex in relation to security needs, budget constraints, and this new stockpile plan.[235]

The planned reductions were those presented by President Bush in May 2004 to cut the total nuclear stockpile almost in half by 2012.

Hobson recommended a new Sustainable Stockpile Initiative and urged DOE to conduct a systematic review of the nuclear weapons complex over the next 25 years to be submitted to Congress in April 2005.[236] In 2005 and 2006 Congress cut funding for the MPF and other new NNSA facilities until a new long-term plan for a consolidated nuclear weapons complex and a detailed long-term nuclear stockpile plan were produced.[237] Formal legislation in the National Defense Authorization Act for FY2007 directed DOE and DOD to develop a plan to transform the nuclear weapons complex to achieve a responsive infrastructure by 2030, maintain the safety, reliability and security of the nuclear arsenal, continue LEP programmes that the Nuclear Weapons Council considered necessary, consolidate disposition of special nuclear materials within the complex to reduce security costs, reduce duplication within the complex, rapidly dismantle inactive nuclear weapons and reduce the size of the stockpile.[238] Hobson's successor, Representative Pete Visclosky, considered a programme to increase the long-term safety and reliability of warheads as part of the process to further consolidate the production complex and reduce the overall nuclear stockpile. The Act therefore directed DOE and DOD to develop plans to produce RRWs as necessary by 2012 with steady-state production by 2025.[239]

NNSA's response was twofold: a major programme to produce several types of Reliable Replacement Warhead that might at some point entirely replace the existing arsenal of Cold War-era warheads; and a detailed to plan to consolidate the nuclear weapons by 2030, labelled Complex-2030 – a successor to Complex-21.[240] The RRW programme was integral to the consolidation and modernisation effort: 'we see stockpile transformation as "enabling" transformation to a responsive infrastructure, and a responsive infrastructure as essential to reducing total stockpile numbers and associated costs'.[241] NNSA's plans rested on formal concerns about the long-term viability of the LEP approach, a stated need to improve the 'responsiveness' of the complex, a stated need to reduce security costs for protecting special nuclear materials within the complex (costs that had risen considerably after 9/11) and a stated need to increase the security of nuclear warheads after 9/11.[242] The plans were endorsed at the highest level in a joint statement by the Secretaries of Energy, Defense and State on 'National Security and Nuclear Weapons: Maintaining Deterrence in the 21st Century' issued in July 2007. The statement declared that further stockpile reductions could only take place with a responsive nuclear infrastructure otherwise the risks associated with further reductions would be too great. The RRW concept would allow these risks to be managed whilst reducing the need to return to nuclear testing. It urged Congress to fund the transformation of the complex and RRW programme in order to realise the benefits of a credible nuclear deterrent at low levels of weapons.[243]

The Complex-2030 plan was informed by a study by the Secretary of Energy's Advisory Board (SEAB) released in October 2005.[244] The report made three main recommendations. First, development of a Consolidated Nuclear Production Center (CNPC) to produce all the components for the nuclear explosive package in nuclear warheads, including uranium components, plutonium pits, high explosives and assembly and disassembly facilities. Under the SEAB plan the Y-12 and Pantex plants would close and the nuclear laboratories would be much reduced in size. Second, prompt development of a family of 2,200 RRWs to completely replace the current stockpile of LEP warheads by 2030 and reduce operating costs. Third, it argued for the continuous modernisation of successive versions of RRWs in five-yearly cycles in a nuclear weapons complex engaged in 'steady state design, production and dismantlement' of nuclear warheads.[245] The SEAB report argued that the status quo of the Complex-21 infrastructure and LEP warhead process was technically and financially untenable since the Cold War stockpile 'does not have the surety controls or the operating margins that the DOD desire' and that 'future [warhead] maintenance and surveillance cost liabilities are unbounded'.[246] This was based on the assumption that the LEP process would become increasingly expensive and difficult in the future and cost much more than designing and certifying a family of RRWs and establishing new production lines to build thousands of new warheads without nuclear testing.[247]

NNSA's Complex-2030 plan envisaged less radical change and would not involve the closure of any major complex facilities. All uranium operations will be carried out at Y-12 with all HEU consolidated at the new Highly-Enriched Uranium Materials Facility (HEUMF). A new Uranium Processing Facility (UPF) would also be built. All plutonium operations will be carried out at a new Consolidated Plutonium Center (CPC) that will produce 125 pits per year by 2022, replacing plans for the MPF. In the meantime LANL will be supported to produce 30–50 pits per year up to 2012. All plutonium operations at LANL and LLNL will be transferred to the CPC after 2022. The RRW programme requires a pit manufacturing capability well beyond the 30–50 per year capacity envisioned for LANL. Tritium operations will continue at SRS, a new facility will be built for non-nuclear component production by 2012 and warhead assembly and disassembly operation will be conducted at a modernised Pantex plant. Special Nuclear Materials that require significant security protection measures will be consolidated to fewer locations within existing sites to reduce burgeoning security costs. Many warheads in the active reserve and inactive stockpiles will be dismantled as part of the strategy leading to a much smaller nuclear arsenal by 2030 and a new Office of Transformation will be established in NNSA to oversee the transition to Complex-2030. NNSA rejected the SEAB study's recommendation for a new CNPC on cost and logistical grounds.[248]

NNSA argued that this modernisation process together with an RRW programme would produce the capabilities-based responsive infrastructure called for in the 2001 NPR allowing America to rely 'less on "inventory" and more on "capability to produce"'.[249] For the head of the SEAB study David Overskei, this meant developing a smaller, more agile, innovative and potent complex 'so feared and so respected that no nuclear weapon is ever used; that is the true metric of successful deterrence'.[250]

The Reliable Replacement Warhead programme

RRWs will be re-engineered and remanufactured warheads based on previously tested designs to replace existing Cold War-era warheads, although they are often referred to as 'new' warheads.[251] This stands in contrast to the LEP programme designed to maintain existing warheads by replacing defective parts and upgrading others, whilst minimising changes to the nuclear explosive package.[252] Current plans envisage two RRWs. The first, RRW-1, would replace some of the W76 warheads on the Trident II (D5) SLBM fleet – the mainstay of the operational nuclear arsenal. RRW-1 could also be designed for use on both SLBMs and ICBMs.[253] The Nuclear Weapons Council approved formation of a joint DOD–DOE Project Officers Group (POG) for the RRW programme in March 2005 and launched a design competition for two teams from LANL and LLNL.[254] The first production unit was planned for deployment by 2012–2014 with full production by 2022 when a new Consolidated Plutonium Center (CPC) would be fully operational, subject to congressional funding and support.[255] A final RRW-1 design was approved in November 2006 to allow NNSA to conduct detailed design and cost studies. A second RRW design study for RRW-2 was also initiated to 'define concepts for replacement warheads to existing and future air-delivered systems' for which congressional funding was requested for 2007. NNSA argues that two RRW designs are needed to guard against failure in one system.[256]

The case for the RRW was made in 2005 by NNSA head Linton Brooks. He argued that the existing stockpile was wrong technically because current warheads been designed to maximise yield whilst minimising size and weight, were not designed for longevity and were not designed to minimise demands on the nuclear weapons complex. It was wrong militarily because current warheads could not defeat HDBTs, were unsuited to destruction of biological and chemical munitions (suggesting that the RRW programme and Complex-2030 plan would lead to RNEP-type weapons for these missions), and did not make full use of precision guidance technology.[257] The stockpile was wrong politically because it was too large, due to the stated need to retain a hedge stockpile because of the lack of a suitably responsive infrastructure. Finally, the stockpile was wrong from a physical security perspective since some warheads and complex facilities were judged to lack sufficient physical security characteristics after 9/11.[258]

NNSA's strategy provides for continuation of LEP efforts as approved by the NWC alongside development of RRW warheads.[259] It envisages a nuclear weapons complex in transition to the Complex-2030 infrastructure supporting a stockpile in transition from an all-LEP arsenal to a mixture of RRWs and LEP warheads by 2030. Only then will NNSA decide whether to move to an all-RRW stockpile which may take another decade.[260] The Complex-2030 report states that the majority of ICBMs, SLBMs, bombs and cruise missiles will have RRWs by 2030.[261] Plans also envisage a process of continuous RRW design, production and deployment by a consolidated and modernised nuclear weapons complex.[262]

NNSA argues that an RRW programme and a Complex-2030 infrastructure will increase confidence in the deployed nuclear stockpile and confidence in the ability of the complex to respond to future problems in a timely fashion and allow a dramatic reduction in the size of the overall nuclear stockpile. It will also enhance nuclear design skills and transfer them to a new generation of experts as a matter of urgency and take full advantage of the success of the SSP to develop 'safer, more secure, more reliable, and cost-effective' warheads without nuclear testing that are easier to manufacture and maintain.[263]

By undertaking a new round of nuclear cuts the RRW and Complex-2030 plans will demonstrate that America is not engaged in a new nuclear build-up and is complying with its obligations under the NPT to reduce its nuclear arsenal and reduce the salience of nuclear weapons.[264] Brooks argued that the RRW programme would in no way 'hamper our efforts to advance global non-proliferation' and have no effect on the nuclear weapons policies of 'rogue' states.[265] RRW would also ensure the credibility of extended deterrence guarantees to allies and reduce allies' incentives for acquiring their own nuclear arsenals.[266]

Congress initially funded the RRW programme in 2004 to 'improve the reliability, longevity and certifiability of existing weapons and their components'.[267] Subsequent legislation established additional goals to increase confidence in warheads without nuclear testing, increase ease of manufacture, reduce costs associated with maintaining the nuclear arsenal, enhance the safety and security of warheads, and reduce the use of environmentally hazardous substances in the warhead programme.[268] Congress envisaged a nuclear stockpile by 2025–2030 significantly smaller than the stockpile planned for 2012 under the Moscow Treaty. It would comprise mainly RRWs, as they replace existing LEP warheads therefore requiring a much smaller LEP programme.[269] Congress subsequently cut funding for the W76 and W80 warhead LEPs for FY 2006 and in May 2006 the NWC directed that the W80 LEP be deferred indefinitely.[270]

Criticisms of Complex-2030 and RRW

Critics claimed the RRW programme was not essential to further consolidation and modernisation of the complex and that the Complex-2030 plan was a plan for modernisation with no major consolidation of the complex.[271] They maintain that the problems with the LEP approach have been overstated. Ten years of investment in the SSP has produced significant results that allow NNSA to predict the life cycle of warhead components, understand warhead deterioration and how to deal with it and to successfully extend the safety and reliability of existing warheads.[272] The LEP approach can continue to successfully maintain existing nuclear warheads, as evidenced by eleven successful annual stockpile assessments since 1996, and confidence has increased in the ability of the SSP to certify the health of the stockpile.[273] As more SSP facilities come online the SSP's ability to predict, detect and resolve problems will increase. As a result, future rounds of life extension for existing warheads could in fact be much easier and less expensive than the current LEPs.[274] It is important to note that prior to congressional pressure in 2005 to provide a coherent long-term plan for the complex and the stockpile NNSA officials expressed few concerns about the long-term effectiveness of the LEP process. In fact in 2007 NNSA officials insisted that SSP was working and the stockpile was safe and reliable – only that it *might* not remain that way based on current processes.[275] Supporters of the LEP approach also question why the Navy would want to use a new, untested warhead to replace the W76 that has been effective for several decades. They argue that NNSA has invested billions in LANL's TA-55 facility to produce and certify pits for the W88 Trident SLBM warhead and that the W88 provides a hedge against the failure of the W76 such that no new replacement warhead is required.[276]

Critics also argue that any new RRWs will undoubtedly suffer 'birth defects' that may yet require nuclear testing to eliminate. This may be exacerbated by the requirement to produce new plutonium pits for RRWs rather than relying on existing pits. Critics point to another report by the JASON group in August 2007, which argued that more concept and design work was needed on how any future RRW would be certified without nuclear testing.[277] In contrast such defects have been removed from existing warheads through previous nuclear testing and the SSP. Many doubt that NNSA could produce such 'perfect' RRWs with readily certifiable new pits to time and cost given its past record of poor management and cost overruns. The Government Accountability Office (GAO) also argued that producing RRWs whilst refurbishing a significant portion of the stockpile through LEPs and continuing to dismantle retired warheads 'will be a difficult and costly undertaking'.[278] DOE estimates that Complex-2030 will cost $150 billion. GAO believes this too low and has advised Congress to request a more accurate budget from DOE.[279] Senator Feinstein summed up the criticism in stating that there are no problems with the safety and reliability of the nuclear arsenal, there are no new formal military requirements for new warheads for new missions, plutonium pits have been shown to have a life span of up to 100 years, there is no risk of a need to return to nuclear testing and there is no evidence that the RRW programme will reduce costs.[280]

Critics also insist that production of new RRWs will undermine American leadership on nuclear non-proliferation. As the House Appropriations Committee stated in 2007, 'a particularly troubling issue for the Committee related to the RRW proposal is the contradictory U.S. policy position of demanding other nations give up their nuclear ambitions while the U.S. aggressively pursues a program to build new nuclear warheads'.[281] Senator Pete Domenici, Ranking Member of both the Senate Energy and Natural Resources Committee and Energy and Water Development Appropriations Subcommittee, also warned that the new programme 'would send American nuclear deterrence strategy in a new, unknown, direction' and cautioned restraint.[282] Former Secretary of Defense William Perry argued before Congress in 2007 that the administration should 'defer action on the RRW program' since this would 'put us in a stronger position to lead the international community in the continuing battle against nuclear proliferation'.[283]

The Complex-2030 and RRW plans were born from conflicting demands. Congress was interested in consolidating and modernising the complex to reduce reliance on nuclear weapons, steering NNSA away from development of new nuclear weapons such as RNEP, ensuring the long-term reliability of a much smaller nuclear arsenal, eliminating any need to return to nuclear testing, and saving money. NNSA, on the other hand, wanted to consolidate and modernise the complex in ways that would make it much more responsive to future nuclear weapons requirements, as set out in the 2001 NPR, with the RRW programme as the linchpin of the transformation. As Levine argues:

> The RRW program was shaped not by a single vision but by the competing demands of an anxious nuclear complex with powerful allies, an administration determined to build a robust weapons infrastructure, and an outspoken Republican congressman [Hobson] keen to rein in costs.[284]

By the end of 2007 Congress' demands had still not been met and influential members continued to greet the rationales presented by NNSA for the RRW and Complex-2030 plans with scepticism. They remained unconvinced that the administration had conducted a thorough review of the long-term direction of the nuclear complex and size and purpose of the overall nuclear stockpile as requested. Government statements on RRW were littered with 'ifs' and 'maybes': the LEP process *might* not be sustainable; minor changes *might* accumulate and reduce confidence in the stockpile; the RRW programme *might* reduce costs and *might* result in warheads that are easier to produce, maintain and certify; the LEP approach could *potentially* increase uncertainty warhead safety and reliability; and the RRW programme *might* allow a substantial reduction in the reserve stockpile.[285] There are no numbers to substantiate claims that RRW is cheaper, safer and more reliable than LEP, or vice versa.[286]

Senator Feinstein, for example, stated:

> The lack of any definitive analysis of strategic assessment defining the objectives of a future nuclear stockpile makes it impossible to weigh the relative merits of investing billions of taxpayer dollars in new nuclear weapons production activities ... currently there exists no convincing rationale for maintaining the large numbers of existing Cold War nuclear weapons, much less producing additional warheads.[287]

A 2006 report by the American Association for the Advancement of Science (AAAS) also noted:

> In the absence of detailed plans on scope, schedule, and costs, however, it is not possible to make judgments on the trade-offs in the weapons and the complex among stockpiles with varying mixes of legacy and LEP weapons and RRWs. Such assessments can be made only when stockpile requirements have been set and cost and schedule predictions have been made in response to those requirements.[288]

Without such plans the RRW and Complex-2030 plans would not be funded. Chair of the Energy and Water Development Appropriations Subcommittee, Peter Visclosky, remarked in 2007, 'there is a need for a comprehensive nuclear defense strategy and stockpile plan to guide transformation and downsizing of the stockpile nuclear weapons complex; and until progress is made on this crucial issue, there will be no new facilities or Reliable Replacement Warhead'.[289] In December 2007 Congress passed authorisation and appropriations bills for FY 2008 that stripped all funding from the RRW programme. It also mandated a Strategic Posture Commission to report in 2008 and a new Nuclear Posture Review to be submitted by the next administration with the next Quadrennial Defense Review in 2009 to determine the overall long-term direction of nuclear weapons policy, stockpile and production infrastructure. The House of Representatives Committee on Appropriations noted that its FY2008 omnibus appropriations bill 'prohibits the development of a reliable replacement warhead until the president develops a strategic nuclear weapon plan to guide transformation and downsizing of the stockpile and nuclear weapons complex'.[290]

Conclusion

In George W. Bush's first term it was clear that the START process was in serious difficulty and that major problems were likely to be encountered over START III. It was also clear that the administration felt America had been left strategically exposed to the threat from WMD-armed 'rogue' states. Nuclear weapons policy under Bush was subsequently defined by the reconceptualisation of strategic stability and the functioning of nuclear deterrence that was set out in the 2001 NPR and the Moscow Treaty and attempts to revitalise the nuclear weapons production complex.

The new posture set out in the 2001 NPR criticised Clinton's commitment to a Cold War conception of strategic stability. It argued that the START process and ABM treaty were adversarial and counter-productive to a cooperative relationship with Russia and increasingly irrelevant in the post-Cold War world. Strategic stability no longer depended on how Russia organised its nuclear arsenal and extensive bilateral arms control treaties and the necessity of mutual vulnerability for stability was rejected. Reciprocal unilateral nuclear force reductions were sufficient and extensive missile defences would be deployed to defend against WMD-armed 'rogue' states, possibly in cooperation with Russia. This was presented as a 'new strategic framework' based on the Moscow Treaty and confidence-building measures to smooth the transition from the practices and understandings of a Cold War concept of strategic stability to a new post-MAD relationship.

Planning for a contingency involving a nuclear conflict with Russia was only downgraded from an immediate to a potential contingency and the administration remained committed to a modernised nuclear triad, retention of a nuclear hedge, and a prompt launch on warning counter-force operational posture. The reductions under the Moscow Treaty were also contingent upon successful development and deployment of a suite of new strategic capabilities set out in the 2001 NPR's 'new triad'. It is notable that the only reductions made by the administration in its first term were those set out in the 1994 NPR. Further reductions in operationally deployed forces were announced in 2006 and 2007 to meet Moscow Treaty requirements together with plans to reduce the reserve.

The 'new strategic framework' was both praised and criticised as a welcome or dangerous break with previous practice. Conservatives in Congress, the new administration and outside government were dissatisfied with nuclear weapons policy under Clinton. This was demonstrated by the 1999 vote against the CTBT, legislation keeping force levels at START I, pressure to abandon the ABM treaty and the version of strategic stability it represented, and criticism over the state of the nuclear weapons production complex. With Bush in office, the START process and the ABM treaty abandoned with minimal political cost and the targeting of WMD-armed 'rogue' states made more explicit, conservatives in and out of Congress endorsed the strategic nuclear force reductions in the Moscow Treaty.[291]

Critics regarded the abandonment of the formal arms control process, the determination to deploy missile defences at the expense of the ABM treaty, explicit nuclear threats to 'rogue' states and the initiatives launched under the NPR as dangerously destabilising. They argued that the 'new strategic framework' had been constructed largely to support conservative Cold War policies applied to a new era and that the administration's policies rested on downgrading multilateralism and seeking security through far greater reliance on unfettered military superiority and flexibility. As the Bush administration entered its final years in 2007 and 2008 it became increasingly clear that Moscow was unconvinced by the 'new strategic framework' rhetoric, with major disagreements over a successor agreement to START I and American missile defence deployments in Europe.

The Bush administration's reconceptualisation of strategic stability completed the shift towards a much greater focus on WMD-armed 'rogue' states in nuclear weapons policy and away from a long-standing focus on a nuclear deterrent relationship with Russia based on mutual assured destruction that proscribed 'destabilising' missile defences. This was based on a shift in thinking on strategic deterrence from deterrence by punishment applied to major powers and peer competitors and towards tailored deterrence by denial targeted at 'rogue' states, particularly their mobile WMD and HDBTs, in an era of strategic uncertainty reinforced by 9/11. This necessitated a flexible, capabilities-based approach involving a range of strategic offensive and defensive capabilities that freed American strategic deterrence posture from the constraints of Cold War arms control agreements but also, it was argued, reduced its dependence on nuclear weapons. This was reflected in operational planning practices that saw the SIOP replaced by a range of nuclear and conventional strategic strike plans. The development of conventional strategic weapons in support of STRATCOM's new global strike mission was an important part of this shift. Critics argued that this would increase the salience of nuclear weapons in international politics, increase the risk of nuclear use and spur nuclear proliferation. More worryingly, the administration also appeared to institutionalise the concept of pre-emptive military planning, including nuclear pre-emptive actions against WMD-armed 'rogues'.

Nuclear force reductions therefore came at a price, as they did throughout the Cold War. In this case the price was full deployment of missile defences, new conventional strategic capabilities, a revitalised nuclear weapons complex, and new or modified nuclear capabilities. Nevertheless, the changes were far from wholesale. The roles assigned to nuclear weapons mirrored those at the end of the Clinton administration, even if the emphasis was different. In addition nuclear forces continued to be modernised, sustained at relatively high levels in between those of START II and III, and on high alert. Russia's nuclear force still remained one of the primary factors determining the size and posture of deployed and reserve nuclear force, reflected in the continued commitment to a strategic nuclear triad, including a large ICBM fleet and a major responsive hedge force.

Many of these arguments and rationales were not new but reflected much of the second theme in nuclear weapons policy at the end of the Cold War. The emphasis was on war-fighting denial strategies, maximum flexibility, distrust in the utility of arms control processes, the necessity of missile defences, and the importance of demonstrating the credibility of American military strength. This was supplemented by the concept of dissuasion – the idea that the mere deployment of specific American capabilities would dissuade other states from investing in WMD or ballistic missile programmes.

The future of the nuclear arsenal was increasingly dependent on the health of the weapons complex. Nuclear weapons policy under Bush was shaped by major efforts to revitalise the complex and establish a 'responsive' infrastructure for future nuclear requirements. NNSA continued to suffer major problems with SSP facilities, the major warhead LEP schedule and re-establishing lost capabilities through the lengthy Complex-21 consolidation process. Congressional dissatisfaction with the administration's nuclear weapons policy, the size of the nuclear stockpile and plans for the nuclear weapons complex meant that new initiatives set out in the 2001 NPR would not be funded until DOD and DOE produced a clear and detailed long-term plan for the nuclear stockpile and the complex. The administration responded with the Complex-2030 and RRW plans, both of which proved controversial and met significant congressional resistance with all funding for the RRW and much of the funding for Complex-2030 plans cut by Congress for FY 2008. With further major nuclear reductions linked to a revitalised complex the long-term future of American nuclear forces remains unclear in the absence of consensus between the White House and Congress.

6 Post-Cold War trends in nuclear weapons policy

A number of long-term interrelated trends emerge from a detailed examination of American nuclear weapons policy since the end of the Cold War. These trends reveal significant continuity *and* change and together with the 15 decisions identified in chapter three represent the evolution of post-Cold War nuclear weapons policy.

Consolidation and modernisation of strategic nuclear forces

In the early 1990s President George H. W. Bush took a number of steps to adjust nuclear weapons policy following the end of the Cold War. The primary means of adjustment was a long-term process of consolidating and modernising the Cold War legacy nuclear force within strictures imposed by Congress. Since then successive Nuclear Posture Reviews, National Security Strategies and STRATCOM force structure studies have recommended reducing nuclear forces to end up with a specific triad of strategic nuclear weapons. This comprised 500 Minuteman III ICBMs, 18 and then 14 Ohio-class SSBNs equipped with Trident II (D5) SLBMs and B-2 and B-52 long-range bombers equipped with nuclear cruise missiles and strategic nuclear gravity bombs, all complemented by a limited arsenal of non-strategic tactical nuclear weapons. This has seen a reduction in deployed strategic nuclear forces from approximately 13,000 in 1990 to around 5,800 in 2004. By 2012 America plans to deploy between 1,700 and 2,200 strategic nuclear warheads with an estimated reserve force of 2,000 warheads. These nuclear delivery systems have all undergone major life extension and modernisation programmes. Warheads have also been refurbished and modernised to make them much more accurate, with more flexible range and targeting capability.

The exact constitution of the post-Cold War triad was established in the very early 1990s when Cold War legacy nuclear weapon systems were withdrawn, cancelled or scaled-down to reflect geo-strategic changes in Europe, congressional budgetary pressure to reduce defence spending and a nuclear weapons production complex that was becoming increasingly incapable of supporting a vast, diverse nuclear weapons enterprise. Calls to rethink the deployment of a strategic triad have been resisted, in particular arguments for eliminating the

ICBM leg. The triad force structure was argued to provide the necessary flexibility, redundancy and survivability in nuclear forces for policy requirements. These requirements have involved maintaining at least nuclear parity with Russia and nuclear superiority over all other potential adversaries, the ability to defeat many thousands of strategic targets, and the ability to launch on warning of attack.

The consolidation process has come at a price. In the early 1990s the price for nuclear force reductions was deployment of the B-2, a mobile ICBM capability, modernisation of strategic nuclear forces and maintenance of a large nuclear reserve force. Congress curtailed the B-2 and scrapped mobile ICBM programmes but the latter two developments went ahead. In the 1990s the price exacted by the Republican-controlled Congress was full deployment of a national missile defence system, a price Clinton was not prepared to pay. Under President George W. Bush the 'risks' associated with consolidating deployed nuclear forces had to be offset through a national missile defence system, new conventional strategic capabilities and a revitalised production complex.

An important feature of this trend has been the codification of nuclear force consolidation and modernisation in agreements with Russia including the PNIs, START I, START II and the Moscow Treaty. The purpose has not been to reduce nuclear weapons *per se* but to enhance the prevailing definition of 'strategic stability' by enhancing confidence, transparency and predictability. A key feature has been attaining the decades-long goal of de-MIRVing the Russian ICBM fleet, later abandoned by George W. Bush. These agreements have generally codified nuclear force reductions America was likely to make anyway. Successive administrations have resisted negotiating agreements that would have undermined the maintenance and modernisation of the consolidated triad force structure it had been working towards since the end of the Cold War. This was seen in changes to warhead accounting rules in the proposed START III agreement and later the Moscow Treaty.

A nuclear 'hedge'

The concept of a nuclear 'hedge' reserve force emerged in the early 1990s driven by two perceived needs: first to guard against a resurgent Russia; and second to guard against the failure of a warhead type as the Cold War legacy arsenal was consolidated and modernised. The first few years of the post-Cold War period were marked by uncertainty in the stability and long-term direction of US-Soviet/Russian strategic relations, particularly as the Soviet Union disintegrated. In the early 1990s the concept of a cautionary nuclear hedge emerged to guard against the possibility of a resurgent and confrontational Soviet Union/Russia. It was founded on early post-Cold War scepticism about Soviet/Russian nuclear weapons policy, strategic force modernisation and commitment to democratic reform. The hedge concept was formally codified in the 1994 NPR with a reserve force designed to be redeployed to reconstitute a

START I nuclear arsenal within a three-year timeframe as nuclear forces steadily reduced to START II levels over the 1990s.

The continued existence of a Russian nuclear arsenal of sufficient size and sophistication to threaten the survivability of America's nuclear force and the destruction of the United States was seen as a major existential threat. It was this capability, rather than the intentions of the Russian leadership, that required maintenance of the nuclear 'hedge' to ensure an equally large, diverse and sophisticated nuclear arsenal that would permanently preclude the possibility of strategic nuclear inferiority to Russia. The warming of relations in the 1990s and regular declarations of a new cooperative relationship did little to undermine this rationale. Even the 'new strategic framework' articulated by George W. Bush only downgraded Russia from an expected to a potential contingency still requiring a hedge, or responsive, force should relations break down.

As relations with Russia improved through the 1990s and deployed forces were reduced under the START I treaty, the rationale for retaining a nuclear hedge shifted from guarding against a resurgent Russia to providing an acceptable degree of redundancy within the ageing nuclear stockpile in the absence of a fully functioning production base and nuclear testing. America no longer had the ability to develop and produce existing or new warheads following the closure of a number of sites and the loss of key capabilities such as nuclear testing, plutonium pit production, tritium operations and uranium component fabrication. A hedge of fully functional nuclear warheads was therefore considered a crucial insurance against the failure of a warhead type that could affect a large proportion of the operational nuclear stockpile. The need to insure against the possibility of warhead failure increased as the number and variety of nuclear weapons steadily declined.

A third rationale that has received less attention is the need to retain a significant gap between American nuclear forces and the nuclear forces of other nuclear weapon states, particularly China. America seeks to dissuade China, and others, from any consideration of competing with it in a nuclear arms race by retaining a relatively large deployed nuclear force and a surge capability to rapidly increase the size of the deployed force through the hedge reserve force.

America will likely retain a significant nuclear hedge force until there is a decisive move away from a counter-force nuclear targeting doctrine focused on Russia and towards a more minimal nuclear deterrent posture, and/or until a fully operational nuclear weapons production complex is re-established with the capability to mass produce nuclear weapons without nuclear testing.

Regional nuclear targeting

Almost immediately after the end of the Cold War attention began to shift in America's national security discourse away from the Soviet Union/Russia towards the perceived threat from unpredictable Third World states in key regions arming themselves with WMD and ballistic missiles. America was determined not to allow these states the potential to deter regional intervention in defence of its interests, forces or allies. Four states in particular were singled out: Iran, Iraq, Libya and North Korea. Countering the threat from these 'rogue' states provided a cohesive new paradigm to guide conventional and nuclear force posture and requirements after the Cold War. It provoked a shift in nuclear contingency planning away from prevailing in a long nuclear war with Russia to limited nuclear strikes against regional WMD-armed adversaries and new thinking on the role of nuclear weapons and nuclear deterrence. This was shaped by the 1991 Gulf War, the 1993–1994 crisis over North Korea's nuclear weapons programme, and the diffusion of missile and WMD expertise, technology and materials from the former Soviet Union. Counter-proliferation missions for use of nuclear weapons against 'rogue' states were steadily institutionalised through the 1990 Reed Report, official doctrine statements from the JCS, and reportedly in the 1997 PDD-60, the 2001 NPR and the 2002 NSPD-17. The increased targeting of 'rogue' states was also facilitated by the development of a far more flexible 'adaptive planning' nuclear targeting apparatus to allow a much more rapid response to quickly emerging contingencies.

The new focus on WMD-armed 'rogues' led to 'studied ambiguity' over the circumstances under which America would use nuclear weapons in response to a chemical or biological weapons attack. The potential for a nuclear response to such attacks was made more explicit by the George W. Bush administration. Under George W. Bush the focus of nuclear planning shifted further away from the threat posed by Russia, culminating in the 'new strategic relationship' that was codified in the 2002 Moscow Treaty and the downgrading of a potential nuclear conflict with Russia to a secondary planning contingency in the 2001 NPR. The threat from WMD-armed 'rogue' states, however, was accentuated to the point where it dominated the 2001 NPR, the 2002 National Security Strategy and the post-9/11 national security discourse.

A shift in role of nuclear forces and nuclear deterrence

The shift in strategic threat perception away from Russia and towards WMD-armed 'rogue' states was marked by a fourth trend that deserves its own status: a shift in the declaratory purpose of nuclear forces and a rethinking of the functioning of nuclear deterrence in relation to these 'rogues'.

America's nuclear weapons have traditionally been assigned the roles of constituting a central deterrent of Soviet/Russian nuclear forces with the capacity for fighting a major nuclear war should deterrence fail and providing an extended nuclear deterrent to allies in NATO and East Asia. These roles have decreased in prominence as the threat from Russia's nuclear arsenal has faded to be superseded by three others. First, the deterrence, and pre-emptive destruction if necessary, of the WMD arsenals and leadership infrastructure of 'rogue' states; second to serve as a disincentive to dissuade such states from developing WMD or competing in a nuclear arms race; and third to act as a general purpose 'insurance' against unforeseen developments that could seriously threaten American security in an increasingly uncertain strategic security environment.

The assignment of these roles to American nuclear forces has occurred alongside a reappraisal of the functioning of nuclear deterrence. A view developed in the United States that Cold War-era nuclear deterrence could not be credibly applied to the emerging 'rogue' state threat. It was not considered credible to threaten the leadership of such states with catastrophic nuclear devastation using high-yield nuclear weapons in retaliation for a WMD attack against the American homeland, its forces or allies. Deterrence through the threat of punishment that could decimate the society and population of a 'rogue' state did not rest easily with those who considered these populations to be in some way 'victims' or 'hostages' to the whims of a dictatorial leadership.[1]

It was argued instead that deterrence of 'rogue' states should shift from deterrence by punishment to deterrence by denial. This appeared to include planning for the pre-emptive use of nuclear weapons under the George W. Bush administration. This required deployment of new military capabilities capable of dramatically reducing the utility and effect of a 'rogue' leadership's WMD and ballistic missiles. These included missile defences, conventional counter-proliferation capabilities, rapid global strike capabilities, a much improved intelligence and targeting infrastructure, and new or modified nuclear weapons. This would, it was argued, reduce pressure to resort to nuclear weapons in a major conflict by providing the White House with credible non-nuclear options. In this context the concept of strategic deterrence expanded in the post-Cold War period beyond just nuclear deterrence to a capabilities-based approach incorporating conventional and nuclear offensive and defensive capabilities.

This represented an important shift in nuclear weapons policy and planning, but not a fundamental change. America still remained committed to a nuclear deterrence posture that evolved during the Cold War that required a large, diverse nuclear force, nuclear primacy over any adversary or set of adversaries in order to control the escalation of a nuclear conflict, a counter-force doctrine to hold a vast array of enemy targets at risk with forces on high alert and capable of launching on warning of an attack. This view of nuclear posture has shown considerable endurance within the nuclear policy community, albeit in a more relaxed mode since the collapse of the Soviet Union.[2]

Pressure for new nuclear weapons

Pressure for new or modified nuclear weapons remained consistent throughout the post-Cold War period. This trend was primarily a function of the shift in threat perception to WMD-armed 'rogue' states and was largely based on the argument that threatening a 'rogue' adversary with high-yield Cold War-era nuclear weapons lacked credibility. The focus of this pressure was on new or modified precision-guided low-yield nuclear warheads, or 'mini nukes' and 'micro-nukes', and earth-penetrating warheads, or 'bunker busters', to hold at risk chemical and biological weapons agents, mobile ballistic missiles, and hardened and deeply buried bunkers containing WMD, WMD facilities, or leadership infrastructure. Pressure to develop these nuclear capabilities gained momentum as the 'rogue' state threat and a deterrence by denial capabilities-based approach came to dominate strategic planning. The PLYWD programme to develop a new precision low-yield warhead, the development of the B61-11 bomb for improved earth-penetrating nuclear capability, the RNEP programme and the Advanced Concepts Initiative to explore low-yield warhead designs reflect this trend.

An additional part of the drive to develop new or modified nuclear warheads was the desire to retain nuclear weapons expertise (and funding) at the nuclear weapons laboratories. The nuclear policy community insisted that the maintenance of nuclear weapons research and design skills was a crucial component of the nuclear 'hedge'. Retaining this expertise, weapons scientists and technicians required researching and designing new or modified nuclear warheads, if not actually developing, testing and deploying them.

The need for new low-yield and earth-penetrating nuclear capabilities and research and design programmes to retain nuclear weapons expertise was supported by some in Congress whilst others provided sustained resistance. In 1993 the PLYWD project was halted by a congressional ban on research and design on new low-yield warheads below five kilotons, and the RNEP and Advanced Concepts Initiatives were questioned and not fully funded, with RNEP abandoned in 2005. The 1993 congressional ban was repealed at the Bush administration's request in 2003 but it is notable that no new or modified nuclear weapons were fielded by the George W. Bush administration, which had highlighted the importance of these capabilities in its 2001 NPR.

Opposition to prohibitive constraints on strategic deterrence posture

President George H. W. Bush, the Republican-controlled Congress under Clinton, and President George W. Bush have all resisted attempts to constrain America's strategic deterrence capabilities, particularly the capability to test nuclear weapons, deploy national missile defences, and develop low-yield and earth-penetrating nuclear weapons. Less opposition was directed towards the START treaties since these largely codified planned nuclear force reductions.

Pressure mounted in the early 1990s from the Democratic-controlled Congress for a zero-yield test ban to halt the further development of new nuclear weapons, stem nuclear proliferation and ensure a successful 1995 NPT Review Conference where a decision would be taken on whether or not to extend the NPT indefinitely. This was vehemently opposed by the Bush administration that insisted on the need for nuclear tests to ensure the unequivocal safety, security and reliability of the nuclear stockpile and the credibility of nuclear deterrent threats. Republican critics denied the non-proliferation benefits of the CTBT and refuted arguments that the Stockpile Stewardship Program would ameliorate treaty-based constraints by providing an adequate substitute for physical testing. Clinton's decision to end all nuclear testing and sign the CTBT sparked fierce and enduring debate throughout the post-Cold War period that peaked with the Senate voting down the treaty in 1999.

The emergence of the WMD-armed 'rogue' state threat led to increasing calls for extensive national and theatre missile defences. This was enhanced by the use of Scud missiles by Iraq in the 1991 Gulf War, the proliferation of ballistic missile technology to Iran and other potential 'rogues' and the unannounced launch of a long-range ballistic missile by North Korea in 1998. This had an indirect but significant impact on nuclear force structure by undermining the START nuclear arms control process. America appeared to be moving towards significant cooperation with Russia on missile defence technology under George H. W. Bush that would either involve major changes to the ABM treaty or its abandonment. President Clinton took a different position and placed the ABM treaty at the centre of strategic stability with Russia alongside the START process. Both Clinton and Yeltsin linked the START process and entry into force of START II to continued adherence to the ABM treaty and codified this in the 1997 Joint Statements at Helsinki.

The Republican-controlled Congress denied such a linkage and refused to accept the necessity of any constraints on American missile defence programmes. As the 1990s progressed momentum developed in Congress to deploy missile defences regardless of the impact on the ABM treaty and START II as the 'rogue' state threat grew and the Russian threat receded. As a result the START process ground to a halt and START II remained in limbo from 1996 when it was ratified by Congress until it was finally put to rest in 2002 with the signing of the Moscow Treaty. The Moscow Treaty further relaxed constraints on America's deterrence posture by allowing maximum flexibility in the configuration of its nuclear arsenal.

The Republican-controlled Congress under Clinton and both Bush presidencies also resisted constraints on research and development for new or modified low-yield and earth-penetrating warheads, demonstrated by the lifting of the 1993 ban on such research in 2003. The Clinton administration also resisted pressure not to deploy the B61-11 earth-penetrating bomb amid accusations that it was a new weapon whose deployment would spur further nuclear proliferation.

A revitalised but decaying nuclear weapons complex

The seventh trend is the revitalisation of the decaying nuclear weapons production complex that was crumbling and heavily polluted with radioactive contamination at the end of the Cold War. The complex had to be consolidated, some sites closed, key capabilities lost and plans for new projects abandoned. The institutionalisation of the concept of a nuclear 'hedge', consensus on the modernisation of the strategic triad, and the establishment of the Stockpile Stewardship Program and major warhead life extension programmes has led to a slow consolidation and rebuilding of a functioning production complex. This has revolved around the Complex-21 infrastructure consolidation and regeneration plan, construction of a suite of major new facilities for the SSP, such as the National Ignition Facility and the Tritium Extraction

Facility, and re-establishment of plutonium pit, tritium and uranium component production capabilities.

Nevertheless, the complex has been plagued by environmental and technical problems that DOE and NNSA have struggled to keep up with. For some this has constituted a form of 'structural disarmament'. Consolidation and modernisation of the complex and warhead refurbishment and dismantlement have progressed at a slow pace and the management of the complex and the SSP have been subject to regular congressional and independent criticism. Under George W. Bush the maintenance of a robust and 'responsive' nuclear weapons complex was deemed an essential part of the new triad outlined in the 2001 NPR and reductions of deployed nuclear weapons and the size of the reserve force were linked to the health of the complex.

The consolidation and modernisation of the production complex has been closely linked to the fierce debate over the ban on nuclear testing and the end of new nuclear weapons design and production. A growing concern since the end of the Cold War has been the erosion of nuclear weapons expertise and the impact of these developments on the ability of the complex to maintain a safe and reliable Cold War legacy nuclear stockpile over the long term. NNSA developed the controversial Complex-2030 and RRW plans in response to sustained congressional criticism about the viability of the massive warhead LEP plan and to provide long-term plans for the nuclear stockpile and production complex and environmental, management, security and long-term planning problems. The future of these programmes and the stockpile and complex as a whole remains uncertain.

Long timelines

Post-Cold War changes in nuclear weapons policy, force structure and capabilities have been characterised by long timelines. The first stage of the post-Cold War consolidation and modernisation process has taken 17 years: the retirement of the MX, the back fitting of all 14 remaining SSBNs to take the Trident II (D5) SLBM and the conversion of four SSBNs to conventional roles was completed in 2007. The next stage of force consolidation will occur between 2005 and 2012 when America will reduce its operationally deployed strategic nuclear force to between 1,700–2,200 under the Moscow Treaty and its total nuclear stockpile to between 4,600 warheads.

The time taken to reduce Cold War nuclear forces to levels agreed in the early 1990s was tied to securing entry into force of START II. This was delayed by the time taken to secure entry into force of START I and major disagreement over the deployment of missile defences. The arms reduction process was finally resuscitated through the 2002 Moscow Treaty. As a result nuclear forces scheduled for deactivation following the signing of START II in 1994 and the 1994 NPR lingered in operationally deployed status until 2001/2002 when their retirement began.

It also took seven years for formal nuclear weapons policy guidance to be changed at the presidential level. For the first seven years of the post-Cold War era nuclear weapons policy was based on Reagan's 1981 guidance. During this first seven years the 1994 NPR was completed, new Nuclear Weapons Employment Policy guidance was issued by DOD, the JCS updated the nuclear appendix to the Joint Strategic Capabilities Plan several times and published new nuclear doctrine twice in 1993 and 1995.

The pace of dismantling nuclear weapons has also proved to be a long and costly process restricted by the dismantling capacity of the Pantex facility.[3] Dismantlement of a warhead type takes years of process, hazard and safety analysis requiring complicated procedures, time and resources and costing a lot more than storing warheads after retirement.[4] The general degradation of the nuclear weapons industrial complex was an additional complicating factor. Former STRATCOM commander Eugene Habiger commented in 2002 that the 'capacity to dismantle nuclear weapons has been seriously degraded since the mid-1990s'.[5] Over 12,000 warheads were dismantled between 1990 and 2000 but it will take up to 16 years to dismantle warheads retired in the stockpile reduction announced in 2004.[6]

The development of new capabilities in the nuclear weapons production complex has also been time consuming, with the production of the first certified plutonium pit since 1988 occurring in 2007, the first new tritium processed in 2007 and major SSP facilities such as the DARHT and NIF slipping further behind schedule and costing millions more than projected. Although the nuclear weapons complex is being revitalised, it will take many more years for the key facilities of the SSP to become operational, perhaps up to 20 years after they were first authorised in 1993 for some of the larger projects.

The warhead refurbishment programme is also a lengthy and difficult process. For example, the first stage of the W76 SLBM warhead refurbishment plan was approved by the DOD-DOE Nuclear Weapons Council in 2000 after a multi-year effort to assess the health of the warhead and develop refurbishment options to extend the life of the warheads by an additional 30 years.[7] A first refurbished unit is planned for 2008 with the first stage of refurbishment to be applied to two-thirds of the W76 arsenal by 2012 and the second stage applied by 2022.[8]

No nuclear disarmament

One overarching trend governs those identified so far: a total commitment to the long-term retention of a sophisticated nuclear arsenal. At the 2000 NPT Review Conference the nuclear weapon states agreed to an 'unequivocal undertaking … to accomplish the total elimination of their nuclear arsenals'.[9] The Clinton administration may have been sincere when it signed up to this long-term goal, but an equally unequivocal undertaking within America's defence establishment to retain nuclear weapons well into the future will have to be overcome before that goal can be realised. The logic of nuclear disarmament has been strongly resisted by all three post-Cold War administrations, despite statements from the Clinton administration suggesting it was actively working towards that goal.

Nuclear disarmament is simply not part of America's nuclear weapons policy discourse. It does seem likely that its nuclear forces will continue to be reduced, although this will probably coincide with the deployment of new nuclear and non-nuclear offensive and defensive strategic capabilities. Nevertheless, America will endeavour to maintain a sophisticated triad or perhaps a dyad of strategic nuclear forces to match Russia's, assure allies, dissuade China from engaging in a nuclear arms race and threaten regional 'rogues'.

All of these long-term post-Cold War trends are interlinked at a number of levels, with some contradictory outcomes. The concept of a nuclear hedge is linked to the existential threat posed by Russia's nuclear arsenal, modernisation and consolidation of nuclear forces, nuclear testing and the state of the nuclear weapons production complex.

The START arms control process is linked to missile defence and the threat from WMD-armed 'rogue' states, the ABM treaty, modernisation and consolidation of nuclear forces, Russian suspicion of American missile defence and strategic superiority motives.

New or modified nuclear weapons are linked to WMD-armed 'rogue' states, nuclear weapons expertise, nuclear testing, counter-proliferation war-fighting doctrine, a capabilities-based approach to deterrence by denial, and nuclear non-proliferation.

Dependency on nuclear weapons in strategic planning is linked to conventional strategic capabilities, missile defences, the blocked START process, modernisation of nuclear forces, a shift to deterrence by denial vis-à-vis 'rogue' states, and the state of the nuclear weapons production complex.

The consolidation of nuclear forces is linked to strategic force modernisation, new targeting infrastructure, new or modified nuclear weapons, missile defences, conventional strategic capabilities, and the START process, PNIs and Moscow Treaty.

Finally, revitalising the nuclear weapons production complex is linked to nuclear weapons expertise, nuclear testing, new nuclear weapons, a nuclear hedge and modernisation of nuclear forces.

This chapter has identified and examined a number of trends that emerge from the analysis of nuclear weapons policy in the previous three chapters. It argues that the key decisions and trends identified and examined represent the evolution of nuclear weapons policy since the end of the Cold War. A number of competing ideas, beliefs, meanings and understandings emerge from analysis of these decisions, trends and the debates. The next chapter examines the substance of these competing ideas and their effect on the evolution of nuclear weapons policy.

7 The influence of ideas on nuclear weapons policy

Analysis of nuclear weapons policy tends to draw on realist theory in which national security and survival are the first and foremost concern of all states in an international system of 'relentless security competition'.[1] States constantly struggle for power because with it comes influence and a greater capacity to ensure national security and state survival in an uncertain and anarchic international environment. The struggle for power and security inevitably results in conflictual relations and power is generally defined in terms of the material, particularly military, capabilities of a state *relative* to the capabilities of other states and the political power to coerce and control other states.[2] It is therefore considered logical and rational for states to maximise their military and political power vis-à-vis their competitors because it is in their national interest to do so if they want to survive. Failure to act 'rationally' in an anarchic international system could undermine the very survival of the state.[3]

Realist theory, with its focus on states, material capabilities and security defined in military terms, therefore explains and in fact prescribes the accumulation of military power as a necessary and rational activity to protect the state from the many, varied and inevitable confrontations it will have with other powerful states. In the nuclear age the relative size and strength of nuclear arsenals became a central feature of military capabilities, power and influence in international politics. During the Cold War American nuclear weapons policy was explained as a necessary response to the imperatives of an international anarchic system in which it had to constantly seek a favourable nuclear balance of power to counter the Soviet Union and avoid the political coercion that would surely result from an inferior nuclear force. Game theory was used to develop hypotheses about the military-political interaction between America and the Soviet Union in Cold War crises. 'Strategic realists' developed models of nuclear deterrence based on the rationalist logic of game theory to explain and inform American nuclear weapons policy and strategy.[4] Traditional accounts of nuclear weapons policy have therefore focused on material military capabilities and the relative balance of these capabilities between major powers. They have generally defined theories of nuclear deterrence as logical and rational and used these to explain and guide policy.

This analysis takes a different approach. It argues that examining the domestic political discourse on nuclear weapons policy is crucial to understanding how and why policy has evolved since the end of the Cold War, rather than examining the military capabilities of America's actual and potential adversaries and how these capabilities affect the 'logic' of nuclear deterrence and the composition and purpose of American nuclear forces. International events, issues and material capabilities matter enormously, but their significance is in their interpretation within the domestic political discourse.

This approach draws on constructivist theory within the wider school of International Relations theory.[5] Constructivist theory argues that 'ideational' factors such as interests, identities, values and norms are essential to understanding international politics rather than just material factors. It emphasises the importance of problematising ideas, interests, identities and meanings rather than taking them as given and the importance of examining how they are constructed in a particular social and historical context. Constructivism also argues that particular collective understandings and meanings can become institutionalised and accepted as 'normal'. These institutionalised understandings can provide an interpretative framework for understanding the world and a road map for policy action.[6] They can determine how external changes and events are interpreted, what information is considered relevant and how interests, threats and desired outcomes are defined.[7] Policy outcomes are not dictated by rational cost-benefit calculations to maximise particular pregiven national interests, but by a sense of what is 'appropriate' according to prevailing institutionalised understandings.[8] Policy outcomes and policy evolution are therefore highly dependent on the set of ideas and beliefs that constitute the dominant interpretive framework and dominant images of the world that are shared by a policy-making elite.[9]

Power through a critical constructivist lens is understood as the authority to legitimise and define what constitutes 'normal' understandings, meanings and practices. The relationship between knowledge and political power is therefore of primary importance and what is deemed 'rational' is 'only the expression of the temporary hegemony of a particular political discourse'.[10] In this context the idea of deducing a 'correct' nuclear weapons policy as an objective, rational response to the external international environment is rejected. It is instead something that is constructed through institutionalised collective understandings and practices.[11] Realist theory, in contrast, argues that ideational factors such as interests, understandings and identities are at best derived from the distribution of material capabilities and at worst have no relevance or independent explanatory power.[12]

A number of case studies that have concluded that shared idea sets, discourses or belief systems play a pivotal role in national security policy-making, including nuclear weapons policy. These include Spinardi's study of why the U.S. Navy opted for a hard-target counter-force capability in the Trident II (D5) SLBM; Tannenwald's analysis of a normative 'nuclear taboo' in America against nuclear use; Mehan *et al.*'s examination of nuclear weapons discourse under the Reagan administration; Cooper's exploration of the role of discourse in constructing the threat from weapons of mass destruction and 'rogue' states; Rhodes' examination of American strategic adjustment in the 1880s and 1890s; and Mutimer's study of the construction of the threat of WMD proliferation through analysis of metaphor and discourse.[13]

A focus on ideas sets and discourses is also particularly appropriate for nuclear weapons policy because of the absence of empirical data on the functioning of nuclear deterrence and nuclear use in a crisis and the impact and credibility of nuclear threats in international politics. As a result these issues have always been debated conceptually. Robert Jervis, for example, argues that in the absence of nuclear war many arguments about nuclear strategy simply cannot be verified and nuclear strategy has remained hypothetical and based on certain sets of logic rather than evidence.[14] Walter Slocombe, former Under Secretary of Defense for Policy for President Clinton, also argues that, 'Discussion of nuclear weapons is almost entirely done in theoretical and conceptual terms. This has an important influence on how nuclear weapons decisions are made'.[15]

The absence of empirical evidence has allowed much greater scope for the power of ideas and concepts to shape perceptions of nuclear reality. Jervis argues that on key issues such as the credibility of nuclear threats there is no reality to be described independent of policy-makers' beliefs and that doctrines and beliefs shape rather than describe reality. He also argues that the construction of problems affecting nuclear strategy by analysts and policy-makers has been arbitrary.[16] The theories that did emerge to influence nuclear weapons policy during the Cold War were dominated by rationalist, realist conceptions of international politics that led to a 'scientisation of nuclear strategy' based on an illusion of precision and exactness.[17] These theories were not value free and technocratic but reflected distinct ideas and understandings about nuclear weapons, the Soviet Union, vulnerability, and a tendency to 'fantasize about Soviet military power'.[18]

More recently Lodal has presented three competing strategic visions of nuclear weapons policy, labelled 'more arms control', 'undefeatable active defense' and 'nuclear abolition'.[19] Krepon has drawn a distinction between two view-points: conciliators who believe strongly in reassurance, preventive diplomacy, downgrading nuclear weapons and the role of strong international anti-proliferation norms; and dominators who believe cooperation and coercion are based on military strength, a clear willingness to use it, and maximum freedom of action for the unilateral use of force, including nuclear weapons.[20] Others have divided the debate between 'maximalists' and 'minimalists', 'marginalisers' and 'traditionalists', and 'minimalist' and 'neo-traditional' views.[21]

Three competing 'idea sets'

The previous chapters have identified and examined the key decisions and long-term trends that represent the evolution of American nuclear weapons policy since the end of the Cold War. These decisions and trends reflect significant continuity as well as change, but this has not been linear. It has instead reflected competing interpretations of a set of contested concepts that have directly and indirectly affected policy. These concepts include the role of or meanings assigned to:

- Strategic stability in relation to the nuclear balance with Russia, nuclear arms controls, assured destruction and mutual vulnerability and missile defences;
- Nuclear deterrence in relation to potential peer adversaries, international stability at the major power level, the relevance of strategic military balances and regional WMD-armed adversaries;
- A prompt launch on warning posture based on a strategic triad to deter a first-strike and limit damage in the event of an attack;
- Maintaining quantitative and qualitative nuclear superiority above all potential adversaries, perhaps even Russia and its relationship to US military and political hegemony and alliance commitments;
- Maintaining a nuclear 'hedge' through a reserve nuclear stockpile and a responsive 'warm' nuclear weapons production complex;
- Developing and articulating 'credible' regional nuclear war-fighting plans for WMD-armed adversaries and developing tailored nuclear weapons for the task;
- The effect of nuclear restraint through non-testing, nuclear reductions and minimal new warhead and production capability initiatives on non-proliferation, arms control, nuclear superiority and alliance commitments;
- Finally, the nuclear arms reductions process in the context of nuclear superiority, relations with Russia, strategic stability, non-proliferation and nuclear force modernisation and transformation.

The broad discourse in America on nuclear weapons policy comprises competing interpretations of these contested concepts and the assignment of different meanings and roles to American nuclear weapons in a range of contexts. There is structure to this discourse, however, and competing interpretations can be usefully ordered into three distinct but overlapping nuclear weapons 'policies' that have all enjoyed partial success since the end of the Cold War. Each competing 'policy' comprises a set of collective ideas and understandings based on an internally coherent interpretation of these contested concepts. Each set of ideas is in turn informed by different images of international politics and America's role in the world. These are often referred to as 'grand strategies' and tend to be listed as isolationism, liberal internationalism, political realism and primacy.[22] Each idea set therefore creates or constructs a different strategic reality for American nuclear weapons and simplifies the many problems and concepts around nuclear weapons policy.[23]

The evolution of policy since the end of the Cold War has therefore been guided by the competition between these three 'idea sets' with particular policy outcomes and actions reflecting the dominance of an idea set within the overall discourse. This competition has been facilitated by the disintegration of the central paradigm governing nuclear forces and strategic behaviour during the Cold War and the absence of a compelling and unifying post-Cold War strategic threat to guide nuclear weapons policy. This has led to dissonance, partisan division and a breakdown in the loose Cold War consensus on the role and utility of nuclear weapons in American national security policy. This is discussed further in the following chapter.[24]

This chapter examines these three competing idea sets and presents them as an analytical tool for understanding the key decisions and trends identified, the debates around them and the change and continuity they represent, rather than objective truths that provide complete explanation. They are not mutually exclusive but their emphases, broad interpretations, collective understandings of causal relationships, the meanings they assign to political and material developments and their prescriptions for change are distinct.

Idea set 1: managing the drawdown of Cold War nuclear forces[25]

The first idea set emphasises American nuclear weapons in the context of the post-Cold War nuclear drawdown process with Russia. Goldstein and Keohane present three types of shared ideas that can be important determinants of policy: worldviews that are 'embedded in the symbolism of a culture and deeply affect modes of thought and discourse' and are closely tied to identities; principled beliefs that comprise normative ideas 'for distinguishing right from wrong and just from unjust'; and causal beliefs about 'cause and effect relationships which derive authority from the shared consensus of recognized elites'.[26]

The two primary principled beliefs underpinning the first idea set are that the main strategic threat to America is Russia's nuclear arsenal and that a strong nuclear defence must be maintained to avoid coercion in a relationship characterised by mutual assured destruction. The primary causal belief is that the most effective way of reducing the threat (primarily the fear of a nuclear first-strike and nuclear coercion) is through bilateral strategic nuclear arms control and a Cold War-era deterrence posture.[27] The primary mechanism is the START process and continued adherence to the ABM treaty. The primary world view underpinning this idea set is a political realist perspective that views the nuclear drawdown process in the context of enhancing a Cold War definition of strategic stability.

Strategic stability

This idea set concentrates on enhancing a Cold War conception of strategic stability. The most appropriate means is through strategic nuclear arms control to verifiably reduce or eliminate Russian strategic nuclear forces that might incentivise a nuclear first-strike in the event of a crisis, in particular MIRVed ICBMs, in exchange for limited American strategic nuclear concessions.[28] Strategic nuclear parity is a vital component of strategic stability and efforts to reduce strategic nuclear forces unilaterally are generally resisted. The purpose of strategic arms control is therefore to increase stability and national security rather than simply to reduce armaments.[29] Maintaining strategic stability is essential to ensure neither side will seek a strategic advantage over the other.[30] This reflects a 'rationalisation' of Cold War nuclear planning and posture constructs.[31]

This particular understanding of strategic nuclear arms control in the post-Cold War era provides a roadmap for carefully and cautiously managing the nuclear drawdown process. It also provides an acceptable framework for the military decline of the Soviet Union/Russia and a means of instilling cooperation and predictability into a historically adversarial relationship.[32] This was the dominant stated purpose of the START process articulated by the G. H. W. Bush and Clinton administrations. In this context other arms control measures, such as the CTBT, are criticised for undermining strategic stability by weakening the perceived credibility of America's nuclear arsenal. START III was criticised for taking arms control beyond managing relations with a well-armed adversary and towards reductions for reductions' sake.[33]

Four additional principled and causal beliefs form part of this idea set. First, arms control must be complemented by modernisation of a consolidated, survivable strategic nuclear triad for the foreseeable future. It is essential that nuclear forces remain technologically superior to allow maximum military preparedness in the event of a crisis and to ensure continued deterrence of the Russian nuclear arsenal as the arms reduction process proceeds.[34] This was a crucial part of the definition of strategic stability employed by the G. H. W. Bush and Clinton administrations. Arguments to reduce forces to a dyad by eliminating the ICBM fleet or to de-alert portions of the nuclear force do not conform to this idea set since they would undermine this conception of strategic stability.[35] Force modernisation also requires a fully functioning nuclear weapons production complex and limited nuclear testing to ensure the safety, security and reliability of nuclear warheads.

Second, strategic stability still required a Cold War-era deterrence posture, albeit a slightly more relaxed version based on a consolidated nuclear force.[36] This is based on modernisation of strategic nuclear forces to enhance counter-force capabilities to ensure full destruction of the many thousands of strategic targets in the SIOP and thousands of weapons on high alert ready to launch on warning of attack.[37] This would have seen full deployment of the Trident II (D5) SLBM, rail mobile MX Peacekeeper ICBM, small ICBM and a much larger fleet of B-2 stealth bombers and Advanced Cruise Missiles. Very deep cuts in nuclear weapons are opposed.

Third, this idea set's interpretation of strategic stability is founded on mutual vulnerability to nuclear devastation characterised by mutual assured destruction or a 'balance of nuclear terror'. In this context the long-term management of the arms reduction process requires continued treaty-based bilateral strategic nuclear reductions and adherence to the ABM treaty, modified or not.[38] This idea set reflects the Cold War belief that extensive and non-treaty compliant American missile defence deployments will undermine the strategic nuclear reductions process based on the logic and reality of mutual assured destruction.[39]

Fourth, a nuclear 'hedge' force had to be established and maintained as a form of insurance against the rapid deterioration of relations with Russia and the emergence of a hostile Russian leadership seeking to coerce the United States and its allies through nuclear brinkmanship.[40] Advocates of a revitalised nuclear weapons complex within this idea set also couch their argument in the context of a 'hedge', premised on the fact that Russia still has a 'warm' production complex capable of producing nuclear warheads, whereas America does not.[41] This was articulated by the first Bush administration and formalised in the 1994 NPR under Clinton.

The purpose of nuclear weapons

The primary objective of this idea set is therefore to design a long-term nuclear deterrence strategy that hedges against the emergence of a revanchist Russian leadership whilst improving relations with Moscow to maximise predictability and minimise the prospect of nuclear threats or even nuclear use in a crisis.[42] A Cold War concept of strategic stability is central. The management of nuclear force reductions through the START process takes priority over competing nuclear threat reduction and deterrence or defence priorities that could undermine it. Radical changes to nuclear weapons policy are avoided and a 'wait and see' approach is adopted before any further marginalisation of nuclear weapons in national security strategy.[43]

The purpose of American nuclear weapons is to deter and if necessary fight and win a major conflict with a peer competitor or other major power, particularly Russia. American nuclear forces and nuclear deterrence are understood to be an essential ingredient in fostering long-term international stability at the major power level, which constitutes a vital national interest.[44] One of the most important meanings assigned to nuclear weapons is that they not only deter nuclear use by others, but restrain war itself by massively increasing the costs of all-out warfare through assured destruction.[45] Secondary roles are the provision of extended deterrence guarantees to allies and deterrence of regional adversaries. Confidence in the functioning of nuclear deterrence is high, requiring few, if any, new capabilities.

The G. H. W. Bush and Clinton administrations adhered strongly to much of this idea set. The Clinton White House in particular remained committed to the Cold War concept of mutual assured destruction, the START process and the ABM treaty as the basis for its interpretation of strategic stability.[46] This is reflected in post-Cold War force structure reviews by SAC and STRATCOM and Clinton's National Security Strategies and DOD annual reports. The outcomes of the 1994 NPR in particular were based on adherence to the 'traditional metrics of "strategic stability"' of this first idea set.[47]

This idea set steadily declined in influence in the 1990s as nuclear deterrence and the composition of nuclear forces became much less central to America's evolving relationship with Russia. The uncertainty and flux of the early 1990s passed and the START process and mutual vulnerability enshrined in the ABM treaty assumed less urgency and relevance in American conceptions of strategic stability.[48] Krepon argues that by the end of the Clinton administration the language of mutual assured destruction was 'archaic, an ancient language rarely spoken and barely understood' with Cold War conceptions of strategic stability 'antiquated beyond repair'.[49]

Nevertheless, belief in the necessity and utility of the START process as an abiding national interest and arguments that Russia's nuclear arsenal presented the greatest strategic threat to the United States remained strong. The mutual assured destruction paradigm was still a necessary basis for strategic stability with Russia in light of its massive nuclear arsenal. A lot may have changed with the end of the Cold War, but this idea set posits that not *enough* has changed to warrant a decisive move away from the this paradigm and its understanding of strategic stability.[50] In 2000 Democratic presidential candidate Al Gore insisted that arms control, strategic force modernisation and missile defences must be based on negotiated agreements otherwise strategic stability would be dangerously undermined. The ABM treaty was a prerequisite for further reductions and nuclear reductions could only take place within the START process. Unilateral measures were deemed destabilising.[51] The existential threat from Russia's large nuclear arsenal remained a major concern that could not be addressed other than through a robust American nuclear force and orderly management of continued nuclear reductions. This was later reflected in criticisms levelled at the Moscow Treaty, pressure to negotiate an agreement to replace START when it expires in 2009 and tensions over American missile defence deployments in Europe.

Idea set 2: responding to nuclear proliferation through progress in arms control and disarmament[52]

The second two idea sets highlight American nuclear weapons in the context of the proliferation of nuclear weapons and ballistic missiles to hostile authoritarian or dictatorial regimes. The nuclear threat posed by Russia is still important, but Russia is viewed as a necessary partner in dealing with WMD-armed 'rogue' states and their potential terrorist allies through cooperative international actions and through increasing the security of its own Cold War legacy nuclear forces and infrastructure. The difference between these two idea sets is in the interpretation of the most effective response to the threat.

The two primary principled beliefs underpinning the second idea set are that the main strategic national security threat is ballistic missiles and WMD (particularly nuclear weapons) in the hands of hostile 'rogue' states and that American nuclear weapons are of declining political and military utility in international security. The primary causal belief is that the most effective means of reducing the threat is through multilateral arms control and significant marginalisation of nuclear weapons. The primary mechanism is the Nuclear Non-Proliferation Treaty (NPT). The primary world view underpinning this idea set is a liberal internationalist perspective that views cooperative security mechanisms, institutions and norms as a firm basis for national security and strategic stability, albeit in conjunction with a robust military posture.

This idea set argues that arms control and the nuclear non-proliferation regime, encompassing the NPT, CTBT, START process, prospective Fissile Material Cut-off Treaty (FMCT), export control regimes and cooperative threat reduction measures, are the essential tools for combating nuclear proliferation. The structures and norms of the non-proliferation regime are invaluable and must be supported as a high priority that is firmly in America's national interest. Actions that undermine the regime should be avoided.[53] One of the starkest reflections of this idea set was issued by the National Academy of Sciences in their 1997 report *The Future of U.S. Nuclear Weapons Policy*. It was also articulated in the Goodpaster Committee report and is reflected in Krepon's 'conciliator' and Sloss' 'minimalist' views.[54]

The detrimental effect of American nuclear weapons policy on non-proliferation

The underlying understanding of this idea set is that constraints on American nuclear forces and doctrine through arms control and non-proliferation agreements and regimes translate into direct and indirect constraints on nuclear proliferation based on the principles of cooperative security, i.e. there exists a strong link between American nuclear weapons policy actions and the success or failure of wider efforts to control and mitigate the effects of nuclear proliferation. As Panofsky and Bunn argue, in nuclear matters 'self restraint is self interest'.[55] This logic maintains that it is simply not possible to persuade other states not to acquire or further develop nuclear weapons capabilities whilst America and the other nuclear weapon states retain large and sophisticated nuclear arsenals and are seen to derive significant security benefits from them.[56] American reliance on nuclear weapons increases the threats to national security in a proliferating world by undermining non-proliferation efforts and legitimising the possession of nuclear weapons.[57] Post-Cold War adherence to a mutual assured destruction relationship with Russia also perpetuates a 'nuclear paradigm' that reinforces the salience of nuclear weapons.[58] A programme to massively reduce and marginalise nuclear weapons in American national security will have a 'salutary' effect on nuclear proliferation.[59] In this context both the START process and the CTBT have been portrayed as non-proliferation measures. Non-proliferation norms had an important impact on Clinton's negotiation of a zero-yield test ban.[60]

Alarmist predictions that the failure to negotiate and implement broad bilateral and multilateral nuclear constraints will unleash a cascade of nuclear proliferation and/or a new nuclear arms race often accompany this idea set. Du Preez, for example, insists that the 2001 NPR will fatally undermine the NPT and encourage further proliferation.[61] Kimball warns of a 'renewed, global nuclear arms competition if the CTBT and other nuclear risk reduction efforts are not finalized'.[62] Others argue that deployment of missile defences and abandonment of the ABM treaty will result in a spiral of nuclear proliferation from Russia to China to India to Pakistan and perhaps the wider Middle East.

A minimum deterrence posture

The role of nuclear weapons and nuclear deterrence is interpreted as a credible and necessary means of preventing nuclear conflict between the major powers, as reflected in the first idea set. This second idea set, however, generally advocates a nuclear posture of 'minimum' deterrence to reflect the declining political and military utility of nuclear weapons. Nuclear weapons are no longer an emblem of American power or the linchpin of its security and status and they can be safely marginalised with little negative effect on American interests, security and status.[63]

Nuclear weapons are judged to serve no function other than to deter a nuclear attack by another state and should be restricted to a minimal or background deterrent role.[64] This view was vigorously expressed by Robert McNamara in 1983 when he declared that 'nuclear weapons serve no military purpose whatsoever. They are totally useless – except only to deter one's opponent from using them'.[65] Any wider remit is not credible and will increase the salience of nuclear weapons in international relations and undermine nuclear non-proliferation efforts.[66] Declaratory policy and operational planning to punish or even preemptively attack WMD-armed 'rogue' states using American nuclear weapons is considered deeply counter productive.[67] As a result America should adopt a 'no-first use' policy stating that it will never use nuclear weapons first in a conflict and seek further cooperative marginalisation of nuclear forces with Russia and the other nuclear weapon states.[68] The 1991 Gulf War is used to demonstrate the irrelevance of nuclear weapons to national security strategy and war-fighting after the Cold War given the supremacy of American conventional capabilities.[69]

The minimum deterrence posture envisages a decisive shift away from Cold War practices of extensive counter-force targeting, high alert rates, multiple roles for nuclear weapons and substantial nuclear forces. The size of America's nuclear arsenal and its reserve 'hedge' force are considered excessive and anathema to non-proliferation objectives that seek to reduce the international salience of nuclear weapons. America should therefore massively reduce its deployed and reserve nuclear forces to a small, survivable second strike capability based on SLBMs and perhaps long-range bombers rather than a large triad of strategic forces.[70] Some modernisation is deemed necessary and acceptable to achieve a smaller, robust and reliable arsenal. Modernisation of the triad to provide enhanced counter-force capabilities is criticised.[71]

American leadership is required to unilaterally reduce its nuclear arsenal to START III levels and then down to between a thousand and a few hundred nuclear warheads.[72] Some advocate abandoning the START process because it reflects the outdated logic of mutual assured destruction that perpetuates a dangerous and adversarial relationship with Russia.[73] Dramatic reductions are necessary to support the non-proliferation regime, but advocates of this idea set tend to accept the difficulties of abolition.[74] An important distinction must therefore be made between this idea set that seeks only to reduce and marginalise nuclear forces and abolitionist arguments that seek to eliminate and outlaw nuclear weapons.[75] These understandings are reflected in the push by the Democratic-controlled Congress in the early 1990s to reduce nuclear forces to much lower levels and curtail strategic counter-force nuclear modernisation programmes, criticism of the 1994 NPR as a lost opportunity for more radical change, and pressure towards the end of the Clinton administration to move unilaterally to START II force levels and even START III.

The logic of this idea set also maintains that any 'new' or unconstrained nuclear weapons initiatives are provocative acts that will only increase the salience of nuclear weapons, the potential for renewed nuclear testing, and undermine the non-proliferation regime. This, it is argued, would spark a new international round of nuclear tests and the development of a new generation of nuclear weapons igniting the old or a new arms race. Efforts to reinvigorate the nuclear weapons complex and to resume testing are generally resisted. The congressional ban on new low-yield nuclear weapons research and design in 1993 and opposition to new tritium and plutonium pit production capabilities, RNEP, the Advanced Concepts Initiative and the Complex-2030 and RRW plans reflect this idea set.

National missile defences are also opposed and adherence to the ABM treaty advocated because of the perceived negative impact on the START reduction process. The negative impact on China's perception of its strategic security should America withdraw from the treaty (which it did in 2002) and deploy national missile defences is also cited. This interpretation claims that the insecurities generated by missile defence could lead to a new arms race with Russia and/or an Asian nuclear arms race involving China, America, India and Pakistan, and possibly extending to Japan and South Korea, that would cripple the NPT.[76]

The importance assigned to nuclear non-proliferation greatly increased immediately after the end of the Cold War under the first Bush administration. Nuclear non-proliferation was also a major focus of the Clinton White House, which placed considerable emphasis on a multilateral world order based on strong international institutions as the basis of American national security.[77] In the early 1990s Clinton and other senior members of his DOD stated that America could dramatically reduce and marginalise its nuclear weapons, adjust deterrence policy to the new post-Cold War world and replace mutual assured destruction with mutual cooperation.[78] Under Clinton the START I treaty came into force, START II was signed, the NPT was extended, Kazakhstan, Ukraine and Belarus joined the NPT as non-nuclear weapons states, the CTBT was negotiated, a de-targeting agreement was reached with Russia, and an agreement was reached with North Korea in 1994 to freeze its nuclear weapons programme. To some these actions represented 'an open-ended intent to move in the direction of nuclear disarmament'.[79] Nevertheless, Clinton soon abandoned his initial idealism and embraced a more realist approach to strategic security that reflected the first idea set and the opportunity to decisively reduce and marginalise American nuclear forces was lost.[80]

A sense of a fresh opportunity steadily grew throughout 2007 following the *Wall Street Journal* editorial by Senator Sam Nunn, former Secretaries of State Henry Kissinger and George Shultz and former Secretary of Defense William Perry in January 2007 and their follow-up in January 2008. These influential figures argued that:

> Nuclear weapons today present tremendous dangers, but also an historic opportunity. U.S. leadership will be required to take the world to the next stage – to a solid consensus for reversing reliance on nuclear weapons globally as a vital contribution to preventing their proliferation into potentially dangerous hands, and ultimately ending them as a threat to the world.[81]

They advocated ratification of the CTBT, de-alerting nuclear forces, reducing deployed nuclear arsenals and negotiating an FMCT. This was also reflected in Democratic presidential candidate Barack Obama's contention that America should seek a world without nuclear weapons, that he would work with Russia to take their ballistic missiles off high alert and negotiate an FMCT.[82]

Idea set 3: responding to nuclear proliferation by reorienting Cold War nuclear weapons policy to a post-Cold War war-fighting policy[83]

The third idea set has a different interpretation of the appropriate response to the threat from the proliferation of WMD and ballistic missiles to 'rogue' states. Its primary principled belief is that American nuclear weapons have a clear role to play in addressing this threat. The primary causal belief is that the most effective means of reducing the threat is through a robust military posture to deter and defeat 'rogue' states and deny any advantage that might be gained by their possession of WMD and ballistic missiles. The primary mechanism is development and deployment of conventional and nuclear offensive and defensive strategic military capabilities and flexible operational plans for retaliatory or pre-emptive attack. The primary world view underpinning this idea set is a more hard-line neo-conservative or 'American primacy' perspective that views military strength and unilateral defence as a firm basis for American national security and stability in conjunction with preventive diplomacy and interventionist activities with coalitions of the willing.[84]

Maximise role of nuclear weapons in counter-proliferation

The key post-Cold War strategic deterrence challenge, as Payne argues, is:

> The demanding mission of 'deterring the deterrent' of a desperate challenger – that is, preventing a regional leader of a regime that is losing a con-

ventional war to an American-led coalition from using WMD in a desperate bid to save what seems to be a lost cause.[85]

For Payne and this third idea set, American nuclear weapons have a vital role to play in this challenge and efforts to maximise the role of nuclear weapons in deterring and if necessary defeating WMD-armed 'rogue' states should be prioritised. It has also been asserted after 9/11 that nuclear weapons can play a role in deterring nuclear terrorism. For some, the threat posed by WMD-armed 'rogue' states is even greater than that posed by the Soviet Union.[86] The marginalisation of nuclear weapons under Clinton is criticised. This view is most succinctly and clearly presented in the 2001 *Rationales and Requirements* report of the National Institute for Public Policy that served as the basis for the 2001 NPR.[87]

The third idea set presents the post-Cold War era as a 'second nuclear age' defined by the emergence of the new 'rogue' state nuclear threat.[88] These regional 'rogues' may not or will not be as deterrable or 'rational' (however measured) as the Soviet Union/Russia.[89] Cold War-style deterrence is therefore considered potentially unworkable against these 'rogues' and deterrence by punishment should be replaced by deterrence by denial tailored for individual cases. This should be based on maximum strategic flexibility and strategies that may include pre-emptive attack.[90] America should not accept a condition of mutual assured destruction with regional states that could limit its freedom of action in key regions.

America must continue to deter major powers that possess large and sophisticated WMD capabilities but it must also actively *defend* against WMD-armed 'rogue' states through war-fighting counter-force strategies.[91] Ideas of 'no-first use' and negative security guarantees that explicitly state that American would not use nuclear weapons in response to a chemical or biological weapon attack are generally rejected.[92] This reflects the Cold War idea set that sought to escape the condition of mutual assured destruction with the Soviet Union through nuclear counter-force superiority, 'implementable' flexible limited nuclear attack options, and missile defences.[93] Robert Joseph, Keith Payne and Colin Gray are important advocates of this position.[94]

Force structure and capabilities

This understanding of strategic deterrence has generated 'capabilities-based' force structure requirements. Threats of using high-yield nuclear weapons in a regional context are no longer considered credible and continued reliance on such threats carries the possibility that America will be 'self-deterred' in a regional crisis.[95] The only viable alternative is the deployment of regional war-fighting capabilities to negate the strategic capabilities of 'rogue' states. Only through such capabilities can America *credibly* threaten regional adversaries whose stakes in a conflict may include regime survival, and thereby deter and coerce as necessary.[96]

America's nuclear arsenal can be cut from bloated Cold War levels and reliance on nuclear weapons can be reduced but only if the arsenal is modernised, a major reserve is retained and new capabilities are added.[97] This includes a consolidated but modernised Cold War strategic triad; a modernised nuclear planning and targeting system to establish a rapid, adaptive, global, highly accurate, strategic nuclear and conventional strike capability for counter-proliferation missions; development of new low-yield and earth-penetrating nuclear weapons for targeting 'rogue' states' WMD and command and control facilities; maintenance of a robust nuclear weapons production complex, including an ongoing testing programme to enable production of specialised new weapons; and deployment of missile defences to support deterrence by denial, war-fighting and counter-proliferation missions. Particular attention is paid to missile defences and the strategic imperative of moving beyond the ABM treaty and developing low-yield and earth-penetrating warheads.[98] The deployment of the B61-11, the RNEP, ACI and RRW initiatives reflect this approach. Nuclear testing and a rejuvenated nuclear weapons complex are deemed vital to a reliable and credible nuclear arsenal, as argued by the first Bush administration and congressional opponents of the test ban.

The 2001 NPR fully endorsed this approach, although arguments reflecting this idea set and advocating these capabilities emerged soon after the end of the Cold War.[99] This was also reflected in a number of important official documents including the Reed Report, the 1993, 1996 and 2005 JCS nuclear doctrine statements and reportedly in PDD-60 in 1997 and NSPD-14 and NSPD-17 in 2002.

Arms control and non-proliferation are anachronistic

This idea set interprets concepts of arms control and non-proliferation quite differently. It embraces the utility of military force in dealing with post-Cold War nuclear threats rather than reinvigorating multilateral arms control.[100] The logic of this idea set argues that arms control and the non-proliferation regime cannot deal with the difficult cases of nuclear proliferation and should not constrain America in its attempts to address these threats for the good of the international community.[101] 'Rogue' states should be isolated, challenged and ultimately have their regimes removed if they do not comply with American demands to abandon their WMD programmes.

Bilateral nuclear arms control is an astrategic and increasingly anachronistic tool designed only to manage the end of the Cold War nuclear arms race with little wider relevance.[102] The START process is defunct, the ABM treaty is an irrelevant hindrance and missile defences are prioritised over efforts to secure further treaty-based nuclear force reductions with Russia. These Cold War treaties and processes lock America into the doctrine of mutual assured destruction. They represent an illusory path to security that must be abandoned by de-coupling American and Russian nuclear forces.[103]

The NPT is interpreted solely as a tool for combating nuclear proliferation, a confidence building measure rather than a source of binding commitments, and often regarded as having little value and relevance to the second nuclear age. The abolition of nuclear weapons envisaged by the treaty will *never* occur.[104] Clinton's 'philosophy of cooperative security' and 'overdependence on arms control' is criticised for undermining American national security and nuclear deterrent threats.[105] Harold Brown and John Deutch, former Secretary and Deputy Secretary of Defense respectively, responded to the January 2007 Nunn, Perry, Kissinger and Schultz *Wall Street Journal* editorial with a commentary entitled 'The Nuclear Disarmament Fantasy' which claimed that 'hope is not a policy, and, at present, there is no realistic path to world free of nuclear weapons'.[106] Advocates of this idea set instead support 'coalitions of the willing' and US-led initiatives such as the Proliferation Security Initiative to combat WMD proliferation and challenge 'rogue' states. They also argue in favour of increased cooperation with Russia and China to deal with 'rogue' states.[107]

Nuclear primacy

This idea set considers American nuclear primacy over all nuclear weapon states including Russia as both possible and necessary to finally escape the constraints and dilemmas of mutual assured destruction.[108] Nuclear primacy and a nuclear posture geared towards the credible deterrence of 'rogue' states and freed of multilateral and bilateral constraints are considered a very positive contribution to world security and a mark of American preeminence and leadership.[109] This is part of a wider 'primacist' world-view that dictates that what is good for America is necessarily good for the world because of the benign nature of American global power.[110]

This again requires a relatively large and sophisticated nuclear triad, a nuclear reserve force and a modern, if consolidated, nuclear weapons production complex capable of designing, producing and testing new nuclear weapons. Deep reductions in nuclear forces are opposed. This idea set considers American nuclear weapons to be already hugely marginalised (too much in fact) and cautions against any further delegitimisation in national security strategy.[111] Severe doubt is cast on arguments that very low numbers of nuclear weapons or even nuclear disarmament would bring lasting security. It would instead undermine America's international status and spur proliferation by emboldening 'rogue' states (including China for some) to seek a degree of military parity with America and lead allies to rethink their nuclear status.[112] For Gray, peace is best secured through 'a healthy disproportion of competitive armament' in favour of status quo states, namely America and its Western allies, and America should err on the size of its nuclear arsenal being too large rather than too small.[113]

Lieber and Press and Krepon argue that America has now achieved nuclear primacy through counter-force modernisation of strategic nuclear forces, development of missile defence capabilities, and the degradation of Russian strategic nuclear forces, including early warning and command and control infrastructure. It is unclear what *use* nuclear primacy might be to the United States or the relevance of this development to its relationship with Russia other than the vague notion of 'dissuasion' articulated in the 2001 NPR.[114] This stands in contrast to the first idea set that remains committed to the Cold War precepts of mutual assured destruction.[115]

American nuclear weapons policy and non-proliferation

This idea set argues that American nuclear weapons and missile defence policies and actions have no effect on non-proliferation apart from through extended deterrence security guarantees to allies that reduce their incentives to develop independent nuclear capabilities.[116] Links between American nuclear weapons policy and its effect on nuclear non-proliferation are heavily exaggerated and based on a false belief in the maxims of a mechanistic action-reaction cycle.[117] It is argued that the CTBT and START process have done little to stem proliferation and that withdrawal from the ABM treaty had no detrimental effect on international security.[118] Changes to American policy such as those announced in the 2001 NPR, deployment of missile defences, development of new nuclear weapons, or even massive reductions in America's arsenal will not spur or reduce nuclear proliferation, as has been claimed.[119]

This idea set sees further potential for new nuclear missions and nuclear force modernisation that will have no effect on the nuclear programmes of other states or the wider non-proliferation regime. Motivations behind the nuclear weapons decisions of other governments are based on regional ambitions, status and prestige, domestic politics and perhaps American conventional capabilities – but not its nuclear force.[120] Sagan describes these opposing views between the second and third idea sets as a clash between a security-oriented strategy in which American nuclear weapons play a major role in national security and extended deterrence, and a norms-oriented strategy to delegitimise nuclear weapons and their acquisition.[121]

Conclusion

The end of the Cold War opened up debate about the meanings assigned to American nuclear weapons and the dominant interpretations of the key concepts that inform nuclear weapons policy. This encompassed competing interpretations of the role and requirements of nuclear weapons, strategic arms control, the role of missile defences, the evolving 'mutual assured destruction' relationship with Russia, the credibility of nuclear deterrence, budgetary pressures, non-proliferation goals, and the rise of WMD-armed 'rogue' states. More widely, it involved competing views of international politics and American self-identity and its vital interests. Circumstantial and theoretical evidence existed to support divergent sets of ideas, amplified by the absence of firm empirical data. A broad political post-Cold War consensus on the role of American nuclear weapons and the future of nuclear weapons policy was not forthcoming after the collapse of the Soviet Union, but a discourse of competing idea sets emerged instead. As Halperin argues, 'The 1990s came to be characterised more by competing images, which did not provide the broad framework for national security decisionmaking that had previously guided the process'.[122]

The three idea sets identified and the competition between them provide a compelling analytical framework for *understanding* the evolution of nuclear weapons policy. It is the competition between different interpretations of contested concepts, between different collective understandings and shared ideas, that has driven policy. All three idea sets have enjoyed some success over the post-Cold War period. As a result nuclear weapons policy cannot be described as linear, rational and internally consistent. It has instead been subject to the relative power of competing and often contradictory ideas whose effect on policy outcomes and degree of institutionalisation is a function of domestic political processes. This is explored further in the next chapter.

Different shared idea sets construct different versions of reality for American nuclear weapons policy based on particular worldview, principled, and causal beliefs, to use Goldstein and Keohane's model. Dominant idea sets naturalise particular interpretations of key concepts, interests and identities, the assignment of particular meanings to material factors and political events, and particular understandings of appropriate behaviour. Other practices and idea sets are excluded as illegitimate, irrational or inappropriate. This constructs a version of reality in which a particular nuclear weapons 'policy' or idea set becomes reified as natural and normal to the exclusion of alternative interpretations and understandings. Each idea set declares what nuclear weapons policy should *really* be based on and how it should be understood and explained, what it should comprise, and how it should be implemented for the benefit of American national security.

The power to shape debate on specific issues and construct a particular version of reality by establishing an idea set and its collective understandings as the dominant view within the nuclear weapons policy discourse is crucial. Policy evolution is therefore *explained* by the relative political salience of each idea set in the policy-making process at different decision points. Only by understanding how dominant interpretations of concepts, practices and events have been constructed can particular policy outcomes and trends be explained. Understanding and explaining American nuclear weapons policy must therefore look to this 'ideational' competition rather than any inherent characteristics of material factors or 'natural' structural imperatives of the international political system, as realist theory postulates. External political and material factors and changes matter hugely, but their significance is in their interpretation and the meanings assigned to them.

A discourse of three idea sets

These three idea sets constitute the mainstream discourse on nuclear weapons policy. Together they set the broad parameters for debate on the many aspects of policy. Each idea set excludes and includes particular shared understandings, but the mainstream discourse as a whole also exhibits these characteristics. They all assert that American nuclear forces can and should safely be reduced, although for different reasons. They accept that the spread of nuclear weapons to 'rogue' states (and construction of that term varies) is a, if not the, major threat to America and its vital interests. For all three the construction of the WMD-armed 'rogue' state, as well as the construction of the threat from a resurgent nuclear-armed Russia, has legitimised the continued possession and development of nuclear weapons after the Cold War. All accept some degree of nuclear force and production complex modernisation and deployment of missile defences. None of the idea sets interpret the contested concepts associated with nuclear weapons policy in such a way as to advocate unilateral nuclear disarmament or a large nuclear re-armament programme. Finally, all accept at the very least an enduring background role for nuclear weapons to deter major power aggression. As former head of Lawrence Livermore National Laboratory, Herb York, observed in 2005, 'the main use for nuclear weapons remains to deter the use of nuclear weapons by others. That has wide support within the defense community. Everything else is controversial'.[123]

This mainstream discourse has also excluded a fourth set of ideas advocating nuclear disarmament. This idea set is closely linked to the second. It argues for nuclear disarmament generally with, but sometimes even without, the coordinated disarmament of the other nuclear weapon states. It gained momentum in the mid-1990s with powerful statements from influential figures such as Paul Nitze, General George Lee Butler and General Charles Horner, together with a statement in 1996 in favour of abolition signed by 58 retired generals and admirals from 17 countries and a statement in 1998 signed by 120 former civilian leaders from 46 countries, including Jimmy Carter and Mikhail Gorbachev.[124] It coincided with the report of the Canberra Commission on the Elimination of Nuclear Weapons, the Henry L. Stimson Center's Goodpaster Committee report on eliminating weapons of mass destruction and the 1996 Advisory Opinion of the International Court of Justice on 'The Legality of the Threat or Use of Nuclear Weapons'. These, and a number of other studies and articles, examined how nuclear disarmament might feasibly be accomplished and presented arguments as to why it is necessary.[125]

The primary arguments are that the only rational purpose for nuclear weapons is to deter a nuclear attack, a purpose that would become irrelevant through nuclear disarmament. Nuclear weapons cannot deter regional powers or chemical or biological weapons and conventional munitions offer a viable substitute for a range of nuclear missions. Nuclear use is inevitable either through deliberate or accidental use as weapons proliferate and therefore nuclear disarmament would make the world a safer place. Nuclear war cannot be controlled or limited and the threat or use of nuclear weapons against civilians is morally wrong. In essence 'a policy that seeks to marry possession with non-proliferation is not coherent and is divided against itself' and will ultimately fail.[126] Nuclear disarmament is generally regarded by all three idea sets within the mainstream discourse as infeasible and/or destabilising, even by those who advocate deep reductions in American nuclear forces.[127]

The rise of the third idea set

The first idea set dominated American nuclear weapons policy for much of the 1990s. This version of nuclear weapons policy is often accepted as normal or natural, particularly within the policy community in DOD and the armed services. It is firmly linked to dominant Cold War understandings of nuclear weapons policy that required a sophisticated, large nuclear arsenal configured to launch on warning of attack in order to maintain strategic stability. American nuclear superpower identity was tied to these understandings, which produced a set of interests and collective meanings that defined appropriate behaviour and became institutionalised during the Cold War as 'normal'. As Smith argues, 'it seems somehow illogical, but maintaining this relatively stable and manageable "balance of terror" became an accepted role for U.S. strategic forces and any departure from it could (and did, with the end of the Cold War), produce discomfort'.[128]

If this first idea set is seen to represent American nuclear weapons policy in its entirety, as it often is, then it can be argued that there has been significant policy continuity from the Cold War to the post-Cold War period because the first idea set has changed little. If, on the other hand, nuclear weapons policy is associated with the mainstream discourse as a whole in which three competing idea sets have all had an impact, then post-Cold War nuclear weapons policy must be characterised by both continuity and change.

In fact a key conclusion that can be drawn from this analysis is that the third idea set has grown in prominence and began to dominate the nuclear weapons policy discourse from the late 1990s onwards. This has been a gradual process through the post-Cold War period. Goodby, for example, claimed even in 1990 that arms control with the Soviet Union was already 'slipping down the national and international agenda' with missile defence and WMD proliferation claiming priority.[129] This idea set has many links to understandings of nuclear weapons policy articulated by the Reagan administration in the early 1980s, which advocated a renewed drive for strategic superiority, considered parity with the USSR a result of liberal weakness, defined the Soviet Union as an aggressive state intent on developing the capability to win a nuclear war, criticised the doctrine of mutual assured destruction and often led to exaggerated beliefs about Soviet power and intentions.[130]

The election of George W. Bush and the transformation agenda of Secretary of Defense Donald Rumsfeld accelerated the rise of the third idea set through the 2001 NPR that was based in large part on the *Rationale and Requirements* study conducted by the National Institute for Public Policy and Joseph and Lehman's study *US Nuclear Policy in the 21st Century*. The group of conservative defence intellectuals behind these studies successfully incorporated their ideas into government policy. Parallels can be drawn with the impact of the Committee on the Present Danger that informed the Reagan administration's nuclear weapons policy and interpretation of the Soviet threat. The Committee's emphasis on military power, a hostile attitude towards arms control, and accusations of a decade of neglect through détente mirror the views of the National Institute for Public Policy and other conservative organisations that informed the strategic security positions of the George W. Bush administration.[131]

The collective understandings, ideas and meanings of this idea set have been steadily institutionalised. As Smith argues, the administration's new strategic framework and new strategic triad will create new organisations and capabilities, a new core mission set, and new planning, command and control concepts and processes. These will institutionalise the changes set out in the 2001 NPR as the appropriate response to the 'second nuclear age'.[132] This represents a shift to a second phase of post-Cold War nuclear weapons policy, the first phase having been dominated by the first idea set and consistently challenged by the second.[133] Nevertheless, sustained congressional resistance to the initiatives set out in the 2001 NPR and the resurgence of the second idea set in 2007 symbolised by the Nunn, Perry, Shultz and Kissinger *Wall Street Journal* editorials may undermine the rise of the third idea set when the next Nuclear Posture Review is conducted in 2009 by a new administration.

A final important implication of this analytical framework is that problems affecting nuclear policy can be addressed by *reconceptualising* a situation or an issue rather than by changing the material reality.[134] Jervis, for example, argues that Reagan successfully defused anxiety about American nuclear inferiority in the early 1980s that he blamed on President Carter by arguing that he had rectified the balance, even though he simply continued his predecessor's nuclear procurement programmes.[135] It can be similarly argued that George W. Bush attempted to reconceptualise the meanings assigned to Russian nuclear weapons and America's strategic relationship with Russia by articulating a 'new strategic framework'. This was exemplified by the manner in which the deployment of MIRVed ICBMs by Russia was suddenly no longer considered strategically destabilising after having been the central focus of the START process for much of the 1990s. Whichever version of nuclear weapons policy has been or may become the accepted orthodoxy its collective understandings and shared ideas are not natural, normal or inevitable. They are a construction based on a particular interpretation of key concepts and a particular definition of appropriate behaviour situated within in a particular social and historical context.

8 Domestic politics and nuclear weapons policy

Understanding the evolution of American nuclear weapons policy requires detailed examination of competing interpretations of a set of contested concepts that constitute that policy. The previous chapter ordered these competing interpretations into three discrete idea sets within the mainstream nuclear weapons policy discourse. The understandings of each idea set have all been accepted at the highest levels of government at different times since the end of the Cold War. All three have therefore affected nuclear weapons policy at different times on different issues.

This conceptual framework, however, offers only partial understanding. In order to fully understand the evolution of policy this framework must be placed within a domestic political context to provide an account of the domestic factors that have affected the relative political salience of different idea sets at different times. It is at the domestic level where competing views are debated, where meanings are assigned, where idea sets are institutionalised, and where decisions are made, adjusted or overturned. It is also at the domestic level where political constraints on radical change are located and where political compromise, confrontation and expenditure of political capital on nuclear weapons policy occur. This chapter examines the effect of domestic political processes on nuclear weapons policy and draws on the insights of theories of bureaucratic politics and organisational processes.[1]

Policy inertia

Organisational interests and bureaucratic politics

Policy is not made in a vacuum but in the context of existing organisational practices, dominant shared conceptions of an issue, and the legacy of previous budget and programming decisions. Senior policy-makers, including the president, are forced to rely on these organisational structures and practices for formulating and implementing policy.[2] This inescapable dependence has led to a body of theory on bureaucratic politics, institutions, group dynamics, and organisational behaviour, and the impact of these domestic political factors on foreign and defence policy outcomes.[3] Some aspects of this field focus on the role of individual officials in policy-making with particular emphasis on the psychology of decision-making during crises.[4] Others concentrate on the overall policy-making process, in particular the effect of bureaucratic politics and organisational behaviour on routine decisions.[5]

Theories of bureaucratic politics and organisational behaviour argue that government is not a single unitary actor but comprises a conglomerate of competitive, loosely allied organisations, such the Department of Energy or the Air Force.[6] Policy is not made solely by elected or appointed officials but also by the bureaucracy in a dynamic and complex process of policy-making and implementation.[7] Policy-making is a competitive game involving coalitions, compromises and conflict on a host of issues based on different conceptions of national, organisational and personal interests.[8] Bureaucracies and bureaucrats are driven by the interests of their organisation and are involved in unceasing competition over their bureaucratic interests.[9] These interests are based on budget resources, personnel, access to senior policy-makers, career progression, autonomy and core missions. Two of the most powerful determinants of bureaucratic behaviour are organisational self-preservation to retain the organisation's core identity or 'essence' and budget, which is often considered a primary indicator of organisational strength.[10]

Government policy is therefore a political product determined by the pulling and hauling of these competing interests and procedures rather than a single strategic master plan.[11] According to this approach, where an official is placed in the bureaucracy defines their perceptions, interests and actions. This leads to the dictum commonly referred to as Miles' Law: where you stand (on an issue) depends on where you sit (in the bureaucracy).[12] Previous chapters demonstrate that many different organisations and agencies are involved in nuclear weapons policy and that policy-making and budgeting processes can be intensely political.

Officials are generally socialised into a particular set of values and interests attached to the organisation they are in.[13] An organisation's essence, Hudson argues, will lead to a 'distinctive organizational culture, with norms of dress behaviour, thinking and value prioritization'.[14] Studies of bureaucratic group dynamics, notably Irving Janis' work on 'groupthink', suggest that pressure to conform to an organisational viewpoint through fear of ostracism is powerful.[15] As individuals are socialised into government organisations they quickly come to support 'the set of shared images prevalent in the bureaucracy' and avoid conflictual actions. Career officials that have been involved in a particular area for a long time become committed to a particular doctrine and exhibit 'ideological thinking', defined as 'a very abstract and extensive belief pattern that is internally consistent and tends to be extremely stable'.[16] These shared images and belief patters often conflate organisational and national interests such that advancing organisational interests also means advancing national interests.[17]

Interests also transcend organisational boundaries. In fact theory suggests that policy is often made within semi-autonomous 'power clusters' that deal with a specific area such as nuclear weapons policy. These clusters can constitute so-called 'iron triangles' comprising administrative agencies, members of congressional committees, and organised interest groups or contractors. These clusters identify policy issues, shape policy alternatives, advocate changes and are involved in policy implementation.[18]

Organisations tend to acquire and supply information and knowledge, present particular options for policy choices and implement policies in ways that support their organisational interests and procedures.[19] These often reflect a set of standard operating procedures (SOPs) that determine how information is processed, how problems, solutions and consequences are constructed and prioritised, how resources are allocated, how threats are perceived and how policy is implemented. Organisations often favour policy choices that reflect their preferences and predispositions to the extent that organisational priorities, particularly budget resources, can come before an administration's stated or perceived needs.[20] A contemporary example of this is seen in preparations for the forthcoming 2009 Quadrennial Defense Review and the jockeying of the armed services to position themselves for the budget battles ahead.[21] More broadly the institutional posture of the Pentagon, for example, leans heavily towards military solutions to national security issues, which directly and indirectly influences its organisational behaviour and the mind-set of those within it.[22] In the bureaucratic politics paradigm, the organisation or person whose position prevails can be more important than *which* position prevails. Consequently the relative political-bureaucratic power of different groups involved in the policy-making process and their ability to shape the discourse on an issue is as relevant as the nature of their arguments.[23]

Resistance to change

Since policy-making is largely the result of bargaining and compromise in an effort to build consensus, policy outcomes tend to result in only incremental change over an extended period and resistance to an overall change in policy direction. This may be based on opposition to a particular policy or generic characteristics of large bureaucracies that militate against change.[24] Hill maintains that conservatism is an 'iron law of bureaucracies' according to models of organisational behaviour, whilst Halperin states that bureaucracies 'are basically inert' and only move when pushed hard and persistently.[25]

A number of propositions support this conclusion. The work of Charles Lindblom, for example, suggests that policy is made by 'muddling through' and taking only incremental and reversible steps.[26] Prospect theory suggests that policy-makers care far more about potential losses than gains and are therefore prepared to take greater risks to maintain a status quo. Well-established and accepted components of American national security policy remain relatively uncontroversial until an administration seeks to change direction, which can then cause reactive resistance in the bureaucracy, armed services and Congress.[27] Change can be implemented slowly or not at all and bureaucracies can, according to Rhodes, 'stonewall, procrastinate, prevaricate, or feign compliance' if decisions do not go their way.[28] In particular, changes that are perceived to undermine essential programmes, missions, SOPs, and organisational morale – the 'essence' of an organisation and its identity – as well as its budget will be fiercely resisted and deemed infeasible.[29]

Policy issues are rarely decided once and for all but are regularly revisited as compromises unravel.[30] The endless revisiting of a given issue by the multiple departments and agencies involved in national security policy often ensures that policy evolves at a glacial pace. It takes a considerable amount of time for each organisation to study, analyse, coordinate or implement a policy initiative.[31] Interagency consensus often requires lowest common denominator policy-making to ensure that policy 'fits' with respective organisations' SOPs and the preferences of entrenched bureaucracies, which precludes policy innovation.[32] This 'sequential decision-making' often involves the same officials dealing with the same competing interpretations of an issue.[33] As issues are revisited convictions about the issue and appropriate means of addressing it become stronger to the extent that major policy change requires a very costly and highly visible failure or a major success with 'recognisable reorganising consequences'.[34] Policy therefore tends to evolve incrementally.

Leadership and change

Sustained senior political leadership by the President, Secretary of Defense or National Security Advisor and a constructive relationship with Congress is required to challenge and overcome bureaucratic resistance to change and competing understandings of a national security issue and appropriate responses.[35] This requires the will to invest political capital in an issue, the capacity to push changes through the political system, clarity of purpose, articulation of an overall policy framework and a clear understanding of the bureaucratic interests involved.[36] Consensus must be built with key members of competing power clusters whose goals and values must be reconciled before decisions can be successfully made and implemented.[37] In the absence of senior political leadership, particularly presidential leadership, the imperatives (or determinism) of bureaucratic politics and organisational behaviour can have a decisive effect on policy outcomes.[38]

Some examples of where senior-level involvement led to important changes in nuclear weapons policy are President Bush's PNIs to remove American and Soviet tactical nuclear weapons from potential theatres of war; Secretary of Defense Dick Cheney's concerted drive to dramatically reduce targets in the SIOP in the early 1990s; President Clinton's determination to negotiate a zero-yield CTBT and the end of nuclear testing; and President George W. Bush's effort to reconceptualise America's relationship with Russia and remove nuclear weapons as a defining feature of that relationship.

If senior political leaders are interested and involved in an issue they are more likely to seek to reduce the power of the bureaucracy.[39] In a study of American policy towards China Garrison argues that the degree of presidential involvement 'correlates closely with the ability of an administration to overcome patterns of bureaucratic politics'.[40] Nevertheless, building consensus can take time. President George H. W. Bush, for example, delayed completion of START I negotiations on entering office until a firm consensus was reached amongst the senior political actors and organisations involved. Newman argues that this internal consensus was as important to the success of START as the actual US–Soviet negotiations.[41] Consensus may, however, require ambiguous policies that avoid substantial costs to organisational interests and do not challenge the dominant understandings of an entrenched bureaucracy. This can leave organisations free to continue operating as they have in the past by implementing policy to suit existing SOPs and perspectives.[42]

Political disinterest in nuclear weapons policy

The literature on organisational processes and bureaucratic politics suggests that any significant shift in American nuclear weapons policy would require sustained leadership interest in change and the political will to see it through. Since the end of the Cold War, however, nuclear weapons policy has been characterised by a growing lack of interest and attention by senior executive, congressional and military leaders. Immediately after the Cold War fiscal, political, strategic, safety and security pressures quickly combined to dramatically reduce the role of nuclear weapons in national security policy and planning.[43] Nuclear weapons force structure, policy and planning had been intimately tied to the Cold War confrontation with the Soviet Union. The demise the of Cold War and the rapid emergence of a range of other national security challenges for which a nuclear-focused national security strategy was judged inappropriate led to a marked reduction in senior-level political attention and interest in nuclear weapons issues at the executive, congressional and military level.

The absence of senior-level attention has consequently allowed bureaucratic interests and understandings to have a considerable impact on the evolution of policy over the post-Cold War period.

This is supported by 35 interviews conducted in 2005 and 2006 with current and former officials involved in American nuclear weapons policy and experts that have studied nuclear weapons in detail for many years through several changes of government. A number of shared views emerged from these interviews that provide important insights into the evolution of nuclear weapons policy. First, nuclear weapons policy since the end of the Cold War has suffered a growing lack of senior political and military interest based on the view that nuclear weapons matter far less to national security than in the past and that no major procurement decisions have been required. Second, this has led to a drifting and neglected nuclear weapons policy and a sense of bureaucratic inertia. Third, this has been exacerbated by the absence of bipartisan consensus on the long-term future of nuclear weapons policy that has stymied implementation of the 2001 Nuclear Posture Review (NPR).

The executive

The status quo outcome of the 1994 NPR provides a compelling example of the absence of senior-level attention and how such absence can reinforce the views of an entrenched bureaucracy. When the Clinton administration came to power in 1993 many observers expected significant change in nuclear weapons policy for a number of reasons. The Democratic-controlled Congress that had terminated or curtailed a number of major nuclear weapons programmes under George H. W. Bush now had a Democrat in the White House. Clinton supported a ban on nuclear testing and further nuclear reduction and appointed Congressman Les Aspin, chair of the House Armed Services Committee, as Secretary of Defense. Aspin had argued for major changes to what he considered an outdated nuclear weapons policy in a 1992 paper entitled *From Deterrence to Denuking: Dealing with Proliferation in the 1990s*.[44] Statements by Aspin and Assistant Secretary of Defense for International Security Policy Ashton Carter suggested that the possibility of a nuclear weapons-free world should be taken seriously. In addition Energy Secretary Hazel O'Leary's openness initiative seemed to signal a shift away from Cold War practices and the secrecy surrounding nuclear weapons policy (these issues are examined in chapter four).

When the 1994 NPR was announced many who favoured change considered it 'the moment of maximum opportunity for the president to establish a nuclear legacy consonant with emerging security challenges' and make a significant shift in policy.[45] There was considerable disappointment when the NPR codified the status quo advocated by the DOD bureaucracy and JCS and previously set out in the SAC and STRATCOM force structure studies in the early 1990s.

Critics have argued that there was little or no leadership desire to change the direction of nuclear weapons policy from the Secretary of Defense, National Security Council, STRATCOM, JCS or the President. According to Nolan, Clinton and his close advisers never indicated that they had a stake in the outcome of the review and Aspin's resignation in December 1993 significantly reduced the level of senior political interest in the review.[46] The NPR was not a priority for Aspin's replacement, William Perry, or his deputy, John Deutch. Instead issues such as Bosnia and the Cooperative Threat Reduction Program with Russia dominated DOD's agenda.[47] Without senior-level interest, leadership and attention it was almost inevitable that the commitment to a status quo posture largely based on the previous chapter's first idea set and firmly linked to Cold War understandings of nuclear weapons policy would continue to dominate nuclear policy and planning.[48] Nolan surmises that this 'vacuum in senior-level leadership and White House authority conspired with the reflexive reluctance of career officials to accept unfamiliar concepts that tested deeply held beliefs and entrenched ways of conducting policy'.[49] White House reluctance to challenge the JCS and DOD bureaucracy was compounded by Clinton's difficult relationship with the military from the very beginning of his administration over the issue of homosexuals in the military and military intervention in Somalia.[50] With hindsight it was clear that any serious review and change of policy must be presidentially ordained and overseen and certified by senior military officials who are convinced of the need for change.[51]

The lack of senior-level political interest continued after the NPR.[52] Clinton had little desire to challenge the military and judged nuclear weapons to be an issue not worth spending political capital on, which, as Halperin argues, should be 'carefully husbanded and used shrewdly' for priority issues.[53] Nuclear weapons were viewed as a residue of the Cold War to be cleaned up rather than an issue on which to take new initiatives. Instead, issues such as Haiti, Somalia, Bosnia, non-proliferation and relations with Russia and China were much higher national security priorities. What political capital Clinton wanted to spend on nuclear weapons policy issues was spent on extension of the NPT in 1995 and negotiation of the CTBT in 1996.[54] The George W. Bush White House has also given nuclear weapons policy a relatively low priority. Interest peaked around the 2001 NPR, as it did in 1994, but the issue soon fell off the leadership's agenda as competing priorities took precedence, in particular the war on terrorism and the war in Iraq.[55]

Given the depth and breadth of issues the Pentagon leadership has to deal with and the lack of time to deal with anything but priority issues, those that are considered secondary are pushed down into the civilian bureaucracy. Nuclear weapons policy quickly became a second or third order priority for the Pentagon after the Cold War and received little senior-level attention in DOD other than the two NPRs, the CTBT vote and periodic nuclear force structure reviews.[56] As the Defense Science Board reported in 2006:

> Since the end of the Cold War, with the escalation of other national security challenges, nuclear matters have slipped even further toward the edge of DOD's mainstream attention … the nuclear-dedicated organizations were disestablished, vitiated, or tasked with additional missions that, in various degrees, submerge the nuclear weapons activities.[57]

This was summed up by one academic who has followed and been directly involved in nuclear weapons policy, who stated there are simply not that many people in Washington that care about nuclear weapons policy any more.[58]

Congress

Interest and attention has also faded considerably in Congress where nuclear weapons policy has become the province of a few congressional committees and subcommittees and influential personalities with divergent views on the subject.[59] During the Cold War the armed services, weapons manufacturers and members of Congress supported nuclear weapons programmes and mutually reinforced each other's positions creating so-called 'iron triangles' that political opponents often found hard to resist. With the termination or curtailing of nuclear weapons programmes after the fall of the Soviet Union this process diminished considerably. Congress is generally a responsive and conservative institution reluctant to initiate major change and challenge the status quo on nuclear weapons policy.[60] From the early 1990s onwards there was no unifying sense in Congress that a major shift in nuclear weapons policy and planning was required or that the issue had much traction with the electorate, with little corresponding interest in instigating change.[61] Nevertheless, Congress influenced policy through the annual budget authorisation and appropriations process that provides funding for nuclear force structure, modernisation programmes and the nuclear weapons production complex, as well as its deliberations on the merits of arms control agreements and missile defence programmes.[62] Congressional activity on nuclear weapons policy has been influential and at times decisive but it has been episodic and centred on a few specific issues driven by a few members of Congress. This was exemplified by the RNEP debate under George W. Bush.[63]

The growing lack of attention to and interest in nuclear weapons policy was compounded and in part constituted by a sense throughout the 1990s and early 2000s that no major decisions on replacing ageing systems or fielding new capabilities were required in order to maintain a reliable background nuclear deterrent. Walter Slocombe, former Under Secretary of Defense for Policy in the Clinton administration, stated in 2006 that 'the level of attention accorded to nuclear weapons has considerably faded with the diminishing role of nuclear weapons in national strategy, and the concomitant long "holiday" in the procurement of any major nuclear weapon delivery system'.[64] The nuclear weapons complex needed attention in the early 1990s but the Complex-21 restructuring programme and heavy investment in the Stockpile Stewardship Program were seen to have addressed that issue. Whilst it was accepted that important decisions would eventually be needed, the political and strategic risks of not doing anything were not high enough to warrant sustained leadership attention or a major shift in policy.[65] With no major decisions required and diminishing leadership interest in American nuclear forces there were few incentives for senior policy-makers or congressional leaders to shift nuclear weapons policy in a new direction.[66]

Military disinterest in nuclear weapons policy

There has also been a waning interest in nuclear weapons within the armed forces for a variety of reasons. Soon after the collapse of the Soviet Union nuclear weapons were no longer considered central to addressing the post-Cold War national security threats facing the nation. They were increasingly viewed as obsolete and disdained as 'an embarrassing military artefact' of the Cold War.[67] The armed services have gradually de-emphasised and reduced the salience of nuclear weapons in military strategy. There has, for example, been little role for nuclear weapons in the three post-Cold War Quadrennial Defense Reviews in 1997, 2001 and 2006 that have shaped military posture since the mid-1990s.[68] Budgetary pressure halted any further nuclear modernisation and promoted cuts across the board in superfluous, expensive, single-use military capabilities in the early 1990s. Nuclear weapons have since become progressively drowned out in terms of money and the volume of debate compared to the massive lobbies and interest groups around other key defence capabilities. In fact resource competition within DOD has had a decisive effect on the direction of nuclear weapons policy since the Joint Staff has been reluctant to spend money on items not regarded as particularly useful, such as nuclear weapons.[69]

The post-Cold War senior military leadership has had far less interaction with nuclear weapons compared to their Cold War predecessors and less interest in nuclear roles and requirements. An interviewee who has been heavily involved in nuclear weapons policy argued that there were now no advocates in the military for nuclear weapons because they are not a priority, they are not 'big ticket' items, and there is a strong institutional bias amongst senior military leaders against them.[70] With fewer and fewer incentives to pursue a nuclear career in the armed services and no single dedicated nuclear career track, nuclear missions became secondary missions for most personnel assigned to them.[71] As Joseph and Lehman argued in 1998, 'career military personnel today generally view the nuclear career fields as being out of the mainstream and having uncertain futures'.[72] Deputy Secretary of Defense John Hamre also stated that 'in the last five to eight years, there's been just a significant reduction in interest of our best and brightest in this career field'.[73] One of the key findings of a 2001 SAIC report for DOD's Defense Threat Reduction Agency was that there was 'a perceived lack of senior DOD leadership attention to "things nuclear".'[74]

The reduced interest in pursuing a nuclear career has led to dwindling nuclear policy and planning expertise in the services, and there has been little military interest in taking forward the initiatives outlined in the 2001 NPR.[75] In 2005 former head of STRATCOM Eugene Habiger stated that the seven years it took for formal presidential nuclear weapons guidance to be changed after the Cold War through PPD-60 was an indication of how far behind military thinking the civilian policy planners were in DOD.[76] Nevertheless, the military did not advocate nuclear disarmament and it continued to spend time and money sustaining the nuclear force, but little more than was necessary.[77]

This reflects some of the propositions of theories of bureaucratic politics and organisational behaviour. Smith, for example, argues that military organisations develop a 'core cultural essence around their central, defining operational mission sets' and seek to marginalise or even expel peripheral mission sets that are believed to reduce resources and attention on core missions. Halperin and Clapp maintain that organisations struggle hardest for those capabilities viewed as intrinsic to its essence, and resist efforts to take away functions deemed vital to its essence. Conversely organisations are often indifferent to functions not seen as part of their essence.[78] The core nuclear mission and new initiatives established in the 2001 NPR have not been a primary mission and lack advocacy from a powerful organisation within the armed services or within the Office of the Secretary of Defense (OSD).[79] Budgetary and resource allocation issues have also been influential. The only organisation for whom nuclear weapons are part of its core essence is NNSA. It is perhaps for this reason that one interviewee commented that Linton Brooks, then head of NNSA, was seen as the primary advocate of nuclear weapons policy issues rather than a DOD or military official.[80]

Institutional de-emphasis of nuclear weapons

Post-Cold War relegation of nuclear weapons policy down the Pentagon's hierarchy of priorities is seen most clearly in the organisational downgrading of the nuclear mission. In the early 1990s consideration was given to disbanding the Defense Nuclear Agency that was responsible for characterising the impact of nuclear weapons effects and nuclear stockpile management, amongst other nuclear weapons functions.[81] The Agency was reorganised and retitled the Defense Special Weapons Agency (DSWA) in 1996.[82] In 1998 the new Defense Threat Reduction Agency (DTRA) was established which amalgamated DSWA, the Cooperative Threat Reduction programme, the On-Site Inspection Agency, and Defense Technology Security Administration.[83] The nuclear weapons mission was only one of four core missions for the new agency, whose primary focus was on deterring, reducing and countering WMD.[84]

Within the OSD the position of Deputy Assistant Secretary of Defense for Nuclear Forces and Arms Control Policy with responsibility for nuclear weapons policy has evolved to reflect the steady de-emphasis of nuclear weapons. Under George H. W. Bush the position was responsible for the formulation of DOD policy with respect to strategic offensive forces, targeting and arms control and theatre nuclear forces and arms control. Under George W. Bush the position evolved into Deputy Assistant Secretary of Defense for Forces Policy with responsibility for conventional strategic forces, ballistic missile defence and the use of space systems for military purposes as well as nuclear weapons.[85] In addition, for much of Clinton's second term the position of Assistant to the Secretary of Defense for Nuclear, Chemical and Biological Defense Programs (ATSD(NBC)) was left vacant. The ATSD(NCB) was the principal staff assistant and adviser to the Secretary and Deputy Secretary of Defense for all matters concerning nuclear weapons policy and staff director of the Nuclear Weapons Council.[86] Leaving the position unfilled left no single point of contact in DOD on nuclear weapons issues.[87]

Under George W. Bush STRATCOM has also expanded its portfolio of missions beyond nuclear weapons to six primary mission areas, only one of which is nuclear deterrence. This dilution of the military's focus on nuclear weapons meant that STRATCOM could no longer be counted on as a firm advocate on nuclear weapons issues. Where STRATCOM was once totally oriented towards nuclear operations, nuclear deterrence and war-fighting, these missions now fall under the Global Strike and Integration (GSI) Joint Functional Component Command (JFCC) along with conventional global strike capabilities. JFCC GSI is one of five JFCCs through which STRATCOM exercises command authority.[88]

As a result of these changes a number of reports and interviewees contend that there is no organisational focal point for nuclear weapons policy. In 1998

Joseph and Lehman argued that the reorganisation of the Defense Department in the late 1990s left it 'unclear which, if any, organization is the focal point for nuclear issues'.[89] In 2001 Woolf reported the views of Clinton's critics that 'there is little senior-level involvement in DOD in planning for nuclear forces and no center of expertise for nuclear policy issues'.[90] That same year the new Secretary of Defense Donald Rumsfeld stated that there was now little interest in nuclear weapons in the military: 'there's ... really not any lobby for nuclear weapons. Our military has never really been terribly interested in them ... strategic nuclear weapons have been kind of an orphan in the defense establishment in the United States'.[91] A senior DOE official involved in nuclear weapon policy for many years argued that there was now no natural home for nuclear weapons policy in DOD.[92] Another senior official involved in nuclear weapons policy in the George W. Bush administration stated that there was no clear centre for nuclear weapons policy issues within the OSD and described the nuclear policy operation as being in 'bad shape'.[93]

Nuclear conservatism and neglect

Bureaucratic inertia and nuclear conservatism

Accounts of post-Cold War nuclear weapons policy have often been characterised by bureaucratic inertia.[94] This inertia is derived from a combination of the embedded organisational interests of the nuclear policy community in favour of the nuclear status quo based on the first idea set and the generic nature of bureaucratic politics. Two issues are often used to highlight the effect of bureaucratic inertia and conservatism on nuclear weapons policy. First, at the end of the Cold War it was clear that organisational processes had led to bloated targeting requirements for nuclear forces. The Single Integrated Operational Plan (SIOP) had effectively become divorced from political guidance.[95] George Lee Butler, head of SAC and later STRATCOM, was astonished at the full extent of the target base and concluded that something had gone seriously wrong with the targeting process. Planning assumptions were judged to be flawed and arbitrary and based on worst case target assessment and worst case scenarios for the reliability of American nuclear weapons leading to exaggerated targeting requirements and a massive nuclear arsenal.[96] Organisational practices were judged to be a, if not the, major cause of this outcome. Senator William Cohen, later Clinton's Defense Secretary, criticised 'institutional arrangements that excessively concentrate in a single locus decisionmaking regarding deterrence requirements, targeting objectives and operational needs. It produces unrealistically high weapon "requirements", distorts procurement decisions'.[97]

The second example is the outcome of the 1994 NPR. Sauer argues that advocacy of significant change was precluded by the bureaucratic interests of the mid-level officials that led the NPR, the SOPs of the organisations involved in nuclear weapons policy and planning, particularly in the military, vested personnel and budgetary interests in the nuclear weapons complex and a desire to retain the organisational prestige of nuclear missions. Any significant change to nuclear policy and planning would have challenged the 'essence' and autonomy of the key organisations involved.[98] 'Less nuclear weapons would have meant less money, less personnel, less prestige and less autonomy for the bureaucracies dealing with nuclear weapons'.[99] Nolan too argues that bureaucratic resistance to change had an important impact on the NPR. Delegating the work for the NPR to the Pentagon bureaucracy and mid-ranking officials virtually guaranteed that radical change would not be forthcoming and that existing policies and practices would be supported.[100]

Nevertheless Nolan takes a broader view than Sauer and argues that it is not accurate to attribute the outcome of the NPR solely to bureaucratic inertia. She argues that the extreme political sensitivity of nuclear policy and planning has resulted in the conservatism of the nuclear policy community and resistance to major policy change.[101] This conservatism is based on a number of factors: an enduring commitment to the assumptions and beliefs of a maximum deterrent counter-force posture that reflects much of the first idea set described in the previous chapter; a general caution induced by the uniquely destructive nature of nuclear weapons and ultimate security guarantee they are seen to provide; early post-Cold War scepticism about the irreversibility of Soviet/Russian nuclear weapons policy and democratic and economic reform; a sense that American nuclear weapons played a major part in 'winning' the Cold War; uncertainty about the future strategic security environment and the decisive role American nuclear forces *might* be required to play; general military resistance to changes that reduce readiness and capability; the difficulty of reversing decisions on force structure, nuclear complex capabilities and warhead numbers and capabilities due to long lead times and the political and fiscal impact of procuring new nuclear weapons facilities and capabilities; and generic explanations of organisational resistance to change based on protection of autonomy, prestige, budgets, operating procedures and personnel.[102] In addition many officials involved in national security see continuity in national security policy as essential because of the lasting impact of policy on allies, adversaries and international stability.[103] This is supported by a number of interviewees who argued that nuclear weapons policy is dealt with in a very conservative manner not so much because of bureaucratic political dynamics but because of the extreme consequences of getting policy decisions wrong and the difficulty of reversing them.[104]

As William Owens, the former vice chairman of the JCS who was centrally involved in the 1994 NPR, highlighted in 2002:

> Military institutions are by nature conservative, cautious of fads, and hesitant to rush headlong into change. Their conservatism is founded on experience, for they have learned, often very painfully, what can happen when they make the wrong changes and that they could be expected to deliver weapons while in the 'midst of change.' So, while the risks of being defeated in mankind's deadliest competition (WAR) drive militaries to

innovate, those same risks inhibit accelerated change and rapid innovation. History suggests that there rarely are revolutions in the way we conduct national defense, and that is even more true in matters of nuclear weapons their doctrine, and the theory of use.[105]

A neglected nuclear weapons policy

The combination of these factors has led to the widespread characterisation of nuclear weapons policy as drifting, lacking coherence, based on ad hoc decisions when needed and episodic and contentious congressional impact on single issue items.[106] Nuclear weapons policy has been politically, fiscally and intellectually neglected and gradually de-emphasised in national security strategy since the end of the Cold War because it was generally considered safe to do so.[107] As a consequence nuclear weapons policy has been defined by the bureaucratic momentum of Cold War understandings of nuclear weapons policy and planning reflected in the first and to an extent the third idea sets of the previous chapter.[108] The absence of presidential attention to nuclear weapons policy has meant that policy has been subject to bureaucratic political dynamics rather than a sustained and coherent strategic view.[109]

The perceived neglect of nuclear weapons policy has been criticised in a number of official reports. The Defense Science Board's 1993 report *Task Force on the Defense Nuclear Agency* found that 'the Services are not fully maintaining nuclear-related skills to meet future DOD-wide needs. In some cases, the Services are withdrawing from supporting nuclear competence beyond immediate operational needs'.[110] DTRA's 2002 official organisational history states that by the mid-1990s, there was 'a perception among defense experts that the programs and infrastructure needed to sustain the nation's strategic nuclear forces and weapons were in decline' and that DOD's and DOE's institutional focus on sustaining the nuclear force needed to be revitalised.[111]

From 1996 to 1998 General Larry Welch, former Air Force Chief of Staff, led the Defense Science Board task force on *Sustaining the Nuclear Deterrent*. Welch reported that there had been little effort to revitalise institutional support within DOD for maintaining a robust nuclear arsenal. The report highlighted the Joint Vision 2010, 1997 and 1998 JCS Posture Statements to Congress and the USAF Global Engagement plan as examples of official strategy documents that made little or no mention of the nuclear mission and reported that 'this apparent lack of emphasis on the nuclear deterrent has been oft noted in nuclear forces and support activities'.[112] It stated that there was very little interest in nuclear weapons policy at senior levels in the White House and DOD and that activity at the Nuclear Weapons Council was minimal.[113] It expressed concern about the trend of putting nuclear deterrence and counter-proliferation missions together as a single set of responsibilities in which the latter was increasingly prioritised.[114] It argued that there was no central focus for nuclear policy-making and that policy functions were fragmented with responsibilities divided between various offices in OSD together with reduced senior-level attention in the military services. It also claimed that DWSA had made little progress in sustaining expertise and revitalising institutional support for the nuclear mission. Finally, it concluded that STRATCOM had stepped in to fill the vacuum to perform some functions neglected during the drawdown of nuclear forces and reduced interest in nuclear matters but that this had been piecemeal with no clear charter.[115]

The 1998 report by the National Defense University and Lawrence Livermore National Laboratory, *U.S. Nuclear Policy in the 21st Century*, warned that without 'concerted and continuing high-level attention to the policies and programs supporting its nuclear forces, the U.S. deterrent posture will continue to erode'.[116] In particular the declining focus on nuclear weapons would result in 'critical expertise shortfalls' in key nuclear policy areas, a trend compounded by the view that 'the career military today generally view the various nuclear career fields as out of the mainstream ... which poses significant obstacles to the ability to recruit and train necessary nuclear expertise ... it is imperative that senior-level attention be given to these issues today'.[117] The report argued that cancellation or curtailment of almost all nuclear force modernisation programmes after the Cold War meant that 'nuclear force matters no longer demand the continuous involvement of senior leaders' with little clarity as to which, if any, organisation was the focal point for nuclear issues within DOD.[118] The authoritative report concluded that 'the most important problem is the lack of sufficient high-level attention to nuclear matters in the Executive Branch and in the Congress' and that there was dwindling experience in the executive and legislative branches on nuclear deterrence and nuclear weapons policy issues. They advocated an organisational change to establish a well staffed high-level nuclear advocate office within OSD.[119]

Finally, in 2006 the Defense Science Board argued that 'competent and committed structure for nuclear weapons within the DOD needs to be re-established'.[120] It also criticised DOE for failing to provide 'a comprehensive, coherent, funded plan or capability to sustain a reliable, safe, secure and credible stockpile of nuclear weapons for the long term'.[121]There has also been sustained concern over the lack of political and financial support for the warhead refurbishment programme, SSP activities and revitalising the nuclear weapons production complex considered essential to sustaining America's nuclear arsenal.[122]

No consensus for implementing the 2001 NPR

Incentives to change nuclear weapons policy have been significantly reduced by the absence of broad bipartisan post-Cold War consensus on the future of nuclear weapons policy and the long-term role and requirements of nuclear weapons. This is reflected in the three competing idea sets examined in the previous chapter. This absence of consensus has affected and been affected by the sense that no major procurement decisions were needed, the secondary importance of nuclear weapons policy to senior political and military leaders, and a conservative inertia within the nuclear policy bureaucracy. There have consequently been few incentives to entice sustained investment of scarce political capital by senior political leaders in government and Congress to overcome either the reality of the nuclear weapons policy presented by the nuclear policy community or the divergent views within and between Congress and the executive.[123] When decisions have been required the management of these domestic divisions was, according to Nolan, 'an increasingly important determinant of policy choices'.[124] Overcoming these divisions would require a compelling strategic vision for American nuclear forces to be articulated at the highest levels of government. There have been incentives for incremental change to adapt nuclear weapons policy to the post-Cold War environment. These have ranged from reducing the perceived risk of nuclear conflict, reducing spending, reinforcing the non-proliferation regime through American restraint, reorienting military forces and posture to new strategic realities and redressing the impact of ageing complex facilities, warheads, delivery platforms and expertise. Occasional senior-level executive, congressional and military engagement has therefore been forthcoming, but there has been little sustained desire to take policy in a different direction following the end of the Cold War.[125]

As the 1990s drew to a close, however, there was growing acknowledgement that major decisions were needed on the future of the nuclear weapons production complex.[126] The George W. Bush administration sought to change nuclear weapons policy to reflect some of the force structure requirements that stem from the third idea set and to address issues affecting the production complex by forging a consensus for action that was reflected in the 2001 NPR.[127] The lack of senior-level interest and advocacy, the absence of broad political consensus and substantially reduced debate in Washington on nuclear weapons policy have meant that the advocates of the 2001 NPR have had little success in securing the necessary resources from Congress to implement change, despite the growing predominance of the third idea set within the nuclear weapons policy discourse.[128] This has been compounded by a view that the nuclear policy community failed to sell the 2001 NPR strategy to Congress and make it a priority issue in DOD. The war on terrorism, Iraq, missile defence and force transformation have all taken precedence.[129]

In 2006 the Defense Science Board concluded that the Cold War consensus on the need for nuclear weapons no longer existed and that 'while the national security leadership has clearly declared a need to sustain a credible nuclear deterrent, this has not been accompanied by a clear and coherent national approach to doing this for the long term'.[130] It argued that five years after the 2001 NPR 'progress in achieving the goals of the New Triad remains elusive' due to obstacles ranging from the decline of the nuclear weapons production complex, decline in nuclear weapons expertise, lack of high-level official attention to nuclear weapons issues and congressional opposition.[131] Gormley similarly argued in 2005 that 'little if anything tangible has occurred with respect to integrating the nuclear and non-nuclear component of the new triad' and that there was considerable uncertainty about long-term plans for deploying global strike forces.[132] Maaranen also noted that the responsive DOD–DOE nuclear infrastructure remains 'the least well-defined, most poorly understood and arguably least effectively implemented component of the new triad' and that DOD's nuclear weapons industrial base and DOE's nuclear weapons production complex needed 'significant investment of political influence and scarce dollars for more than a decade'.[133] The senior political leadership required to get Congress on board and get the NPR's initiatives funded has been absent. There appears to have been marked reluctance to spend political capital in attempting to forge a consensus on the NPR and invite a divisive debate in Congress.[134]

The nuclear policy community itself appears divided between the first and third idea sets with those advocating change through the 2001 NPR caught between the incumbent 'nuclear priesthood' and senior-level disinterest. As Under Secretary of Defence for Policy, Douglas Feith, noted in 2002 in the context of the 2001 NPR:

> There is an enormous investment that people have made over decades in Cold War thinking. And there is, as you all know, a 'priesthood' that has focused on arms control notions and strategic stability concepts during the Cold War. And it is very hard for people who have invested decades of intellectual energy and, for that matter, emotional energy, in these kinds of strategic concepts, to abandon them and think about these issues in a new way.[135]

Nuclear weapons policy needs executive, congressional, military, and bureaucratic advocates but it is currently considered a second or third level issue with no clear institutional focal point. Whilst this has given Pentagon bureaucrats more freedom to operate and implement incremental changes according to a dominant idea set, it has constrained their ability to secure new resources to implement more significant change when deemed necessary.[136] It is noteworthy that the George W. Bush administration has failed to deploy any new or modified nuclear weapons due to congressional opposition and an unwillingness to spend political capital on forging a consensus on nuclear procurement and deployment plans.

The inability or reluctance of the Bush administration to forge a consensus has left a leadership vacuum on nuclear weapons policy. As a result members of Congress have stepped in to take the lead, as they have done in the past, for example in creating NNSA. This has allowed a few members of Congress to direct the debate on nuclear weapons policy, often informed by the second idea set.[137] This has manifested itself primarily through consistent calls from Congress for the administration to set out a long-term vision for nuclear weapons policy. Congress has refused to fund any 'new' nuclear weapon initiatives such as RNEP, ACI, MPF, RRW and Complex-2030 until it is convinced that the administration has a viable and affordable long-term nuclear weapons strategy that further reduces force numbers and the salience of nuclear weapons in national security strategy.[138] A lasting consensus may be forged around results of the Strategic Posture Commission due to report to Congress at the end of 2008 and the next Nuclear Posture Review due to be completed in 2009.

Conclusion

The preceding chapter argued that competing interpretations of a set of contested concepts have largely defined the evolution of nuclear weapons policy after the Cold War through the construction of different realities for American nuclear weapons. This chapter began with the argument that understanding nuclear weapons policy requires not only identification and examination of competing idea sets but also examination of the domestic political context in which the competition is set. The mainstream discourse on nuclear weapons policy that comprises the three competing idea sets must be placed within this context to provide a more complete understanding.

Analysis of the domestic political context identifies a number of important factors that have shaped the evolution of policy. There is indeed an incumbent or entrenched view of nuclear weapons policy that has been regularly articulated by officials within the military and OSD bureaucracy throughout the 1990s and into the new century. The views of this nuclear policy community have at times been at odds with administration policy, such as over a zero-yield nuclear test ban, and with the views of powerful members of Congress. This entrenched view can most commonly be associated with the first idea set and reflects many of the precepts of Cold War nuclear weapons policy. It has also been institutionalised in organisational processes and interests reflected the outcome of the 1994 NPR. The first idea set has not been accepted uniformly across the military and OSD bureaucracy, but it appears from the evidence that it dominated the nuclear weapons discourse and policy outcomes for much of the 1990s.

It is clear that senior-level administration, congressional and military interest in, and attention to, nuclear weapons policy and planning has reduced significantly since the end of the Cold War. This is unsurprising given that the Cold War confrontation was defined by a major strategic Soviet threat that all but evaporated in the early 1990s, that a number of different post-Cold War national security threats and challenges have arisen and taken priority for which American nuclear weapons offer no immediate solution and that no major nuclear procurement decisions were required through the 1990s. Attention and interest in nuclear weapons policy has waned as the relevance of nuclear weapons to the most pressing national security challenges of the post-Cold War period has faded. The absence of high-level interest allowed the entrenched idea set most commonly associated with the OSD bureaucracy to persist relatively unchallenged for much of the 1990s until it came under challenge from the third idea set that shared many of its tenets.

The reality and complexity of bureaucratic life suggests that there are genuine difficulties in shifting policy even with senior-level attention and widespread support from Congress and those involved in the policy-making process. This supports the contention that changes in national security policy generally occur incrementally due in part to the nature of government bureaucracy, as well as resistance to changes that challenge organisational interests and identities that may have coalesced around institutionalised idea sets. There also appears to be a general military and political inclination towards conservatism and reversibility in national security policy decisions, particularly with regard to nuclear weapons. This originates in part from the nature of nuclear weaponry and long timelines involved in weapons procurement and materials production processes and in part from a conservative idea set.

Change requires sustained high-level leadership and the building of consensus on the long-term role, effect and requirements of nuclear weapons that has broken down over the post-Cold War period. This requires overcoming a dominant idea set and the vested organisational interests of the armed services and OSD bureaucracy and forging a durable consensus on a divisive issue with an activist Congress. The absence of consensus, the entrenched views of the bureaucracy, the judgement that no major decisions were needed, and the relatively low priority accorded to nuclear weapons policy have served as major disincentives to senior-level investment of political capital to forge such a consensus.

Finally, although the third idea set has gained increased prominence in the discourse on nuclear weapons policy and although these domestic political factors may have given the military and OSD bureaucracy greater scope to modify nuclear weapons policy, they have constrained the changes sought in the 2001 NPR. These changes are generally acknowledged to require bipartisan congressional support and high-level military and administration attention, neither of which has been forthcoming.

Discussion of the domestic political context of national security policy invariably refers to the literature on American governmental politics that incorporates theories of bureaucratic politics, organisational behaviour and the decision-making processes of senior politicians. This body of literature has been applied to nuclear weapons policy since the end of the Cold War on a number of occasions, but most notably to the 1994 NPR. A common assertion present in a number of books, journal articles, and interviews conducted for this research is that reference to the 'bureaucratic inertia' of the Cold War views of an incumbent 'nuclear priesthood' provides sufficient explanation of the post-Cold War evolution of nuclear weapons policy. Some analysts tend to draw a line there, whilst others concede that the evolution of nuclear weapons policy has been more complex than this relatively straightforward argument suggests.

A crucial question in attempting to fully understand the evolution of nuclear weapons policy is the extent to which it is idea sets or political processes that have decisively shaped the debate and policy outcomes. The governmental politics approach suggests that competing policy preferences and policy outcomes are based on and determined by organisational behaviour and bureaucratic politics, particularly personal and organisational interests such as autonomy, prestige, personnel, budgets, missions and influence. In this context idea sets (or mindsets, belief systems, or worldviews) are primarily instrumental in that they are used by policy-makers to justify policy outcomes. The organisation or bureaucrats whose interests prevail are what matters rather than the substance of the idea set associated with those interests.

This model is too simplistic for a number of reasons. First, evidence suggests that policy-makers, including bureaucrats and members of Congress, are motivated in the first instance largely by conviction.[139] This has been evidenced in post-Cold War nuclear weapons policy through a number of decisions. These include the decision by President George H. W. Bush to withdraw large numbers of tactical nuclear weapons, congressional pressure to restrict strategic nuclear weapons modernisation programmes in the early 1990s, Clinton's decision to pursue a zero-yield nuclear test ban, his decision to pursue START III, and congressional pressure to reinvigorate the nuclear weapons production complex, including the establishment of NNSA. Bureaucratic and organisational factors are certainly important here, but the understandings at the heart of competing idea sets dominate. Second, the fact that nuclear weapons policy has slipped far down White House, OSD, military and congressional agendas and that no major new nuclear weapons systems have been procured since the end of the Cold War has significantly reduced the nuclear weapons budget and the degree of vested interests in nuclear weapons policy and planning compared to the 'iron triangles' of nuclear weapons advocacy during the Cold War. Third, when reference is made to bureaucratic inertia in the context of nuclear weapons policy the referent is the continuing relevance of a dominant idea set rather than an intrinsically bureaucratic or organisational position. Hill, for example, argues that competing bureaucratic views within the policy elite and the politics of policy-making are important but 'must not be mistaken for the more profound forms of politics which arise from clashes between differing value systems and sets of social interests', whilst Rhodes insists that it is not bureaucratic politics that affects policy but 'the competition of ideas for intellectual hegemony'.[140]

Nevertheless, organisational processes and bureaucratic politics do matter, but not in an either/or dichotomy. To dominate the discourse and have an effect on policy outcomes a particular idea set becomes institutionalised and embedded in organisational practices.[141] It is the process of institutionalisation that establishes ways of doing things, ways of interpreting issues and events, particular values and norms as 'normal' and creates barriers to the entry of competing ideas. Institutionalised ideas sets become resistant to change because they become bound up in organisational processes, identities and interests that are founded upon the belief that the dominant idea set provides the 'right' answers to the challenges faced by government. In this context change requires leadership to transform or replace a particular policy, or even a dominant idea set, and its associated organisational and bureaucratic identities and interests. New or adjusted identities and interests will subsequently coalesce around a transformed or adjusted policy, or idea set, and construct a different reality for American nuclear weapons.

At the same time idea sets can be reinforced by and adjusted to reflect bureaucratic politics and organisational behaviour. In this sense idea sets can be used instrumentally to rationalise and justify organisational and bureaucratic interests. In the extreme adherence to a dominant idea set may continue because it supports powerful parochial interests with little or no consideration given to the relevance of the idea set to national security.[142] In post-Cold War nuclear weapons policy interests and identities emerged around programmes and issues such as the Stockpile Stewardship Program and non-testing. They have also been sustained around the concept of a nuclear triad and they have been sustained and built up around strategic nuclear reductions through arms control or unilateral initiatives and missile defences. Bureaucratic and organisational factors will always be part of the nuclear weapons policy-making process. The political power of a dominant idea set stems from both its substance, which includes its historical background, and the organisational and bureaucratic identities and interests formed around it. In the process of forging consensus to reach a policy outcome, however, it is competing idea sets that are the determining factor.

Conclusion

Since the fall of the Soviet Union American nuclear weapons policy has lacked a long-term sense of direction. It has been subject to competing understandings of a range of concepts that constitute 'policy' in its broadest sense. This includes declaratory nuclear policy, operational nuclear policy, strategic threat perceptions, force structure, the nuclear weapons production complex and nuclear arms control.

This book attempts to provide a detailed understanding of the evolution of American nuclear weapons policy since the end of the Cold War and in doing so to provide some signposts for its likely future direction. The signposts are explored after a brief overview of the ground covered so far.

Decisions and trends

This study has progressed through three stages of analysis and reaches a number of conclusions. It first identified a number of key decisions and long-term interrelated trends that have constituted the evolution of policy based on detailed analysis of the general purpose of American nuclear forces, nuclear arms control, nuclear force structure and the nuclear weapons production complex under George H. W. Bush, Bill Clinton and George W. Bush.

The 15 key decisions identified are: ratification of START I in 1991; the 1991 and 1992 Presidential Nuclear Initiatives; establishment of Strategic Command in 1992; the 1992 nuclear test moratorium and negotiation of the CTBT in 1996; formulation of the Complex-21 plan for the nuclear weapons production complex; the congressional ban on new low-yield nuclear weapons research in 1993; signing of START II in 1994; establishment of the Stockpile Stewardship Program in 1993; the outcomes of the 1994 Nuclear Posture Review; nuclear posture changes in the 1997 Presidential Decision Directive 60; the 1997 US–Russian Helsinki agreements; the outcomes of the 2001 Nuclear Posture Review; the 2002 Moscow Treaty; formation of a new Strategic Command in 2002; and the 2005/2006 Reliable Replacement Warhead and Complex-2030 plans.

The long-term trends identified are: the steady consolidation and modernisation of strategic forces to arrive at a specific strategic nuclear triad;

emergence of the concept of a nuclear 'hedge'; a decisive shift in nuclear policy away from the Soviet Union/Russia and towards WMD and ballistic missile-armed 'rogue' states; a shift from deterrence by punishment for peer competitors to deterrence by denial for 'rogue' states; consistent pressure for new or modified nuclear weapons; sustained and decisive opposition to constraints on strategic deterrence posture; gradual revitalisation of the decaying nuclear weapons production complex; long timelines for many aspects of nuclear weapons policy; and a final trend of an enduring commitment to the long-term retention of a sophisticated nuclear arsenal.

Three 'idea sets'

The second stage of analysis identified and explored three discrete sets of ideas about nuclear weapons policy that represent the above decisions and trends and provide a compelling analytical tool for understanding the evolution of policy. These 'idea sets' comprise competing understandings of a set of concepts that constitute nuclear weapons policy and have different things to say about what American nuclear weapons are for, what the nuclear arsenal and production complex should look like, and how nuclear arms control, non-proliferation and deterrence operate. The three idea sets are described as: 'management' – managing the drawdown of Cold War nuclear forces; 'restraint' – responding to nuclear proliferation through progress in arms control and disarmament; and 'war-fighting' – responding to nuclear proliferation by reorienting Cold War nuclear weapons policy to a post-Cold War war-fighting policy.

Dominant idea sets naturalise particular interpretations of key concepts, interests and identities, the assignment of particular meanings to material factors and political events, and specific definitions of appropriate behaviour. In this context the power to shape the debate on specific issues and construct a particular version of what is 'normal' by embedding an idea set as the orthodox view within the discourse on nuclear weapons policy is crucial.

These three idea sets constitute the mainstream discourse on nuclear weapons policy and all three have enjoyed some success over the post-Cold War period. The first idea set dominated the discourse for much of the 1990s. The second idea set never took firm hold in the discourse as some expected or hoped it might under Clinton. The third idea set, which shares much with the first, has grown in prominence since the late 1990s when it began to dominate the nuclear weapons policy discourse. This has been a gradual process through the post-Cold War period that was accelerated under the G. W. Bush administration to the point where the understandings of the third idea set were firmly institutionalised, particularly through the 2001 NPR. A fourth set of ideas based on the logic of nuclear disarmament has been largely excluded from the mainstream discourse other than experiencing a brief rise to prominence in the mid-1990s.

American nuclear weapons policy and the long confrontation with the Soviet Union were deeply entwined. The collapse of one deeply affected the other and the end of the Cold War opened up debate about the meanings assigned to American nuclear weapons and understandings of the key concepts that inform nuclear weapons policy. Considerable tension emerged between the breakdown of the loose consensus on nuclear weapons policy within America's national security discourse and a powerful commitment to 'nuclearism' – the argument that America could not be safe without a massive, flexible, and superior nuclear arsenal – around which identities and interests had coalesced.[1]

This 'nuclearism' that directed America to retain a sophisticated, large nuclear arsenal configured to launch on warning of attack continued to form the core of 'normal' nuclear weapons policy in the Department of Defense and the armed services after the Cold War. It forms the heart of the first idea set and to a significant extent the third. If this first idea set is seen to represent nuclear weapons policy in its entirety, as it often is, then it can be argued that there has been significant policy continuity from the Cold War to the post-Cold War period because the first idea set has itself changed little. If nuclear weapons policy is associated with the broad mainstream discourse in which three competing idea sets have all had an impact, then post-Cold War nuclear weapons policy must be characterised by both continuity and change. Furthermore, the version of American nuclear weapons policy commonly associated with the first idea set is not natural or inevitable but a social construction based on a range of collective understandings and particular interpretations of key concepts informed by the 'realist' paradigm.

Politics, interest and consensus

The final stage of the analysis placed this 'ideational framework' in the context of domestic political factors that have largely constrained major change. The competing idea sets that constitute the mainstream discourse do not exist in a political vacuum and policy outcomes are not based solely on the relative merits of 'ideational' factors. Instead, nuclear weapons policy, like all issues in government, is subject to bureaucratic political bargaining and the effects of organisational behaviour on the policy-making process.

Generic characteristics of bureaucratic politics and organisational behaviour have inhibited major change allowing the first idea set to dominate nuclear weapons policy for much of the 1990s, giving rise to a sense of bureaucratic inertia. This has been reinforced by a general conservatism regarding changes to nuclear weapons policy.

Nuclear weapons policy has also been affected by a marked reduction in senior-level executive, military and congressional interest and attention. Nuclear deterrence dynamics and strategic military balances steadily became less relevant to the major national security issues and problems faced by America after the Cold War. Nuclear weapons policy was soon relegated as a priority and left to the nuclear weapons policy bureaucracy to tend, whilst being subject to episodic congressional and senior-level executive involvement. This has led to a marked institutional de-emphasis of nuclear weapons in DOD and STRATCOM and considerable difficulty in ensuring effective DOE/NNSA management of the nuclear mission. As a result there has been no real focal point for nuclear weapons issues in the Pentagon from the mid-1990s onwards. This has been compounded by a sense that no major procurement decisions were needed on nuclear weapons policy in order to maintain a background nuclear deterrent – a broadly accepted position across the three competing idea sets.

There has been little broad consensus on the long-term roles and requirements of American nuclear weapons over the post-Cold War period, as demonstrated by the identification of three competing idea sets. The absence of consensus has shaped and been shaped by reduced senior-level attention and interest and institutional de-emphasis of the nuclear mission. These factors have led to a widespread characterisation of nuclear weapons policy as drifting, neglected and lacking a coherent long-term strategy. Major policy change will therefore require sustained senior-level political and military involvement and expenditure of political capital to forge a consensus between the entrenched bureaucratic 'nuclear priesthood', senior administration and military leaders, and Congress. This is evidenced by the difficulties encountered in implementing the 2001 NPR.

Three propositions

Three core propositions emerge from this analysis that underpin a full understanding of the evolution of American nuclear weapons policy since the end of the Cold War. First, nuclear weapons policy has not proceeded in a linear, rational and internally consistent direction since the end of Cold War. It has instead been subject to the relative power of competing and often contradictory idea sets. Nuclear weapons policy does not reflect an objective, rational response to the external international environment but is constructed through institutionalised collective understandings and practices. International political issues, events and material capabilities matter hugely, but their significance is in their interpretation and the meanings assigned to them through the lens of different idea sets.

Second, policy has entered a second post-Cold War phase under President George W. Bush. A series of shifts in different aspects of nuclear weapons policy throughout the 1990s were institutionalised under George W. Bush and the institutionalisation of these changes represents a new phase in policy signified by the rise to prominence of the third of the three idea sets identified.

Third, domestic political processes have constrained major shifts in policy since the end of the Cold War. Bureaucratic politics and organisational processes have had a crucial impact on policy outcomes, the institutionalisation of competing idea sets and the salience of nuclear weapons policy and planning in national security strategy. The effect of different idea sets on policy outcomes is a function of domestic political processes and the relative political power of different conceptions of nuclear weapons policy at different times on different issues.

Future directions

These three propositions indicate that understanding the future direction of policy will require close attention to the evolution of competing idea sets, the policy-makers and organisations that can operationalise them and domestic political constraints. With this in mind a number of signposts for the likely future direction of nuclear weapons policy emerge.

A regional war-fighting nuclear posture

The third idea set has ascended to prominence in the discourse on nuclear weapons policy. Future decisions will most likely reflect its interpretations of the contested concepts that constitute policy. America will gradually develop and deploy a modified low-yield and/or earth-penetrating nuclear warhead and conventional strategic delivery vehicles should congressional opposition ease. The institutionalisation of this idea set can be conceived as a second phase in post-Cold War nuclear weapons policy based on deterrence by denial oriented towards regional WMD-armed 'rogue' states and possibly terrorist groups.

Further marginalisation and force reductions

The rise to prominence of the third idea set will be constrained by the domestic political factors identified. In particular, nuclear weapons will be further marginalised in national security policy and planning. The nuclear mission will continue to be de-emphasised organisationally within DOD and the military and continue its retreat from the heart of relations with Russia. Rationales for new nuclear production complex capabilities, new nuclear warhead capabilities and new nuclear delivery vehicles will struggle to compete in the contemporary fiscal environment, the defence budget planning and programming process and a political environment characterised by the absence of consensus. Without senior-level political attention and military and congressional support it is likely that policy will continue to be characterised as 'benign neglect' by many. For some this will be positively beneficial, for others deeply worrying.

By the end of the first term of the G. W. Bush administration the consolidation and modernisation of the Cold War legacy arsenal to the specific strategic triad envisaged in the early 1990s was all but complete. Deployed and reserve nuclear arsenals are likely to continue to shrink with further reductions after the Moscow Treaty expires in 2012. Frank Miller, one of the primary architects of nuclear weapons policy in DOD throughout the 1980s and 1990s, argued in 2005 that America should reduce deployed and non-deployed nuclear stockpiles significantly below current holdings and those established in the Moscow Treaty.[2]

Two factors will have a significant impact. First, there is considerable scepticism about the wisdom of trying to sustain a relatively large, expensive Cold War legacy nuclear arsenal indefinitely in which political and military confidence will eventually erode, according to the dominant view. Pressures on the complex may be eased by retiring more deployed and reserve weapons and warhead types regardless of whether the RRW and Complex-2030 plans receive long-term congressional support. Second, forthcoming decisions on replacing current ageing strategic nuclear delivery vehicles, particularly the ICBM fleet, will be contentious. Current plans envisage deployment of a new ICBM by 2018, a new SLBM and SSBN by 2029, a new cruise missile by 2030 and a new long-range bomber by 2040. The case for a 450-strong ICBM may prove particularly difficult and a much smaller ICBM fleet may be procured. This may have multiple warheads, mobility, accommodate conventional and nuclear payloads, or involve a common sea-based and land-based ballistic missile. The nuclear weapons policy community will attempt to condition further reductions on a programme to mass produce Reliable Replacement Warheads, new conventional or dual-capable strategic delivery vehicles, progress on other initiatives set out in the 2001 NPR and perhaps limited explosive testing.

Congressional support and the absence of consensus

Decisions on the long-term sustainment of the nuclear arsenal and its roles and requirements will need long-term congressional support. This has not been forthcoming in an era of competing idea sets, the absence of consensus, and the absence of political will at the highest levels to forge a consensus. Future nuclear policy decisions will therefore likely be ad hoc and driven largely by events and domestic politics. These decisions will probably be informed by the third idea set and made in response to material factors, such as the ability of the production complex to support the deployed and reserve arsenals and ageing nuclear delivery vehicles; congressional budgetary pressure and opposition to new nuclear initiatives; and the domestic and international political value of further reductions in deployed nuclear forces.[3]

An absence of consensus will likely continue until the political balance of power shifts between the White House and Congress, the gravity of the decisions needed makes them a priority for the executive, or a unifying strategic threat emerges that is widely perceived to require a major and sustained strategic nuclear deterrent response. A long-term absence of consensus could, as Krepon argues, lead to the unravelling of support both for nuclear weapon programmes and future arms control measures.[4] The 2008 Strategic Posture Commission and the 2009 Nuclear Posture Review provide an opportunity to forge a new consensus.

Nuclear superiority not nuclear disarmament

American nuclear weapons are here to stay, at least in some configuration, and will likely adhere to a number of Cold War policy precepts. Whilst political trends suggest further marginalisation and non-consensus within the discourse, the parameters of the discourse suggest that nuclear disarmament is not an option, either through deliberate actions or long-term neglect. Nuclear weapons will continue to be imbued with powerful meanings as an ultimate 'insurance' background deterrent in an uncertain world in which America must retain military hegemony for global stability.

The defence establishment will strive to remain second to none in nuclear capability informed by a realist perspective that places utmost value in military strength. This may not prove too difficult as political, technological and budgetary constraints drive Russian nuclear forces down despite ongoing modernisation and China retains a comparatively modest nuclear arsenal. American nuclear primacy and the credibility of a general nuclear deterrent threat will continue to be seen as an important if background part of the military supremacy that underpins its hegemony. This will, however, remain in tension with the perception that nuclear weapons offer no easy or relevant solution to pressing contemporary international security problems, continued political and military disinterest in American nuclear weapons and declaratory commitments to work towards nuclear disarmament under the NPT.

Commitment to Cold War nuclear policy precepts

It is unlikely that America will move away from a prompt, launch on warning counter-force nuclear posture and a triad of strategic nuclear forces. The deployment of missile defence systems and strategic conventional global strike assets will complement, rather than replace, strategic nuclear forces and current posture. As Nolan argues, 'it will be a long time before the chiefs [JCS] – and certainly STRATCOM – believe that defenses take the place of prompt response'.[5] Nuclear posture will only change dramatically if new presidential guidance instructs the JCS to no longer plan to respond to a surprise nuclear first-strike that requires America to quickly retaliate by comprehensively destroying the majority of an adversary's strategic targets.[6] Nevertheless, additional reductions in deployed nuclear forces could entail a further move away from Cold War operational planning precepts and reduce the number of weapons on 'hard' alert.

Nuclear weapons policy and non-proliferation

A particularly vexatious and contentious issue is the degree to which American nuclear weapons policy actions and decisions affect the decisions of other states in terms of their WMD and ballistic missile programmes or in terms of their willingness to assist America in achieving its non-proliferation goals. Opinion is deeply divided on the long-term effect on the NPT of America's overriding and enduring commitment to a nuclear national security policy and nuclear superiority. This is reflected in the three idea sets and lies at the heart of a number of nuclear weapons policy issues around which consensus has withered.

Nevertheless, the argument that American nuclear policy decisions have no wider impact on the non-proliferation regime is difficult to make. America is not a passive bystander and its policies shape attitudes and understandings about nuclear weapons in national security policy and in international relations more generally, even if they do not directly cause other states to either procure or abandon nuclear forces or other WMD. America's policy decisions and actions can play a significant part in marginalising or reinforcing the role of nuclear weapons in international politics in the minds of others.[7] The real question is how much and whether it matters. In the context of the NPT American decisions on developing new or modified warheads for regional war-fighting, enhancing test readiness, building a Modern Pit Facility or retaining a major nuclear reserve force will be cited as further evidence that the nuclear weapon states are intent on retaining nuclear weapons indefinitely, that the 'double standard' many see at the heart of the NPT remains firm, and that the NPT cannot and will not deliver the nuclear disarmament that many of its signatories want.

One crucial issue will be any decision to resume limited nuclear testing. If major defects are detected in the existing nuclear stockpile that could undermine nuclear posture, pressure to resume limited nuclear testing could increase dramatically, particularly if the Nevada Test Site is maintained at an advanced state of readiness. The RRW programme may also eventually result in a limited resumption of explosive tests. This would, however, be an extremely contentious decision both domestically and internationally and could legitimise renewed nuclear testing by other nations.

Possibilities for change

Nuclear weapons policy changed considerably over the post-Cold War period as the trends identified suggest, although aspects of operational nuclear posture remain close to Cold War assumptions and practices. Since 1990 deployed nuclear forces have been reduced by roughly three-quarters, total forces including reserves have been cut by a half and over 12,000 warheads dismantled. In 1990 the United States deployed a total of approximately 12,300 strategic nuclear warheads and 7,800 non-strategic warheads giving a total stockpile in the region of 21,000 warheads. By 2012 America will deploy between 1,700 and 2,200 operational strategic warheads, around 400 non-strategic warheads and retain a reserve of approximately 2,000 warheads leaving a total nuclear stockpile in the region of 4,600 warheads.[8] Nuclear testing, fissile material production, and new warhead design and production have also been terminated. In addition, operational nuclear planning has experienced some change towards a more relaxed Cold War deterrence posture and there has been a wholesale shift to regional nuclear planning. Interest and attention paid to American nuclear forces by senior policy-makers, military officials and legislators has also faded considerably.

The constructed and 'ideational' nature of nuclear weapons policy also means that further change is possible through reconceptualising orthodox understandings that inform policy to fit contemporary interpretations of strategic 'reality'. The George W. Bush administration attempted to do this with the Cold War conception of strategic stability by articulating a 'new strategic framework' with Russia. The potential for reconceptualisation seems particularly relevant with nuclear weapons policy given the absence of concrete empirical data on the functioning of nuclear deterrence. Change can therefore occur by reconceptualising collective understandings, practices and causal relationships without the dramatic geo-political upheavals of the end of the Cold War. A break-down in consensus on an institutionalised set of collective understandings that sustains a particular set of practices, identities and interests can lead to a critical examination of those understandings. As identities and interests are re-conceptualised new practices may be adopted that change the practices, identities and interests of others. Mehan *et al.* argue that Soviet President Mikhail Gorbachev reconceptualised the Soviet Union's relationship with America and changed Moscow's practices according to a new set of identities and interests. This undermined American threat perceptions and dominant understandings of the role of American nuclear forces and nuclear deterrence.[9]

Finally, policy will continue to evolve and change according to a complex mix of competing idea sets within the mainstream discourse, the power of Cold War nuclear identities, interests and practices, the conservatism of the nuclear policy community, congressional budgetary pressure and opposition, decreasing political and military interest and attention and an absence of consensus. Incremental change will be the norm, but a more fundamental reconceptualisation is inherently possible.

Notes

Introduction

1 Walker, W. (2000), 'Nuclear Order and Disorder', *International Affairs*, vol. 76, no. 4.
2 (2003), 'Differentiation and Defense: An Agenda for the Nuclear Weapons Program', United States House of Representatives Policy Committee Subcommittee on National Security and Foreign Affairs, Washington, D.C., p. 3.
3 Butler, G. L. (1993), *Prepared Posture Statement of Gen. Lee Butler, Commander in Chief, United States Strategic Command*, Hearing before the Senate Committee on Armed Services, 22 April 1993, Government Printing Office, Washington, D.C., p. 405.
4 Sloss is a national security consultant who spent 20 years as a government official serving in the Bureau of the Budget, the Department of State, the Department of Defense, and the Arms Control and Disarmament Agency and directed a major study on American nuclear strategy in 1978. He has written frequently on nuclear weapons policy. Sloss, L. (2001), 'Deterrence, Defenses, Nuclear Weapons and Arms Control', *Comparative Strategy*, vol. 20, no. 5, pp. 435, 439.
5 Smith, S. (2005), 'The Contested Concept of Security', in Booth, K. (ed.) *Critical Security Studies and World Politics*, London, Lynne Rienner, p. 38.

1 The policy-making process

1 Jordan, A. A., Mazarr, M. J. and Taylor, W. J. (1999), *American National Security*, Baltimore, Johns Hopkins University Press, pp. 217–219.
2 Miall, H. (1987), *Nuclear Weapons: Who's in Charge?*, Basingstoke, Macmillan Press, pp. 79–80.
3 (2005), 'U.S. Commission on National Security/21st Century – National Security Strategy and Policy Development', in Bolt, P. J., Coletta, D. V. and Shackelford, C. G. (eds) *American Defense Policy*, 8th edn, Johns Hopkins University Press, Baltimore, p. 161.
4 Jordan, Mazarr and Taylor, *American National Security*, pp. 221–223.
5 Smith, H. P. (1997), *Testimony of Harold P. Smith, Assistant to the Secretary of Defense for Atomic Energy*, Hearing before the Senate Committee on Appropriations, 3 May 1990, Government Printing Office, Washington, D.C., pp. 27–30.
6 Smith, H. (1995), *Testimony by Dr. Harold P. Smith, Assistant to the Secretary of Defense for Atomic Energy*, Hearing before the Senate Committee on Armed Services, 16 May 1995, Government Printing Office, Washington, D.C., p. 220.
7 Cohen, W. (1997), *Nuclear Weapon Systems Sustainment Programs*, Washington, D.C., Department of Defense; (1999), *Stockpile Stewardship Program: 30-Day Review*, Washington, D.C., U.S. Department of Energy, pp. 3–4.
8 Cohen, W. (1997), *Nuclear Weapon Systems Sustainment Programs.*

9 Harahan, J. P. and Bennett, R. J. (2002), *Creating the Defense Threat Reduction Agency*, Washington, D.C., U.S. Department of Defense, p. 20.
10 Halperin, M. H. and Clapp, P. A. (2006), *National Security Policy-Making*, Washington, D.C., Brookings Institution Press; (1998), 'Joint Statement on Common Security Challenges at the Threshold of the Twenty-First Century', 2 September 1998, *Weekly Compilation of Presidential Documents, vol. 34, no. 36, pp. 1667–1730*, Government Printing Office, Washington, D.C.
11 Jordan, Mazarr and Taylor, *American National Security*, p. 192.
12 Slocombe, W. (2006), *Democratic Control of Nuclear Weapons*, Geneva, Policy Paper, no. 12, Geneva Centre for the Democratic Control of Armed Forces, p. 24.
13 Miller, F. (1997), *Testimony of Franklin C. Miller, Acting Assistant Secretary of Defense for International Security Policy*, Hearing before the Senate Committee on Appropriations, 3 May 1990, Government Printing Office, Washington, D.C., p. 24.
14 (2005), 'Joint Doctrine for Nuclear Operations (draft)', U.S. Joint Chiefs of Staff, Washington, D.C.; Kristensen, H. (2006), *U.S. Changes Name of Nuclear War Plan*, The Nuclear Information Project, Washington, D.C. Retrieved from http://www.nukestrat.com/us/stratcom/siopname.htm on 15 February 2007; Woolf, A. (2006), 'U.S. Nuclear Weapons: Changes in Policy and Force Structure', January 2006, Congressional Research Service, Washington, D.C., p. 16.
15 Conahan, F. C. (1991), *Strategic Weapons: Nuclear Weapons Targeting Process*, Washington, D.C., Government Printing Office.
16 Slocombe, *Democratic Control of Nuclear Weapons*, p. 21.
17 Herzfeld, C. (1990), *Testimony of Dr. Charles Herzfeld, Chairman, Nuclear Weapons Council*, Hearing before the House of Representatives Committee on Armed Services, 20 March 1990, Government Printing Office, Washington, D.C., p. 405; (1998), 'Nuclear Weapons: Key Nuclear Weapons Component Issues are Unresolved', November 1998, U.S. General Accounting Office, Washington, D.C., p. 3; Smith, *Testimony by Dr. Harold P. Smith, Assistant to the Secretary of Defense for Atomic Energy*, 16 May 1995, p. 220.
18 (2005), 'Department of Defense Directive: Defense Threat Reduction Agency', 28 November 2005, U.S. Department of Defense, Washington, D.C.
19 Bongiovi, R. P. (2001), *Testimony by Major General Robert P. Bongiovi, Acting Director, Defense Threat Reduction Agency*, Hearing before the Senate Committee on Armed Services, 12 July 2001, Government Printing Office, Washington, D.C.
20 DTRA FY2005 budget justification: Appropriation/Budget Activity, RDT&E, Defense-Wide/Applied Research – BA2 'Nuclear Programs', February 2004.
21 Cohen, *Nuclear Weapon Systems Sustainment Programs*.
22 Clinton, W. J. (1997), 'Message to the Senate Transmitting the Comprehensive Nuclear Test-Ban Treaty and Documentation, 22 September 1997', *Weekly Compilation of Presidential Documents, vol. 33, no. 39, pp. 1371–1429*, Government Printing Office, Washington, D.C.
23 Jordan, Mazarr and Taylor, *American National Security*, p. 94.
24 Lindsay, J. M. (1991), *Congress and Nuclear Weapons*, Baltimore, The Johns Hopkins University Press, pp. 41–45; 'U.S. Commission on National Security/21st Century – National Security Strategy and Policy Development' in Bolt, Coletta and Shackelford, *American Defense Policy*, p. 168.
25 (2001), 'Conference Report on H.R. 2311, Energy and Water Development Appropriations Act, 2002', *Congressional Record (House of Representatives)*, 30 October 2001, p. H7492.
26 Halperin and Clapp, *National Security Policy-Making*, pp. 314–315.
27 (2005), 'U.S. Commission on National Security/21st Century – National Security Resource Allocation', in Bolt, P. J., Coletta, D. V. and Shackelford, C. G. (eds) *American Defense Policy*, 8th edn. Johns Hopkins University Press, Baltimore, p. 177.

28 Jordan, Mazarr and Taylor, *American National Security*, pp. 126, 137; Halperin and Clapp, *National Security Policy-Making*, p. 343.
29 Sarkesian, S. C., Williams, J. A., *et al.* (2005), 'The Military Establishment, the President, and Congress', in Bolt, P. J., Coletta, D. V. and Shackelford, C. G. (eds) *American Defense Policy*, 8th edn. Johns Hopkins University Press, Baltimore, p. 146.
30 Jordan, Mazarr and Taylor, *American National Security*, p. 126.
31 Hartung, W. D. and Reingold, J. (2002), *About Face: The Role of the Arms Lobby In the Bush Administration's Radical Reversal of Two Decades of U.S. Nuclear Policy*, New York, World Policy Institute.
32 Slocombe, *Democratic Control of Nuclear Weapons*, p. 24.
33 (2008), *The Budget Process – The Historical Context*, OSD Comptroller iCenter, Department of Defense, Retrieved from http://www.defenselink.mil/comptroller/Icenter/budget/histcontext.htm on 7 January 2008.
34 Jordan, Mazarr and Taylor, *American National Security*, p. 207.
35 Johnson, S. E. (2005), 'The New PPBS Process to Advance Transformation', in Bolt, P. J., Coletta, D. V. and Shackelford, C. G. (eds) *American Defense Policy*, 8th edn. Johns Hopkins University Press, Baltimore, pp. 180–181; 'U.S. Commission on National Security/21st Century – National Security Resource Allocation' in Bolt, Coletta and Shackelford, *American Defense Policy*, pp. 172–175.
36 Ibid. p. 176.
37 Lindsay, *Congress and Nuclear Weapons*, p. 49; 'U.S. Commission on National Security/21st Century – National Security Resource Allocation' in Bolt, Coletta and Shackelford, *American Defense Policy*, pp. 177–178.

2 American nuclear weapons policy at the end of the Cold War

1 Powaski, R. E. (2000), *Return to Armageddon: The United States and the Nuclear Arms Race, 1981–1999*, New York, Oxford University Press, pp. 72–73.
2 See MccGwire on the construction of the Soviet threat that laid the foundations for the Cold War. MccGwire, M. (2001), 'The Paradigm That Lost its Way', *International Affairs*, vol. 77, no. 4; McCauley, M. (2004), *Russia, America and the Cold War*, London, Longman, p. 38.
3 George F. Kennan's strong views of the Soviet Union's intentions and capabilities, set out in his famous 'Long Telegram' from the American embassy in Moscow in 1946, were particularly influential. Schwartzman, D. (1988), *Games of Chicken: Four Decades of U.S. Nuclear Policy*, London, Praeger, pp. 22–23.
4 Brodie, B. (ed.) (1946), *The Absolute Weapon: Atomic Power and World Order*, New York, Harcourt, Brace and Company; Mandelbaum, M. (1979), *The Nuclear Question: The United States and Nuclear Weapon, 1946–1976*, Cambridge, Cambridge University Press, p. 19.
5 McGwire, 'The Paradigm That Lost its Way', pp. 788–790.
6 Powaski, *Return to Armageddon*, p. 71.
7 Schwartzman, *Games of Chicken: Four Decades of U.S. Nuclear Policy*, p. 39.
8 Freedman, L. (1989), *The Evolution of Nuclear Strategy*, Basingstoke, Macmillan Press, p. 63.
9 Ibid. p. 140; Mandelbaum, *The Nuclear Question*, pp. 51, 66.
10 Freedman, *The Evolution of Nuclear Strategy*, pp. 83–87, 216–219. See Kahn, H. (1968), *On Escalation: Metaphors and Scenarios*, Baltimore, Penguin on the concepts of 'escalation dominance' and a 'ladder of escalation' central to the theory of a flexible response strategy.
11 Mandelbaum, *The Nuclear Question*, p. 66.
12 Freedman, *The Evolution of Nuclear Strategy*, pp. 218, 244; Schwartzman, *Games of Chicken*, p. 89.
13 Mandelbaum, *The Nuclear Question*, p. 115.

14 Freedman, *The Evolution of Nuclear Strategy*, pp. 349, 359.
15 *Harold Brown*, U.S. Department of Defense, Washington, D.C. Retrieved from http://www.defenselink.mil/specials/secdef_histories/bios/brown.htm on 17 January 2007; Schwartzman, *Games of Chicken*, pp. 151–152.
16 Alarmist estimates claimed the USSR would soon have 2,500 ICBMs and would be able to destroy 95 per cent of the US ICBM fleet in a first-strike. Schwartzman, *Games of Chicken*, p. 111.
17 Freedman, *The Evolution of Nuclear Strategy*, p. 410. Set out in national security decision directive 13 (NSDD-13) in 1981.
18 Schwartzman, *Games of Chicken*, pp. 110, 157.
19 Gaddis, J. L. (1997), *We Now Know: Rethinking Cold War History*, Oxford, Clarendon Press, p. 125.
20 Freedman, *The Evolution of Nuclear Strategy*, p. 413.
21 In 1984 the Senate refused to appropriate funds for anti-satellite weapons development and passed an amendment calling for the President to attempt to gain ratification of the Threshold Test Ban Treaty, the Partial Nuclear Test Ban Treaty and to resume negotiations for a CTBT. Powaski, *Return to Armageddon*, pp. 45, 247.
22 Goodby, J., 'Looking Back: The 1986 Reykjavik Summit', *Arms Control Today*, vol. 36, no. 7 (September 2006).
23 Robert McNamara, Secretary of Defense from 1961–1968, argued in 1983 that 'nuclear weapons serve no military purpose whatsoever. They are totally useless – except only to deter one's opponent from using them'. McNamara, R. S. (1983), 'The Military Role of Nuclear Weapons: Perceptions and Misperceptions', *Foreign Affairs*, vol. 62, no. 1, p. 79.
24 Freedman, *The Evolution of Nuclear Strategy*, pp. 335–339, 410.
25 Lebow, R. and Stein, J. (1994), *We all Lost the Cold War*, Princeton N.J., Princeton University Press, pp. 350, 363. Keohane and Nye argue that the first order effect of nuclear deterrence is to deny effective offensive power to a superpower opponent, but the second to gain political influence. Keohane, R. and Nye, J. (1989), *Power and Interdependence*, London, HarperCollins, p. 28.
26 Kull, S. (1988), *Minds at War: Nuclear Reality and the Inner Conflicts of Defense Policymakers*, New York, Basic Books, p. 114.
27 Waltz, K. (1993), 'The Emerging Structure of International Politics', *International Security*, vol. 18, no. 2, p. 47.

3 Nuclear weapons policy under George H. W. Bush

1 (1991), 'A START Briefing Book', *Bulletin of the Atomic Scientists*, vol. 47, no. 9 (November 1991).
2 Powaski, R. E. (2000), *Return to Armageddon: The United States and the Nuclear Arms Race, 1981–1999*, New York, Oxford University Press, pp. 139–144; Woolf, A. (1996), 'Nuclear Arms Control and Nuclear Threat Reduction: Issues and Agenda', October 1996, CRS Issue Brief, Congressional Research Service, Washington, D.C., pp. 3–4.
3 (2001), 'START Treaty Final Reductions, 5 December 2001', Bureau of Arms Control, U.S. Department of State, Washington, D.C.
4 Pell, C. (1992), 'Committee Approval of the START Treaty', *Congressional Record (Senate)*, 2 July 1992, pp. S9751–S9752.
5 Helms, J. (1991), 'The START Treaty must be Postponed', *Congressional Record (Senate)*, 25 October 1991, p. S15247; Wallop, M. (1991), 'The ABM Treaty', *Congressional Record (Senate)*, 6 June 1991, pp. S7255–S7259; Craig, L. (1992), 'The START Treaty', *Congressional Record (Senate)*, 30 September 1992, pp. S15861–S15864.
6 Arbatov, A. (1991), 'We Could Have Done Better', *Bulletin of the Atomic*

Scientists, vol. 47, no. 9 (November 1991); Powaski, *Return to Armageddon*, pp. 124–125.

7 Mendelsohn, J. (1991), 'Senate will Grouse then Ratify', *Bulletin of the Atomic Scientists*, vol. 47, no. 1 (January/February 1991).

8 Albright, H., Zamora, T., *et al.* (1990), 'Turn off Rocky Flats', *Bulletin of the Atomic Scientists*, vol. 46, no. 5 (June 1991).

9 Nitze, P. H. (1991), 'START is no Place to Stop', *Washington Post*, 14 August 1991.

10 Stark, P. (1992), 'The President Should Continue to Pursue the Policy Goals set forth in the Nuclear Weapons Reduction Act', *Congressional Record (Extension of Remarks)*, 17 June 1992, p. E1874.

11 Powaski, *Return to Armageddon*, p. 102.

12 McCain, J. (1993), 'Senate Resolution 54 – Commending President Bush on Conclusion of the START II Treaty', *Congressional Record (Senate)*, 2 February 1993, p. S1050.

13 Bush, G. H. W. (1990), 'Soviet–United States Joint Statement on Future Negotiations on Nuclear and Space Arms and Further Enhancing Strategic Stability', 1 June 1990, George Bush Presidential Library, Texas; Hadley, S. J. (1990), *Testimony of Stephen J. Hadley, Assistant Secretary of Defense for International Security Policy*, Hearing before the House of Representatives Committee on Armed Services, 21 March 1990, Government Printing Office, Washington, D.C., p. 291; (1991), *The Future of the U.S.-Soviet Nuclear Relationship*, Washington, D.C., National Academy Press, p. 31.

14 Nunn, S. (1990), 'A Broader Agenda for the Summit', *Congressional Record (Senate)*, 24 May 1990, p. S6998.

15 Arbatov, 'We Could Have Done Better'.

16 Powaski, *Return to Armageddon*, p. 149.

17 (1992), *Fact Sheet on the Charter for American–Russian Partnership and Friendship, 17 June 1992*, The White House, Washington, D.C. Retrieved from http://www.fas.org/spp/starwars/offdocs/b920617k.htm on 2 March 2007; Christopher, W. (1993), *Testimony of Hon. Warren Christopher, Secretary of State*, Hearing before the Senate Committee on Foreign Relations, 11 May 1993, Government Printing Office, Washington, D.C., p. 3.

18 Powaski, *Return to Armageddon*, p. 124.

19 Jeremiah, D. E. (1991), *Testimony of Adm. David E. Jeremiah, Vice Chairman, Joint Chiefs of Staff*, Hearing before the House of Representatives Committee on Armed Services, 6 March 1991, Government Printing Office, Washington, D.C.

20 See letter from Lawrence Eagleburger, Acting Secretary of State, to Senator George Mitchell, Senate Majority Leader. Mitchell, G. (1992), 'Protocol to the Treaty with the Union of Soviet Socialist Republics on the Reduction and Limitation of Strategic Offensive Arms – Treaty Doc., no. 102–32', *Congressional Record (Senate)*, 29 September 1992, pp. S15502–S15503.

21 Cheney, R. B. (1992), *Testimony by Richard B. Cheney, Secretary of Defense*, Hearing before the Senate Committee on Armed Services, 28 July 1992, United States Senate, Washington, D.C., p. 13; Powaski, *Return to Armageddon*, p. 145.

22 Jeremiah, D. E. (1992), *Testimony by Adm. David E. Jeremiah*, Hearing before the House of Representatives Committee on Armed Services, 30 April 1992, Government Printing Office, Washington, D.C.; Bush, G. H. W. and Scowcroft, B. (1998), *A World Transformed*, New York, Alfred A. Knopf, pp. 544–545.

23 Arkin, W. and Norris, R. (1991), 'Nuclear Notebook', *Bulletin of the Atomic Scientists*, vol. 47, no. 4 (May 1991).

24 Harkin, T. (1990), 'Senator Sasser's Proposals for Defense Spending', *Congressional Record (Senate)*, 3 May 1990, p. H346; Pease, D. (1990), 'Peace Dividend', *Congressional Record (House of Representatives)*, 7 February 1990, p. H346;

Dorgan, B. (1991), 'Time for President Bush to Start Domestic Program at Home', *Congressional Record (House of Representatives)*, 30 July 1991, p. H5984.

25 Gore, A. (1991), 'Nuclear Weapons', *Congressional Record (Senate)*, 7 October 1991, p. S14468.

26 Daalder, I. and Terriff, T. (eds) (1993), *Rethinking the Unthinkable: New Directions for Nuclear Arms Control*, London, Frank Cass, p. 12.

27 Woolf, A. (2004), 'Non-Strategic Nuclear Weapons', September 2004, Congressional Research Service, Washington, D.C.; Millot, M. D. (1994), 'Facing the Emerging Reality of Regional Nuclear Adversaries', *The Washington Quarterly*, vol. 17, no. 3, p. 53.

28 Representative Lee Hamilton maintained that 'the most astonishing aspect of the President's initiative is his call for a unilateral reduction of U.S. armaments. In one stroke, he scrapped much of the now obsolete nuclear doctrine and Cold War thinking of the past four decades. He has paved the way for a new approach'. Hamilton, L. (1991), 'The President's Arms Control Speech', *Congressional Record (Extension of Remarks)*, 9 October 1991, p. E3331.

29 Bush, G. H. W. (1991), 'Presidential Initiative on Nuclear Arms', 27 September 1991, Government Printing Office, Washington, D.C.; Cheney, *Testimony by Richard B. Cheney, Secretary of Defense*, 28 July 1992, p. 12; Bush and Scowcroft, *A World Transformed*, pp. 542–544; Cimbala, S. (1996), *Clinton and Post-Cold War Defense*, Westport, CT, Praeger, p. 2.

30 Miller, F. (1990), *Testimony of Franklin C. Miller, Deputy Assistant Secretary of Defense for Nuclear Forces*, Hearing before the Senate Committee on Armed Services, 3 May 1990, Government Printing Office, Washington, D.C.

31 Thurmond, S. (1990), 'The Savannah River Site Restart and New Production Reactor', *Congressional Record (Senate)*, 21 June 1990, p. S8450.

32 McClure, J. (1990), 'Reports of Three New Soviet Violations of the INF Treaty Show a Continuing Need for a United States Compliance Policy for Proportionate Response', *Congressional Record (Senate)*, 5 April 1990, p. S4165; Livingston, B. (1991), 'SDI – Now More Than Ever', *Congressional Record (Extension of Remarks)*, 27 April 1990, p. E1271; Inouye, D. (1990), 'Looking to the Future: American Defense Posture in a Changing World', *Congressional Record (Senate)*, 12 June 1990, p. S7838.

33 Butler, G. L. (1991), *Testimony of Gen. George L. Butler*, Hearing before the Senate Committee on Appropriations, 7 May 1991, Government Printing Office, Washington, D.C.

34 Rice, D. (1990), 'The Manned Bomber and Strategic Deterrence: the U.S. Air Force Perspective', *International Security*, vol. 15, no. 1, p. 101.

35 Bush and Scowcroft, *A World Transformed*, pp. 12–13.

36 Powell, C. (1992), *Testimony by Gen. Colin L. Powell, Chairman Joint Chiefs of Staff*, Hearing before the Senate Committee on Armed Services, 28 July 1992, Government Printing Office, Washington, D.C.; Bush, G. H. W. (1990), 'Remarks to Strategic Air Command Personnel', February 8, 1990, U.S. Government Printing Office, Washington, D.C.

37 Tuck, J. (1990), *Testimony of John C. Tuck, Acting Assistant Secretary for Defense Programs*, Hearing before the Senate Committee on Armed Services, 23 May 1990, Government Printing Office, Washington, D.C.

38 Paulsen, R. A. (1994), *The Role of Nuclear Weapons in the Post-Cold War Era*, Maxwell Air Force Base, Alabama, Air University Press, p. xiii; Nolan, J. E. (1999), *An Elusive Consensus: Nuclear Weapons and American Security After the Cold War*, Washington D.C., Brookings Institution Press, p. 31.

39 Arkin and Norris, 'Nuclear Notebook', (December 1991); Frank Miller, former Principal Deputy Assistant Secretary of Defense and a career bureaucrat centrally involved in nuclear weapons policy, interviewed in (2005), *U.S. Strategic Nuclear*

Policy: An Oral History (Unclassified DVD), Albuquerque, NM, Sandia National Laboratories, Part 4.

40 Kristensen, H. (2001), *The Matrix of Deterrence: U.S. Strategic Command Force Structure Studies*, Berkeley, CA, The Nautilus Institute.

41 (2004), *History of the United States Strategic Command: 1 June 1992–2 October 2002*, Offut Air Force Base, Nebraska, Strategic Command, p. 26.

42 Ibid., p. 26.

43 Dixon, A. (1990), 'Reexamining U.S. Defense Strategy', *Congressional Record (Senate)*, 3 May 1990, p. S5624; Rice, D. B. (1990), *The Case for the B-2*, Hearing before the Senate Committee on Armed Services, 6 June 1990, Government Printing Office, Washington, D.C., p. 364; Gottemoeller, R. (1992), *Strategic Arms Control in the Post-START Era*, London, Brasseys for the IISS, p. 43.

44 Ball, D. and Toth, R. (1990), 'Revising the SIOP: Taking War-Fighting to Dangerous Extremes', *International Security*, vol. 14, no. 4, p. 90; Gottemoeller, *Strategic Arms Control in the Post-START Era*, p. 103.

45 Bush, G. H. W. (1991), 'Remarks at the United States Air Force Academy Commencement Ceremony in Colorado Springs, Colorado', *Public Papers of the Presidents, George Bush – 1992 vol. 1*, 29 May 1991, Government Printing Office, Washington, D.C.; Welch, L. (1990), *Testimony of Gen. Larry D. Welch, Chief of Staff, U.S. Air Force*, Hearing before the Senate Committee on Armed Services, 28 February 1990, Government Printing Office, Washington, D.C.

46 Cheney, *Testimony by Richard B. Cheney, Secretary of Defense*, 28 July 1992, p. 16; Correll, J. T. (1991), 'The New Defense Strategy', *Air Force Magazine*, vol. 74, no. 7 (July 1991).

47 See McCain, J. (1990), 'The Need for a New Strategic Focus on Power Projection', *Congressional Record (Senate)*, 2 August 1990, pp. S11549–S11553; Hansen, J. (1991), 'National Defense Authorization Act for Fiscal Years 1992 and 1993', *Congressional Record (House of Representatives)*, 20 May 1991, p. H3182; Exon, J. J. (1990), 'Areas for United States–Soviet Cooperation', *Congressional Record (Senate)*, 6 June 1991, p. S7285.

48 Stockton, P. (1991), 'The New Game on the Hill: The Politics of Arms Control and Strategic Force Modernization', *International Security*, vol. 16, no. 2; Nunn, S. (1990), 'Defense Budget Blanks', *Congressional Record (Senate)*, 22 March 1990, p. S2965.

49 Gates, R. (1991), *Testimony of Robert M. Gates, Director, Central Intelligence Agency*, Hearing before the Defense Policy Panel of the House of Representatives Committee on Armed Services, 11 December 1991, Government Printing Office, Washington, D.C.

50 *The Future of the U.S.–Soviet Nuclear Relationship*, p. 2.

51 See Nunn, S. (1990), 'Implementing a New Military Strategy: The Budget Decisions', *Congressional Record (Senate)*, 20 April 1990, p. S4652 on PNIs; Leahy, P. (1991), 'National Defense Authorization Act for Fiscal Year 1992 and 1993 – Conference Report', *Congressional Record (Senate)*, 21 November 1991, pp. S17393–S17405 on the B-2; Hunter, D. (1992), 'The Republican Congress – A Manifesto for Change in the House of Representatives', *Congressional Record (House of Representatives)*, 30 January 1992, and Butler, G. L. (1992), *Prepared Statement of Gen. Lee Butler*, Hearing before the House of Representatives Committee on Armed Services, 8 April 1992, Government Printing Office, Washington, D.C. on ICBMs and SSBNs. For detail on the congressional coalition to terminate or restrict the B-2 see Aspin, L. (1990), 'Do We Need the B-2?' *Congressional Record (House of Representatives)*, 23 July 1990, pp. H5329–H2534.

52 Butler, *Testimony of Gen. George L. Butler*, 7 May 1991, p. 973.

53 Brower, M. (1990), 'B-2: New Numbers, Old Arguments', *Bulletin of the Atomic Scientists*, vol. 46, no. 5 (June 1990); Arkin, W. and Norris, R. (1992), 'Nuclear Notebook', *Bulletin of the Atomic Scientists*, vol. 48, no. 1 (January/February 1992).

54 Perry, W. (1996), *Annual Report to the President and the Congress*, Washington, D.C., Department of Defense; Arkin, W. and Norris, R. (1994), 'Estimated U.S. and Soviet/Russian Nuclear Stockpiles, 1945–94', *Bulletin of the Atomic Scientists*, vol. 50, no. 6 (November/December 1994), p. 58.
55 Ball and Toth, 'Revising the SIOP', p. 85.
56 Kristensen, H. (2003), *Changing Targets II: A Chronology of U.S. Nuclear Policy Against Weapons of Mass Destruction*, Washington, D.C., Greenpeace, p. 11; Nolan, J. (2000), 'Preparing for the 2001 Nuclear Posture Review', *Arms Control Today*, vol. 30, no. 9 (November 2000).
57 *History of the United States Strategic Command*, Strategic Command, p. 27; Jeremiah, *Testimony of Adm. David E. Jeremiah*, 6 March 1991, pp. 55–58.
58 Mandelbaum, M. (1995), 'Lessons of the Next Nuclear War', *Foreign Affairs*, vol. 74, no. 2, p. 34.
59 May, M. (1992), *Testimony of Michael May*, Hearing before the House of Representatives Committee on Armed Services, 8 April 1992, Government Printing Office, Washington, D.C.; Reed, T. (1992), *Testimony of Thomas C. Reed*, Hearing before the House of Representatives Committee on Armed Services, 8 April 1992, Government Printing Office, Washington, D.C.
60 Sloss, L. (1991), 'U.S. Strategic Forces After the Cold War: Policies and Strategies', *The Washington Quarterly*, vol. 14, no. 4, p. 147.
61 Klare, M. (1995), *Rogue States and Nuclear Outlaws*, New York, Hill and Wang.
62 Callahan, D. (1994), *Between Two Worlds: Realism, Idealism, and American Foreign Policy After the Cold War*, New York, HarperCollins, pp. 97, 156. See also CIA Director Robert Gates *Testimony of Robert M. Gates, Director, Central Intelligence Agency*, and the 1990 JCS Net Assessment in Inouye 'Looking to the Future: American Defense Posture in a Changing World', p. S7838.
63 Bush, G. H. W. (1992), 'Remarks and a Question-and-Answer Session in Billings, Montana', *Public Papers of the Presidents, George Bush – 1992 vol. 2, pp. 1983–1991*, 25 October 1992, Government Printing Office, Washington, D.C.
64 Kerry, J. (1992), 'American Agenda for the New World Order: A. Cementing the Democratic Foundation; B. Forging a New Strategy of Containment', *Congressional Record (Senate)*, 30 June 1992, p. S9177.
65 Levin, C. (1992), 'Address to Center for Naval Analyses Conference', *Congressional Record (Senate)*, 19 May 1992, p. S6917.
66 Kristensen, *Changing Targets II*, p. 7.
67 Arkin, W. and Norris, R. (1992), 'Tiny Nukes for Tiny Minds', *Bulletin of the Atomic Scientists*, vol. 48, no. 3 (April 1992); Arkin, W. (1994), 'Nuclear Posture and the NPT', *F.A.S. Public Interest Report*, vol. 47, no. 5 (September/October 1994).
68 Powaski, *Return to Armageddon*, p. 86.
69 Kristensen, H. (1997), 'Targets of Opportunity: How Nuclear Planners Found New Targets for Old Weapons', *Bulletin of the Atomic Scientists*, vol. 53, no. 5 (September/October 1997).
70 Kristensen, H. and Handler, J. (1996), 'The USA and Counter-Proliferation: a New and Dubious Role for U.S. Nuclear Weapons', *Security Dialogue*, vol. 27, no. 4; Paulsen, *The Role of Nuclear Weapons in the Post-Cold War Era*.
71 Arkin, W. (1995), 'The Last Word', *Bulletin of the Atomic Scientists*, vol. 51, no. 3 (May/June 1995).
72 Kristensen, *Changing Targets II*, p. 9.
73 Frank, B. (1991), 'The Middle East Crisis and the Fiscal Year 1992 Military Budget', *Congressional Record (Extension of Remarks)*, 5 February 1991, p. E411.
74 Powell, C. (1995), *My American Journey*, New York, Ballantine Books, pp. 486 and 472; Bush and Scowcroft, *A World Transformed*, p. 463; Baker, J. (1995), *The Politics of Diplomacy*, New York, Putnam Adult, p. 359.

75 Biden, J. (1992), 'START: The Imperative of Deeper Cuts', *Congressional Record (Senate)*, 23 January 1992, p. S281.
76 Stark, P. (1992), 'The Nuclear Weapons Reduction Act of 1992', *Congressional Record (House of Representatives)*, 19 May 1992, p. H3435.
77 Warner, J. (1990), 'National Defense Authorization Act for Fiscal Year 1991', *Congressional Record (Senate)*, 4 August 1990, p. S12344.
78 Bush, G. H. W. (1991), 'Remarks to Raytheon Missile Systems Plant Employees in Andover, Massachusetts', *Public Papers of the Presidents, George Bush – 1992 vol. 1*, 15 February 1991, Government Printing Office, Washington, D.C.; Kyl, J. (1990), 'The Strategic Defense Initiative', *Congressional Record (House of Representatives)*, 21 March 1990, p. H997; McCain, J. (1990), 'National Defense Authorization Act for Fiscal Year 1991', *Congressional Record (Senate)*, 2 August 1990, p. S11552.
79 Dornan, R. (1991), 'Scud Attacks Give Hint of Future – Patriot Successes Prove Value, Need of Missile Defense', *Defense News*, 25 February 1991.
80 Cooper, H. (1991), *Testimony of Henry F. Cooper, Director, Strategic Defense Initiative Organization*, Hearing before the Subcommittee of the Senate Committee on Appropriations, 7 May 1991, Government Printing Office, Washington, D.C.; Hadley, S. J. (1990), *Testimony of Stephen J. Hadley, Assistant Secretary of Defense for International Security Policy*, Hearing before the Senate Committee on Armed Services, 20 June 1990, Government Printing Office, Washington, D.C.
81 Cooper, H. F. (1992), 'Limited Ballistic Missile Strikes: GPALS Comes up with an Answer', *NATO Review*, vol. 40, no. 3 (June 1992).
82 Cooper, *Testimony of Henry F. Cooper*, 7 May 1991.
83 Smith, R. J. (1992), 'U.S. Moves Away From ABM Treaty – '72 Pact Was Omitted From List Applicable to Ex-Soviet States', *Washington Post*, 25 January 1992; Cheney, *Testimony by Richard B. Cheney, Secretary of Defense*, 28 July 1992, pp. 12–13.
84 Dole, B. (1990), 'Strategic Defenses in the 1990's', *Congressional Record (Senate)*, 9 March 1990, p. S2690; Helms, J. (1991), 'The ABM Treaty is Obsolete', *Congressional Record (Senate)*, 24 April 1991, p. S4932; Kyl, J. (1990), 'Cooperative Transition to Strategic Defenses', *Congressional Record (Extension of Remarks)*, 1 May 1990, p. E1293.
85 Aspin, L. (1991), 'The Future of Defense', *Congressional Record (Extension of Remarks)*, 3 October 1991, p. E3279; Gore, A. (1991), 'The Antiballistic Missile Treaty', *Congressional Record (Senate)*, 23 July 1991, p. S10594; Pell, C. (1992), 'President's Nuclear Initiatives', *Congressional Record (Senate)*, 29 January 1992, p. S560.
86 Nunn, S. (1991), 'National Defense Authorization Act for Fiscal Year 1992 and 1993 – Conference Report', *Congressional Record (Senate)*, 21 November 1991, p. S17394; Powaski, *Return to Armageddon*, p. 126.
87 Hadley, S. J. (1992), *Testimony of Stephen J. Hadley, Assistant Secretary of Defense for International Security Policy*, Hearing before the Senate Committee on Armed Services on 'Department of Defense Authorization for Appropriations for Fiscal Year 1993 and the Future Years Defense Program', 20 May 1992, United States Senate, Washington, D.C., pp. 488–489. For further details of US–Soviet/Russian discussions on a joint missile defence system see Lehman, R. F. (1999), *Testimony of Ronald F. Lehman*, Hearing before the Senate Committee on Foreign Relations, 5 May 1999, Government Printing Office, Washington, D.C., and Hadley, S. J. (1999), *Testimony of Stephen J. Hadley*, Hearing before the Senate Committee on Foreign Relations, 13 May 1999, Government Printing Office, Washington, D.C.
88 Albright, D. (1991), *Testimony of David Albright*, Hearing before the House of Representatives Committee on Armed Services, 18 April 1991, Government Printing Office, Washington, D.C., p. 829.

89 Olshanksky, S. J. and Williams, R. G. (1990), 'Culture Shock at the Weapons Complex', *Bulletin of the Atomic Scientists*, vol. 46, no. 8 (September 1990); Hecker, S. (1992), *Testimony by Dr. Siegfried Hecker, Director, Los Alamos National Laboratory*, Hearing before the Senate Committee on Armed Services, 27 March 1992, Government Printing Office, Washington, D.C.
90 Isaacs, J. (1991), 'What a Difference a Year Makes', *Bulletin of the Atomic Scientists*, vol. 47, no. 1 (January/February 1991); Rowberg, R. (2001), 'The Department of Energy's Tritium Production Program', *CRS Report for Congress*, 8 November 2001, Congressional Research Service, Washington, D.C., pp. 3–4.
91 Watkins, J. (1992), *Testimony of Admiral James D. Watkins, Secretary of Energy U.S. Department of Energy*, Hearing before the Senate Committee on Armed Services, 6 May 1992, Government Printing Office, Washington, D.C. For details see Tuck, J. (1991), *Testimony of John Tuck, Under Secretary of Energy*, Hearing before the Senate Committee on Governmental Affairs, 25 February 1991, Government Printing Office, Washington, D.C., pp. 72–76.
92 Claytor, R. (1992), *Testimony of Richard A. Claytor, Assistant Secretary of Energy for Defense Programs*, Hearing before the Senate Committee on Governmental Affairs, 25 February 1992, Government Printing Office, Washington, D.C.
93 Claytor, R. (1992), *Testimony of Richard Claytor*, Hearing before the House of Representatives Committee on Armed Services, 30 April 1992, Government Printing Office, Washington, D.C., p. 14.
94 Norris, R. and Arkin, W. (1991), 'Beating Swords into Swords', *Bulletin of the Atomic Scientists*, vol. 46, no. 10 (November 1991); Herzfeld, C. (1991), *Testimony of Dr. Charles Herzfeld, Director of Defense Research and Engineering and Chairman of the Council*, Hearing before the House of Representatives Committee on Armed Services, 6 March 1991, Government Printing Office, Washington, D.C., p. 53.
95 Albright, Zamora and Lewis, 'Turn off Rocky Flats'.
96 Jeremiah, *Testimony by Adm. David E. Jeremiah*, 30 April 1992, p. 1010.
97 Gaffney, F. (1991), *Self-Imposed Structural Disarmament: The Sorry State of the DOE Weapons Complex*, Hearing before the House of Representatives Committee on Armed Services, 18 April 1991, Government Printing Office, Washington, D.C., p. 818; Thurmond, S. (1991), *Testimony of Hon. Strom Thurmond, U.S. Senator from the State of South Carolina*, Hearing before the Senate Committee on Governmental Affairs, 25 February 1991, Government Printing Office, Washington, D.C., p. 3.
98 Albright, *Testimony of David Albright*, p. 828.
99 Dowler, T. and Howard, J. (1991), 'Countering the Well Armed Tyrant: a Modest Proposal for Small Nuclear Weapons', *Strategic Review*, vol. 19, no. 4.
100 Arkin, W. (1993), 'Nuclear Junkies: Those Lovable Little Bombs', *Bulletin of the Atomic Scientists*, vol. 49, no. 6 (July/August 1993).
101 Fenstermacher, D. (1991), 'Arms Race, the Next Generation', *Bulletin of the Atomic Scientists*, vol. 47, no. 2 (March 1991).
102 Reed *Testimony of Thomas C. Reed*, p. 401; Barker, R. (1990), *Testimony of Robert B. Barker, Assistant to the Secretary of Defense (Atomic Energy)*, Hearing before the Senate Committee on Armed Services, 17 September 1990, Government Printing Office, Washington, D.C., p. 45.
103 *Cheney*, *Testimony by Richard B. Cheney, Secretary of Defense*, 28 July 1992, p. 16; Watkins, *Testimony of Admiral James D. Watkins*, 6 May 1992.
104 Barker, R. (1992), *Testimony by Robert B. Barker, Assistant to the Secretary of Defense (Atomic Energy)*, Hearing before the Senate Committee on Armed Services, 27 March 1992, Government Printing Office, Washington, D.C., pp. 43–44; Tuck, *Testimony of John C. Tuck, Acting Assistant Secretary for Defense Programs*, 23 May 1990, p. 171.

105 Barker, *Testimony by Robert B. Barker*, 27 March 1992, p. 147.

106 Lehman, R. F. (1990), *Testimony of Robert F. Lehman, Director, U.S. Arms Control and Disarmament Agency*, Hearing before the Senate Committee on Armed Services, 17 September 1990, Government Printing Office, Washington, D.C., p. 151; Barker, R. (1991), *Testimony of Robert B. Barker, Assistant to the Secretary of Defense (Atomic Energy)*, Hearing before the Senate Committee on Armed Services, 9 May 1991, Government Printing Office, Washington, D.C., p. 81.

107 Fascell, D. B. (1990), 'Conference Report on H.R. 4739, National Defense Authorization Act for Fiscal Year 1991', *Congressional Record (House of Representatives)*, 24 October 1990, p. H13516; Green, S. W. (1990), 'National Defense Authorization Act Fiscal Year 1991', *Congressional Record (House of Representatives)*, 11 September 1990, p. H7318; Markey, E. (1990), 'In Support of the Bosco Amendment', *Congressional Record (Extension of Remarks)*, 19 September 1990, p. E2934.

108 Mitchell, G. (1992), 'Energy and Water Development Appropriations Act', *Congressional Record (Senate)*, 3 August 1992, p. S11171.

109 Fascell, 'Conference Report on H.R. 4739', p. H13516; Harkin, T. (1991), 'Senate Concurrent Resolution 1 – Relative to Underground Nuclear Explosions', *Congressional Record (Senate)*, 16 January 1991, p. S961; Gorton, S. (1990), 'Threshold Test Ban and Peaceful Nuclear Explosions Treaties', *Congressional Record (Extension of Remarks)*, 1 October 1990, p. S14299.

110 Kopetski, M. (1992), 'Nuclear Weapons Testing Must Come to a Stop', *Congressional Record (House of Representatives)*, 25 March 1992, p. H1723; Mitchell, G. (1992), 'The Latest U.S. Nuclear Test', *Congressional Record (Senate)*, 23 June 1992, p. S8577. On the new policy see Cheney, *Testimony by Richard B. Cheney, Secretary of Defense*, 28 July 1992, p. 17; Barker, *Testimony by Robert B. Barker*, 27 March 1992, p. 146.

111 Mitchell, 'Energy and Water Development Appropriations Act', p. S11180.

112 Isaacs, J. (1992), 'Reports: Nuclear Testing: the Senate that can say No', *Bulletin of the Atomic Scientists*, vol. 48, no. 8 (October 1992); Iakimets, V. and Suleimenov, O. (1992), 'New Tests Means New Nukes', *Bulletin of the Atomic Scientists*, vol. 48, no. 8 (October 1992). For details of the legislation and the vote see Representative Fascell, D. B. (1992), 'U.S. Arms Control Policy in the Post Cold War Era', *Congressional Record (Extension of Remarks)*, 3 October 1992, p. E2949.

113 See statement by John Nuckolls, Director of Lawrence Livermore National Laboratory in Nuckolls, J. (1990), *Testimony of John Nuckolls*, Hearing before the House of Representatives Committee on Armed Services, 27 February 1990, Government Printing Office, Washington, D.C., p. 168.

114 In Paulsen, *The Role of Nuclear Weapons in the Post-Cold War Era*, p. 44.

115 For example the 1991 National Academy of Sciences study, *The Future of the US-Soviet Nuclear Relationship*, proposed a radical a reduction in nuclear forces to between 1,000 and 3,000 weapons. Rothstein, L. (1991), 'Reports', *Bulletin of the Atomic Scientists*, vol. 47, no. 9 (November 1991).

4 Nuclear weapons policy under Bill Clinton

1 Lockwood, D. (1993), 'On Clinton's Calendar', *Bulletin of the Atomic Scientists*, vol. 49, no. 1 (January/February).

2 See statement by head of Strategic Command Admiral Chiles, H. G. (1995), *Questions and Responses, Adm. Henry G. Chiles, USN, Commander in Chief, U.S. Strategic Command*, testimony before the Senate Committee on Armed Services, 23 February 1995, Government Printing Office, Washington, D.C.

3 (1994), Nuclear Forces, Post-1994, Strategic Advisory Group paper for Henry Chiles, Commander, Strategic Command (ed.).

4 Kaminski, P. (1995), 'Sustaining the U.S. Nuclear Deterrent in the 21st Century', *Prepared remarks of Paul G. Kaminski, Undersecretary of Defense for Acquisition and Technology, at the U.S. Strategic Command Strategic Systems Industrial Symposium, Offutt Air Force Base, 30 August 1995*, Department of Defense, Washington, D.C.

5 (1993), 'Doctrine for Joint Nuclear Operations', Joint Chiefs of Staff, Washington, D.C., p. II-2.

6 Perry, W. (1995), *Annual Report to the President and the Congress*, Washington, D.C., Department of Defense; Bleek, P. (2000), 'Joint Chiefs of Staff 'Uncomfortable' With START III Reductions Below 2,000–2,500', *Arms Control Today*, vol. 30, no. 5 (June 2000); Butler, G. L. (1993), *Prepared Posture Statement of Gen. Lee Butler, Commander in Chief, United States Strategic Command*, Hearing before the Senate Committee on Armed Services, 22 April 1993, Government Printing Office, Washington, D.C., p. 406.

7 Arkin, W. and Norris, R. (1997), 'Nuclear Notebook: U.S. Strategic Forces, End of 1996', *Bulletin of the Atomic Scientists*, vol. 53, no. 1 (January/February 1997).

8 Arkin, W. and Norris, R. (2000), 'Nuclear Notebook: U.S. Nuclear Forces 2000', *Bulletin of the Atomic Scientists*, vol. 56, no. 3 (May/June 2000).

9 Kaminski, P. and Fiester, C. (1995), *DOD News Briefing*, Department of Defense, Washington, D.C. Retrieved from http://www.defenselink.mil/transcripts/1995/t020795_tkaminsk.html; Perry, W. (1994), *Questions and Answers*, Hearing before the Senate Committee on Armed Services, 2 February 1994, Government Printing Office, Washington, D.C.; Woolf, A. (1997), 'Nuclear Weapons in U.S. Defense Policy: Issues for Congress', July 1997, CRS Issue Brief, Congressional Research Service, Washington, D.C.

10 Kristensen, H. (2001), *The Matrix of Deterrence: U.S. Strategic Command Force Structure Studies*, Berkeley, CA, The Nautilus Institute; Kristensen, H. (2001), 'The Unruly Hedge: Cold War Thinking at the Crawford Summit', *Arms Control Today*, vol. 31, no. 10 (December 2001).

11 Cohen, W. (1997), *Nuclear Weapon Systems Sustainment Programs*, Washington, D.C., Office of the Secretary of Defense.

12 Mello, G. (1998), 'That Old Designing Fever', *Bulletin of the Atomic Scientists*, vol. 56, no. 1 (January/February 2000); Perry, W. (1996), *Annual Report to the President and the Congress*, Washington, D.C., Department of Defense; Chiles, *Questions and Responses, Adm. Henry G. Chiles*, 23 February 1995.

13 (1998), 'Report of the Defense Science Board Task Force on Nuclear Deterrence', October 1998, Department of Defense, Washington, D.C.

14 See Cohen, *Nuclear Weapon Systems Sustainment Programs*; Arkin, W. (2001), 'Nuclear Notebook', *Bulletin of the Atomic Scientists*, vol. 57, no. 2 (March/April 2001).

15 Chelimsky, E. (1992), *'The US Nuclear Triad: GAO's Evaluation of the Strategic Modernization Program', Statement of Eleanor Chelimsky, Assistant Comptroller General, Program Evaluation and Methodology Division*, Washington, D.C., U.S. General Accounting Office; Fascell, D. B. (1992), 'The U.S. Strategic Nuclear Triad', *Congressional Record (Extension of Remarks)*, 21 July 1992, p. E2179.

16 Perry, W. (1997), *Testimony of William J. Perry*, Hearing before the Senate Committee on Governmental Affairs, 10 June 1997, Government Printing Office, Washington, D.C., p. 51.

17 Habiger, E. E. (1997), *Questions and Responses*, Hearing before the Senate Committee on Armed Services, 13 March 1997, Government Printing Office, Washington, D.C.; Mies, R. W. (2000), *Questions and Reponses, Adm. Richard W. Mies, USN, Commander in Chief, United States Strategic Command*, Hearing before the Senate Committee on Armed Services, 23 May 2000, Government Printing Office, Washington, D.C.

18 Owens, W. A. and Deutch, J. (1994), *Questions and Responses, Adm. William A. Owens, USN, Vice Chairman, Joint Chiefs of Staff, Dr. John Deutch, Deputy Secretary of Defense*, Hearing before the Senate Committee on Armed Services, 22 September 1994, Government Printing Office, Washington, D.C., p. 9.

19 (1994), 'Press Conference with Secretary of Defense William J. Perry, General Shalikashvili, Chairman JCS, Deputy Secretary of Defense John Deutch, Kenneth Bacon, ATSD-PA', 22 September 1994, Department of Defense, Washington, D.C.; Tolin, T. (1994), *Nuclear Posture Review Key Issues, Brig. Gen. Tony Tolin, Deputy Director, Strategy and Policy, J5*, Retrieved from http://www.nautilus.org/archives/nukestrat/USA/Npr/jcssag031594.pdf.

20 Krepinevich, A. F. and Kosia, S. M. (1998), 'Smarter Bombs, Fewer Nukes', *Bulletin of the Atomic Scientists*, vol. 54, no. 6 (November/December 1998).

21 (1998), *U.S. Commitment to the Treaty on the Non-Proliferation of Nuclear Weapons, 22 April 1998*, Department of State, Washington, D.C. Retrieved from http://dosfan.lib.uic.edu/acda/factshee/wmd/nuclear/npt/commnpt.htm on 12 January 2005; 'Press Conference with Secretary of Defense William J. Perry, General Shalikashvili, Chairman JCS, Deputy Secretary of Defense John Deutch, Kenneth Bacon, ATSD-PA', Department of Defense.

22 (1994), *DOD Recommends Reduction in Nuclear Force, 22 September 1994*, U.S. Department of Defense, Washington, D.C. Retrieved from http://www.nautilus.org/archives/nukestrat/USA/Npr/dodpr092294.pdf.

23 Carey, B. (1994), *U.S. Adopting New Nuclear Weapons Policy, 23 September 1994*, U.S. Information Agency, Washington, D.C. Retrieved from http://www.globalsecurity.org/wmd/library/news/usa/1994/77054321–77059383.htm on 24 February 2007.

24 Nuclear Forces, Post-1994. Strategic Advisory Group.

25 Arkin, W. and Norris, R. (1995), 'Nuclear Notebook: U.S. Nuclear Weapons Stockpile, July 1995', *Bulletin of the Atomic Scientists*, vol. 51, no. 4 (July/August).

26 Woolf, A. (2004), 'U.S. Nuclear Weapons: Changes in Policy and Force Structure', February 2004, Congressional Research Service, Washington, D.C., p. 30; Arkin, W. and Norris, R. (1995), 'Nuclear Notebook: U.S. Strategic Forces, End of 1994', *Bulletin of the Atomic Scientists*, vol. 51, no. 1 (January/February 1995); Arkin and Norris, 'Nuclear Notebook: U.S. Strategic Forces, End of 1996'.

27 Woolf, A. (2004), 'Non-Strategic Nuclear Weapons', September 2004, Congressional Research Service, Washington, D.C.

28 (2004), *History of the United States Strategic Command: 1 June 1992–2 October 2002*, Offut Air Force Base, Nebraska, Strategic Command, p. 33.

29 (1995), *Nuclear Posture Review [extract from the 1995 Annual Defense Report]*, Federation of American Scientists, Washington, D.C. Retrieved from http://www.fas.org/nuke/guide/usa/doctrine/dod/95_npr.htm on 5 February 2003.

30 (1994), *Overview of Nuclear Posture Review (NPR) Results, 22 September 1994*, Strategic Command, Retrieved from http://www.nukestrat.com/us/reviews/usstratcom0994.pdf on 23 February 2007.

31 Deutch, J. (1994), *Additional written answers by the Department of Defense*, Hearing before the Senate Committee on Armed Services, 22 September 1994, Government Printing Office, Washington, D.C.

32 (1995), 'A National Security Strategy of Engagement and Enlargement', The White House, Washington, D.C.

33 Cohen, W. (1997), *Report of the Quadrennial Defense Review*, Washington, D.C., Office of the Secretary of Defense, U.S. Department of Defense; Cohen, W. (1997), 'Special: The Secretary's Message – Report of the Quadrennial Defense Review', *Joint Force Quarterly*, vol. 17, Summer 1997, p. 12.

34 (1997), 'A National Security Strategy for A New Century', The White House, Washington, D.C.

35 (1998), 'A National Security Strategy for A New Century', The White House, Washington, D.C.
36 Aspin, L. (1990), 'From Deterrence to Denuking: Dealing with Proliferation in the 1990s', *House Armed Services Committee*, February 18, 1990; Cimbala, S. (1996), *Clinton and Post-Cold War Defense*, Westport, CT, Praeger, p. 54.
37 Deutch, J. (1994), *Questions and Responses, Dr. John Deutch, nominee to be Deputy Secretary of Defense*, Hearing before the Senate Committee on Armed Services, 10 March 1994, Government Printing Office, Washington, D.C., p. 423. See exchange between Deutch and Senator Carl Levin in Owens and Deutch, *Questions and Responses, Adm. William A. Owens, Dr. John Deutch*, 22 September 1994.
38 Perry, *Annual Report to the President and the Congress.*
39 'Press Conference with Secretary of Defense William J. Perry, General Shalikashvili, Chairman JCS, Deputy Secretary of Defense John Deutch, Kenneth Bacon, ATSD-PA', Department of Defense.
40 Sauer, T. (2005), *Nuclear Inertia: US Nuclear Weapons Policy after the Cold War*, London, I.B. Taurus, pp. 11–14.
41 Nolan, J. E. (1999), *An Elusive Consensus: Nuclear Weapons and American Security After the Cold War*, Washington D.C., Brookings Institution Press, pp, 41–58; Daalder, I. (1995), 'What Vision for the Nuclear Future?' *The Washington Quarterly*, vol. 18, no. 2, p. 128; Krepon, M. (2001), 'Moving Away from MAD', *Survival*, vol. 43, no. 2 (Summer 2001), p. 86.
42 Boldrick, M. R. (1995), 'The Nuclear Posture Review: Liabilities and Risks', *Parameters*, vol. XXV, no. 4. For statements by Butler see Butler, G. L. (1996), *Speech to the National Press Club, Washington, D.C., 4 December 1996*, Retrieved from http://www.wagingpeace.org/articles/1996/12/04_butler_abolition-speech.htm on 12 March 2007 and Butler, G. L. (1997), 'The General's Bombshell: Phasing out the U.S. Nuclear Arsenal', *The Washington Quarterly*, vol. 20, no. 3. On Horner see Schell, J. (1998), *The Gift of Time*, London, Granta Books.
43 (1996), *Report of the Canberra Commission on the Elimination of Nuclear Weapons*, Canberra, Commonwealth of Australia, p. 9.
44 (1996), *Legality of the Threat or use of Nuclear Weapons, Advisory Opinion of 8 July 1996*, International Court of Justice, The Hague. Retrieved from http://www.icj-cij.org/icjwww/idecisions/isummaries/iunanaummary960708.htm on 4 April 2007.
45 Gormley, D. and Mahnken, T. (2000), 'Facing Nuclear and Conventional Reality', *Orbis*, vol. 44, no. 1, pp. 110–112.
46 Cimbala, *Clinton and Post-Cold War Defense*, p. 58.
47 Payne, K. (1998), *Testimony by Dr. Keith Payne*, Hearing before the Senate Committee on Armed Services, 31 March 1998, Government Printing Office, Washington, D.C., p. 503; On Thurmond's views see (1994), *Briefing on the Results of the Nuclear Posture Review*, Hearing before the Senate Committee on Armed Services, 22 September 1994, 22 September 1994, Government Printing Office, Washington, D.C., pp. 3–4.
48 Carter, A., Perry, W. *et al.* (1992), *A New Concept of Cooperative Security*, Washington, D.C., The Brookings Institution, p. 12.
49 Clinton, W. J. (1995), 'Remarks to the Nixon Center for Peace and Freedom Policy Conference 1 March 1995', *Weekly Compilation of Presidential Documents, vol. 31*, no. *9, pp. 315–359*, Government Printing Office, Washington, D.C.; Levin, C. (1996), 'Treaty with the Russian Federation on Further Reduction and Limitation of Strategic Offensive Arms (The START II Treaty)', *Congressional Record (Senate)*, 26 January 1996, p. S483.
50 Maintaining nuclear forces at START II levels would require substantial investment to replace ageing strategic nuclear delivery vehicles. Moscow's preference was to move immediately to START III levels of 1,500–2,000 warheads, well below

START II. Habiger, E. E. (1997), *DOD News Briefing, 4 November 1997, Commander-in-Chief, Strategic Command, Press Conference*, U.S. Department of Defense, Washington, D.C. Retrieved from http://www.defenselink.mil/transcripts/1997/t11071997_thabiger.html on 2 March 2007.

51 Bunn, G. and Rhinelander, J. (1997), 'The Duma-Senate Logjam on Arms Control: What Can Be Done?' *Non-Proliferation Review*, vol. 5, no. 1, p. 74.

52 Graham, T. (1993), *Testimony of Thomas Graham, Jr*, Hearing before the Senate Committee on Foreign Relations, 18 May 1993, Government Printing Office, Washington, D.C., p. 33; Sorokin, K. (1994), 'Russia After the Crisis: the Nuclear Strategy Debate', *Orbis*, vol. 38, no. 1, pp. 30–33.

53 Lepingwell, J. (1995), 'START II and the Politics of Arms Control in Russia', *International Security*, vol. 20, no. 2; Mendelsohn, J. (1997), 'The Current and Future US-Russian Nuclear Arms Control Agenda', *Disarmament Diplomacy*, vol. 19 (October 1997).

54 Kyl, J. (1995), 'Treaty with the Russian Federation on Further Reduction and Limitation of Strategic Offensive Arms (The START II Treaty)', *Congressional Record (Senate)*, 22 December 1995, p. S19213; Helms, J. (1999), 'National Missile Defense Act of 1999', *Congressional Record (Senate)*, 5 March 1999, p. S2630.

55 Thurmond, S. (1995), 'Treaty with the Russian Federation on Further Reduction and Limitation of Strategic Offensive Arms (The START II Treaty)', *Congressional Record (Senate)*, 22 December 1995, p. S19209.

56 Cohen, S. (2006), 'The New American Cold War', *The Nation*, 10 July 2006; Aubin, S. (2001), 'Clinton's Legacy of Strategic Instability', *Strategic Review*, vol. 29, no. 2, p. 34; Walt, S. M. (2000), 'Two Cheers for Clinton's Foreign Policy', *Foreign Affairs*, vol. 79, no. 2, p. 70.

57 Lepingwell 'START II and the Politics of Arms Control in Russia', p. 90; Pushkov, A. (1993), 'Letter from Eurasia: Russia and America: the Honeymoon's Over', *Foreign Policy*, no. 93 (Winter 1993/1994).

58 (1997), 'Russia–United States Joint Statement on Parameters on Future Reduction in Nuclear Forces, 21 March 1997', *Weekly Compilation of Presidential Documents, vol. 33*, no. *12, pp. 373–397*, Government Printing Office, Washington, D.C.

59 Holum, J. D. (1997), *Statement of John D. Holum, Director U.S. Arms Control And Disarmament Agency to the United Nations General Assembly in the First Committee General Debate, 14 October 1997*, U.S. Department of State, Washington, D.C. Retrieved from http://dosfan.lib.uic.edu/acda/speeches/holum/unga1.htm on 5 March 2007. See also the statement by Russian Defense Minister Igor Rodionov in (1997), *DoD News Briefing, Secretary of Defense William S. Cohen, May 13, 1997*, U.S. Department of Defense, Washington, D.C. Retrieved from http://www.defenselink.mil/transcripts/1997/t051397_t0513coh.html on 3 March 2007.

60 Helms, J. (2000), 'Negotiations with Russia on a Revised U.S.-Soviet ABM Treaty', *Congressional Record (Senate)*, 26 April 2000, p. S2895.

61 *History of the United States Strategic Command*, Strategic Command, p. 58; Bunn and Rhinelander, 'The Duma–Senate Logjam on Arms Control', p. 81.

62 Krepon, M. (2003), *Cooperative Threat Reduction, Missile Defense and the Nuclear Future*, New York, Palgrave Macmillan, p. 33.

63 Habiger, E. E. (1996), *Questions and Responses*, Hearing before the Senate Committee on Armed Services, 1 February 1996, Government Printing Office, Washington, D.C., p. 80; 'Report of the Defense Science Board Task Force on Nuclear Deterrence', p. 15.

64 Chiles, *Questions and Responses, Adm. Henry G. Chiles*, 23 February 1995; Christopher, W. (1995), *Testimony of Secretary of State Christopher*, Hearing before the Senate Committee on Foreign Relations, 31 January 1995, Government Printing Office, Washington, D.C., p. 10.

65 Holum, J. D. (1995), *Testimony of John D. Holum*, Hearing before the Senate Committee on Foreign Relations, 31 January 1995, Government Printing Office, Washington, D.C., p. 35.

66 *U.S. Commitment to the Treaty on the Non-Proliferation of Nuclear Weapons*, Department of State.

67 Christopher, *Testimony of Secretary of State Christopher*, 31 January, 1995, p. 12; Dorgan, B. (1999), 'National Missile Defense Act of 1999', *Congressional Record (Senate)*, 16 March 1999, p. S471.

68 Graham, *Testimony of Thomas Graham, Jr*, 18 May 1993, p. 33; Slocombe, W. (1995), *Testimony of Walter B. Slocombe, Under Secretary of Defense for Policy*, 17 May 1995, Government Printing Office, Washington, D.C., p. 14.

69 Perry, W. and Shalikashvili, J. M. (1995), 'Support START II's Nuclear Reductions', *Defense Issues*, vol. 10, no. 25.

70 (1994), 'Moscow Declaration, 14 January 1994', *Weekly Compilation of Presidential Documents, vol. 30*, no. *3, pp. 55–134*, Government Printing Office, Washington, D.C.; Butler *Prepared Posture Statement of Gen. Lee Butler*, 22 April 1993, p. 406.

71 Habiger, E. E. (1997), *Testimony of Gen. Eugene E. Habiger, U.S. Air Force, Commander in Chief, U.S. Strategic Command*, Hearing before the Senate Committee on Armed Services, 13 March 1997, Government Printing Office, Washington, D.C., p. 725.

72 *History of the United States Strategic Command*, Strategic Command, p. 49.

73 (1997), *PDD/NSC 60: Nuclear Weapons Employment Policy Guidance, November 1997*, Federation of American Scientists, Washington, D.C. Retrieved from http://www.fas.org/irp/offdocs/pdd60.htm on 3 March 2007.

74 Arkin, W. and Kristensen, H. (1998), 'Dangerous Directions', *Bulletin of the Atomic Scientists*, vol. 54, no. 2 (March/April 1998); Cerniello, C. (1997), 'Clinton Issues New Guidelines on U.S. Nuclear Weapons Doctrine', *Arms Control Today*, vol. 27, no. 8 (November/December 1997); Payne, K. (1998), 'Post-Cold War Requirements for U.S. Nuclear Deterrence Policy', *Comparative Strategy*, vol. 17, no. 3 (July–September 1998), p. 252.

75 Kristensen, H. (2003), *Changing Targets II: A Chronology of U.S. Nuclear Policy Against Weapons of Mass Destruction*, Washington, D.C., Greenpeace, p. 4.

76 Clinton, W. J. (1998), 'Remarks Prior to Discussions with Prime Minister Ryutaro Hashimoto of Japan and an Exchange with Reporters in Birmingham, United Kingdom, 15 May 1998', Government Printing Office, Washington, D.C.; (2000), 'Joint Statement: Strategic Stability Cooperation Initiative Between the United States of America and Russian Federation, 6 September 2000', *Weekly Compilation of Presidential Documents, vol. 36*, no. *36, pp. 1997–2024*, Government Printing Office, Washington, D.C.

77 Starr, B. (1998), 'New US-Russian Arms Control Talks Imminent', *Jane's Defence Weekly*, vol. 29, no. 10 (11 March 1998), p. 3.

78 For an outline of the issues to be negotiated under a START III see Mendelsohn, 'The Current and Future US-Russian Nuclear Arms Control Agenda'.

79 See Holum, J. D. (1998), *Remarks to the Carnegie Moscow Center Moscow by John D. Holum, Director, Arms Control And Disarmament Agency, 23 April 1998*, U.S. Arms Control and Disarmament Agency, Washington, D.C. Retrieved from http://dosfan.lib.uic.edu/acda/speeches/holum/moscow.htm on 3 March 2007; Mies, R. W. (2000), *Testimony of Adm. Richard W. Mies, USN, Commander in Chief, United States Strategic Command*, Hearing before the Senate Committee on Armed Services, 23 May 2000, Government Printing Office, Washington, D.C., p. 11; Habiger, E. E. (1998), *Testimony of Gen. Eugene E. Habiger, U.S. Air Force, Commander in Chief, U.S. Strategic Command*, Hearing before the Senate Committee on Armed Services, 31 March 1998, Government Printing Office, Washington, D.C., p. 534.

80 (2000), *Questions submitted by Senator John Warner*, Hearing before the Senate Committee on Armed Services, 23 May 2000, Government Printing Office, Washington, D.C., p. 38; Koch, A. (2000), 'DOD Seeks Arms Limit Changes', *Jane's Defence Weekly*, vol. 33, no. 22 (31 May 2000).

81 Habiger, *Testimony of Gen. Eugene E. Habiger, U.S. Air Force, Commander in Chief, U.S. Strategic Command*, p. 658; Slocombe, W. (2000), *Testimony of Walter B. Slocombe, Under Secretary of Defense for Policy*, 23 May 2000, Government Printing Office, Washington, D.C., p. 8.

82 Kerrey, B. (2000), 'Nuclear Weapons', *Congressional Record (Senate)*, 4 April 2000, p. S2139.

83 Younger, S. (2000), 'Nuclear Weapons in the 21st Century', Los Alamos National Laboratory, Los Alamos, NM.

84 Kerrey, B. (1999), 'National Defense Authorization Act for Fiscal Year 2000', *Congressional Record (Senate)*, 26 May 1999, pp. S5990–S5991; Levin, C. (1999), 'National Defense Authorization Act for Fiscal Year 2000', *Congressional Record (Senate)*, 26 May 1999, p. S6022; Domenici, P. (1998), 'Nuclear Issues', *Congressional Record (Senate)*, 11 February 1998, p. S635.

85 Furse, E. (1995), 'Cuts in Nuclear Arsenals Needed', *Congressional Record (Extension of Remarks)*, 9 May 1995, p. E982.

86 (1997), *The Future of U.S. Nuclear Weapons Policy*, Washington, D.C., National Academy Press.

87 (1997), 'Transforming Defense: National Security in the 21st Century', 1 December 1997, National Defense Panel, Washington, D.C., p. 50.

88 Kerrey, 'National Defense Authorization Act for Fiscal Year 2000', p. S5991.

89 Perry, W. (1994), *Testimony of William J. Perry*, Hearing before the Senate Committee on Armed Services, 2 February 1994, Government Printing Office, Washington, D.C., p. 101.

90 Owens and Deutch, *Questions and Responses, Adm. William A. Owens, Dr. John Deutch*, 22 September 1994, p. 58; Bailey, K. C. and Barish, F. (1999), 'De-alerting of U.S. Nuclear Forces: a Critical Appraisal', *Comparative Strategy*, vol. 18, no. 1, p. 6.

91 Owens and Deutch, *Questions and Responses, Adm. William A. Owens, Dr. John Deutch*, 22 September 1994, p. 58; Mies, R. W. (1998), *Questions and Responses*, Hearing before the Senate Committee on Armed Services, 31 March 1998, Government Printing Office, Washington, D.C., p. 364.

92 (1996), 'National Defense Authorization Act for Fiscal Year 1997', *Congressional Record (Senate)*, 18 June 1996, p. S6321; (1996), 'Treaty with the Russian Federation on Further Reduction and Limitation of Strategic Offensive Arms (The START II Treaty)', *Congressional Record (Senate)*, 26 January 1996, p. S461.

93 See Bacon, K. H. (1997), *DOD News Briefing: Mr. Kenneth H. Bacon, ASD (PA), 1 April 1997*, U.S. Department of Defense, Washington, D.C. Retrieved from http://www.defenselink.mil/transcripts/1997/t040197_t0401asd.html on 23 February 2005; (1997), *Report of the Quadrennial Defense Review*, Department of Defense, Washington, D.C. Retrieved from http://www.defenselink.mil/pubs/qdr/ on 2 March 2007, Section III.

94 Kerrey, B. (2000), 'National Defense Authorization Act for Fiscal Year 2001', *Congressional Record (Senate)*, 6 June 2000, pp. S4543–46; Woolf, A. (2001), 'U.S. Nuclear Weapons: Policy, Force Structure and Arms Control Issues', 12 January 2001, Congressional Research Service, Washington, D.C., p. 21; (1999), 'USA Sets Sights on Unilateral Nuclear Cuts', *Jane's Defence Weekly*, vol. 31, no. 2 (13 January 1999), p. 63. On the costs involved see Warner, E. (1999), *Testimony of Edward L. Warner, III, Assistant Secretary of Defense for Strategy and Threat Reduction*, 14 April 1999, Government Printing Office, Washington, D.C., p. 359 and Senator Kerrey, B. (1999), 'The Department of Defense Appropriations Bill for Fiscal Year 2000', *Congressional Record (Senate)*, 9 June 1999, p. S6781.

95 Clinton, W. J. (1993), 'The President's News Conference, 23 March 1993', *Weekly Compilation of Presidential Documents vol. 29*, no. *12, pp. 457–501*, Government Printing Office, Washington, D.C.

96 Clinton, W. J. (1993), *Background Briefing by Senior Administration Official, 31 March 1993*, The White House, Washington, D.C. Retrieved from http://clinton6.nara.gov/1993/03/1993–03–31-background-briefing-on-yeltsin-summit.html on 1 March 2006.

97 'Moscow Declaration, 14 January 1994', Government Printing Office.

98 (1998), 'Joint Statement on Common Security Challenges at the Threshold of the Twenty-First Century, 2 September 1998', *Weekly Compilation of Presidential Documents, vol. 34*, no. *36, pp. 1667–1730*, Government Printing Office, Washington, D.C.

99 'Joint Statement: Strategic Stability Cooperation Initiative', Government Printing Office.

100 Perry, W. (1995), *'Pursuing a Strategy of Mutual Assured Safety', Remarks delivered by Secretary of Defense William Perry, National Press Club, 5 January 1995*, Department of Defense, Washington, D.C. Retrieved from http://www.defenselink.mil/Speeches/Speech.aspx?SpeechID=817 on 12 February 2007; DeLaski, K. (1994), *U.S. Detargets all Strategic Nuclear Missiles*, U.S. Department of Defense, Washington, D.C. Retrieved from http://www.globalsecurity.org/wmd/library/news/usa/1994/8690221–8693415.htm on 22 February 2007; (1995), *1995 Annual Report of the U.S. Arms Control and Disarmament Agency*, Arms Control and Disarmament Agency, Washington, D.C. Retrieved from http://dosfan.lib.uic.edu/acda/reports/chap1.htm on 2 March 2007.

101 Habiger, E. E. (1996), *Testimony of Gen. Eugene E. Habiger, USAF, Commander in Chief, U.S. Strategic Command*, Hearing before the Senate Committee on Armed Services, 21 March 1996, Government Printing Office, Washington, D.C.; *History of the United States Strategic Command*, p. 51; Habiger, E. E. (1998), *DOD News Briefing, Tuesday, 16 June 1998, General Eugene Habiger, Commander of U.S. Strategic Command*, U.S. Department of Defense, Washington, D.C. Retrieved from http://www.defenselink.mil/transcripts/1998/t06231998_t616hab2.html on 23 February 2007.

102 Payne, K. (1997), *Testimony of Keith Payne, President, National Institute for Public Policy*, Hearing before the Senate Committee on Governmental Affairs, 13 March 1997, Government Printing Office, Washington, D.C., p. 11; Flournoy, M. and Murdock, C. (1998), *Revitalizing the U.S. Nuclear Deterrent*, Washington, D.C., Center for Strategic and International Studies, p. 31.

103 Shalikashvili, J. M. (1994), 'Speech at the Retired Officers' Association, Cincinnati, Ohio, 26 September 1994', U.S. Joint Chiefs of Staff, Washington, D.C.

104 Perry, *Annual Report to the President and the Congress.*

105 Mies, R. W. (1999), *Testimony by Adm. Richard W. Mies, USN, Commander in Chief, United States Strategic Command*, Hearing before the Senate Committee on Armed Services on, 14 April 1999, Government Printing Office, Washington, D.C. p. 364; 'Report of the Defense Science Board Task Force on Nuclear Deterrence', p. 13.

106 Lepingwell, 'START II and the Politics of Arms Control in Russia', pp. 72–73; Sorokin, 'Russia After the Crisis', pp. 24–26; Sokov, N. (1996), 'Russia's Approach to Nuclear Weapons', *The Washington Quarterly*, vol. 23, no. 3, p. 109. It was reported that in 1997 Yeltsin approved a new military doctrine that explicitly authorised the first-use of Russian nuclear weapons in response to a major conventional attack. Benson, S. (1998), 'Competing Views on Strategic Arms Reduction', *Orbis*, vol. 42, no. 4, p. 596. Berlin, D. (2001), 'The Growing Nuclear Weapons Threat: An Assessment of U.S. Strategic Options', *Strategic Review*, vol. 29, no. 2, p. 26.

107 Lake, A. (1995), 'A Year of Decision: Arms Control and Nonproliferation in 1995', *Non-Proliferation Review*, vol. 2, no. 2, p. 55; Nolan, *An Elusive Consensus*, p. 72.

108 Carey, B. (1993), *U.S. Begins 'Counter-Proliferation' Against Mass Weapons, 7 December 1993*, U.S. Information Agency, Washington, D.C. Retrieved from http://www.globalsecurity.org/wmd/library/news/usa/1993/45215398–45219581.htm on 24 February 2007.

109 Shalikashvili, J. M. (1998), '"Strategy for the 90's: Building on the Past – Looking to the Future", Remarks at the National Defense University, Fort McNair, 2 February 1994', U.S. Joint Chiefs of Staff, Washington, D.C. See also Cohen, W. (1997), *Annual Report to the President and the Congress*, Washington, D.C., Department of Defense and Shalikashvili, J. M. (1997), *National Military Strategy, 1997: Shape, Respond, Prepare Now – A Military Strategy for a New Era*, Washington, D.C., U.S. Joint Chiefs of Staff.

110 Perry, W. (1996), *Proliferation: Threat and Response*, Washington, D.C., Department of Defense; Perry, W. (1996), *DOD News Briefing, Secretary of Defense William J. Perry, 11 April 1996*, Department of Defense, Washington, D.C. Retrieved from http://www.defenselink.mil/transcripts/1996/t041196_t0411asd.html on 23 February 2005.

111 Aspin, L. (1993), *Speech to the National Academy of Sciences, 7 December 1993*. Retrieved from http://www.fas.org/irp/offdocs/pdd18.htm on 12 February 2007; Cambone, S. and Garrity, P. (1994), 'The Future of U.S. Nuclear Policy', *Survival*, vol. 36, no. 4 (Winter 1994/1995), pp. 88–89.

112 'Doctrine for Joint Nuclear Operations', pp. I–3; (1996), 'Doctrine for Joint Theater Nuclear Operations', Joint Chiefs of Staff, Washington, D.C., p. I-2; Cerniello 'Clinton Issues New Guidelines on U.S. Nuclear Weapons Doctrine', p. 26; and *History of the United States Strategic Command*, p. 37. See also Starr, B. (1993), 'Targeting Rethink May Lead to Non-Nuclear STRATCOM Role', *Jane's Defence Weekly*, vol. 19, no. 21 (22 May 1993), p. 19.

113 (1998), *Nuclear Operations, Air Force Doctrine Document 2–1.5*, Maxwell AFB, AL, Air Force Doctrine Center, p. vi.

114 Kristensen, H. (1998), 'Nuclear Futures: Proliferation of Weapons of Mass Destruction and US Nuclear Strategy', British American Security Information Council, London; Kristensen, H. (1997), 'Targets of Opportunity: How Nuclear Planners Found New Targets for Old Weapons', *Bulletin of the Atomic Scientists*, vol. 53, no. 5 (September/October 1997); Sauer, *Nuclear Inertia*, p. 52.

115 Butler *Prepared Posture Statement of Gen. Lee Butler*, 22 April 1993, p. 406; Kristensen, *Changing Targets II*, pp. 12–13.

116 Chiles, H. G. (1994), *Questions and Responses, Vice Adm. Henry G. Chiles, USN, nominee to be Commander in Chief, U.S. Strategic Command*, Hearing before the Senate Committee on Armed Services, 9 February 1994, Government Printing Office, Washington, D.C., pp. 220–221; Kristensen, 'Nuclear Futures', p. 11; Chiles, *Questions and Responses, Adm. Henry G. Chiles*, 23 February 1995.

117 Mitchell, J. T. (1993), *Testimony of Rear Adm, John T. Mitchell, USN, Director, Strategic Systems Program Office*, Hearing before the Senate Committee on Armed Services, 11 May 1995, Government Printing Office, Washington, D.C.

118 Kaminski, 'Sustaining the U.S. Nuclear Deterrent in the 21st Century'.

119 'Doctrine for Joint Nuclear Operations', Joint Chiefs of Staff, p. 3.12 and Cimbala, *Clinton and Post-Cold War Defense*, p. 55. It was reported that DOE spent $2 million in fiscal year 1993 on Phase I conceptual studies for low-yield nuclear weapons. Spratt, J. (1993), 'National Defense Authorization Act for Fiscal Year 1994', *Congressional Record (House of Representatives)*, 28 September 1993, p. H7065.

120 Medalia, J. (2004), *Nuclear Weapon Initiatives: Low-Yield R&D, Advanced Concepts, Earth Penetrators, Test Readiness*, Washington, D.C., Congressional Research Service, p. 6.

121 Ibid., p. 9.
122 Bacon, K. H. (1996), *DOD News Briefing, Mr. Kenneth H. Bacon, ASD (PA), 23 April 1996*, U.S. Department of Defense, Washington, D.C. Retrieved from http://www.defenselink.mil/transcripts/1996/t042396_tbrfg-42.html.
123 Mello, G. (1997), 'New Bomb, No Mission', *Bulletin of the Atomic Scientists*, vol. 53, no. 3 (May/June 1997); Smith, H. (1995), *Memorandum for Assistant Secretary for Defense Programs: Replacement of the B53 Strategic Gravity Bomb, 18 July 1995*, U.S. Department of Defense, Washington, D.C. Retrieved from http://www.nukestrat.com/us/afn/95–19h_DOD071895.pdf on 3 March 2007.
124 Robinson, C. P. (1999), *Testimony of C. Paul Robinson, Director, Sandia National Laboratories*, Hearing before the Senate Committee on Armed Services, 26 February 1999, Government Printing Office, Washington, D.C.
125 Mello, 'New Bomb, No Mission'; Pike, J. (2004), *B61*, Globalsecurity.org, Washington, D.C. Retrieved from http://www.globalsecurity.org/wmd/systems/b61.htm on 23 November 2004.
126 (1995), *A Modification of the B61 is Expected to Replace the B53, 20 September 1995*, Department of Energy, Washington, D.C. Retrieved from http://www.nukestrat.com/us/afn/DOEpr092095.pdf on 27 February 2007.
127 Barker, R. (1997), *Testimony of Robert Barker*, Hearing before the Senate Committee on Governmental Affairs, 27 October 1997, Government Printing Office, Washington, D.C., p. 52; Robinson *Testimony of C. Paul Robinson*, 26 February 1999, p. 128.
128 Markey, E. (2000), 'Conference Report on H.R. 4205, Floyd D. Spence National Defense Authorization Act for Fiscal Year 2001', *Congressional Record (House of Representatives)*, 11 October 2000, p. H9641; Tauscher, E. (2000), 'Conference Report on H.R. 4205, Floyd D. Spence National Defense Authorization Act for Fiscal Year 2001', *Congressional Record (House of Representatives)*, 11 October 2000, p. H9657.
129 *U.S. Commitment to the Treaty on the Non-Proliferation of Nuclear Weapons*, Department of State.
130 Cerniello, 'Clinton Issues New Guidelines'.
131 Kristensen, 'Targets of Opportunity'; 'Nuclear Forces, Post-1994', Strategic Advisory Group. See also STRATCOM's Strategic Advisory Group 1995 report cited in Kristensen, H. (2000), 'U.S. Nuclear Strategy Reform in the 1990s', Nautilus Institute, Berkeley, CA, p. 16.
132 For a useful overview of the missile defence debate under Clinton from an anti-missile defence perspective see Hartung, W. D. and Ciarrocca, M. (2000), 'Star Wars II: Here We Go Again', *The Nation*, 19 June 2000 and Powaski, R. E. (2000), *Return to Armageddon: The United States and the Nuclear Arms Race, 1981–1999*, New York, Oxford University Press, pp. 183–194.
133 Holum, J. D. (1993), *Speech by the Honorable John D. Holum, Director U.S. Arms Control and Disarmament Agency at the Arms Control Association Annual Dinner, 13 December 1993*, U.S. Department of State, Washington, D.C. Retrieved from http://dosfan.lib.uic.edu/acda/speeches/holum/holum2.htm on 23 February 2007.
134 Clinton, W. J. (1994), 'Joint Statement on Strategic Stability and Nuclear Security, 29 September 1994', Government Printing Office, Washington, D.C.
135 For details of the demarcation agreement see (1997), 'Russia–United States Joint Statement Concerning the Anti-Ballistic Missile Treaty, 21 March 1997', *Weekly Compilation of Presidential Documents, vol. 33*, no. *12, pp. 373–397*, Government Printing Office, Washington, D.C.
136 Roberts, G. (1995), 'An Elegant Irrelevance: the Anti-Ballistic Missile Treaty in the New World Disorder', *Strategic Review*, vol. 23, no. 2 (Spring 1995).
137 Cochran, T. (1998), 'American Missile Protection Act', *Congressional Record (Senate)*, 12 May 1998, p. S4640; Kyl, J. (1995), 'National Defense', *Congressional Record (Senate)*, 28 July 1995, p. S10866.

138 (1998), *Report of the Commission to Assess the Ballistic Missile Threat to the United States*, Retrieved from http://www.fas.org/irp/threat/missile/rumsfeld/ on 4 April 2007.
139 Payne, K. (1999), *Testimony of Dr. Keith B. Payne*, Hearing before the Senate Committee on Foreign Relations, 5 May 1999, Government Printing Office, Washington, D.C.
140 Dornan, R. (1994), 'Conference Report on S. 2182 National Defense Authorization Act for Fiscal Year 1995', *Congressional Record (House of Representatives)*, 17 August 1994, p. H8558; Kyl 'Treaty with the Russian Federation on Further Reduction and Limitation of Strategic Offensive Arms (The START II Treaty)', p. S19210. See also the text of the 1995 Missile Defense Act at (1995), 'Department of Defense Authorization Act for Fiscal Year 1996', *Congressional Record (House of Representatives)*, 12 September 1995, p. S13386.
141 Aubin, 'Clinton's Legacy of Strategic Instability'; Thurmond, S. (1996), 'Treaty with the Russian Federation on Further Reduction and Limitation of Strategic Offensive Arms (The START II Treaty)', *Congressional Record (Senate)*, 26 January 1996, p. S476.
142 Payne, *Testimony of Keith Payne, President, National Institute for Public Policy*, 13 March 1997, p. 9; Habiger, E. E. (1999), *Testimony of Gen. Eugene E. Habiger, Former Commander in Chief, U.S. Strategic Command*, Hearing before the Senate Committee on Foreign Relations, 5 May 1999, Government Printing Office, Washington, D.C., p. 139. Glaser and Fetter list six Russian concerns about American missile defence plans and long-term confidence in the retaliatory capability of the Russian nuclear arsenal in Fetter, S. and Glaser, C. (2001), 'National Missile Defense and the Future of U.S. Nuclear Weapons Policy', *International Security*, vol. 26, no. 1, pp. 74–75.
143 See letter from JCS chairman John Shalikashvili to Senator Sam Nunn in 1996 in, Levin, C. (1996), 'Defend America Act Increases Nuclear Threat', *Congressional Record (Senate)*, 23 May 1996, p. S5628, a letter from Shalikashvili to Senator Carl Levin in June 1995 in Glenn, J. H. (1995), 'National Defense Authorization Act for Fiscal Year 1996', *Congressional Record (House of Senate)*, 6 September 1995, p. S12655 and statement by National Security Advisor Robert Bell in Nunn, S. (1996), 'Defend America Act of 1996 – Motion To Proceed', *Congressional Record (Senate)*, 3 June 1996, p. S5688.
144 Nunn, S. (1995), 'National Defense Authorization Act for Fiscal Year 1996 – Conference Report', *Congressional Record (Senate)*, 15 December 1995, p. S18702; Senator Biden, J. (1995), 'National Defense Authorization Act for Fiscal Year 1996', *Congressional Record (Senate)*, 6 September 1995, p. S12658; and Senator Levin, C. (1995), 'National Defense Authorization Act for Fiscal Year 1996 – Conference Report', *Congressional Record (Senate)*, 19 December 1995, p. S18886.
145 Inhofe, J. (1996), 'Treaty with the Russian Federation on Further Reduction and Limitation of Strategic Offensive Arms (The START II Treaty)', *Congressional Record (Senate)*, 26 January 1996, p. S468; Smith, B. (1996), 'Treaty with the Russian Federation on Further Reduction and Limitation of Strategic Offensive Arms (The START II Treaty)', *Congressional Record (Senate)*, 26 January 1996, p. S473; Kyl, J. (1996), 'Defend America Act of 1996 – Motion to Proceed', *Congressional Record (Senate)*, 4 June 1996, p. S5715.
146 Roberts, B. (2001), 'The Road Ahead for Arms Control', in Lennon, A. (ed.) *Contemporary Nuclear Debates*, Cambridge, MA, The MIT Press.
147 Helms, 'Negotiations with Russia on a Revised U.S.–Soviet ABM Treaty', p. S2894; Woolf, A. (2001), 'Arms Control after START II: Next Steps on the US–Russian Agenda', 22 June 2001, Congressional Research Service, Washington, D.C., pp. 9, 19. On Clinton's reluctance see Clinton, W. J. (1999), 'The President's News Conference, 14 October 1999', *Weekly Compilation of Presidential Docu-*

ments, vol. 35, no. *41, pp. 1991–2064*, Government Printing Office, Washington, D.C.

148 Clinton, W. J. (2000), 'Remarks to the Russian State Duma in Moscow, 5 June 2000', *Weekly Compilation of Presidential Documents, 2000 vol. 36*, no. *23, pp. 1271–1329*, Government Printing Office, Washington, D.C.

149 Cohen, W. (1998), *DOD News Briefing, 30 April 1998*, U.S. Department of Defense, Washington, D.C. Retrieved from http://www.defenselink.mil/transcripts/1998/t04301998_t430cohe.html on 5 April 2006; Slocombe, W. (1999), *Address by Walter B. Slocombe, Under Secretary of Defense for Policy to the Center for Strategic and International Studies Statesmen's Forum, 5 November 1999*, U.S. Department of Defense, Washington, D.C. Retrieved from http://www.defenselink.mil/transcripts/1998/t04301998_t430cohe.html on 5 April 2006.

150 By mid-1993 Russia and France had announced testing moratoria and Britain was dependent upon America's Nevada Test Site.

151 Clinton, W. J. (1993), 'The President's Radio Address, 3 July 1993', *Weekly Compilation of Presidential Documents, vol. 29*, no. *27, pp. 1229–1296*, Government Printing Office, Washington, D.C.

152 Medalia, J. (2004), *Nuclear Testing and Comprehensive Test Ban: Chronology Starting September 1992*, Washington, D.C., Congressional Research Service, pp. 1–3.

153 Smith, R. J. (1993), 'White House Studies Nuclear Test Limits', *Washington Post*, 30 April 1993.

154 Clinton, 'Remarks to the Nixon Center'; *1995 Annual Report of the U.S. Arms Control and Disarmament Agency*, chapter 1. See statements supporting the CTBT by ACDA Director John Holum, Secretary of Defense William Cohen, JCS chairman Henry Shelton, Secretary of Energy Bill Richardson and Secretary of State Madeleine Albright: Holum, J. D. (1998), *Testimony of ACDA Director and Acting Under Secretary of State John Holum*, Hearing before the Senate Committee on Governmental Affairs, 18 March 1998, Government Printing Office, Washington, D.C.; Cohen, W. and Shelton, H. (1999), *Joint Prepared Statement by William S. Cohen an Gen. Henry H. Shelton*, Hearing before the Senate Committee on Armed Services, 6 October 1999, Government Printing Office, Washington, D.C.; Richardson, B. (1999), *Testimony by Secretary Bill Richardson*, Hearing before the Senate Committee on Armed Services, 7 October 1999, Government Printing Office, Washington, D.C.; Albright, M. (1999), *Testimony of Madeleine K. Albright*, Hearing before the Senate Committee on Foreign Relations, 7 October 1999, Government Printing Office, Washington, D.C.

155 Clinton, 'The President's Radio Address, July 3, 1993'.

156 Mallin, M. (1995), 'CTBT and NPT: Options for U.S. Policy', *Non-Proliferation Review*, vol. 2, no. 2, p. 4.

157 Exon, J. J. (1996), 'The Comprehensive Test Ban Treaty', *Congressional Record (Senate)*, 11 September 1996, p. S10279; Kennedy, E. (1996), 'Treaty With the Russian Federation on Further Reduction and Limitation of Strategic Offensive Arms (The Start II Treaty)', *Congressional Record (Senate)*, 26 January 1996, p. S468; Pell, C. (1996), 'World Leaders Sign Test Ban Treaty', *Congressional Record (Senate)*, 25 September 1996, p. S11277.

158 (1993), 'Nuclear Testing Moratorium', *Congressional Record (Senate)*, 25 May 1993, p. S6410.

159 (1995), 'National Defense Authorization Act for Fiscal Year 1996', *Congressional Record (Senate)*, 4 August 1995, pp. S11368–S11369.

160 Biden, J. (1997), 'Comprehensive Test Ban Treaty', *Congressional Record (Senate)*, 10 September 1997, p. S9059.

161 Daschle, T. (1997), 'The Comprehensive Test Ban', *Congressional Record*

(Senate), 1 October 1997, p. S10268; Reed, J. (1997), 'The Comprehensive Test Ban Treaty and the 34th Anniversary of President Kennedy's Call for the Vigorous Pursuit of Peace', *Congressional Record (Senate)*, 10 June 1997, p. S5433; Senator Biden, J. (1998), 'Nuclear Non-Proliferation and Senate Ratification of the Comprehensive Nuclear Test-Ban Treaty', *Congressional Record (Senate)*, 30 July 1998, p. S9421.

162 Pell, 'World Leaders Sign Test Ban Treaty', p. S11277.

163 (1999), 'Nuclear Test Ban Vote Set for October', *Associated Press*, 2 October 1999; Durbin, R. (1999), 'Comprehensive Test Ban Treaty', *Congressional Record (Senate)*, 30 September 1999, p. S11674.

164 Helms, J. (1999), 'Comprehensive Test Ban Treaty', *Congressional Record (Senate)*, 6 October 1999, p. S12070; Kyl, J. (1993), 'National Defense Authorization Act for Fiscal Year 1994', *Congressional Record (House of Representatives*, 29 September 1993, p. H7211; Bailey, K. C. (1998), *Testimony of Dr. Kathleen C. Bailey*, Hearing before the Senate Committee on Governmental Affairs, 18 March 1998, Government Printing Office, Washington, D.C., pp. 54–65.

165 Warner, J. (1999), 'Comprehensive Test Ban Treaty', *Congressional Record (Senate)*, 6 October 1999, p. S11672.

166 Mitchell, G. (1993), 'Senate Concurrent Resolution 9 – Urging The President to Negotiate a Comprehensive Nuclear Weapons Test Ban', *Congressional Record (Senate)*, 4 February 1993, p. S1494.

167 Warner 'Comprehensive Test Ban Treaty', p. S12090; Helms 'Comprehensive Test Ban Treaty', p. S12070; Spence, F. (1994), 'National Defense Authorization Act for Fiscal Year 1995', *Congressional Record (House of Representatives)*, 8 June 1994, p. H4194; Bryan, R. (1995), 'National Defense Authorization Act for Fiscal Year 1996', *Congressional Record (Senate)*, 4 August 1995, p. S11363.

168 Abraham, S. (1999), 'Comprehensive Nuclear Test Ban Treaty', *Congressional Record (Senate)*, 14 October 1999, p. S12630; Barker, R. (1992), *Testimony by Robert B. Barker, Assistant to the Secretary of Defense (Atomic Energy)*, Hearing before the Senate Committee on Armed Services, 27 March 1992, Government Printing Office, Washington, D.C., pp. 48–49.

169 Clinton, W. J. (1998), 'Remarks at Los Alamos National Laboratory in Los Alamos, New Mexico, 3 February 1998', *Weekly Compilation of Presidential Documents, vol. 34*, no. *6, pp. 175–225*, Government Printing Office, Washington, D.C. CTBT safeguards were: continuation of a robust science-based SSP; maintenance of modern nuclear laboratory facilities and programmes to attract and retain nuclear weapons expertise; maintenance of the basic capability to resume nuclear tests if needed; continuation of a comprehensive programme to improve CTBT monitoring capabilities, operations and intelligence on global nuclear weapons programmes; an annual stockpile certification process embodied in domestic law; and acceptance that the President, in consultation with Congress, would be prepared to withdraw from the CTBT to conduct whatever testing might be required if a major problem arose with the safety or reliability of a nuclear weapon type that the Secretaries of Defense and Energy consider to be critical to the nuclear arsenal. Clinton, W. J. (1997), 'Message to the Senate Transmitting the Comprehensive Nuclear Test-Ban Treaty and Documentation, 22 September 1997', *Weekly Compilation of Presidential Documents, vol. 33*, no. *39, pp. 1371–1429*, Government Printing Office, Washington, D.C.

170 Clinton, 'Message to the Senate Transmitting the Comprehensive Nuclear Test-Ban Treaty and Documentation'; Cohen, *Nuclear Weapon Systems Sustainment Programs*.

171 Medalia *Nuclear Testing and Comprehensive Test Ban: Chronology Starting September 1992*, p. 4; Biden, J. (1999), 'Ratifying the Comprehensive Test Ban Treaty', *Congressional Record (Senate)*, 27 July 1999, p. S9321.

172 Kimball, D. (1999), 'How the U.S. Senate Rejected CTBT Ratification', *Disarmament Diplomacy*, no. 40 (September/October 1999).

173 For an account of how Senators Kyl and Helms galvanised Republican opposition to the CTBT see Lowry, R. (1999), 'Test-Ban Ban: How the Treaty Went Down', *National Review*, 8 November 1999, Diebel, T. (2002), 'The Death of a Treaty', *Foreign Affairs*, vol. 18, no. 5 and Kimball, 'How the U.S. Senate Rejected CTBT Ratification'.

174 (1999), 'Clinton, Senate Take Treaty Dispute to the Brink', *Reuters*, 12 October 1999; Clinton, W. J. (1999), *Statement by the President, 13 October 1999*, The White House, Washington, D.C. Retrieved from http://www.acronym.org.uk/ctbt/ctbreact.htm on 22 November 2006.

175 Paine, C. (2004), *Weaponeers of Waste*, Washington, D.C., Natural Resources Defense Council, p. 5.

176 (1993), *PDD-15: Stockpile Stewardship, November 1993*, Federation of American Scientists, Washington, D.C. Retrieved from http://www.fas.org/irp/offdocs/pdd_steward.htm on 4 March 2007.

177 (1999), *Stockpile Stewardship Program: 30-Day Review*, Washington, D.C., U.S. Department of Energy, pp. 2–3.

178 (1995), 'The Stockpile Stewardship and Management Program: Maintaining Confidence in the Safety, Reliability of the Enduring U.S. Nuclear Weapon Stockpile', Department of Energy, Washington, D.C.

179 Hecker, S. S. (1997), *Testimony by Dr. Siegfried S. Hecker, Director, Los Alamos National Laboratory*, Hearing before the Senate Committee on Armed Services, 19 March 1997, Government Printing Office, Washington, D.C., pp. 206–207; Collina, T. and Kidder, R. (1994), 'Shopping Spree Softens Test-Ban Sorrows', *Bulletin of the Atomic Scientists*, vol. 50, no. 4 (July/August 1994).

180 Curtis, C. (1994), *Prepared Statement by Charles B. Curtis, Under Secretary of Energy*, Hearing before the Senate Committee on Armed Services 'Department of Defense Authorization for Appropriations for Fiscal Year 1995 and the Future Years Defense Program', 3 May 1994, United States Senate, Washington, D.C., p. 265; Reis, V. (1995), *Testimony by Dr. Victor Reis, Assistant Secretary for Defense Programs, Department of Energy*, Hearing before the Senate Committee on Armed Services, 16 May 1995, United States Senate, Washington, D.C., p. 213.

181 Caldicott, H. (2002), *The New Nuclear Danger: George W. Bush's Military-Industrial Complex*, New York, The New Press, p. 47.

182 Bailey, *Testimony of Dr. Kathleen C. Bailey*, p. 64; Joseph, R. and Lehman, R. (1998), 'U.S. Nuclear Policy in the 21st Century', *Strategic Forum*, no. 145 (August 1998), pp. 4–5; Robinson, *Testimony of C. Paul Robinson*, 26 February 1999, p. 129.

183 'Report of the Defense Science Board Task Force on Nuclear Deterrence', p. 52.

184 'The Stockpile Stewardship and Management Program', Department of Energy; Collina and Kidder, 'Shopping Spree Softens Test-Ban Sorrows'.

185 For full details of these processes see Reis, V. (1997), *Testimony of Dr. Victor Reis*, 27 October 1997, Government Printing Office, Washington, D.C., p. 28; Cohen, W. (1999), *Joint Prepared Statement By William S. Cohen and Gen. Henry H. Shelton*, Hearing before the Senate Committee on Armed Services, 6 October 1999, Government Printing Office, Washington, D.C., p. 18; Smith, H. (1996), *Testimony by Dr. Harold P. Smith*, Hearing before the Senate Committee on Armed Services, 13 March 1996, Government Printing Office, Washington, D.C., p. 196; and Reis, V. (1997), *Testimony of Dr. Victor Reis, Assistant Secretary of Energy for Defense Programs*, 29 October 1997, Government Printing Office, Washington, D.C., p. 36.

186 *Stockpile Stewardship Program: 30-Day Review*, pp. 2–10.

187 Beckner, E. (2002), *Testimony of Dr. Everett Beckner, Deputy Administrator for Defense Programs, National Nuclear Security Administration*, Hearing before the

Senate Committee on Armed Services, 10 April 2002, Government Printing Office, Washington, D.C.

188 *Stockpile Stewardship Program: 30-Day Review*, Department of Energy, pp. 3–6; (1999), 'The Stockpile Stewardship Program. Fact Sheet Released by the Bureau of Arms Control, 8 October 1999', U.S. Department of State, Washington, D.C.

189 (2003), 'Infrastructure Plan for the NNSA Nuclear Complex', April 2003, U.S. National Nuclear Security Administration, Washington, D.C., p. 6.

190 Beckner, E. (1993), *Testimony of Dr Everett Beckner, Acting Assistant Secretary for Defense Programs*, Hearing before the House Committee on Armed Services, 28 April 1993, Government Printing Office, Washington, D.C., p. 12; 'The Stockpile Stewardship and Management Program', Department of Energy.

191 For full details of the plan see O'Leary, H. (1993), *Testimony of Hazel O'Leary, Secretary of Energy*, 18 May 1993, Government Printing Office, Washington, D.C. and Reis, V. (1996), *Testimony by Dr. Victor Reis*, Hearing before the Senate Committee on Armed Services, 13 March 1996, Government Printing Office, Washington, D.C.; *Stockpile Stewardship Program: 30-Day Review*, Department of Energy.

192 *Stockpile Stewardship Program: 30-Day Review*, Department of Energy, pp. 6–14.

193 Smith, *Testimony by Dr. Harold P. Smith*, p. 196.

194 'National Defense Authorization Act for Fiscal Year 1997', p. S6369.

195 For details see Reis, V. (1999), *Testimony of Dr. Victor Reis, Assistant Secretary of Energy for Defense Programs*, 26 February 1999, Government Printing Office, Washington, D.C.; Cerniello, C. (1998), 'DOE Plans to Obtain Tritium from Existing Civilian Reactors', *Arms Control Today*, vol. 28, no. 3 (November/December 1998); Kyl, J. (1998), 'Strom Thurmond National Defense Authorization Act for Fiscal Year 1999 – Conference Report', *Congressional Record (Senate)*, 30 September 1998, p. S11172; O'Leary, H. (1996), *Testimony by Hazel O'Leary, Secretary of Energy*, 16 April 1996, Government Printing Office, Washington, D.C., p. 882.

196 Reis, V. (1998), *Testimony of Dr. Victor Reis, Assistant Secretary of Energy for Defense Programs*, 19 March 1998, Government Printing Office, Washington, D.C., p. 182; Reis, *Testimony of Dr. Victor Reis*, 26 February 1999.

197 Spence, 'National Defense Authorization Act for Fiscal Year 1995', p. H4197.

198 Browne, J. C. (1999), *Testimony of Dr. John C. Browne, Director, Los Alamos National Laboratory*, Hearing before the Senate Committee on Armed Services, 26 February 1999, Government Printing Office, Washington, D.C.

199 Reis, *Testimony of Dr. Victor Reis*, 19 March 1998, p. 182; (1998), 'Nuclear Weapons: Key Nuclear Weapons Component Issues are Unresolved', November 1998, U.S. General Accounting Office, Washington, D.C., p. 4.

200 'Report of the Defense Science Board Task Force on Nuclear Deterrence', pp. 48–49.

201 'Nuclear Weapons: Key Nuclear Weapons Component Issues are Unresolved', pp. 2–4.

202 Beckner, *Testimony of Dr Everett Beckner*, April 28, 1993, p. 23.

203 In 1996 the Senate Armed Services Committee Report on the National Defense Authorization Act for FY 1997 also expressed concern about the ability of the Department of Defense to maintain the necessary expertise to sustain the nuclear arsenal without nuclear testing. Cohen, *Nuclear Weapon Systems Sustainment Programs.*

204 Hecker, S. S. (1994), *Testimony by Dr. Siegfried S. Hecker, Director, Los Alamos National Laboratory*, Hearing before the Senate Committee on Armed Services, 3 May 1994, Government Printing Office, Washington, D.C., p. 284.

205 *Stockpile Stewardship Program: 30-Day Review*, Department of Energy, pp. 7–9.

206 Spence, F. (1994), 'The Clinton Administration and Nuclear Weapons Policy: Benign Neglect or Erosion by Design?' *Congressional Record (House of Represen-*

tatives), 8 June 1994, p. H4196; Kyl, J. (1994), 'National Defense Authorization Act for Fiscal Year 1995', *Congressional Record (House of Representatives)*, 18 May 1994, p. H3542.

207 See statements by Senators Thurmond and Kempthorne in *Briefing on the Results of the Nuclear Posture Review*, pp. 3–5.

208 Aftergood, S. (2000), 'Openness and Secrecy at the Department of Energy after the China Espionage Investigations', *F.A.S. Public Interest Report*, vol. 53, no. 1.

209 (1995), *A Review of the Department of Energy Classification Policy and Practice*, Washington, D.C., National Academy of Sciences, p. 1.

210 Boldrick, 'The Nuclear Posture Review: Liabilities and Risks', p. 88.

211 Gray, P. (1994), 'Reports: O'Leary v. Deutch', *Bulletin of the Atomic Scientists*, vol. 50, no. 6 (November/December 1994).

212 (1995), *Report of the Task Force on Alternative Futures for the National Laboratories*, Washington, D.C., Department of Energy.

213 (2000), 'Nuclear Skills Retention Measures within the Department of Defense and Department of Energy', November 2000, Washington, D.C.

214 Richanbach, P. H., Graham, D. R., *et al.* (1997), *The Organization and Management of the Nuclear Weapons Program.*, Alexandria, Institute for Defense Analysis.

215 Drell, S. D. and Jeanloz, R. (1999), *Remanufacture*, McLean, The MITRE Corporation, JASON Program Office, p. 1; 'Report of the Defense Science Board Task Force on Nuclear Deterrence', p. 23.

216 Thornberry, M. (1999), 'Calling for Creation of the Nuclear Security Administration', *Congressional Record (House of Representatives)*, 7 June 1999, p. H3743.

217 Warner *Testimony of Edward L. Warner, III, Assistant Secretary of Defense for Strategy and Threat Reduction*, p. 359; 'Nuclear Skills Retention Measures within the Department of Defense and Department of Energy', p. v.

218 (1999), 'FY 1999 Report of the Panel to Assess the Reliability, Safety, and Security of the United Sates Nuclear Stockpile', November 1999, Washington, D.C., p. ES-2.

219 Domenici, P. (1999), 'National Defense Authorization Act for Fiscal Year 2000 – Conference Report – Continued', *Congressional Record (Senate)*, 21 September 1999, p. S11103.

220 See the report of the Cox Commission, Cox, C. (1999), *Report of the Select Committee on U.S. National Security and Military/Commercial Concerns with the People's Republic of China*, Washington, D.C., Government Printing Office.

221 1999), 'Science at its Best; Security at its Worst: A Report on Security Problems at the U.S. Department of Energy', June 1999, The President's Foreign Intelligence Advisory Board, Washington, D.C.; Stearns, C. (1999), 'Release of Rudman Report', *Congressional Record (House of Representatives)*, 22 June 1999, United States Congress, Washington, D.C., p. H4668.

222 Gordon, J. A. (2001), *Speech to the LANL Foundation, John A. Gordon, Administrator, NNSA, 25 August 2001*, U.S. National Nuclear Security Administration, Washington, D.C. Retrieved from http://www.nnsa.doe.gov/docs/speeches/2001/2001–08–25-LANL_Foundation_Speech.pdf on 4 March 2007.

223 Ibid.; Gordon, J. A. (2000), *Testimony of Gen. John A Gordon, Administrator, National Nuclear Security Administration*, Hearing before the House Committee on Armed Services on 'Status of the National Nuclear Security Administration', 11 July 2000, United States Senate, Washington, D.C., p. 12.

224 Bohlen, A. (2003), 'The Rise and Fall of Arms Control', *Survival*, vol. 45, no. 3 (Autumn 2003), p. 30. Krepon emphasises this point in Krepon *Cooperative Threat Reduction, Missile Defense and the Nuclear Future*, pp. 25–26.

225 Woolf, 'U.S. Nuclear Weapons: Changes in Policy and Force Structure', p. 2.

226 (2002), *Table of U.S. Nuclear Warheads*, Natural Resources Defense Council, New York. Retrieved from http://www.nrdc.org/nuclear/nudb/datab9.asp on 24 November 2004.

5 Nuclear weapons policy under George W. Bush

1 These issues are explored further in chapter 7.
2 Reports included Payne, K. (2001), *Rationale and Requirements for U.S. Nuclear Forces and Arms Control*, Fairfax, VA, National Institute for Public Policy; Joseph, R. and Lehman, R. (1998), *U.S. Nuclear Policy in the 21st Century: A Fresh Look at National Strategy and Requirements*, Washington, D.C., National Defense University and Lawrence Livermore National Laboratory; Flournoy, M. and Murdock, C. (1998), *Revitalizing the U.S. Nuclear Deterrent*, Washington, D.C., Center for Strategic and International Studies, and (1998), 'Report of the Defense Science Board Task Force on Nuclear Deterrence', October 1998, Department of Defense, Washington, D.C.
3 Bush, G. W. (1999), *'A Distinctly American Internationalism', 19 November 1999*, Ronald Reagan Presidential Library, Simi Valley, California. Retrieved from http://www.fas.org/news/usa/1999/11/991119-bush-foreignpolicy.htm on 17 May 2006; Isaacs, J. (2001), 'The Ones to Watch', *Bulletin of the Atomic Scientists*, vol. 57, no. 2 (March/April 2001).
4 Bush, G. W. (2001), 'Remarks at the National Defense University, 1 May 2001', The White House, Washington, D.C.
5 (2001), *Background Briefing on the Quadrennial Defense Review, 14 June 2001*, U.S. Department of Defense, Washington, D.C. Retrieved from http://www.defenselink.mil/transcripts/2001/t06142001_t614bckg.html on 2 March 2007; Woolf, A. (2006), 'U.S. Nuclear Weapons: Changes in Policy and Force Structure', January 2006, Congressional Research Service, Washington, D.C., p. 2. The requirement to conduct an NPR was established in law in the 2000 National Defense Authorization Act for Fiscal Year 2001.
6 Bush, G. W. (2001), 'The President's News Conference With President Vladimir Putin of Russia, 13 November 2001', The White House, Washington, D.C.
7 Excerpts available at http://www.globalsecurity.org/wmd/library/policy/dod/npr.htm.
8 Brooks, L. (2004), ''Beyond the War on Terrorism', Speech to the Heritage Foundation Conference, 12 May, 2004', U.S. Department of Energy, Washington, D.C.
9 Rumsfeld, D. (2002), *Annual Report to the President and the Congress*, Washington, D.C., U.S. Department of Defense, chapter 7.
10 Ibid., chapter 7; Admiral James Ellis (2005), *U.S. Strategic Nuclear Policy: An Oral History (Unclassified DVD)*, Albuquerque, NM, Sandia National Laboratories, disk 4.
11 Brooks, L. (2003), *Questions and Responses*, Hearing before the Senate Committee on Foreign Relations, 8 April 2003, Government Printing Office, Washington, D.C., p. 176.
12 Allard, W. (2003), 'Energy and Water Development Appropriations Act, 2004', *Congressional Record (Senate)*, 16 September 2003, p. S11522.
13 Crouch, J. D. (2001), *Special Briefing on the Nuclear Posture Review, 9 January 2002*, U.S. Department of Defense, Washington, D.C. Retrieved from http://www.defenselink.mil/transcripts/2002/t01092002_t0109npr.html on 2 March 2007.
14 (2005), 'Joint Doctrine for Nuclear Operations (draft)', U.S. Joint Chiefs of Staff, Washington, D.C., p. I.1.
15 Rumsfeld, D. (2002), *Testimony by Donald H. Rumsfeld, Secretary of Defense*, Hearing before the Senate Committee on Armed Services, 25 July 2002, Government Printing Office, Washington, D.C., p. 7.
16 Cartwright, J. (2004), *Advance Questions for Lieutenant General James E. Cartwright for Commander, United States Strategic Command*, Hearing before the Senate Committee on Armed Services, 8 July 2004, Government Printing Office,

Washington, D.C., p. 16; Mies, R. W. (2001), *Testimony of Adm. Richard W. Mies, USN, Commander in Chief, United States Strategic Command*, Hearing before the Senate Committee on Armed Services, 11 July 2001, Government Printing Office, Washington, D.C., p. 3.

17 (2002), *Nuclear Posture Review (Excerpts)*, Globalsecurity.org, Washington, D.C. Retrieved from http://www.globalsecurity.org/wmd/library/policy/dod/npr.htm on 24 November 2004, p. 16.

18 Rumsfeld, *Annual Report to the President and the Congress*, chapter 7.

19 It was reported that in January 2001 the Air Force reviewed the Chinese Integrated Strategic Operation Plan or CHISOP, a Joint Chiefs of Staff nuclear targeting plan in the event of armed conflict with China. China was removed from the SIOP in 1982 to reflect a normalisation of relations but STRATCOM reportedly reinstated China in the SIOP in 1998 following Clinton's PDD-60 guidance. Arkin, W. (2001), 'The Last Word: Targeting China', *Bulletin of the Atomic Scientists*, vol. 51, no. 4 (July/August 2001); Kristensen, H. (2001), *The Matrix of Deterrence: U.S. Strategic Command Force Structure Studies*, Berkeley, CA, The Nautilus Institute.

20 (2004), *History of the United States Strategic Command: 1 June 1992–2 October 2002*, Offut Air Force Base, Nebraska, Strategic Command, p. 70.

21 Woolf, 'U.S. Nuclear Weapons: Changes in Policy and Force Structure', p. 18.

22 *Nuclear Posture Review (Excerpts)*, p. 16.

23 Rumsfeld, D. (2003), *Remarks as delivered by Secretary of Defense Donald H. Rumsfeld at the Hoover Institution Board of Overseers, 25 February 2003*, U.S. Department of Defense. Retrieved from http://www.defenselink.mil/speeches/2003/sp20030225-secdef0084.html on 27 January 2004.

24 Wolfowitz, P. (2001), *Testimony of Deputy Secretary of Defense Paul Wolfowitz*, Hearing before the Senate Committee on Armed Services, 4 October 2001, Government Printing Office, Washington, D.C.

25 Rumsfeld, D. (2002), *Testimony of U.S. Secretary of Defense Donald H. Rumsfeld before the House Armed Services Committee regarding Iraq (Transcript), 18 September 2005*, U.S. Department of Defense, Washington, D.C. Retrieved from http://www.defenselink.mil/speeches/2002/s20020918-secdef2.html on 22 July 2005.

26 Ritchie, N. and Rogers, P. (2007), *The Political Road to War with Iraq*, London, Routledge. Key statements defining the new paradigm included President Bush's January 2002 State of the Union address that described North Korea, Iran and Iraq 'an axis of evil, arming to threaten the peace of the world' (Bush, G. H. W., 2002, *President Delivers State of the Union Address, 29 January 2002*, The White House, Washington, D.C. Retrieved from http://www.whitehouse.gov/news/releases/2002/01/iraq/20020129–11.html on 27 January 2004), his speech at the US Military Academy at West Point in June 2002, Bush, G. W. (2002), *President Bush Delivers Graduation Speech at West Point, 1 June 2002*, The White House, Washington, D.C. Retrieved from http://www.whitehouse.gov/news/releases/2002/06/20020601–3.html on 19 February 2004 and the speech by Vice President Dick Cheney to the Veterans of Foreign Wars in August 2002 (Cheney, D., 2002, *Vice President Cheney's Speech to the Veterans of Foreign Wars, 26 August 2002*, Project for a New American Century, Retrieved from http://www.newamericancentury.org/iraq-082602.htm on 19 February 2004).

27 (2002), 'The National Security Strategy of the United States of America', The White House, Washington, D.C., p. 15.

28 (2002), 'National Strategy to Combat Weapons of Mass Destruction', The White House, Washington, D.C.

29 Rumsfeld, D. (2001), *Testimony by Donald H. Rumsfeld, Secretary of Defense*, Hearing before the House Committee on Armed Services, 21 June 2001, Government Printing Office, Washington, D.C.

30 Rumsfeld, *Annual Report to the President and the Congress*, chapter 7.
31 Cheney, R. B. (2003), *Remarks by the Vice President to the Heritage Foundation, 1 May 2003*, The White House, Washington, D.C. Retrieved from http://www.white-house.gov/news/releases/2003/05/20030501–9.html on 3 March 2007.
32 Wolfowitz, P. (2001), *Testimony of Paul Wolfowitz*, Hearing before the Senate Committee on Armed Services, 27 February 2001, Government Printing Office, Washington, D.C.
33 See Jervis, R. (1984), *The Illogic of American Nuclear Strategy*, Ithaca, Cornell University Press.
34 Payne, K. (1998), 'Post-Cold War Requirements for U.S. Nuclear Deterrence Policy', *Comparative Strategy*, vol. 17, no. 3 (July–September 1998), p. 231.
35 Ibid., p. 261.
36 (2004), 'Report of the Defense Science Board Task Force on Future Strategic Strike Forces', February 2004, Office of the Under Secretary of Defense for Acquisition and Technology, U.S. Department of Defense, Washington, D.C., pp. 2–11.
37 See the Clinton administration's final Department of Defense Annual Report to Congress in Cohen, W. (2001), *Annual Report to the President and the Congress*, Washington, D.C., U.S. Department of Defense; Woolf, 'U.S. Nuclear Weapons: Changes in Policy and Force Structure', p. 41.
38 Buchan, G. C., Matonik, D. *et al.* (2003), *Future Roles of U.S. Nuclear Forces*, Arlington, RAND, p. 38.
39 See statements by Douglas Feith, Under Secretary of Defense for Policy, J.D. Crouch, Assistant Secretary of Defense for International Security Policy, and Admiral Richard Mies, head of STRATCOM. Crouch, *Special Briefing on the Nuclear Posture Review*; Feith, D. J. (2002), *Testimony of Douglas J. Feith Under Secretary of Defense for Policy*, Hearing before the Senate Committee on National Security, 14 February 2002, Government Printing Office, Washington, D.C., and Mies, *Testimony of Adm. Richard W. Mies*,11 July 2001.
40 Brooks, 'Beyond the War on Terrorism,'; Ellis, J. O. (2002), *Testimony of Adm. James O. Ellis, USN, Commander in Chief, United States Strategic Command*, Hearing before the Senate Committee on Armed Services, 14 February 2002, Government Printing Office, Washington, D.C.
41 Feith *Testimony of Douglas J. Feith Under Secretary of Defense for Policy*; Mies, *Testimony of Adm. Richard W. Mies*,11 July 2001, p. 14; Woolf, 'U.S. Nuclear Weapons: Changes in Policy and Force Structure', p. 10.
42 Kristensen, H. (2007), *White House Guidance Led to New Nuclear Strike Plans Against Proliferators, Document Shows*, Strategic Security Blog, Federation of American Scientists, 11 November 2007. Retrieved from http://www.fas.org/blog/ssp/2007/11/white_house_guidance_led_to_ne.php on 2 December 2007; Allen, M. and Gellman, B. (2002), 'Preemptive Strikes Part of U.S. Strategic Doctrine', *Washington Post*, 11 December 2002.
43 (2004), 'The National Military Strategy of the United States: A Strategy for Today; A Vision for Tomorrow', U.S. Joint Chiefs of Staff, Washington, D.C., p. 13.
44 Rumsfeld, *Testimony by Donald H. Rumsfeld, Secretary of Defense*, 21 June 2001.
45 See Payne, K. (1995), 'Post-Cold War Deterrence and Missile Defense', *Orbis*, vol. 39, no. 2 (Spring 1995); Payne, K. (1996), *Deterrence in the Second Nuclear Age*, Kentucky, University of Kentucky Press; Payne, K. (1998), *Testimony by Dr. Keith Payne*, Hearing before the Senate Committee on Armed Services, 31 March 1998, Government Printing Office, Washington, D.C.; Joseph, R. and Lehman, R. (1998), 'U.S. Nuclear Policy in the 21st Century', *Strategic Forum*, no. 145 (August 1998); Joseph, R. (1997), 'Nuclear Deterrence and Regional Proliferators', *The Washington Quarterly*, vol. 20, no. 3.
46 Payne, *Rationale and Requirements.*
47 These include Stephen Hadley, later Deputy National Security Advisor; Robert

Joseph, later Special Assistant to the President and Senior Director for Proliferation Strategy, Counter-proliferation and Homeland Defense in the National Security Council; Stephen Cambone, later Director, Program Analysis and Evaluation, Office of the Secretary of Defense; William Schneider, later chairman of the Pentagon's Defense Science Board and a member of the State Department's Defense Trade Advisory Group; and Ambassador Linton Brooks, later Administrator of NNSA and Under Secretary of Energy for Nuclear Security.

48 Mies, *Testimony of Adm. Richard W. Mies*, 11 July 2001, p. 14.

49 Crouch, *Special Briefing on the Nuclear Posture Review*; *Nuclear Posture Review (Excerpts)*, p. 29.

50 'National Strategy to Combat Weapons of Mass Destruction'.

51 Myers, R. B. (2003), *Posture Statement of General Richard B. Myers, USAF Chairman of the Joint Chiefs of Staff*, Hearing before the House Committee on Armed Services, 5 February 2003, Government Printing Office, Washington, D.C.

52 Ellis, J. O. (2003), *Testimony of Adm. James O. Ellis, USN, Commander in Chief, United States Strategic Command on Command Posture and Strategic Issues*, Hearing before the Senate Committee on Armed Services on, 8 April 2003, Government Printing Office, Washington, D.C.

53 Ellis, J. O. (2002), *Advance Questions for Admiral James O. Ellis, Nominee for position of Commander in Chief, United States Strategic Command*, Hearing before the Senate Committee on Armed Services, 27 September 2002, Government Printing Office, Washington, D.C., p. 209.

54 *History of the United States Strategic Command*, Strategic Command, p. 64; Woolf, 'U.S. Nuclear Weapons: Changes in Policy and Force Structure', pp. 16–18.

55 Norris, R. S., Kristensen, H. M., *et al.* (2004), 'Nuclear Insecurity: A Critique of the Bush Administration's Nuclear Weapons Policies', National Resources Defense Council, Washington, D.C. p. 7.

56 'Joint Doctrine for Nuclear Operations (draft)', Joint Chiefs of Staff, p. III-2.

57 Woolf, 'U.S. Nuclear Weapons: Changes in Policy and Force Structure', pp. 44–45.

58 Bleek, P. (2002), 'Bush Administration Reaffirms Negative Security Assurances', *Arms Control Today*, vol. 32, no. 2 (March 2002).

59 (2003), *New Nuclear Policies, New Weapons, New Dangers*, Arms Control Association, Washington, D.C. Retrieved from http://www.armscontrol.org/factsheets/newnuclearweaponsissuebrief.asp on 18 March 2007.

60 Ellis, *Testimony of Adm. James O. Ellis*, 8 April 2003, p. 9.

61 'Report of the Defense Science Board Task Force on Future Strategic Strike Forces', p. iii.

62 In 1991 Watts examined the issue of conventional strategic weapons to provide the US with strategic options short of nuclear war in Watts, B. D. (1991), 'The Conventional Utility of Strategic Nuclear Forces', *The Washington Quarterly*, vol. 14, no. 4 (Autumn 1991). In 1996 STRATCOM commander Eugene Habiger stated that 'I am aware and support the Services in evaluating the technological feasibility of using conventionally armed ballistic systems. Such a capability could provide valuable options to decision makers.' Habiger, E. E. (1996), *Questions and Responses*, Hearing before the Senate Committee on Armed Services, 1 February 1996, Government Printing Office, Washington, D.C., p. 81. See also Gormley, D. (2005), 'Conventional Force Integration in Global Strike', in Wirtz, J. J. and Larsen, J. A. (eds) *Nuclear Transformation: The New U.S. Nuclear Doctrine*, New York, Palgrave Macmillan, p. 54; Starr, B. (1994), 'Conventional Trident Tests Planned by USN', *Jane's Defence Weekly*, vol. 22, no. 5 (6 August 1994), p. 1.

63 Feith, *Testimony of Douglas J. Feith*, 14 February 2002.

64 'Report of the Defense Science Board Task Force on Future Strategic Strike Forces', p. 5.11. See also arguments in favour of conventionally-armed ICBMs in

Cimbala, S. (2005), *Nuclear Weapons and Nuclear Strategy*, New York, Routledge, p. 46.

65 (2007), *Conventional Prompt Global Strike Capability: Letter Report*, Washington, D.C., National Academy Press, p. 8; Young, C. B. (2006), *Testimony of Charles B. Young, Director, Strategic Systems Programs, U.S. Navy*, Hearing before the Senate Committee on Armed Services, 29 March 2006, Government Printing Office, Washington, D.C., p. 3; Woolf, A. (2007), 'Conventional Warheads for Long-Range Ballistic Missiles: Background and Issues for Congress', June 2007, Congressional Research Service, Washington, D.C.

66 Sokolsky, R. (2002), 'Demystifying the U.S. Nuclear Posture Review', *Survival*, vol. 44, no. 3 (Autumn 2002), p. 139.

67 Grossman, E., 'Prospects Brighten for Army Hypersonic Weapon', *Global Security Newswire*, 8 November 2007.

68 Kristensen, H. (2006), *U.S. Changes Name of Nuclear War Plan*, The Nuclear Information Project, Washington, D.C. Retrieved from http://www.nukestrat.com/us/stratcom/siopname.htm on 15 February 2007; Woolf, 'U.S. Nuclear Weapons: Changes in Policy and Force Structure', p. 16.

69 Payne, K. (2005), 'The Nuclear Posture Review: Setting the Record Straight', *The Washington Quarterly*, vol. 28, no. 3; Rumsfeld, *Annual Report to the President and the Congress*, p. 140.

70 McGinnis, J. S. (2003), *Remarks of J. Sherwood McGinnis, Deputy U.S. Representative to the Conference on Disarmament, to the Second Session of the Preparatory Committee for the 2005 NPT Review Conference, Geneva, Switzerland, 1 May 2003*, U.S. Department of State, Washington, D.C. Retrieved from http://www.state.gov/t/isn/rls/rm/24919.htm on 3 March 2007; Crouch, *Special Briefing on the Nuclear Posture Review*.

71 Wolfowitz, P. (2002), *Wolfowitz Interview with Knight-Ridder, 15 May 2002*, U.S. Department of Defense, Washington, D.C. Retrieved from http://www.defenselink.mil/transcripts/2002/t05172002_t515knt2.html on 2 March 2007.

72 Ellis, *Testimony of Adm. James O. Ellis*, 8 April 2003, p. 9.

73 Cirincione, J. (2002), *Testimony of Joseph Cirincione, Director, Non-Proliferation Project, Carnegie Endowment for International Peace*, Hearing before the Senate Committee on Foreign Relations, 16 May 2002, Government Printing Office, Washington, D.C., p. 48.

74 Turner, S. (2001), 'The Dilemma of Nuclear Weapons in the Twenty-First Century', *Naval War College Review*, vol. LIV, no. 2; Wurst, J. and Burroughs, J. (2001), 'Ending the Nuclear Nightmare: a Strategy for the Bush Administration', *World Policy Journal*, vol. XVIII, no. 1.

75 Cirincione, *Testimony of Joseph Cirincione*, p. 48.

76 Knopf, J. W. (2005), 'Nuclear Tradeoffs: Conflicts Between U.S. National Security and Global Nonproliferation Efforts', in Wirtz, J. J. and Larsen, J. A. (eds) *Nuclear Transformation: The New U.S. Nuclear Doctrine*, New York, Palgrave Macmillan, pp. 162–170; Woolf, 'U.S. Nuclear Weapons: Changes in Policy and Force Structure', pp. 41–42.

77 Cirincione, *Testimony of Joseph Cirincione*, pp. 48–49.

78 Glaser, C. and Fetter, S. (2005), 'Counterforce Revisited: Assessing the Nuclear Posture Review's New Missions', *International Security*, vol. 30, no. 2. For a detailed critical overview of the NPR see Sokolsky, 'Demystifying the U.S. Nuclear Posture Review'. For a reply to general criticism of the NPR from one of its primary architects, see Payne, 'The Nuclear Posture Review: Setting the Record Straight'.

79 Cirincione, *Testimony of Joseph Cirincione*, p. 50.

80 Owens, W. A. (2002), *Testimony of Adm. William Owens, U.S. Navy (Ret.)*, Hearing before the Senate Committee on Foreign Relations, 16 May 2002, Government

Printing Office, Washington, D.C., pp. 17–18; Habiger, E. E., Nunn, S. *et al.* (2002), 'Still Missing: A Nuclear Strategy', *Washington Post*, 21 May 2002.

81 Frank, B. (2002), 'The President's New Nuclear Posture Paper: How Many Things can we Find Wrong with this Picture?' *Congressional Record (House of Representatives)*, 12 March 2002, p. H790. See statements by Reed, J. (2003), 'National Defense Authorization Act for Fiscal Year 2004 – Continued', *Congressional Record (Extension of Remarks)*, 20 May 2003, United States Congress, Washington, D.C., p. S6690; Feinstein, D. (2003), 'Energy and Water Development Appropriations Act, 2004', *Congressional Record (Senate)*, 15 September 2003, United States Congress, Washington, D.C., p. S11437 and a letter in 2003 to President Bush from Representative Rush Holt and 33 colleagues, Holt, R. (2003), 'Explanation of Vote on Conference Report on FY2004 Defense Authorization Bill', *Congressional Record (Extension of Remarks)*, 23 November 2003, p. E2437.

82 (2002), 'America as Nuclear Rogue', *New York Times*, 12 March 2002; (2002), 'A Twisted Posture', *Boston Globe*, 12 March 2002.

83 Sokolsky, 'Demystifying the U.S. Nuclear Posture Review'.

84 Arkin, W. and Norris, R. (2000), 'Nuclear Notebook: U.S. Nuclear Forces 2000', *Bulletin of the Atomic Scientists*, vol. 56, no. 3 (May/June 2000); Kristensen, H. and Norris, R. (2004), 'Nuclear Notebook: U.S. Nuclear Forces 2004', *Bulletin of the Atomic Scientists*, vol. 60, no. 3 (May/June 2004).

85 Kristensen and Norris, 'Nuclear Notebook: U.S. Nuclear Forces 2004'.

86 Woolf, 'U.S. Nuclear Weapons: Changes in Policy and Force Structure', p. 28; Kristensen and Norris, 'Nuclear Notebook: U.S. Nuclear Forces 2004'.

87 'Report of the Defense Science Board Task Force on Future Strategic Strike Forces', pp. 5–6; Kristensen, H. (2004), *U.S. Nuclear Planning After the 2001 Nuclear Posture Review*, Presentation to the Center for International and Security Studies at Maryland (CISSM), 21 October 2004, University of Maryland; Norris, S and Kristensen, H., U.S. Nuclear Forces, 2006, *Bulletin of the Atomic Scientists*, vol. 63, no. 1 (January/February 2007), pp. 80–81.

88 'Lockheed Martin Receives $135-million Contract Modification from the Navy for Trident II D5 Missile Life Extension', Lockheed Martin, Press Release, 9 April 2007; Kristensen, H. and Norris, R. (2003), 'Nuclear Notebook: U.S. Nuclear Forces 2003', *Bulletin of the Atomic Scientists*, vol. 59, no. 3 (May/June 2003).

89 *Nuclear Posture Review (Excerpts)*; Bleek, P. (2001), 'Pentagon Prepares Modest Cut Backs in Nuclear Arsenal', *Arms Control Today*, vol. 31, no. 6 (July/August 2001); Kristensen and Norris, 'Nuclear Notebook: U.S. Nuclear Forces 2004'.

90 Woolf, 'U.S. Nuclear Weapons: Changes in Policy and Force Structure'.

91 Herbert, A. J. (2003), 'The Future Missile Force', *Air Force Magazine*, vol. 86, no. 10 (October 2003), p. 67; USAF Chief of Staff General Jumper, J. (2002), 'Final Mission Needs Statement (MNS) Land-Based Strategic Nuclear Deterrent', 18 January 2002, Department of Defense, Washington, D.C.

92 (2006), 'Quadrennial Defense Review Report', Department of Defense, Washington, D.C., p. 50; Norris, S. and Kristensen, H., 'U.S. Nuclear Forces, 2006', *Bulletin of the Atomic Scientists*, vol. 63, no. 1 (January/February 2007), p. 80.

93 'Report of the Defense Science Board Task Force on Future Strategic Strike Forces', pp. 5.1–5.2.

94 Kristensen, H. (2007), *Strategic Security Blog, US Air Force Decides to Retire Advanced Cruise Missile, 7 March 2007.* Retrieved from http://www.fas.org/blog/ssp/2007/03/us_air_force_decides_to_retire.php on 12 December 2007.

95 'Quadrennial Defense Review Report', p. 46.

96 *Nuclear Posture Review (Excerpts)*.

97 Woolf, 'U.S. Nuclear Weapons: Changes in Policy and Force Structure', p. 25.

98 Feith, *Statement of Douglas J. Feith*, 14 February 2002.

99 Ibid.; Brooks, 'Beyond the War on Terrorism'.

100 Rumsfeld, *Testimony by Donald H. Rumsfeld, Secretary of Defense*, 21 June 2001.

101 Bose, W. and Pomper, M. (2005), *The U.S. Approach to the 2005 Nuclear Nonproliferation Treaty Review Conference: An ACT Interview with Assistant Secretary of State Stephen Rademaker*, Arms Control Association, Washington, D.C. Retrieved from http://www.armscontrol.org/interviews/20050419_Rademaker.asp on 27 April 2005.

102 D'Agostino, T. P. (2007), *Testimony of Thomas P. D'Agostino Acting Administrator, National Nuclear Security Administration*, Hearing before the Senate Armed Services Committee, 28 March 2007, Government Printing Office, Washington, D.C.

103 'President Bush Approves Significant Reduction in Nuclear Weapons Stockpile', The White House, Washington, D.C., 18 December 2007.

104 Norris, S. and Kristensen, H., 'What's Behind Bush's Nuclear Cuts?', *Arms Control Today*, vol. 34, no. 8 October 2004; Kristensen, H. 'White House Announces (Secret) Nuclear Weapons Cuts', *Strategic Security Blog*, Federation of American Scientists, 18 December 2007. Retrieved from http://www.fas.org/blog/ssp/2007/12/white_house_announces_secret_n.php#more on 7 January 2008.

105 Habiger, E. E. (2002), *Testimony of Gen. Eugene E. Habiger, Former Commander in Chief, U.S. Strategic Command*, Hearing before the Senate Committee on Foreign Relations, 23 July 2002, Government Printing Office, Washington, D.C., p. 144.

106 Bush, G. W. (2002), 'The President's News Conference, 13 March 2002', The White House, Washington, D.C.

107 'Report of the Defense Science Board Task Force on Future Strategic Strike Forces', pp. I.10, 7.11–7.12.

108 These were Payne, *Rationale and Requirements*; Robinson, C. P. (2001), 'Pursuing a New Nuclear Weapons Policy for the 21st Century', Sandia National Laboratory, Livermore, CA; and Younger, S. (2000), 'Nuclear Weapons in the 21st Century', Los Alamos National Laboratory, Los Alamos, N. M. Robinson was Director of the Sandia National Laboratory and Younger was Associate Laboratory Director for Nuclear Weapons at the Los Alamos National Laboratory and later Director of DOD's Defense Threat Reduction Agency (DTRA) under President Bush.

109 Medalia, J. (2004), ''Bunker Busters': Sources of Confusion in the Robust Nuclear Earth Penetrator Debate', 22 September 2004, Congressional Research Service, Washington, D.C., p. 5.

110 See Browne, J. C. (2002), *Testimony of Dr. John C. Browne, Director, Los Alamos National Laboratory*, Hearing before the House Committee on Armed Services, 12 June 2002, Government Printing Office, Washington, D.C. See also C. Paul Robinson, 'exploratory work on advanced concepts will also be necessary to ensure that our design skills are sufficiently challenged for evolving needs in the nation's nuclear forces.' Robinson, C. P. (2002), *Testimony of C. Paul Robinson, Director, Sandia National Laboratories*, Hearing before the House Committee on Armed Services, 12 June 2002, Government Printing Office, Washington, D.C., and Energy Secretary Spencer Abraham, Abraham, S. (2004), *Testimony of Spencer Abraham, Secretary of Energy*, Hearing before the Senate Committee on Armed Services, 23 March 2004, Government Printing Office, Washington, D.C.

111 *Nuclear Posture Review (Excerpts)*, pp. 12–13.

112 Ibid., p. 47.

113 Beckner, E. (2002), *Testimony of Dr. Everett Beckner, Deputy Administrator for Defense Programs, National Nuclear Security Administration*, Hearing before the Senate Committee on Armed Services, 10 April 2002, Government Printing Office, Washington, D.C.

114 Medalia, ''Bunker Busters': Sources of Confusion', p. 10. See statements by Feingold, R. (2003), 'National Defense Authorization Act for Fiscal Year 2004 – Continued', *Congressional Record (Senate)*, 20 May 2003, p. S6674; Durbin, R. (2003),

'National Defense Authorization Act for Fiscal Year 2004 – Continued', *Congressional Record (Senate)*, 20 May 2003, p. S6668.

115 Udall, M. (2003), 'H.R. 1588, Defense Authorization Conference Report', *Congressional Record (Extension of Remarks)*, 20 November 2003, p. E2354. See also Biden, J. (2003), 'Energy and Water Development Appropriations Act, 2004', *Congressional Record (Senate)*, 16 September 2003, p. S11526; Feinstein, D. (2003), 'National Defense Authorization Act for Fiscal Year 2004 – Continued', *Congressional Record (Senate)*, 20 May 2003, p. S6664; Dorgan, B. (2003), 'Nuclear Weapons', *Congressional Record (Senate)*, 15 September 2003, p. S11435.

116 Feinstein, D. (2005), 'National Defense Authorization Act for Fiscal Year 2006', *Congressional Record (Senate)*, 22 July 2005, p. S88726. See also Tauscher, E. (2004), 'National Defense Authorization Act for Fiscal Year 2005', *Congressional Record (House of Representatives)*, 20 May 2004, p. H3415.

117 (2005), *Effects of Nuclear Earth-Penetrator and Other Weapons*, Washington, D.C., National Academy Press, p. 2.

118 (2002), 'Conference Report on H.R. 4546, Bob Stump National Defense Authorization Act for Fiscal Year 2003', *Congressional Record (House of Representatives)*, 12 November 2002, p. H8092.

119 Medalia, ''Bunker Busters': Sources of Confusion', p. 7; (2000), 'National Defense Authorization Act for Fiscal Year 2001', United States Congress, Washington, D.C., Sec. 1044.

120 Kucia, C. (2003), 'Congress Approves Research on New Nuclear Weapons', *Arms Control Today*, vol. 33, no. 5 (June 2003). Letters were sent to Senator John Warner, chair of the Senate Armed Services Committee from Secretary of State Colin Powell, General John Jumper, Chief of Staff of the Air Force, Admiral J. O. Ellis, Commander of the Navy, requesting the ban be repealed. (2003), 'National Defense Authorization Act for Fiscal Year 2004 – Continued', *Congressional Record (Senate)*, 20 May 2003, pp. S6679–S6680.

121 Graham, L. (2003), 'National Defense Authorization Act for Fiscal Year 2004 – Continued', *Congressional Record (Senate)*, 20 May 2003, p. S6669. See also Senator Sessions, J. (2003), 'National Defense Authorization Act for Fiscal Year 2004 – Continued', *Congressional Record (Senate)*, 20 May 2003, p. S6667.

122 Brooks, 'Beyond the War on Terrorism'.

123 Byrd, J. (2002), *Testimony of John Byrd, Director, Plans and Policy, United States Strategic Command*, Hearing before the House Committee on Armed Services, 12 June 2002, Government Printing Office, Washington, D.C.; Rumsfeld, D. (2003), *DOD News Briefing – Secretary Rumsfeld and Gen. Myers, 20 May 2003*, U.S. Department of Defense, Washington, D.C. Retrieved from http://www.defenselink.mil/transcripts/2003/tr20030520-secdef0207.html on 21 March 2007.

124 Smolen, R. L. (2003), *Posture Statement of Robert L. Smolen, USAF, Director, Nuclear and Counterproliferation*, Hearing before the Senate Committee on Armed Services, 8 April 2003, Government Printing Office, Washington, D.C.; Young, C. B. (2003), *Testimony of Charles B. Young, Director, Strategic Systems Programs, U.S. Navy*, Hearing before the Senate Committee on Armed Services, April 8, 2003, Government Printing Office, Washington, D.C.; Ellis, J. O. (2003), *Question and Responses*, Hearing before the Senate Committee on Armed Services on, 8 April 2003, Government Printing Office, Washington, D.C., p. 177.

125 Cartwright, *Advance Questions*, 8 July 2004.

126 Ellis, *Advance Questions*, 27 September 2002, p. 215.

127 Brooks, *Questions and Responses*, 8 April 2003.

128 See Feinstein, D. (2005), 'Congressional Budget for the United States Government for the Fiscal Year 2006', *Congressional Record (Senate)*, 16 March 2005, p. S2760; Feinstein 'National Defense Authorization Act for Fiscal Year 2006', p.

S8724; and Reed, J. (2005), 'National Defense Authorization Act for Fiscal Year 2006', *Congressional Record (Senate)*, 22 July 2005, p. S8722.

129 Clinton, W. J. (2000), 'Remarks at Georgetown University, 1 September 2000', *Weekly Compilation of Presidential Documents, vol. 36, no. 35, pp. 1941–1995*, Government Printing Office, Washington, D.C.

130 Bush, G. W. (2001), 'The President's News Conference With President Vladimir Putin of Russia in Genoa, 22 July 2001', The White House, Washington, D.C.

131 Feith, D. J. (2001), *Media Roundtable with USD (P) Feith, 4 September 2001*, U.S. Department of Defense, Washington, D.C. Retrieved from http://www.defenselink.mil/transcripts/2001/t09052001_t904usdp.html on 12 March 2007.

132 Bush, 'Remarks at the National Defense University'.

133 Bush, G. W. (2001), 'Joint Statement by President George W. Bush and President Vladimir V. Putin of Russia on a New Relationship Between the United States and Russia, 13 November 2001', *Weekly Compilation of Presidential Documents, vol. 37, no. 46, pp. 1631–1685*, Government Printing Office, Washington, D.C.

134 Bush, G. W. (2002), 'Joint Declaration by President George W. Bush and President Vladimir V. Putin on the New Strategic Relationship Between the United States of America and the Russian Federation, 24 May 2002', The White House, Washington, D.C. See also comments by President Putin in (2003), *The President's News Conference With President Vladimir Putin of Russia in St. Petersburg, Russia, 1 June 2003*, Washington, D.C., The White House.

135 'The National Security Strategy of the United States of America', p. 26.

136 Feith, *Testimony of Douglas J. Feith*, 14 February 2002.

137 Rumsfeld, *Testimony by Donald H. Rumsfeld*, 25 July 2002.

138 Wolfowitz, P. (2001), *Press Availability with Deputy Secretary Wolfowitz in Berlin, 10 May 2001*, U.S. Department of Defense, Washington, D.C. Retrieved from http://www.defenselink.mil/transcripts/2001/t05102001_t510dsda.html on 2 March 2007; Rumsfeld, D. (2002), *Background Briefing en route to Moscow, 29 April 2002*, U.S. Department of Defense. Retrieved from http://www.defenselink.mil/transcripts/2002/t04292002_t0429bge.html on 3 March 2007.

139 Rumsfeld, D. (2001), *Secretary Rumsfeld Interview with Finnish Newspaper, 9 June 2001*, U.S. Department of Defense. Retrieved from http://www.defenselink.mil/transcripts/2001/t06112001_t609sdiv.html on 3 March 2007; Rumsfeld, *Testimony by Donald H. Rumsfeld*, 25 July 2002.

140 Feith, *Media Roundtable with USD (P) Feith*.

141 Bush, 'The President's News Conference With President Vladimir Putin of Russia'; Bush, G. W. (2002), 'Message to the Senate Transmitting the Treaty Between the United States of America and the Russian Federation on Strategic Offensive Reductions, 20 June 2002', The White House, Washington, D.C.

142 Bush, 'Message to the Senate Transmitting the Treaty Between the United States of America and the Russian Federation on Strategic Offensive Reductions'.

143 Hadley, S. J. (1999), *Testimony of Stephen J. Hadley*, Hearing before the Senate Committee on Foreign Relations, 13 May 1999, Government Printing Office, Washington, D.C., p. 177; Joseph, R. (1999), *Testimony of Robert G. Joseph*, Hearing before the Senate Committee on Foreign Relations, 13 May 1999, Government Printing Office, Washington, D.C., pp. 199–201.

144 Rumsfeld, D. (2002), *Questions and Responses*, Hearing before the Senate Committee on Armed Services, 25 July 2002, Government Printing Office, Washington, D.C., p. 188; Fetter, S. and Glaser, C. (2001), 'National Missile Defense and the Future of U.S. Nuclear Weapons Policy', *International Security*, vol. 26, no. 1, p. 80.

145 Rumsfeld, D. (2002), *Questions and Responses*, Hearing before the Senate Committee on Armed Services on 'The National Security Implications of the Strategic Offensive Reductions Treaty', July 25, 2002, US Government Printing Office,

Washington, D.C., p. 48; Powell, C. (2002), *Testimony of Colin L. Powell, Secretary of State*, Hearing before the Senate Committee on Foreign Relations, 9 July 2002, Government Printing Office, Washington, D.C., p. 18.

146 Payne, 'The Nuclear Posture Review: Setting the Record Straight', p. 138; Payne, *Deterrence in the Second Nuclear Age*, p. 65.

147 Feith, *Media Roundtable with USD (P) Feith, 4 September 2001*, Retrieved from on; Wolfowitz, P. (2001), *Deputy Secretary Wolfowitz Interview with Business Week, 18 December 2001*, U.S. Department of Defense, Washington, D.C. Retrieved from http://www.defenselink.mil/transcripts/2001/t12212001_t1218bw.html on 2 March 2007.

148 McGinnis, *Remarks of J. Sherwood McGinnis to the Second Session of the Preparatory Committee for the 2005 NPT Review Conference*'; Bush, 'Message to the Senate Transmitting the Treaty Between the United States of America and the Russian Federation on Strategic Offensive Reductions'; Powell, *Testimony of Colin L. Powell*, 9 July 2002, p. 15.

149 (2002), *Background Briefing en route to Moscow, 29 April 2002*, U.S. Department of Defense, Washington, D.C. Retrieved from http://www.defenselink.mil/transcripts/2002/t04292002_t0429bge.html on 12 March 2007.

150 Biden, J. (2001), 'Significant Strategic Issues', *Congressional Record (Senate)*, 15 November 2001, p. S11897; Biden, J. (2001), 'Conference Report Accompanying the National Defense Authorization Act for Fiscal Year 2002 – Continued', *Congressional Record (Senate)*, 13 December 2001, p. S13118.

151 (2002), 'News Transcript: Special Briefing on the Russian Visit', 16 January 2002, Department of Defense, Washington, D.C.

152 Woolf, A. (2002), 'The Nuclear Posture Review: Overview and Emerging Issues', 31 January 2002, Congressional Research Service, Washington, D.C., p. 5.

153 Payne, 'The Nuclear Posture Review: Setting the Record Straight', p. 147.

154 Krepon, M. (2003), *Cooperative Threat Reduction, Missile Defense and the Nuclear Future,* New York, Palgrave Macmillan, p. 238; Kristensen, *U.S. Nuclear Planning After the 2001 Nuclear Posture Review.*

155 Powell, *Testimony of Colin L. Powell*, 9 July 2002, p. 50.

156 Woolf, A. (2003), 'Nuclear Arms Control: the Strategic Offensive Reductions Treaty', Congressional Research Service, Washington, D.C.; Bleek, P. (2002), 'U.S., Russia Sign Treaty Cutting Deployed Nuclear Forces', *Arms Control Today*, vol. 32, no. 5 (June 2002); Boese, W. (2004), 'Bush Plans to cut Atomic Arsenal', *Arms Control Today*, vol. 34, no. 6 (July/August 2004). The START framework did not require any warheads to be destroyed but it did require verifiable destruction of delivery vehicles such as missiles and their silos and long-range bombers.

157 Feith, *Media Roundtable with USD (P) Feith.*

158 Rumsfeld, *Secretary Rumsfeld Interview with Finnish Newspaper.*

159 Fuerth, L. (2001), 'Return of the Nuclear Debate', in Lennon, A. (ed.) *Contemporary Nuclear Debates*, Cambridge, MA, The MIT Press.

160 Krepon, *Cooperative Threat Reduction, Missile Defense and the Nuclear Future*, p. 43.

161 Woolf, A. (2001), 'Arms Control and Strategic Nuclear Weapons: Unilateral vs. Bilateral Reductions', 17 December 2001, Congressional Research Service, Washington, D.C., p. 6; Bleek, P. (2002), 'U.S., Russia Agree to Codify Nuclear Reductions', *Arms Control Today*, vol. 32, no. 2 (March 2002).

162 Lautenberg, F. R. (2003), 'Moscow Treaty', *Congressional Record (Senate)*, 6 March 2003, p. S3220; Kerry, J. (2003), 'Moscow Treaty – continued', *Congressional Record (Senate)*, 6 March 2003, pp. S3233–S3234.

163 Dorgan, B. (2003), 'The So-Called Moscow Treaty', *Congressional Record (Senate)*, 4 March 2003, p S3052.

164 Kerry, 'Moscow Treaty – continued', pp. S3233–S3234.
165 Gottemoeller, R. (2002), 'Arms Control in the New Era', *The Washington Quarterly*, vol. 25, no. 2.
166 Fuerth, 'Return of the Nuclear Debate'.
167 Bush, G. H. W. and Scowcroft, B. (1998), *A World Transformed*, New York, Alfred A. Knopf, p. 53.
168 (2006), 'The National Security Strategy of the United States of America', The White House, Washington, D.C., p. 39.
169 Hildreth, S. and Ek, C. (2007), *Long-Range Ballistic Missile Defense in Europe*, Washington, D.C., CRS Report for Congress, Congressional Research Service.
170 Rumer, E. (2007), *Russian Foreign Policy Beyond Putin*, London, Adelphi Paper 390, International Institute for Strategic Studies.
171 Goldman, S. (2007), *Russian Political, Economic, and Security Issues and U.S. Interests*, Washington, D.C., CRS Report for Congress, Congressional Research Service, p. 16.
172 *U.S. Forces Russia to Modernize Weapons, Putin Says, 31 May 2007*, Global Security Newswire. Retrieved from http://www.nti.org/d_newswire/issues/2007_5_31.html on 12 December 2007.
173 Diakov, A. and Miasnikov, E. (2006), 'ReSTART: The Need for a New U.S.–Russian Strategic Arms Agreement', *Arms Control Today*, vol. 36, no. 7 (September 2006); Shanker, T. and Myers, S. L., 'Stark Differences on Arms Threaten U.S.–Russia Talks', *New York Times*, 10 October 2007.
174 Lugar, R. 'Opening Statement for Strategic Assessment of U.S.-Russian Relations Hearing', Senate Committee on Foreign Relations, 21 June 2007.
175 Rumsfeld *Testimony by Donald H. Rumsfeld, Secretary of Defense*, Rumsfeld, D. (2001), *Media Availability with Secretary of Defense Donald H. Rumsfeld, 26 January 2001*, U.S. Department of Defense, Washington, D.C. Retrieved from http://www.defenselink.mil/transcripts/2001/t01262001_t126mdav.html on 3 March 2007.
176 Feith, D. J. (2001), *Questions and Responses*, Hearing before the Senate Committee on Armed Services, 5 June 2001, Government Printing Office, Washington, D.C.
177 Bush, 'Remarks at the National Defense University'.
178 Bush, 'The President's News Conference With President Vladimir Putin of Russia'.
179 Cambone, S. (2001), *Questions and Responses*, Hearing before the Senate Committee on Armed Services, 27 June 2001, Government Printing Office, Washington, D.C., p. 1107.
180 Boese, W. (2001), 'Congress Responds to Bush Missile Plans Along Party Lines', *Arms Control Today*, vol. 31, no. 5 (June 2001).
181 Sutter, R. (1999), 'China and U.S. Missile Defense Proposals: Reactions and Implications', 17 March 1999, Congressional Research Service, Washington, D.C.
182 Bush, G. W. (2001), 'Remarks Announcing the United States Withdrawal from the Anti-Ballistic Missile Treaty, 13 December 2001', The White House, Washington, D.C.; Woolf, A. (2001), 'Missile Defense, Arms Control, and Deterrence: A New Strategic Framework', 31 October 2001, Congressional Research Service, Washington, D.C., p. 2; Powell *Testimony of Colin L. Powell, Secretary of State*, p. 13.
183 Rumsfeld, D. (2002), *Testimony of Secretary of Defense Donald Rumsfeld*, Hearing before the Senate Committee on Armed Services, 25 July 2002, Government Printing Office, Washington, D.C.
184 Feith, *Media Roundtable with USD (P) Feith.*
185 Bohlen, A. (2003), 'The Rise and Fall of Arms Control', *Survival*, vol. 45, no. 3 (Autumn 2003), p. 30.
186 Woolf, A. and Hildreth, S. (2005), 'Missile Defense: The Current Debate', 19 July 2005, Congressional Research Service, Washington, D.C., p. 1.

187 On the missile threat and the administration's missile defence programmes see Ibid.
188 (2006), 'Complex 2030: An Infrastructure Planning Scenario for a Nuclear Weapons Complex Able to Meet the Threats of the 21st Century', Department of Energy, Washington, D.C.
189 Mies, *Testimony of Adm. Richard W. Mies, USN, Commander in Chief, United States Strategic Command*, p. 20; (2004), 'The National Nuclear Security Administration Strategic Plan', November 2004, U.S. National Nuclear Security Administration, Washington, D.C., p. 7.
190 Feith, *Testimony of Douglas J. Feith*; *Nuclear Posture Review (Excerpts)*; Gordon, J. A. (2002), *Testimony of Gen. John A Gordon, Administrator, National Nuclear Security Administration*, Hearing before the Senate Committee on Armed Services, 14 February 2002, United States Senate, Washington, D.C.
191 Gordon, *Testimony of Gen. John A. Gordon*, 14 February 2002.
192 Foster, J. (2002), *Testimony of John S. Foster, Jr., Panel to Assess the Reliability, Safety and Security of the United States Nuclear Stockpile*, Hearing before the Senate Committee on Foreign Relations, 16 May 2002, Government Printing Office, Washington, D.C., p, 12.
193 'The National Nuclear Security Administration Strategic Plan', p. 20.
194 'The National Nuclear Security Administration Strategic Plan'; (2003), 'Infrastructure Plan for the NNSA Nuclear Complex', April 2003, U.S. National Nuclear Security Administration, Washington, D.C.
195 Schwartz, S. (2001), 'The New-Nuke Chorus Tunes Up', *Bulletin of the Atomic Scientists*, vol. 57, no. 4 (July/August 2001); Foster *Testimony of John S. Foster*, 16 May 2002.
196 Browne, J. C. (2001), *Testimony of Dr. John C. Browne, Director, Los Alamos National Laboratory*, Hearing before the Senate Committee on Armed Services, 25 April 2001, Government Printing Office, Washington, D.C.; Brooks, L. (2004), *Testimony of Ambassador Linton F. Brooks, Under Secretary for Nuclear Security and Administrator, National Nuclear Security Administration*, Hearing before the Senate Committee on Appropriations, 24 March 2004, Government Printing Office, Washington, D.C.; Medalia, J. (2004), 'Nuclear Warhead 'Pit' Production: Background and Issues for Congress', 29 March 2004, Congressional Research Service, Washington, D.C.
197 Paine, C. (2003), 'And Another Thing: It Really is the Pits', *Bulletin of the Atomic Scientists*, vol. 59, no. 5 (September/October 2003); Arkin, W. (2001), 'Nuclear Notebook', *Bulletin of the Atomic Scientists*, vol. 57, no. 2 (March/April 2001).
198 Byrd, *Testimony of John Byrd*, 12 June 2002.
199 Medalia, 'Nuclear Warhead 'Pit' Production', pp. 9 13.
200 Hemley, R. J., Meiron, D. *et al.* (2007), 'Pit Lifetime', The MITRE Corporation JASON Program Office, McClean, VA, p. 1.
201 Medalia, 'Nuclear Warhead 'Pit' Production'; Abraham, S. (2001), *Questions and Responses*, Hearing before the Senate Committee on Armed Services, 8 February 2001, Government Printing Office, Washington, D.C., pp. 44, 53.
202 *Nuclear Posture Review (Excerpts)*.
203 D'Agostino, T. P. (2006), *Testimony of Thomas P. D'Agostino Deputy Administrator for Defense Programs, National Nuclear Security Administration*, Hearing before the House Armed Services Committee, 5 April 2006, Government Printing Office, Washington, D.C.
204 Brooks, L. (2004), *Statement of Ambassador Linton F. Brooks, Under Secretary for Nuclear Security and Administrator, National Nuclear Security Administration*, Hearing before the Senate Committee on Appropriations, March 24, 2004, U.S. Government Printing Office, Washington, D.C.
205 Crouch, *Special Briefing on the Nuclear Posture Review, 9 January 2002*; Ellis, J. O. (2002), *Testimony of Adm. James O. Ellis, USN, Commander in Chief, United*

States Strategic Command on Command Posture, Hearing before the Senate Committee on Armed Services on, 20 March 2002, Government Printing Office, Washington, D.C.

206 Medalia, J. (2007), 'Nuclear Weapons: Comprehensive Test Ban Treaty', 13 June 2007, Congressional Research Service, Washington, D.C., p. 28.

207 Lortie, B. (2001), 'Setting the Scene', *Bulletin of the Atomic Scientists*, vol. 57, no. 2 (March/April 2001); Isaacs, 'The Ones to Watch'.

208 Kennedy, E. (2001), 'Nomination of John Robert Bolton of Maryland to be Under Secretary of State for Arms Control and International Security – Resumed', *Congressional Record (Senate)*, 8 May 2001, p. S4455.

209 Wolfowitz, P. (2001), *Deputy Secretary Wolfowitz Interview with Radio Correspondents, 29 June 2001*, U.S. Department of Defense, Washington, D.C. Retrieved from http://www.defenselink.mil/transcripts/2001/t07022001_t0629dsd.html on 2 March 2007; Spector, L. (2002), 'Ambassador Linton Brooks on U.S. Nuclear Policy', *Non-Proliferation Review*, vol. 9, no. 3.

210 Kimball, D. (1999), 'How the U.S. Senate Rejected CTBT Ratification', *Disarmament Diplomacy*, no. 40 (September/October 1999).

211 Gordon, *Testimony of Gen. John A. Gordon*, 14 February 2002; (2001), 'Letter to Carl Levin and John Warner, Chair and Ranking Minority Member of Senate Armed Services Committee, and to Bob Stump and Ike Skelton, Chair and Ranking Minority of House of Representatives Committee on Armed Services on 'Status of Planning for Stockpile Life Extension', 7 December 2001', U.S. General Accounting Office, Washington, D.C.

212 Paine, C. (2004), *Weaponeers of Waste*, Washington, D.C., Natural Resources Defense Council, p. 44.

213 Gordon, *Testimony of Gen. John A Gordon*, 14 February 2002.

214 Foster, J. (2001), *Testimony of John S. Foster*, Hearing before the House Committee on Armed Services, 26 June 2001, Government Printing Office, Washington, D.C.

215 Ellis, *Testimony of Adm. James O. Ellis, USN*, 20 March 2002.

216 Beckner, *Testimony of Dr. Everett Beckner*, 10 April 2002.

217 'Complex 2030: An Infrastructure Planning Scenario', p. 19.

218 Beckner, *Testimony of Dr. Everett Beckner*, 10 April 2002.

219 O'Brien, K. H., Fearey, B. L. *et al.* (2005), *Sustaining the Nuclear Enterprise – A New Approach*, Lawrence Livermore National Laboratory, Los Alamos National Laboratory, Sandia National Laboratory. Retrieved from http://www.nukewatch.org/facts/nwd/SustainingtheEnterprise.pdf= on 14 June 2007, p. 3.

220 (1999), 'FY 1999 Report of the Panel to Assess the Reliability, Safety, and Security of the United Sates Nuclear Stockpile', November 1999, Washington, D.C., p. ES-2; 'Report of the Defense Science Board Task Force on Future Strategic Strike Forces', p. 1.10.

221 (2006), 'Interim report of the Feasibility and Implementation of the Reliable Replacement Warhead Program', U.S. Department of Defense and U.S. Department of Energy, Washington, D.C., p. 3.

222 Medalia, J. (2007), 'The Reliable Replacement Warhead Program: Background and Current Developments', 12 June 2007, Congressional Research Service, Washington, D.C., p. 11.

223 D'Agostino, *Testimony of Thomas P. D'Agostino*, 28 March 2007; Medalia, 'The Reliable Replacement Warhead Program', p. 1.

224 Medalia, 'The Reliable Replacement Warhead Program', p. 9.

225 Schwartz, 'The New-Nuke Chorus Tunes Up'.

226 Gordon, *Testimony of Gen. John A. Gordon*, 14 February 2002.

227 Hart, G. and Rudman, W. (2001), *Road Map for National Security: Imperative for Change. The Phase III Report of the U.S. Commission on National Security/21st*

Century, Washington, D.C., The United States Commission on National Security/21st Century, p. 37.

228 These were the 1999 Readiness in Technical Base and Facilities (RTBF) programme and the 2001 Facilities and Infrastructure Recapitalization Program (FIRP). (1999), *Stockpile Stewardship Program: 30-Day Review*, Washington, D.C., U.S. Department of Energy, pp. 2.7–2.9 and 'Infrastructure Plan for the NNSA Nuclear Complex', p. 10.

229 Gordon, *Testimony of Gen. John A. Gordon*, 14 February 2002.

230 Gordon, J. A. (2001), *Testimony of Gen. John A. Gordon, Administrator, National Nuclear Security Administration*, Hearing before the Senate Committee on Armed Services on 'Department of Defense Authorization for Appropriations for Fiscal Year 2002', 25 April 2001, United States Senate, Washington, D.C.; Crouch, *Special Briefing on the Nuclear Posture Review*; Robinson, *Testimony of C. Paul Robinson*, 12 June 2002.

231 Paine, *Weaponeers of Waste*, pp. 39–40; Kidder, R. (1997), 'Problems with Stockpile Stewardship', *Nature*, 17 April 1997; (2005), 'Preliminary Results of Review of Stockpile Stewardship Program Scientific Campaigns', 4 April 2005, General Accounting Office, Washington, D.C.

232 Hobson, D. (2003), 'Energy and Water Development Appropriations Act, 2004', *Congressional Record (House of Representatives)*, 18 July 2003, p. H7114.

233 Boese, W. (2006), 'Hobson Aims to Rein in Warhead Program', *Arms Control Today*, vol. 36, no. 4 (May 2006).

234 Visclosky, P. (2003), 'Conference Report on H.R. 2754, Energy and Water Development Appropriations Act, 2004', *Congressional Record (House of Representatives)*, 18 November 2003, p. H11396.

235 Hobson, D. (2004), 'Energy and Water Development Appropriations Act, 2005', *Congressional Record (House of Representatives)*, 25 June 2004, p. H5084.

236 Medalia, J. (2006), 'Nuclear Weapons Complex Reconfiguration: Analysis of an Energy Department Task Force Report', 1 February 2006, Congressional Research Service, Washington, D.C., pp. 1–2; Hobson, D. (2005), 'Energy and Water Development Appropriations Act, 2006', *Congressional Record (House of Representatives)*, 24 May 2005, p. H3780.

237 Medalia, 'The Reliable Replacement Warhead Program', p. 21; Medalia, 'Nuclear Weapons Complex Reconfiguration', p. 27.

238 (2007), 'National Defense Authorization Act for Fiscal Year 2007: Sec. 4214. Plan for Transformation of National Nuclear Security Administration Nuclear Weapons Complex', *Congressional Record (House)*, 10 May 2006, p. H2443; (2007), 'Report on the Plan for Transformation of the National Nuclear Security Administration Nuclear Weapons Complex', U.S. Department of Energy, Washington, D.C., p. i.

239 Medalia, 'The Reliable Replacement Warhead Program', p. 14; Visclosky, P. (2005), 'Energy and Water Development Appropriations Act, 2006', *Congressional Record (House of Representatives)*, 24 May 2005, p. H3784.

240 'Complex 2030: An Infrastructure Planning'.

241 Brooks, L. (2005), *Testimony of Ambassador Linton F. Brooks, Administrator, National Nuclear Security Administration*, Hearing before the Senate Armed Services Committee, 4 April 2005, Government Printing Office, Washington, D.C.; D'Agostino, *Testimony of Thomas P. D'Agostino*, 5 April 2006.

242 D'Agostino, *Testimony of Thomas P. D'Agostino*, 28 March 2007; Aloise, G. (2006), *'Nuclear Weapons: Views on Proposals to Transform the Nuclear Weapons Complex', Statement of Gene Aloise, Director, Natural Resources and Environment before the House of Representatives Subcommittee on Energy and Water Development, Committee on Appropriations*, Washington, D.C., General Accounting Office.

243 (2007), 'National Security and Nuclear Weapons: Maintaining Deterrence in the

21st Century', July 2007, A Statement by the Secretary of Energy, Secretary of Defense and Secretary of State, Washington, D.C.

244 See (2005), 'Recommendations for the Nuclear Weapons Complex of the Future: Report on the Nuclear Weapons Complex Infrastructure Task Force', U.S. Secretary of Energy Advisory Board, Washington, D.C.

245 Overskei, D. O. (2006), *Testimony of Dr. David O. Overskei, Chairman of the Nuclear Weapons Complex Infrastructure Task Force of the Secretary of Energy Advisory Board*, Hearing before the House Armed Services Committee, 4 April 2006, Government Printing Office, Washington, D.C.; 'Recommendations for the Nuclear Weapons Complex of the Future: Report on the Nuclear Weapons Complex Infrastructure Task Force'.

246 Overskei, *Testimony of Dr. David O. Overskei*, 4 April 2006.

247 Medalia, 'Nuclear Weapons Complex Reconfiguration', pp. 35–36.

248 'Complex 2030: An Infrastructure Planning Scenario for a Nuclear Weapons Complex Able to Meet the Threats of the 21st Century'; D'Agostino, *Testimony of Thomas P. D'Agostino*, 5 April 2006; 'Report on the Plan for Transformation of the National Nuclear Security Administration Nuclear Weapons Complex'; and 'Interim report of the Feasibility and Implementation of the Reliable Replacement Warhead Program'.

249 D'Agostino, *Testimony of Thomas P. D'Agostino*, 28 March 2007.

250 Overskei, *Testimony of Dr. David O. Overskei*, 4 April 2006.

251 Medalia, J. (2007), 'Nuclear Warheads: The Reliable Replacement Warhead Program and the Life Extension Program', 16 July 2007, Congressional Research Service, Washington, D.C., p. 5.

252 Medalia, 'The Reliable Replacement Warhead Program', p. 2.

253 'Interim report of the Feasibility and Implementation of the Reliable Replacement Warhead Program', p. 3.

254 Medalia, 'The Reliable Replacement Warhead Program', p. 16.

255 'Report on the Plan for Transformation of the National Nuclear Security Administration Nuclear Weapons Complex', p. 11; Medalia, 'The Reliable Replacement Warhead Program', p. 18.

256 Burg, R. (2007), *Testimony by Maj Gen Roger Burg, USAF*, Hearing before the Senate Armed Services Committee Strategic Forces Subcommittee, 28 March 2007, Government Printing Office, Washington, D.C.; 'Report on the Plan for Transformation of the National Nuclear Security Administration Nuclear Weapons Complex', pp. 26–27.

257 Brooks, L. (2006), 'Presentation by Linton F. Brooks, Administrator, NNSA, on 'The Future of the U.S. Nuclear Weapons Stockpile', Arms Control Association Panel Discussion, 25 January 2006', U.S. Department of Energy, Washington, D.C.

258 Brooks, *Testimony of Ambassador Linton F.* Brooks, 4 April 2005.

259 'Report on the Plan for Transformation of the National Nuclear Security Administration Nuclear Weapons Complex', p. ii.

260 D'Agostino, *Testimony of Thomas P. D'Agostino*, 5 April 2006; Medalia, 'Nuclear Warheads: The Reliable Replacement Warhead Program and the Life Extension Program', p. 28.

261 'Complex 2030: An Infrastructure Planning Scenario for a Nuclear Weapons Complex Able to Meet the Threats of the 21st Century', p. 8.

262 Ibid. p. 9.

263 D'Agostino, *Testimony of Thomas P. D'Agostino*, 28 March 2007; Brooks, 'The Future of the U.S. Nuclear Weapons Stockpile, Arms Control Association Panel Discussion'; (2007), 'NNSA Fact Sheet Reliable Replacement Warhead Program'', March 2007, U.S. Department of Energy, Washington, D.C.

264 D'Agostino, *Testimony of Thomas P. D'Agostino*, 28 March 2007.

265 Brooks, 'The Future of the U.S. Nuclear Weapons Stockpile, Arms Control Association Panel Discussion'.

266 D'Agostino, T. P. (2007), ''The Reliable Replacement Warhead and Future U.S. Nuclear Weapons Program'. Remarks at National Defense University Capitol Hill Breakfast Seminar Series, 9 May 2007', U.S. Department of Energy, Washington, D.C.
267 Medalia, 'The Reliable Replacement Warhead Program', p. 1.
268 See ibid. p. 2 and 'Interim report of the Feasibility and Implementation of the Reliable Replacement Warhead Program', p. 1.
269 Medalia, 'The Reliable Replacement Warhead Program', p. 20.
270 Brooks, L. (2006), *Testimony of Ambassador Linton F. Brooks, Administrator, National Nuclear Security Administration*, Hearing before the Senate Armed Services Committee, 7 March 2006, Government Printing Office, Washington, D.C.; D'Agostino, *Testimony of Thomas P. D'Agostino Acting Administrator, National Nuclear Security Administration;* Pomper, M. (2006), 'Congress Challenges Global Strike Plan', *Arms Control Today*, vol. 36, no. 5 (June 2006).
271 Medalia, 'The Reliable Replacement Warhead Program', p. 65.
272 Ibid., pp. 4–5.
273 Ellis, *Testimony of Adm. James O. Ellis*, 8 April 2003; 'The National Nuclear Security Administration Strategic Plan', p. 9; Medalia, 'Nuclear Warheads: The Reliable Replacement Warhead Program and the Life Extension Program', p. 9.
274 Medalia, 'Nuclear Warheads: The Reliable Replacement Warhead Program and the Life Extension Program', pp. 23, 31.
275 D'Agostino, *Testimony of Thomas P. D'Agostino*, 28 March 2007.
276 Medalia, 'Nuclear Warheads: The Reliable Replacement Warhead Program and the Life Extension Program', p. 24.
277 Hemley, R. J., Meiron, D. *et al.* (2007), 'Reliable Replacement Warhead Executive Summary', The MITRE Corporation JASON Program Office, McClean, VA.
278 Aloise *'Nuclear Weapons: Views on Proposals to Transform the Nuclear Weapons Complex'*, p. 12.
279 (2006), 'Fact Sheet: Complex 2030: DOE's Misguided Plan to Rebuild the U.S. Nuclear Weapons Complex', December 2006, Union of Concerned Scientists, Washington, D.C.
280 Feinstein, D. (2007), 'Statement on Introduced Bills and Joint Resolutions', *Congressional Record (Senate)*, 1 August 2007, p. S10606.
281 Medalia, 'The Reliable Replacement Warhead Program', p. 32.
282 Domenici, P. (2007), 'Our Nuclear Deterrent', *Congressional Record (Senate)*, 19 June 2007, p. S78411.
283 Perry, W. (2007), *Testimony by William Perry*, Hearing before the House Armed Services Committee Strategic Forces Subcommittee, 18 July 2007, Government Printing Office, Washington, D.C.
284 Levine, H. (2007), 'Birth of a Notion', *Bulletin of the Atomic Scientists*, vol. 63, no. 4 (July/August 2007), p. 39.
285 'Interim report of the Feasibility and Implementation of the Reliable Replacement Warhead Program',
286 Medalia 'Nuclear Warheads: The Reliable Replacement Warhead Program and the Life Extension Program', p. 3.
287 Feinstein 'Statement on Introduced Bills and Joint Resolutions', p. S10606.
288 Wagner, R., Williams, E. *et al.* (2007), 'The United States Nuclear Weapons Program: The Role of the Reliable Replacement Warhead', American Association for the Advancement of Science, Washington, D.C., p. 4.
289 Visclosky, P. (2007), 'Energy and Water Development and Related Agencies Appropriations Act, 2008', *Congressional Record (House of Representatives)*, 19 June 2007, p. H6675; Medalia 'The Reliable Replacement Warhead Program: Background and Current Developments', p. 31.
290 *FY 2008 Omnibus Summary: Energy and Water Subcommittee*, Committee on Appropriations, U.S. House of Representatives, 16 December 2007. Retrieved from

http://appropriations.house.gov/pdf/EnergyandWaterOmnibus.pdf on 22 December 2007.

291 Reed, 'National Defense Authorization Act for Fiscal Year 2004 – Continued', p. S6689.

6 Post-Cold War trends in nuclear weapons policy

1 Rumsfeld, D. (2001), *CNN Interview with Secretary Rumsfeld, 1 June 2001*, U.S. Department of Defense. Retrieved from http://www.defenselink.mil/transcripts/2001/t06042001_t0601cnn.html on 3 March 2007.

2 This has been described as a shift from 'MAD' (a posture of mutual assured destruction) to 'half MAD'. Binnendijk, H, and Goodby, J, (eds) 'Introduction' in *Transforming Nuclear Deterrence*, National Defense University Press, Washington, D.C., 1997, p. xiv.

3 Woolf, A. (2001), 'Arms Control and Strategic Nuclear Weapons: Unilateral vs. Bilateral Reductions', 17 December 2001, Congressional Research Service, Washington, D.C., p. 10.

4 Beckner, E. (2002), *Questions and Responses*, Hearing before the Senate Committee on Armed Services, 1 August 2002, Government Printing Office, Washington, D.C., p. 94. On specific difficulties see Hecker, S. (1992), *Testimony by Dr. Siegfried Hecker, Director, Los Alamos National Laboratory*, Hearing before the Senate Committee on Armed Services, 27 March 1992, Government Printing Office, Washington, D.C., p. 168 and Reis, V. (1999), *Testimony of Dr. Victor Reis, Assistant Secretary of Energy for Defense Programs*, 26 February 1999, Government Printing Office, Washington, D.C., p. 7.

5 Habiger, E. E. (2002), *Testimony of Gen. Eugene E. Habiger, Former Commander in Chief, U.S. Strategic Command*, Hearing before the Senate Committee on Foreign Relations, 23 July 2002, Government Printing Office, Washington, D.C., p. 200.

6 Gioconda, T. (2000), *Testimony of Brig. Gen. Thomas Gioconda*, Hearing before the Senate Committee on Armed Services, 25 February 2000, Government Printing Office, Washington, D.C.; Grossman, E. (2007), *U.S. to Reduce Nuclear Stockpile, 19 December 2007*, Global Security Newswire. Retrieved from http://204.71.60.36/d_newswire/issues/2007_12_19.html on 7 January 2008.

7 (2005), *W76–0/Mk4/W76–1/Mk4A*, Globalsecurity.org, Washington, D.C. Retrieved from http://www.globalsecurity.org/wmd/systems/w76.htm on 17 July 2007.

8 Beckner, E. (2002), *Testimony of Dr. Everett Beckner, Deputy Administrator for Defense Programs, National Nuclear Security Administration*, Hearing before the Senate Committee on Armed Services, 10 April 2002, Government Printing Office, Washington, D.C.

9 (2000), *2000 Review Conference of the Parties to the Treaty on the Non-Proliferation of Nuclear Weapons Final Document*, New York. Retrieved from http://disarmament.un.org/wmd/npt/2000FD.pdf on 5 April 2007, p. 14.

7 The influence of ideas on nuclear weapons policy

1 Mearsheimer, J. (1994/1995), 'The False Promise of International Institutions', *International Security*, vol. 19, no. 5, p. 10.

2 Wohlforth, W. (1994/1995), 'Realism and the End of the Cold War', *International Security*, vol. 19, no. 3, p. 107; Smith, S. and Baylis, J. (eds) (2005), *The Globalization of World Politics*, Oxford, Oxford University Press, pp. 208–211; Viotti, P. and Kauppi, M. (1993), *International Relations Theory: Realism, Pluralism, Globalism*, New York, Macmillan, pp. 35–37.

3 Keohane, R. (1986), 'Neorealism and the Study of World Politics', in Keohane, R. (ed.) *Neorealism and its Critics*, New York, Colombia University Press, p. 11; Cox,

R. (1986), 'Social Forces, States and World Orders: Beyond International Relations Theory', in Keohane, R. (ed.) *Neorealism and its Critics*, New York, Colombia University Press, pp. 212–213.

4 Viotti and Kauppi, *International Relations Theory*, p. 36. On rationality and deterrence theory see Zagare, F. (1990), 'Rationality and Deterrence', *World Politics*, vol. 42, no. 2.

5 Key texts include Wendt, A. (1999), *Social Theory of International Politics*, Cambridge, Cambridge University Press; Wendt (1995), 'Constructing International Politics', *International Security*, vol. 20, no. 1; Wendt (1992), 'Anarchy is What States Make of It: The Social Construction of Power Politics', *International Organization*, vol. 46, no. 2; Adler, E. and Haas, P. M. (1992), 'Epistemic Communities, World Order, and the Creation of a Reflective Research Program', *International Organization*, vol. 46, no. 1 (Winter 1992); Checkel, J. (1998), 'The Constructivist Turn in International Relations Theory', *World Politics*, vol. 50, no. 1; Katzenstein, P. J. (ed.) (1996), *The Culture of National Security: Norms and Identity in World Politics*, New York, Columbia University Press; Barnett, M. (2005), 'Social Constructivism', in Smith, S. and Baylis, J. (eds) *The Globalization of World Politics*, 3rd edn. Oxford, Oxford University Press.

6 On the effect of ideas on foreign policy see Checkel, J. T. (1997), *Ideas and International Political Changes: Soviet/Russian Behavior and the End of the Cold War*, New Haven, Yale University Press; MacLean, J. (1988), 'Belief Systems and Ideology in International Relations: a Critical Approach', in Little, R. and Smith, S. (eds) *Belief Systems and International Relations*, Oxford, Basil Blackwell Inc; Goldstein, J. and Keohane, R. O. (1993), 'Ideas and Foreign Policy: An Analytical Framework', in Goldstein, J. and Keohane, R. O. (eds) *Ideas and Foreign Policy: Beliefs, Institutions and Political Change*, Ithaca, Cornell University Press; Dueck, C. (2004), 'Ideas and Alternatives in American Grand Strategy, 2000–2004', *Review of International Studies*, vol. 30, no. 4 (October 2004); Yee, A. S. (1996), 'The Causal Effects of Ideas on Policies', *International Organization*, vol. 50, no. 1 (Winter 1996); and Spear, J. and Williams, P. (1988), 'Belief Systems and Foreign Policy: the Cases of Carter and Reagan', in Little, R. and Smith, S. (eds) *Belief Systems and International Relations*, Oxford, Basil Blackwell Inc.

7 Trubowitz, P. and Rhodes, E. (1999), 'Explaining American Strategic Adjustment', in Trubowitz, P., Rhodes, E. and Goldman, E. O. (eds) *The Politics of Strategic Adjustment: Ideas, Institutions and Interests*, New York, Columbia University Press, p. 17; Little, R. and Smith, S. (eds) (1988), *Belief Systems and International Relations*, Oxford, Basil Blackwell Inc, p. 140; Yee, 'The Causal Effects of Ideas on Policies'.

8 Barnett, 'Social Constructivism', in Smith and Baylis, *The Globalization of World Politics*, p. 259; Checkel 'The Constructivist Turn in International Relations Theory', pp. 326–327.

9 Lawrence, P. (1988), 'Strategic Beliefs, Mythology and Imagery', in Little, R. and Smith, S. (eds) *Belief Systems and International Relations*, Oxford, Basil Blackwell Inc, p. 139.

10 Larsen, H. (1997), *Foreign Policy and Discourse Analysis: France, Britain and Europe*, New York, Routledge, p. 22.

11 Smith, S. (2005), 'The Contested Concept of Security', in Booth, K. (ed.) *Critical Security Studies and World Politics*, London, Lynne Rienner.

12 Katzenstein, P. J. (1996), 'Alternative Perspectives on National Security', in Katzenstein, P. J. (ed.) *The Culture of National Security: Norms and Identity in World Politics*, New York, Columbia University Press.

13 See Spinardi, G. (1990), 'Why the U.S. Navy Went for Hard-Target Counterforce in Trident II', *International Security*, vol. 15, no. 2; Tannenwald, N. (1999), 'The Nuclear Taboo: The United States and the Normative Basis of Nuclear Non-Use', *International Organization*, vol. 53, no. 3; Mehan, H., Nathanson, C. E. *et al.*

(1990), 'Nuclear Discourse in the 1980s: The Unravelling Conventions of the Cold War', *Discourse and Society*, vol. 1, no. 2; Cooper, N. (2006), 'Putting Disarmament Back in the Frame', *Review of International Studies*, vol. 32, no. 2 (April 2006); Rhodes, E. (1999), 'Constructing Power: Cultural Transformation and Strategic Adjustment in the 1890s', in Trubowitz, P., Rhodes, E. and Goldman, E. O. (eds) *The Politics of Strategic Adjustment: Ideas, Institutions and Interests*, New York, Columbia University Press; and Mutimer, D. (1997), 'Reimagining Security: The Metaphors of Proliferation', in Krause, K. and Williams, M. C. (eds) *Critical Security Studies: Concepts and Cases*, London, UCL Press.

14 Jervis, R. (1989), *The Meaning of the Nuclear Revolution: Statecraft and the Prospect of Armageddon*, Ithaca, Cornell University Press, pp. 104, 182.

15 Slocombe, W. (2006), *Democratic Control of Nuclear Weapons*, Geneva, Policy Paper, no. 12, Geneva Centre for the Democratic Control of Armed Forces, p. 7.

16 Jervis *The Meaning of the Nuclear Revolution: Statecraft and the Prospect of Armageddon*, pp. 38, 183; Jervis, R. (1984), *The Illogic of American Nuclear Strategy*, Ithaca, Cornell University Press, p. 54.

17 Lawrence, 'Strategic Beliefs, Mythology and Imagery', in Little and Smith, *Belief Systems and International Relations*, p. 143.

18 Ibid., p. 145.

19 Lodal, J. (2001), *The Price of Dominance: the New Weapons of Mass Destruction and Their Challenge to American Leadership*, New York, Council on Foreign Relations Press, pp. 6–8.

20 Krepon, M. (2003), *Cooperative Threat Reduction, Missile Defense and the Nuclear Future*, New York, Palgrave Macmillan, pp. 106–111.

21 Mazarr, M. (1992), 'Nuclear Weapons After the Cold War', *The Washington Quarterly*, vol. 15, no. 3 (Summer 1992); Cambone, S. and Garrity, P. (1994), 'The Future of U.S. Nuclear Policy', *Survival*, vol. 36, no. 4 (Winter 1994/95); Sloss, L. (1991), 'U.S. Strategic Forces After the Cold War: Policies and Strategies', *The Washington Quarterly*, vol. 14, no. 4.

22 See Mead, W. R. (2002), *Special Providence: American Foreign Policy and How it Changed the World*, London, Routledge; Posen, B. R. and Ross, A. L. (1996), 'Competing Visions for U.S. Grand Strategy', *International Security*, vol. 21, no. 3; and Drezner, D. (2005), 'Values, Interests and American Grand Strategy', *Diplomatic History*, vol. 29, no. 3.

23 Garrison explores this idea in the context of American policy towards China in Garrison, J. (2007), 'Constructing the 'National Interest' in U.S.-China Policy Making: How Foreign Policy Decision Groups Define and Signal Policy Choices', *Foreign Policy Analysis*, vol. 2007, no. 3.

24 Garrity, P. (1991), 'The Depreciation of Nuclear Weapons in International Politics', *Journal of Strategic Studies*, vol. 14, no. 4 (December 1991), p. 498; Krepon, M. (2001), 'Moving Away from MAD', *Survival*, vol. 43, no. 2 (Summer 2001), p. 85; Lodal, *The Price of Dominance*, p. 6.

25 For analysis that reflects all, or a significant part, of this idea set see the section on 'Traditionalists' in Cambone and Garrity 'The Future of U.S. Nuclear Policy', pp. 76–78; (1997), *The Future of U.S. Nuclear Weapons Policy*, Washington, D.C., National Academy Press; Hall, G. M., Capello, J. T., *et al.* (1998), *A Post-Cold War Nuclear Strategy Model*, Colorado, Institute for National Security Studies, U.S. Air Force Academy; Miller, F. (2005), 'Is There a Role for Nuclear Weapons Today?' *Arms Control Today*, vol. 35, no. 6 (July/August); and Cimbala, S. (2006), 'Parity in Peril? The Continuing Vitality of Russian–US Strategic Nuclear Deterrence', *Contemporary Security Policy*, vol. 27, no. 3.

26 Goldstein and Keohane, 'Ideas and Foreign Policy', in Goldstein and Keohane, *Ideas and Foreign Policy*.

27 Fuerth, L. (2001), 'Return of the Nuclear Debate', in Lennon, A. (ed.) *Contempor-*

ary Nuclear Debates, Cambridge, MA, The MIT Press.
28 Garrity 'The Depreciation of Nuclear Weapons in International Politics', p. 484.
29 Schlesinger, J. (2001), 'The Demise of Arms Control?' in Lennon, A. (ed.) *Contemporary Nuclear Debates*, Cambridge, MA, The MIT Press, p. 251.
30 Habiger, E. E. (1997), 'Deterrence in a New Security Environment', *Strategic Forum*, no. 109 (April 1997).
31 Buchan, G. C. (1994), *U.S. Nuclear Strategy for the Post-Cold War Era*, Santa Monica, RAND, p. 48.
32 Goodby, J. E. (1990), 'Can Arms Control Survive Peace?' *The Washington Quarterly*, vol. 13, no. 4 (Autumn 1990), p. 96; Bohlen, A. (2003), 'The Rise and Fall of Arms Control', *Survival*, vol. 45, no. 3 (Autumn 2003), p. 27; Bush, G. H. W. and Scowcroft, B. (1998), *A World Transformed*, New York, Alfred A. Knopf, p. 45.
33 Cambone, S. (2001), 'An Inherent Lesson in Arms Control', in Lennon, A. (ed.) *Contemporary Nuclear Debates*, Cambridge, MA, The MIT Press, p. 298; Clark, M. (2001), 'Seven Worries About START III', *Orbis*, vol. 45, no. 2, p. 175.
34 Slocombe, W. (1991), 'The Continued Need for Extended Deterrence', *The Washington Quarterly*, vol. 14, no. 4, p. 168; Robinson, C. P. and Bailey, K. C. (1997), 'To Zero or Not to Zero: a U.S. Perspective on Nuclear Disarmament', *Security Dialogue*, vol. 28, no. 2, p. 150.
35 Bailey, K. C. and Barish, F. (1999), 'De-alerting of U.S. Nuclear Forces: a Critical Appraisal', *Comparative Strategy*, vol. 18, no. 1, pp. 2, 7.
36 Von Hippel and Fievesen label this 'finite deterrence' Hippel, F. v. and Fievesen, H. (1990), 'Beyond START: How to Make Much Deeper Cuts', *International Security*, vol. 15, no. 1.
37 Sloss, 'U.S. Strategic Forces After the Cold War', p. 150; Blair, B. (1992), 'Targeting and Deterrence', in Gottemoeller, R. (ed.) *Strategic Arms Control in the Post-START Era*, London, Brasseys for IISS, p. 162.
38 Fuerth, 'Return of the Nuclear Debate', in Lennon, *Contemporary Nuclear* Debate, pp. 194–196.
39 See in particular Bundy, M., Smith, G. *et al.* (1984), 'The President's Choice: Star Wars or Arms Control', *Foreign Affairs*, vol. 63, no. 2 (Winter 1984/1985).
40 Sloss, L. (2001), 'Deterrence, Defenses, Nuclear Weapons and Arms Control', *Comparative Strategy*, vol. 20, no. 5, p. 148.
41 Cambone and Garrity, 'The Future of U.S. Nuclear Policy'. p. 82.
42 Glaser, C. (1992), 'Nuclear Policy Without an Adversary: U.S. Planning for the Post-Soviet Era', *International Security*, vol. 14, no. 4, p. 37.
43 Cambone and Garrity, 'The Future of U.S. Nuclear Policy', p. 79.
44 Freedman, L. (1994), 'Great Powers, Vital Interests and Nuclear Weapons', *Survival*, vol. 36, no. 4 (Winter 1994/95), p. 39; Gaddis, J. L. (1994), *The United States and the End of the Cold War*, New York, Oxford University Press, p. 118.
45 Hall, Capello and Lambert, *A Post-Cold War Nuclear Strategy Model*, p. 39; Quinlan, M. (1996), 'The Future of Nuclear Weapons in World Affairs', *The Washington Quarterly*, vol. 20, no. 3, p. 138.
46 Krepon, 'Moving Away from MAD', p. 86; Payne, K. (2001), 'Action–Reaction Metaphysics and Negligence', in Lennon, A. (ed.) *Contemporary Nuclear Debates*, Cambridge, MA, The MIT Press, p. 197.
47 Payne, K. (1998), 'Post-Cold War Requirements for U.S. Nuclear Deterrence Policy', *Comparative Strategy*, vol. 17, no. 3 (July–September 1998), p. 253; Spulak, R. (1997), 'The Case in Favour of Nuclear Weapons', *Parameters*, vol. XXVII, no. 1 (Spring 1997).
48 Bohlen, 'The Rise and Fall of Arms Control', p. 28.
49 Krepon, *Cooperative Threat Reduction, Missile Defense and the Nuclear Future*, p. 26.

50 Hall, Capello and Lambert, *A Post-Cold War Nuclear Strategy Model;* Lodal, *The Price of Dominance*, p. 27.

51 Gore, A. (2000), *Commencement Speech by Vice President Al Gore, United States Military Academy, West Point, 27 May 2000*. Retrieved from http://www.usma.edu/class/2000/GradSpeech00.asp on 14 April 2007.

52 For analysis that reflects all, or a significant part, of this 'idea set' see section on 'Marginalisers' in Cambone and Garrity, 'The Future of U.S. Nuclear Policy', pp. 74–76; Daalder, I. (1993), 'Stepping Down the Thermonuclear Ladder: How Low Can We Go?' in Daalder, I. and Terriff, T. (eds) *Rethinking the Unthinkable: New Directions for Nuclear Arms Control*, London, Frank Cass, pp. 70–80; Goodpaster Committee, (1995), 'The Declining Utility of Nuclear Weapons', *The Washington Quarterly*, vol. 20, no. 3, pp. 91–95; Schell, J. (2000), 'The Folly of Arms Control', *Foreign Affairs*, vol. 79, no. 5 (Sept./Oct. 2000); and Krepon, *Cooperative Threat Reduction, Missile Defense and the Nuclear Future*, pp. 106–111.

53 Schelling, T. C. (2005), 'An Astonishing Sixty Years: the Legacy of Hiroshima', 8 December 2005, The Royal Swedish Academy of Sciences, Stockholm; Keysen, C., McNamara, R. S. *et al.* (1991), 'Nuclear Weapons After the Cold War', *Foreign Affairs*, vol. 70, no. 4, p. 110.

54 *The Future of U.S. Nuclear Weapons Policy*, National Academy; Goodpaster Committee 'The Declining Utility of Nuclear Weapons'; Goodpaster, A. J. (1997), *An American Legacy: Building a Nuclear-Weapon-Free World – Final Report of the Steering Committee Project on Eliminating Weapons of Mass Destruction*, Washington, D.C., Henry L. Stimson Center.

55 Panofsky, W. and Bunn, G. (1994), 'The Doctrine of the Nuclear Weapon States and the Future of Non-Proliferation', *Arms Control Today*, vol., no. July/August, p. 3.

56 Daalder, I. (1995), 'What Vision for the Nuclear Future?' *The Washington Quarterly*, vol. 18, no. 2, p. 139; Perkovich, G. (2003), 'Bush's Nuclear Revolution: a Regime Change in Nonproliferation', *Foreign Affairs*, vol. 82, no. 2 (March/April 2003), p. 2; Dunn, L. A. and Alessi, V. (2000), 'Arms Control by Other Means', *Survival*, vol. 42, no. 4 (Winter 2000/01), p. 130.

57 Blechman, B. and Fisher, C. S. (1994), 'Phase Out the Bomb', *Foreign Policy*, no. 97 (Winter 1994/95); Panofsky and Bunn, 'The Doctrine of the Nuclear Weapon States', p. 7; MccGwire, M. (1994), 'Is There a Future for Nuclear Weapons?' *International Affairs*, vol. 70, no. 2, p. 224.

58 Schell, 'The Folly of Arms Control', p. 32; Schelling, 'An Astonishing Sixty Years'.

59 Carter, A., Perry, W., *et al.* (1992), *A New Concept of Cooperative Security*, Washington, D.C., The Brookings Institution, p. 19.

60 Sagan, S. D. (1996), 'Why Do States Build Nuclear Weapons?' *International Security*, vol. 21, no. 3 (Winter 1996/97), p. 84; Deibel, T. (2002), 'The Death of a Treaty', *Foreign Affairs*, vol. 18, no. 5.

61 Preez, J. D. (2002), 'The Impact of the Nuclear Posture Review on the International Nuclear Nonproliferation Regime', *Non-Proliferation Review*, vol. 9, no. 3 (Winter/Fall 2002), pp. 73–74.

62 Kimball, D. (1999), 'How the U.S. Senate Rejected CTBT Ratification', *Disarmament Diplomacy*, no. 40 (September/October 1999).

63 Gompert, D. (1998), 'Rethinking the Role of Nuclear Weapons', *Strategic Forum*, vol. –, no. 141 (May 1998); Ross, A. L. (2001), 'Thinking About the Unthinkable: Unreasonable Exuberance', *Naval War College Review*, vol. LIV, no. 2.

64 Carter, Perry and Steinbruner, *A New Concept of Cooperative Security*, pp. 8, 19; Daalder, I. and Terriff, T. (eds) (1993), *Rethinking the Unthinkable: New Directions for Nuclear Arms Control*, London, Frank Cass, p. 70.

65 McNamara, R. S. (1983), 'The Military Role of Nuclear Weapons: Perceptions and Misperceptions', *Foreign Affairs*, vol. 62, no. 1, p. 79.

66 Turner, S. (2001), 'The Dilemma of Nuclear Weapons in the Twenty-First Century', *Naval War College Review*, vol. LIV, no. 2; Joseph, R. and Blechman, B. (1997), 'Chapter Two', in Binnendjik, H. and Goodby, J. E. (eds) *Transforming Nuclear Deterrence*, Washington, D.C., National Defense University Press, p. 14; Cimbala, S. (1996), *Clinton and Post-Cold War Defense*, Westport, CT, Praeger, p. 59.
67 Cropsey, S. (1994), 'The Only Credible Deterrent', *Foreign Affairs*, vol. 73, no. 3 (March/April 1994), p. 15.
68 Brown, M. (1996), *Phased Nuclear Disarmament and US Defense Policy*, Washington, D.C., Henry L. Stimson Center, p. 19; Glaser 'Nuclear Policy Without an Adversary: U.S. Planning for the Post-Soviet Era', pp. 35–36; Goodpaster, *An American Legacy*, p. 8.
69 Millot, M. D. (1994), 'Facing the Emerging Reality of Regional Nuclear Adversaries', *The Washington Quarterly*, vol. 17, no. 3, p. 52; Nitze, P. H. (1997), 'Is it Time to Junk Our Nukes?' *The Washington Quarterly*, vol. 20, no. 3 (Summer 1997), p. 98.
70 Lodal, *The Price of Dominance*, p. 35.
71 Glaser 'Nuclear Policy Without an Adversary: U.S. Planning for the Post-Soviet Era', vol. no., p. 59; Keysen, McNamara, *et al.* 'Nuclear Weapons After the Cold War', vol. no., p. 107.
72 Daalder, 'What Vision for the Nuclear Future?', pp. 133–135; Buchan, G. C., Matonik, D. *et al.* (2003), *Future Roles of U.S. Nuclear Forces*, Arlington, RAND, p. xiii; Sokolsky, R. (2002), 'Demystifying the U.S. Nuclear Posture Review', *Survival*, vol. 44, no. 3 (Autumn 2002), p. 184; Lodal, *The Price of Dominance*, p. 84.
73 Daalder, 'Stepping Down the Thermonuclear Ladder' in Daalder and Terriff, *Rethinking the Unthinkable*, p. 74; Gottemoeller, R. (1992), *Strategic Arms Control in the Post-START Era*, London, Brasseys for the IISS, p. 101; Cimbala, S. (2005), *Nuclear Weapons and Nuclear Strategy*, New York, Routledge, p. 44.
74 Dean, J. (1994), 'The Final stage of Nuclear Arms Control', *The Washington Quarterly*, vol. 17, no. 4, pp. 46–50; Krepon, *Cooperative Threat Reduction, Missile Defense and the Nuclear Future*, pp. 240–241.
75 Payne, K. (1998), 'The Case Against Nuclear Abolition and for Nuclear Deterrence', *Comparative Strategy*, vol. 17, no. 1, p. 18.
76 Wurst, J. and Burroughs, J. (2001), 'Ending the Nuclear Nightmare: a Strategy for the Bush Administration', *World Policy Journal*, vol. XVIII, no. 1.
77 Walt, S. M. (2000), 'Two Cheers for Clinton's Foreign Policy', *Foreign Affairs*, vol. 79, no. 2, pp. 63–67.
78 Freedman, 'Great Powers, Vital Interests and Nuclear Weapons', p. 35; Michelsen, N. (1994), 'Presidential Views of Nuclear Trends', *Journal of Strategic Studies*, vol. 17, no. 3 (Summer 1994), p. 264; Carter, Perry and Steinbruner, *A New Concept of Cooperative Security*.
79 Michelsen, 'Presidential Views of Nuclear Trends', p. 265. See also Cambone and Garrity, 'The Future of U.S. Nuclear Policy', p. 74.
80 Walt, 'Two Cheers for Clinton's Foreign Policy', p. 78.
81 Schultz, G., Kissinger, H., *et al.* (2007), 'A World Free of Nuclear Weapons', *Wall Street Journal*, 4 January 2007; Schultz, G., Kissinger, H. *et al.* (2008), 'Toward a Nuclear-Free World', *Wall Street Journal*, 15 January 2008.
82 Stern, A. (2007), 'Obama Would Seek Nuclear Ban', *Reuters*, 3 October 2007.
83 For analysis that reflects all, or a significant part, of this 'idea set' see (2006), 'Report of the Defense Science Board Task Force on Nuclear Capabilities', December 2006, Office of the Under Secretary of Defense for Acquisition and Technology, U.S. Department of Defense, Washington, D.C.; Joseph and Blechman 'Chapter Two', pp. 8–14; Payne, K. (2001), *Rationale and Requirements for U.S. Nuclear Forces and Arms Control*, Fairfax, VA, National Institute for Public Policy; Gray,

C. (1992), *House of Cards: Why Arms Control Must Fail*, Ithaca, Cornell University Press; Payne, K. (1996), *Deterrence in the Second Nuclear Age*, Kentucky, University of Kentucky Press; Lieber, K. and Press, D. (2006), 'The Rise of Nuclear Primacy', *Foreign Affairs*, vol. 85, no. 2 (March/April 2006); and Krepon's description of 'Dominators' in Krepon, *Cooperative Threat Reduction, Missile Defense and the Nuclear Future*, pp. 106–111.

84 See Hurst, S. (2005), 'Myths of Neo-Conservatism: George W. Bush's 'Neo-Conservative' Foreign Policy Revisited', *International Politics*, vol. 42, no. 1; Krauthammer, C. (2004), *Democratic realism: An American Foreign Policy for a Unipolar World*, Washington. D.C., American Enterprise Institute; Monten, J. (2005), 'The Roots of the Bush Doctrine: Power, Nationalism and Democracy Promotion in U.S. Strategy', *International Security*, vol. 29, no. 4.

85 Payne, 'Post-Cold War Requirements for U.S. Nuclear Deterrence Policy', p. 242.

86 Berlin, D. (2001), 'The Growing Nuclear Weapons Threat: An Assessment of U.S. Strategic Options', *Strategic Review*, vol. 29, no. 2, p. 27; (2003), 'Differentiation and Defense: An Agenda for the Nuclear Weapons Program', United States House of Representatives Policy Committee Subcommittee on National Security and Foreign Affairs, Washington, D.C.

87 Payne, *Rationale and Requirements*.

88 On the 'second nuclear age' hypothesis see Bracken, P. (2000), 'The Second Nuclear Age', *Foreign Affairs*, vol. 79, no. 1 (Jan./Feb. 2000); Bracken, P. (2003), 'The Structure of the Second Nuclear Age', *Orbis*, vol. 74, no. 2 (Summer 2003); Gray, C. (1999), *The Second Nuclear Age*, London, Lynne Rienner, and Payne, *Deterrence in the Second Nuclear Age*.

89 Sloss, 'U.S. Strategic Forces After the Cold War', p. 154; Payne, K. (1995), 'Post-Cold War Deterrence and Missile Defense', *Orbis*, vol. 39, no. 2 (Spring 1995); Roberts, G. (1995), 'An Elegant Irrelevance: the Anti-Ballistic Missile Treaty in the New World Disorder', *Strategic Review*, vol. 23, no. 2 (Spring 1995), p. 17.

90 Sloss, 'U.S. Strategic Forces After the Cold War', p. 240; Payne, K. (2005), 'The Nuclear Posture Review: Setting the Record Straight', *The Washington Quarterly*, vol. 28, no. 3, pp. 138–140; Joseph and Blechman, 'Chapter Two' in Binnendjik and Goodby, *Transforming Nuclear Deterrence*, pp. 8–9.

91 Wirtz, J. J. (2000), 'Counterproliferation, Conventional Counterforce and Nuclear War', in Herring, E. (ed.) *Preventing the Use of Weapons of Mass Destruction*, London, Frank Cass, p. 9; Flournoy, M. and Murdock, C. (1998), *Revitalizing the U.S. Nuclear Deterrent*, Washington, D.C., Center for Strategic and International Studies, p. 30.

92 Gompert, 'Rethinking the Role of Nuclear Weapons', pp. 5–6.

93 See Gray, C. and Payne, K. (1980), 'Victory is Possible', *Foreign Policy*, no. 39 (Summer 1980) and Jervis' presentation and critique of Reagan's 'countervailing' nuclear strategy in Jervis, *The Illogic of American Nuclear Strategy*, especially chapter 3.

94 See Gray, C. (1998), 'Deterrence and Regional Conflict: Hopes, Fallacies, and 'Fixes;' *Comparative Strategy*, vol. 17; Gray, C. (2000), 'Deterrence in the 21st Century', *Comparative Strategy*, vol. 19, no. 3; Gray, *House of Cards*; Payne 'Post-Cold War Deterrence and Missile Defense'; Payne, 'Post-Cold War Requirements for U.S. Nuclear Deterrence Policy'; Payne, *Rationale and Requirements for U.S. Nuclear Forces and Arms Control*; Joseph, R. (1997), 'Nuclear Deterrence and Regional Proliferators', *The Washington Quarterly*, vol. 20, no. 3; Joseph, R. and Lehman, R. (1998), 'U.S. Nuclear Policy in the 21st Century', *Strategic Forum*, no. 145 (August 1998); Joseph, R. and Reichart, J. (1998), 'The Case for Nuclear Deterrence Today', *Orbis*, vol. 42, no. 1 (Winter 1998) and Payne, 'The Nuclear Posture Review'.

95 Flournoy and Murdock, *Revitalizing the U.S. Nuclear Deterrent*, p. 9.

96 Powell, R. (2003), 'Nuclear Deterrence Theory, Nuclear Proliferation and National Missile Defense', *International Security*, vol. 27, no. 4 (Spring 2003), pp. 101–103.
97 Krepon, *Cooperative Threat Reduction, Missile Defense and the Nuclear Future*, p. 110.
98 Powell 'Nuclear Deterrence Theory, Nuclear Proliferation and National Missile Defense'; Aubin, S. (2001), 'Clinton's Legacy of Strategic Instability', *Strategic Review*, vol. 29, no. 2.
99 See John Powers, senior policy advisor for strategic planning at the Federal Emergency Management Agency (FEMA), and Joseph Muckerman, director of emergency planning at the Office of the Under Secretary of Defense for Policy, in Muckerman, J. and Powers, J. (1994), 'Rethink the Nuclear Threat', *Orbis*, vol. 38, no. 1 (Winter 1994), p. 106. See also articles by Dowler and Howard, two senior weapons analysts at the Los Alamos National Laboratory, Dowler, T. and Howard, J. (1991), 'Countering the Well Armed Tyrant: a Modest Proposal for Small Nuclear Weapons', *Strategic Review*, vol. 19, no. 4, and Dowler, T. and Howard, J. (1995), 'Stability in a Proliferated World', *Strategic Review*, vol. 23, no. 2 (Spring 1995), pp. 31–33.
100 Bracken, P. (2004), 'Thinking (Again) About Arms Control', *Orbis*, vol. 48, no. 1 (Winter 2004), pp. 149–150.
101 Cooper, 'Putting Disarmament Back in the Frame', p. 355; Dowler and Howard, 'Stability in a Proliferated World', pp. 27–28.
102 Fuerth, 'Return of the Nuclear Debate' in Lennon, *Contemporary Nuclear Debates*, p. 184.
103 Ibid., p. 184; Joseph and Lehman, 'U.S. Nuclear Policy in the 21st Century'. On the illusion of strategic arms control and its fundamentally astrategic nature see Gray, *House of Cards*.
104 Bracken, 'The Structure of the Second Nuclear Age', p. 400; Perkovich, 'Bush's Nuclear Revolution', p. 4; Kitfield, J. (2005), 'The Pros and Cons of New Nuclear Weapons', in Bolt, P. J., Coletta, D. V. and Shackelford, C. G. (eds) *American Defense Policy*, 8th ed. Johns Hopkins University Press, Baltimore, p. 404.
105 Clark, M. T. (1996), 'Arms Control is Not Enough', *Orbis*, vol. 40, no. 1 (Winter 1996), p. 72.
106 Brown, H. and Deutch, J. (2007), 'The Nuclear Disarmament Fantasy', *Wall Street Journal*, 19 November 2007.
107 Joseph and Lehman 'U.S. Nuclear Policy in the 21st Century'.
108 Payne, *Deterrence in the Second Nuclear Age*, 149.
109 Dowler and Howard, 'Stability in a Proliferated World', p. 36; Guthe, K. (2002), *The Nuclear Posture Review: How is the 'New Triad' New?*, Washington, D.C., Center for Strategic and Budgetary Assessments, p. 24.
110 Hurst, 'Myths of Neo-Conservatism'; Krauthammer, *Democratic Realism*.
111 Payne, 'Post-Cold War Requirements for U.S. Nuclear Deterrence Policy', p. 265; Joseph and Reichart, 'The Case for Nuclear Deterrence Today', p. 11.
112 Spulak, 'The Case in Favour of Nuclear Weapons'; Barnett, R. W. (2001), 'What Deters? Strength, not Weakness', *Naval War College Review*, vol. LIV, no. 2 (Spring 2001); Payne, 'The Nuclear Posture Review', p. 143. For a detailed critique of abolitionist arguments see Payne, 'The Case Against Nuclear Abolition and for Nuclear Deterrence'.
113 Gray, *House of Cards*', pp. 77–79; Gray, *The Second Nuclear Age*, p. 148.
114 Lieber and Press, 'The Rise of Nuclear Primacy', pp. 43–53; Krepon, *Cooperative Threat Reduction, Missile Defense and the Nuclear Future*, pp. 188, 238. See also Cohen, S. (2006), 'The New American Cold War', *The Nation*, 10 July 2006.
115 Michelsen, 'Presidential Views of Nuclear Trends', p. 258.
116 Miller, 'Is There a Role for Nuclear Weapons Today?', p. 10; Robinson and Bailey, 'To Zero or Not to Zero', p. 154; Joseph and Lehman, 'U.S. Nuclear Policy in the 21st Century'.

117 Payne, 'Action-Reaction Metaphysics and Negligence' in Lennon, *Contemporary Nuclear Debates*, pp. 198–200.
118 Manning, R. A. (1997), 'The Nuclear Age: the Next Chapter', *Foreign Policy*, vol. 109, (Winter 1997), p. 79; Bracken, 'Thinking (Again) About Arms Control', p. 154; Binnendjik, H. and Goodby, J. E. (1997), 'Introduction', in Binnendjik, H. and Goodby, J. E. (eds) *Transforming Nuclear Deterrence*, Washington, D.C., National Defense University Press, p. xiii.
119 Fetter, S. and Glaser, C. (2001), 'National Missile Defense and the Future of U.S. Nuclear Weapons Policy', *International Security*, vol. 26, no. 1, p. 57; Dowler and Howard, 'Stability in a Proliferated World'.
120 Sokolsky, 'Demystifying the U.S. Nuclear Posture Review', p. 136; Gompert, D., Wilkening, D. A., *et al.* (1995), 'Nuclear First Use Revisited', *Survival*, vol. 37, no. 3 (Autumn 1995), p. 39; Deutch, J. (1992), 'The New Nuclear Threat', *Foreign Affairs*, vol. 71, no. 4 (Fall 1992), p. 130. Payne lists such factors as competing foreign policy goals and defence requirements; inter- and intraservice rivalries, bureaucratic politics, specific character and style of political and social systems, electoral politics, resource availability or limitations, organisational momentum and technological innovation or limitations. Payne, 'Action–Reaction Metaphysics and Negligence' in Lennon, *Contemporary Nuclear Debates*, p. 206.
121 Sagan, 'Why Do States Build Nuclear Weapons?', p. 86.
122 Halperin, M. H. and Clapp, P. A. (2006), *National Security Policy-Making*, Washington, D.C., Brookings Institution Press, p. 12.
123 (2005), *U.S. Strategic Nuclear Policy: An Oral History (Unclassified DVD)*, Albuquerque, NM, Sandia National Laboratories, disk 4, chapter 5.
124 (1996), *Statement on Nuclear Weapons by International Generals and Admirals*. Retrieved from http://www.comeclean.org.uk/articles.php?articleID=27 on 14 April 2007; (1998), *Statement by Heads of State and Civilian Leaders Worldwide*. Retrieved from http://www.comeclean.org.uk/articles.php?articleID=28 on 14 April 2007;Gormley, D. and Mahnken, T. (2000), 'Facing Nuclear and Conventional Reality', *Orbis*, vol. 44, no. 1, pp. 110–112.
125 See Goodpaster, *An American Legacy*, Walker, R. (2000), 'What is to be Done About Nuclear Weapons? A Rejoinder', *Security Dialogue*, vol. 31, no. 2 (June 2000), Butler, G. L. (1997), 'The General's Bombshell: Phasing out the U.S. Nuclear Arsenal', *The Washington Quarterly*, vol. 20, no. 3; Butler, G. L. (1998), *'The Risks of Nuclear Deterrence: From Superpowers to Rogue Leaders', An Address by General George Lee Butler at the National Press Club, 2 February 1998*. Retrieved from http://www.brook.edu/fp/projects/nucwcost/deter.htm on 12 March 2007; Schell, J. (1998), *The Gift of Time*, London, Granta Books; Blechman and Fisher, 'Phase Out the Bomb'; MccGwire 'Is There a Future for Nuclear Weapons?'.
126 Schell, 'The Folly of Arms Control', pp. 23, 40; Gormley, D. (2005), 'Conventional Force Integration in Global Strike', in Wirtz, J. J. and Larsen, J. A. (eds) *Nuclear Transformation: The New U.S. Nuclear Doctrine*, New York, Palgrave Macmillan, p. 112. For an eloquent articulation of this view see Butler, 'The General's Bombshell', p. 132.
127 On the exclusion of nuclear disarmament from mainstream American discourse on nuclear weapons policy as an infeasible and destabilising idea see Schell, 'The Folly of Arms Control', p. 37. See also Glaser, C. (1998), 'The Flawed Case for Nuclear Disarmament', *Survival*, vol. 40, no. 1 (Spring 1998); Deutch, J. (2005), 'A Nuclear Posture for Today', *Foreign Affairs*, vol. 84, no. 1, p. 5; Sloss, 'Deterrence, Defenses, Nuclear Weapons and Arms Control', p. 246; Payne, 'Post-Cold War Requirements for U.S. Nuclear Deterrence Policy', p. 246; Brown, *Phased Nuclear Disarmament and US Defense Policy*, pp. 27–30; and Quinlan, 'The Future of Nuclear Weapons in World Affairs', p. 140.

128 Smith, J. M. (2005), 'The New Strategic Framework, the New Strategic Triad, and the Strategic Military Services', in Wirtz, J. J. and Larsen, J. A. (eds) *Nuclear Transformation: The New U.S. Nuclear Doctrine*, New York, Palgrave Macmillan, p. 133.
129 Goodby, 'Can Arms Control Survive Peace?', p. 100.
130 Lawrence, 'Strategic Beliefs, Mythology and Imagery' in Little and Smith, *Belief Systems and International Relations*, pp. 156–59.
131 Spear and Williams, 'Belief Systems and Foreign Policy' in Little and Smith, *Belief Systems and International Relations*, pp. 203–206; Krepon, *Cooperative Threat Reduction, Missile Defense and the Nuclear Future*, p. 253.
132 Smith, 'The New Strategic Framework' in Wirtz and Larsen, *Nuclear Transformation*, p. 136.
133 Goldfischer discusses 'phases' of nuclear weapons policy from the beginning of the nuclear age with a new and as yet undetermined phase beginning in 1992 in Goldfischer, D. (1998), 'Rethinking the Unthinkable After the Cold War: Toward Long-Term Nuclear Policy Planning', *Security Studies*, vol. 7, no. 4 (Summer 1998). Larsen also argues that the shift in nuclear weapons policy under George W. Bush through the 2001 NPR represents a quiet revolution. Larsen, J. A. (2005), 'Conclusion', in Wirtz, J. J. and Larsen, J. A. (eds) *Nuclear Transformation: The New U.S. Nuclear Doctrine*, New York, Palgrave Macmillan, p. 261.
134 Jervis, *The Meaning of the Nuclear Revolution*, pp. 199, 216.
135 Ibid., p. 216.

8 Domestic politics and nuclear weapons policy

1 Nolan's study of American nuclear policy-making suggests that explanation lies not in external factors but predominantly in a domestic political context. Nolan, J. E. (1999), *An Elusive Consensus: Nuclear Weapons and American Security After the Cold War*, Washington D.C., Brookings Institution Press.
2 Jordan, A. A., Mazarr, M. J. *et al.* (1999), *American National Security*, Baltimore, Johns Hopkins University Press, p. 119.
3 Key texts include Snyder, R. C., Bruck, H. W. *et al.* (eds) (1962), *Foreign Policy Decision-Making: An Approach to the Study of International Politics*, New York, Free Press of Glencoe; Allison, G. (1971), *Essence of Decision: Explaining the Cuban Missile Crisis*, Boston, Little Brown; Halperin, M. H. (1975), *National Security Policy-Making*, Lexington, Mass, D.C. Heath; and Newmann, W. W. (2003), *Managing National Security Policy: The President and the Process*, Pittsburgh, University of Pittsburgh Press.
4 On individual policy-makers and the psychology of decision-making see Hudson, V. M. (2007), *Foreign Policy Analysis: Classic and Contemporary Theory*, New York, Rowan & Littlefield Publishers, chapter two, 'The Individual Decisionmaker: The Political Psychology of World Leaders'.
5 Ibid., p. 89.
6 Allison, *Essence of Decision*.
7 Hill, C. (2003), *The Changing Politics of Foreign Policy*, Basingstoke, Palgrave Macmillan, p. 96.
8 Allison, *Essence of Decision*; Hilsman, R. (1971), *The Politics of Policy Making in Defense and Foreign Affairs*, New York, Harper and Row, pp. 15, 122.
9 Kozak, D. C. (1988), 'The Bureaucratic Politics Approach: The Evolution of the Paradigm', in Kozak, D. C. and Keagle, J. M. (eds) *Bureaucratic Politics and National Security*, Boulder, Lynne Rienner Publishers, pp. 6–7; Jordan, Mazarr *et al. American National Security*, pp. 225–226.
10 Hudson *Foreign Policy Analysis: Classic and Contemporary Theory*, p. 78; Lord, C. (1988), *The President and the Management of National Security*, New York, The Free Press, p. 17.

11 Dougherty, J. E. and Pfaltzgraff, R. L. (2001), *Contending Theories of International Relations: A Comprehensive Survey*, New York, Longman, p. 572.
12 Kozak, 'The Bureaucratic Politics Approach' in Kozak and Keagle, *Bureaucratic Politics and National Security*, p. 7.
13 Hill, *The Changing Politics of Foreign Policy*, p. 88.
14 Hudson, *Foreign Policy Analysis: Classic and Contemporary Theory*, p. 77.
15 Janis, I. (1972), *Victims of Groupthink: A Psychological Study of Foreign-Policy Decisions and Fiascoes*, Boston, Houghton, Mifflin; Hudson, *Foreign Policy Analysis: Classic and Contemporary Theory*, pp. 66–69.
16 Halperin, M. H. and Clapp, P. A. (2006), *National Security Policy-Making*, Washington, D.C., Brookings Institution Press, pp. 13, 22.
17 Jordan, Mazarr, *et al.*, *American National Security*, p. 224.
18 Ogden, D. M. (1988), 'How National Policy is Made', in Kozak, D. C. and Keagle, J. M. (eds) *Bureaucratic Politics and National Security*, Boulder, Lynne Rienner Publishers, pp. 260–266; Shuman, H. E. (1988), 'Congress and the Bureaucracy', in Kozak, D. C. and Keagle, J. M. (eds) *Bureaucratic Politics and National Security*, Boulder, Lynne Rienner Publishers, p. 230.
19 Halperin, *National Security Policy-Making*, p. 15.
20 Allison, *Essence of Decision*; Newmann, *Managing National Security Policy*, p. 20.
21 Muradian, V. (2007), *Is U.S. Army Resisting Irregular War Focus? Early Jockeying For Next QDR Spurs Debate, 10 August 2007*, DefenseNews.com. Retrieved from http://www.defensenews.com/story.php?F=3090743&C=america on 12 December 2007.
22 Sarkesian, S. C. (1989), *U.S. National Security: Policymakers, Processes, and Politics*, Boulder, Lynne Rienner Publishers, p. 78.
23 Jefferies, C. (1988), 'Bureaucratic Politics in the Department of Defense', in Kozak, D. C. and Keagle, J. M. (eds) *Bureaucratic Politics and National Security*, Boulder, Lynne Rienner Publishers, p. 116; Hilsman, *The Politics of Policy Making*, p. 138.
24 Kozak, 'The Bureaucratic Politics Approach' in Kozak and Keagle, *Bureaucratic Politics and National Security*, p. 8; Lord, *The President and the Management of National Security*, p, 11; Hudson, *Foreign Policy Analysis*, p. 81.
25 Hill, *The Changing Politics of Foreign Policy*, p. 93; Halperin and Clapp, *National Security Policy-Making*, p. 99.
26 Kozak, 'The Bureaucratic Politics Approach' in Kozak and Keagle, *Bureaucratic Politics and National Security*, p. 8.
27 Sarkesian, *U.S. National Security*, pp. 65, 130; Sauer, T. (2005), *Nuclear Inertia: US Nuclear Weapons Policy after the Cold War*, London, I.B. Taurus, p. 72.
28 Rhodes, E. (1994), 'Do Bureaucratic Politics Matter?' *World Politics*, vol. 47, no. 1, p. 19.
29 Sarkesian, *U.S. National Security*, pp. 66, 121; Hudson, *Foreign Policy Analysis*, p. 76.
30 Jefferies, 'Bureaucratic Politics in the Department of Defense' in Kozak and Keagle, *Bureaucratic Politics and National Security*, p. 120.
31 Jordan, Mazarr, *et al.*, *American National Security*, p. 120.
32 Newmann, *Managing National Security Policy*, p. 53; Hudson, *Foreign Policy Analysis*, p. 91.
33 Hermann, C. F., Stein, J. G. *et al.* (2001), 'Resolve, Accept, or Avoid: Effects of Group Conflict on Foreign Policy Decisions', *International Studies Review*, vol. 3, no. 3 (Summer 2001), p. 162.
34 Beasley, R. K., Kaarbo, J. *et al.* (2001), 'People and Process in Foreign Policymaking: Insights from Comparative Case Studies', *International Studies Review*, vol. 3, no. 3 (Summer 2001), p. 243.
35 Sarkesian, S. C., Williams, J. A. *et al.* (2005), 'The Military Establishment, the President, and Congress', in Bolt, P. J., Coletta, D. V. and Shackelford, C. G. (eds)

American Defense Policy, 8th edn. Johns Hopkins University Press, Baltimore, p. 149.

36 Sauer, *Nuclear Inertia*, p. 78; Jordan, Mazarr *et al.*, *American National Security*, p. 115.

37 Halperin, *National Security Policy-Making*, p. 16; Sarkesian, *U.S. National Security*, p. 61; Hilsman, *The Politics of Policy Making in Defense and Foreign Affairs*, pp. 136–137.

38 Newmann, *Managing National Security Policy*, p. 22.

39 Ibid., p. 29.

40 Garrison, J. (2007), 'Constructing the 'National Interest' in U.S.–China Policy Making: How Foreign Policy Decision Groups Define and Signal Policy Choices', *Foreign Policy Analysis*, vol. 2007, no. 3, p. 123.

41 Newmann, *Managing National Security Policy*, p. 156.

42 Halperin, *National Security Policy-Making*, p. 5.

43 Garrity, P. (1991), 'The Depreciation of Nuclear Weapons in International Politics', *Journal of Strategic Studies*, vol. 14, no. 4 (December 1991), p. 485.

44 Les Aspin, 'From Deterrence to Denuking: Dealing with Proliferation in the 1990s,' United States Congress, February 1992.

45 Nolan, *An Elusive Consensus*, p. 39.

46 Ibid., pp. 40, 51.

47 Interview with former DOD official involved in nuclear weapons policy, November 2006.

48 Sauer, *Nuclear Inertia*, pp. 110, 166–167.

49 Nolan, *An Elusive Consensus*, p. 103.

50 Cimbala, S. (1996), *Clinton and Post-Cold War Defense*, Westport, CT, Praeger, pp. 132–133; See also Hartung, W. D. (1999), 'Ready For What? The New Politics of Pentagon Spending', *World Policy Journal*, vol. 16, no. 1 (Spring 1999), and Starr, B. (1994), 'Clinton Has Yet to Close Trust Gap, Aspin Says', *Jane's Defence Weekly*, vol. 21, no. 7 (19 February 1994), p. 8.

51 Nolan, *An Elusive Consensus*, p. 107.

52 See also (2005), *U.S. Strategic Nuclear Policy: An Oral History (Unclassified DVD)*, Albuquerque, NM, Sandia National Laboratories, disk 4, chapter 3.

53 Halperin and Clapp, *National Security Policy-Making*, p. 73.

54 Interviews with five independent experts on American nuclear weapons policy, Washington, D.C., June 2005 and October 2006; interview with former senior DOD official involved in nuclear weapons policy, November 2006; interview with former senior NSC official in the Clinton administration, September 2006. See also Michelsen, N. (1994), 'Presidential Views of Nuclear Trends', *Journal of Strategic Studies*, vol. 17, no. 3 (Summer 1994), p. 268.

55 This view was shared by a number of interviewees.

56 Interviews with senior Department of Defense officials in the Clinton administration, October 2006 and September 2006; interviews with academic experts on American nuclear weapons policy, Washington, D.C., September 2006 and October 2006. In fact, Sagan argued in 1989 that nuclear weapons policy was not a high priority due to 'many other pressing issues on the agenda of senior civilian authorities'. Sagan, S. D. (1989), *Moving Targets: Nuclear Strategy and National Security*, Princeton, Princeton University Press, p. 186.

57 (2006), 'Report of the Defense Science Board Task Force on Nuclear Capabilities', December 2006, Office of the Under Secretary of Defense for Acquisition and Technology, U.S. Department of Defense, Washington, D.C., p. 33.

58 Interview with academic expert on American nuclear weapons policy, Maryland, September 2006.

59 Interview with senior Department of Energy official in the G. W. Bush administration, September 2006. See also Representative Ellen Tauscher in (2005), 'Session

on Congress and Nuclear Weapons', *Carnegie International Non-Proliferation Conference, 8 November 2005*, Washington, D.C.

60 Lindsay, J. M. (1991), *Congress and Nuclear Weapons*, Baltimore, The Johns Hopkins University Press, p. 104.

61 Interview with senior aide to Representative involved in nuclear weapons policy in Congress, September 2006; interview with senior Department of Defense official in the Clinton administration, October 2006.

62 Woolf, A. (2001), 'U.S. Nuclear Weapons: Policy, Force Structure and Arms Control Issues', 12 January 2001, Congressional Research Service, Washington, D.C., pp. 33–34.

63 See Stephen Schwartz in 'Session on Congress and Nuclear Weapons'.

64 Slocombe, W. (2006), *Democratic Control of Nuclear Weapons*, Geneva, Policy Paper, no. 12, Geneva Centre for the Democratic Control of Armed Forces.

65 Interview with senior Department of Energy official in the George W. Bush administration, September 2006; interview with independent expert on American nuclear weapons policy, October 2006.

66 Interview with senior Department of Defense official in the Clinton administration, September 2006; interview with former Senator involved in nuclear weapons policy, October 2006.

67 Gray, C. (1999), *The Second Nuclear Age*, London, Lynne Rienner, pp. 41, 160.

68 Interview with State department official in the George W. Bush administration, September 2006.

69 (2002), 'Arms Control Association Panel Briefing at the Carnegie Endowment for International Peace, 22 January 2002', Arms Control Association, Washington, D.C.

70 Interview with senior Strategic Command official in the Clinton administration, September 2006.

71 Smith, J. M. (2005), 'The New Strategic Framework, the New Strategic Triad, and the Strategic Military Services', in Wirtz, J. J. and Larsen, J. A. (eds) *Nuclear Transformation: The New U.S. Nuclear Doctrine*, New York, Palgrave Macmillan, p. 141.

72 Joseph, R. and Lehman, R. (1998), 'U.S. Nuclear Policy in the 21st Century', *Strategic Forum*, vol. –, no. 145 (August 1998). See also (1998), 'Report of the Defense Science Board Task Force on Nuclear Deterrence', October 1998, Office of the Under Secretary of Defense for Acquisition and Technology, U.S. Department of Defense, Washington, D.C., p. 26.

73 Hamre, J. (1998), *DOD News Briefing, Thursday, 11 June 1998, Deputy Secretary of Defense John J. Hamre*, U.S. Department of Defense, Washington, D.C. Retrieved from http://www.defenselink.mil/transcripts/1998/t06231998_t616hab2.html on 23 February 2007.

74 Neary, T., Preisinger, J., Ludka, L. and Sutter, J. (2001), 'Nuclear Deterrence Issues and Options Study: A Baseline Assessment of DOD Staff Nuclear Expertise', 21 December 2001, Defense Threat Reduction Agency, Washington, D.C.

75 Millot, M. D. (1994), 'Facing the Emerging Reality of Regional Nuclear Adversaries', *The Washington Quarterly*, vol. 17, no. 3, p. 66; Cambone, S. and Garrity, P. (1994), 'The Future of U.S. Nuclear Policy', *Survival*, vol. 36, no. 4 (Winter 1994/95), pp. 493–495. Interview with senior Strategic Command official in the Clinton administration, September 2006; interview with Department of Defense official in the G. W. Bush administration, November 2006.

76 (2005), 'Session on Utility of Nuclear Weapons', *Carnegie International Non-Proliferation Conference, 8 November 2005*, Washington, D.C.

77 Interview with senior Department of Defense official in the Clinton administration, October 2006.

78 Halperin and Clapp, *National Security Policy-Making*, pp. 38–39.

79 Smith, 'The New Strategic Framework' in Wirtz and Larsen, *Nuclear Transformation*, pp. 131–132, 138–139.
80 Interview with former DOD official involved in nuclear weapons policy, October 2006.
81 Senator John Warner expressed grave concern at this prospect. Warner, J. (1993), 'Department of Defense Appropriations Act of 1994', *Congressional Record (Senate)*, 14 October 1993.
82 (1997), *Defense Special Weapons Agency 19476–1997: The First 50 Years of National Service*, Washington, D.C., Defense Special Weapons Agency, pp. 27–31.
83 Harahan, J. P. and Bennett, R. J. (2002), *Creating the Defense Threat Reduction Agency*, Washington, D.C., U.S. Department of Defense, p. 10.
84 Ibid., p. 15.
85 Crouch, J. D. (2001), *Media Roundtable with ASD (ISP) Crouch, 28 August 2001*, U.S. Department of Defense, Washington, D.C. Retrieved from http://www.defenselink.mil/transcripts/2001/t08292001_t0828isp.html on 21 March 2007.
86 Smith, H. (1995), *Testimony by Dr. Harold P. Smith, Assistant to the Secretary of Defense (Atomic Energy)*, Hearing before the Senate Committee on Armed Services, 16 May 1995, Government Printing Office, Washington, D.C., p. 220; Cohen, W. (1997), *Nuclear Weapon Systems Sustainment Programs*, Washington, D.C., Department of Defense.
87 (1994), *Department of Defense Directive 5134.8, 8 June 1994*, Department of Defense, Washington, D.C. Retrieved from http://www.dtic.mil/whs/directives/corres/pdf/513408p.pdf on 2 May 2007; Harahan and Bennett, *Creating the Defense Threat Reduction Agency*, p. 14.
88 (2007), *U.S. Strategic Command Fact Sheet: Joint Functional Component Command for Global Strike and Integration*, U.S. Strategic Command. Retrieved from http://www.stratcom.mil/fact_sheets/fact_gsi_print.html on 17 July 2007; (2007), *About STRATCOM: Functional Components*, U.S. Strategic Command, Retrieved from http://www.stratcom.mil/organization-fnc_comp.html on 17 July 2007.
89 Joseph and Lehman, 'U.S. Nuclear Policy in the 21st Century'.
90 Woolf, 'U.S. Nuclear Weapons: Policy, Force Structure and Arms Control Issues', p. 24.
91 Rumsfeld, D. (2001), *Secretary Rumsfeld Media Availability with Russian Journalists, 13 August 2001*, U.S. Department of Defense, Washington, D.C. Retrieved from http://www.defenselink.mil/transcripts/2001/t08132001_t813russ.html on 2 May 2007.
92 Interview with senior Department of Energy official in the George W. Bush administration, September 2006.
93 Interview with DOD official involved in nuclear weapons policy, October 2006.
94 Michelsen, 'Presidential Views of Nuclear Trends', p. 268.
95 Nolan, *An Elusive Consensus*, pp. 28–30.
96 See comments by Butler, Frank Miller, former Deputy Assistant Secretary of Defense for Nuclear Forces and Arms Control Policy, and General Larry Welch, former Air Force chief of staff, in *U.S. Strategic Nuclear Policy: An Oral History (Unclassified DVD)*, disk 4.
97 Cohen, W. (1990), 'Reorienting Defense in the 1990's', *Congressional Record (Senate)*, 5 April 1990, p. S4056.
98 Sauer, *Nuclear Inertia*, pp. 85–86, 124–129.
99 Ibid., p. 99.
100 Nolan, *An Elusive Consensus*, pp. 41–58.
101 Ibid., p. 105.
102 See testimony by Vice Admiral William Owens, in Owens, W. A. (2002), *Testimony of Adm. William Owens, U.S. Navy (Ret.)*, Hearing before the Senate

Committee on Foreign Relations, 16 May 2002, Government Printing Office, Washington, D.C., p. 16; Nolan, *An Elusive Consensus*, pp. 3, 103, 105; and Norquist, D. L. (2005), 'The Defense Budget: Is it Transformational?' in Bolt, P. J., Coletta, D. V. and Shackelford, C. G. (eds) *American Defense Policy*, 8th edn. Johns Hopkins University Press, Baltimore, p. 196.

103 Sarkesian, *U.S. National Security*, p. 60.

104 Interview with former DOD official involved in nuclear weapons policy, October 2006.

105 Owens, *Testimony of Adm. William Owens*, 16 May 2002, p. 16.

106 See Lindsay, *Congress and Nuclear Weapons*, pp. 84–85; Buchan, G. C. (1994), *U.S. Nuclear Strategy for the Post-Cold War Era*, Santa Monica, RAND, p. ix; Cambone and Garrity, 'The Future of U.S. Nuclear Policy', pp. 78–80; and Michelsen, 'Presidential Views of Nuclear Trends', p. 268.

107 Interview with senior Department of Defense official in the Clinton administration, October 2006; interview with senior White House official in the G. H. W. Bush administration, October 2006; interview with independent expert on American nuclear weapons policy, October 2006; Interview with senior Strategic Command official in the Clinton administration, September 2006.

108 Interview with academic expert on American nuclear weapons policy, October 2006.

109 Interview with independent expert on American nuclear weapons policy, October 2006.

110 (1993), 'Report of the Defense Science Board Task Force on the Defense Nuclear Agency', April 1993, Department of Defense, Washington, D.C., p. iii.

111 Harahan and Bennett, *Creating the Defense Threat Reduction Agency*, p. 6.

112 'Report of the Defense Science Board Task Force on Nuclear Deterrence', p. 28.

113 Ibid., pp. 22–23.

114 Ibid., p. 25.

115 Ibid., p. 18.

116 Joseph, R. and Lehman, R. (1998), *U.S. Nuclear Policy in the 21st Century: A Fresh Look at National Strategy and Requirements*, Washington, D.C., National Defense University and Lawrence Livermore National Laboratory, p. 1.2.

117 Ibid., p. 1.23.

118 Ibid., p. 1.26.

119 Ibid., pp. 1.39, 4.6–4.7.

120 'Report of the Defense Science Board Task Force on Nuclear Capabilities', p. 33.

121 Ibid.

122 Wirtz, J. J. (2006), 'Do U.S. Nuclear Weapons Have a Future?' *Strategic Insights*, vol. V, no. 3 (March 2006); Gordon, J. A. (2002), *Testimony of Gen. John A Gordon, Administrator, National Nuclear Security Administration*, Hearing before the Senate Committee on Armed Services, 14 February 2002, United States Senate, Washington, D.C.

123 Interview with senior Department of Energy official in the G. W. Bush administration, September 2006; Hall, G. M., Capello, J. T., *et al.* (1998), *A Post-Cold War Nuclear Strategy Model*, Colorado, Institute for National Security Studies, U.S. Air Force Academy, p. 42; and Nolan, *An Elusive Consensus*, p. 105.

124 Nolan, *An Elusive Consensus*, p. 7.

125 Interview with senior Department of Energy official in the George W. Bush administration, September 2006.

126 Interview with former DOD official involved in nuclear weapons policy in the Clinton administration, September 2006.

127 Interview with former DOD official involved in nuclear weapons policy, October 2006.

128 Interview with senior Strategic Command official in the Clinton administration, September 2006. See statement by Representative Woolsey, L. (2004), 'Smart Security and Energy and Water Appropriations', *Congressional Record (House of Representatives)*, 23 September 2004, p. H7543.
129 Interview with senior Department of Energy official in the George W. Bush administration, September 2006; interview with senior Strategic Command official in the Clinton administration, September 2006.
130 'Report of the Defense Science Board Task Force on Nuclear Capabilities', pp. 2, 19.
131 Ibid., pp. 14–15.
132 Gormley, D. (2005), 'Conventional Force Integration in Global Strike', in Wirtz, J. J. and Larsen, J. A. (eds) *Nuclear Transformation: The New U.S. Nuclear Doctrine*, New York, Palgrave Macmillan, p. 64.
133 Maaranen, S. (2005), 'A Responsive New Triad Infrastructure', in Wirtz, J. J. and Larsen, J. A. (eds) *Nuclear Transformation: The New U.S. Nuclear Doctrine*, New York, Palgrave Macmillan, p. 100.
134 Interview with independent expert on American nuclear weapons policy, May 2005.
135 Feith, D. J. (2002), *Special Briefing on the Russian Visit, 16 January 2002*, U.S. Department of Defense, Washington, D.C. Retrieved from http://www.defenselink.mil/transcripts/2002/t01162002_t0116fcb.html on 12 March 2007.
136 Interviews with independent expert on American nuclear weapons policy, Washington, D.C., October 2006 and September 2006. See also Kristensen, H. and Handler, J. (1996), 'The USA and Counter-Proliferation: a New and Dubious Role for U.S. Nuclear Weapons', *Security Dialogue*, vol. 27, no. 4, p. 393.
137 Interview with independent expert on American nuclear weapons policy, Washington, D.C., October 2006.
138 Interview with expert on American nuclear weapons policy, June 2005; Interview with senior Strategic Command official in the Clinton administration, September 2006.
139 Lindsay, *Congress and Nuclear Weapons*, pp. 19–20, 123.
140 Hill, *The Changing Politics of Foreign Policy*, p. 96; Rhodes 'Do Bureaucratic Politics Matter?', pp. 32, 41.
141 Hudson, *Foreign Policy Analysis*, p. 121.
142 Halperin and Clapp, *National Security Policy-Making*, p. 158.

Conclusion

1 On 'nuclearism' see Lawrence, P. (1988), 'Strategic Beliefs, Mythology and Imagery', in Little, R. and Smith, S. (eds), *Belief Systems and International Relations*, Basil Blackwell Inc, Oxford, p. 142.
2 Miller, F. (2005), 'Is There a Role for Nuclear Weapons Today?' *Arms Control Today*, vol. 35, no. 6 (July/August 2005).
3 This view was expressed by a number of interviewees. Interview with DOD official involved in nuclear weapons policy, October 2006; interview with independent expert on US nuclear weapons policy, October 2006; telephone interview with independent expert on nuclear weapons policy, October 2006; Interview with senior Department of Energy official in the George W. Bush administration, September 2006.
4 Krepon, M. (2001), 'Moving Away from MAD', *Survival*, vol. 43, no. 2 (Summer 2001), p. 86.
5 (2002), 'Arms Control Association Panel Briefing at the Carnegie Endowment for International Peace, 22 January 2002', Arms Control Association, Washington, D.C.
6 This point was made by Halperin in ibid.
7 Rebecca Johnson, Stephen Pullinger and Nicola Butler make this point in the context of the British government's decision to renew its Trident nuclear arsenal in *Worse than*

Irrelevant? British Nuclear Weapons in the 21st Century, Acronym Institute for Disarmament Diplomacy: London, p. 4.
8 Norris, S. and Kristensen, H., 'What's Behind Bush's Nuclear Cuts?', *Arms Control Today*, vol. 34, no. 8 October 2004; Kristensen, H. 'White House Announces (Secret) Nuclear Weapons Cuts', *Strategic Security Blog*, Federation of American Scientists, 18 December 2007. Retrieved from http://www.fas.org/blog/ssp/2007/12/white_house_announces_secret_n.php#more on 7 January 2008; (2002), *Table of U.S. Nuclear Warheads*, Natural Resources Defense Council, New York. Retrieved from http://www.nrdc.org/nuclear/nudb/datab9.asp on 24 November 2004.
9 Mehan, H., Nathanson, C. E. and Skelly, J. M. (1990), 'Nuclear Discourse in the 1980s: The Unravelling Conventions of the Cold War', *Discourse and Society*, vol. 1, no. 2.

Select bibliography

Government publications

(1993), *Doctrine for Joint Nuclear Operations*, Joint Chiefs of Staff, Washington, D.C.

(1994), *Briefing on the Results of the Nuclear Posture Review*, Hearing before the Senate Committee on Armed Services, September 22, 1994, U.S. Government Printing Office, Washington, D.C.

(1995), *The Stockpile Stewardship and Management Program: Maintaining Confidence in the Safety, Reliability of the Enduring U.S. Nuclear Weapon Stockpile*, U.S. Department of Energy Office of Defense Programs, Washington, D.C.

(1996), *Doctrine for Joint Theater Nuclear Operations*, Joint Chiefs of Staff, Washington, D.C.

(1996), W. Perry, *Proliferation: Threat and Response*, Department of Defense, Washington, D.C.

(1997), *Defense Special Weapons Agency 1947–1997: The First 50 Years of National Service*, U.S. Defense Special Weapons Agency, Washington, D.C.

(1997), W. Cohen, *Nuclear Weapon Systems Sustainment Programs*, Department of Defense, Washington, D.C.

(1998), *Report of the Defense Science Board Task Force on Nuclear Deterrence*, Department of Defense, Washington, D.C.

(1999), *FY 1999 Report of the Panel to Assess the Reliability, Safety, and Security of the United Sates Nuclear Stockpile*, November 1999, Washington, D.C.

(1999), *Stockpile Stewardship Program: 30-Day Review*, Department of Energy, Washington, D.C.

(2000), S. Younger, *Nuclear Weapons in the 21st Century*, Los Alamos National Laboratory, Los Alamos, NM.

(2002), J. D. Crouch, *Special Briefing on the Nuclear Posture Review, January 9, 2002*, U.S. Department of Defense, Washington, D.C.

(2004), *History of the United States Strategic Command: June 1, 1992 – October 2, 2002*, United States Strategic Command, Offut Air Force Base, Nebraska

(2004), *Report of the Defense Science Board Task Force on Future Strategic Strike Forces*, Department of Defense, Washington, D.C.

(2005), *Joint Doctrine for Nuclear Operations (draft)*, Joint Chiefs of Staff, Washington, D.C.

(2005), K. H. O'Brien *et al.*, *Sustaining the Nuclear Enterprise – A New Approach*, Lawrence Livermore National Laboratory, Los Alamos National Laboratory, Sandia National Laboratory.

(2006), *Report of the Defense Science Board Task Force on Nuclear Capabilities*, Department of Defense, Washington, D.C.

(2007), *National Security and Nuclear Weapons: Maintaining Deterrence in the 21st Century*, statement by the Secretary of Energy, Secretary of Defense and Secretary of State, Washington, D.C.

(2007), *Report on the Plan for Transformation of the National Nuclear Security Administration Nuclear Weapons Complex*, Department of Energy, Washington, D.C.

Books and journal articles

Adler, E. (1997), 'Seizing the middle ground: constructivism in world politics', *European Journal of International Relations*, vol. 3, no. 3.

Binnendjik, H. and Goodby, J. E. (eds) (1997), *Transforming Nuclear Deterrence*, National Defense University Press, Washington, D.C.

Blechman, B. and Fisher, C. S. (1994), 'Phase Out the Bomb', *Foreign Policy*, no. 97.

Bohlen, A. (2003), 'The Rise and Fall of Arms Control', *Survival*, vol. 45, no. 3.

Bolt, P. J., Coletta, D. V. and Shackelford, C. G. (eds) (2005), *American Defense Policy*, 8th edn, Johns Hopkins University Press, Baltimore.

Bracken, P. (2000), 'The Second Nuclear Age', *Foreign Affairs*, vol. 79, no. 1.

Buchan, G. C. (1994), *U.S. Nuclear Strategy for the Post-Cold War Era*, RAND, Santa Monica.

Buchan, G. C., Matonik, D., Shipbaugh, C. and Mesic, R. (2003), *Future Roles of U.S. Nuclear Forces*, RAND, Arlington.

Bunn, G. and Rhinelander, J. (1997), 'The Duma–Senate Logjam on Arms Control: What Can Be Done?', *Non-Proliferation Review*, vol. 5, no. 1.

Bush, G. H. W. and Scowcroft, B. (1998), *A World Transformed*, Alfred A. Knopf, New York.

Butler, G. L. (1997), 'The General's Bombshell: Phasing out the U.S. Nuclear Arsenal', *The Washington Quarterly*, vol. 20, no. 3.

Checkel, J. T. (1997), *Ideas and International Political Changes: Soviet/Russian Behavior and the End of the Cold War*, Yale University Press, New Haven.

Checkel, J. T. (1998), 'The Constructivist turn in International Relations Theory', *World Politics*, vol. 50, no. 1.

Cimbala, S. (2005), *Nuclear Weapons and Nuclear Strategy*, Routledge, New York.

Clark, M. (2001), 'Seven Worries About START III', *Orbis*, vol. 45, no. 2.

Daalder, I. (1995), 'What Vision for the Nuclear Future?', *The Washington Quarterly*, vol. 18, no. 2.

Daalder, I. and Terriff, T. (eds) (1993), *Rethinking the Unthinkable: New Directions for Nuclear Arms Control*, Frank Cass, London.

Dean, J. (1994), 'The Final stage of Nuclear Arms Control', *The Washington Quarterly*, vol. 17, no. 4.

Deibel, T. (2002), 'The Death of a Treaty', *Foreign Affairs*, vol. 18, no. 5.

Desch, M. C. (1998), 'Culture Clash: Assessing the Importance of Ideas in Security Studies', *International Security*, vol. 23, no. 1.

Deutch, J. (1992), 'The New Nuclear Threat', *Foreign Affairs*, vol. 71, no. 4.

Deutch, J. (2005), 'A Nuclear Posture for Today', *Foreign Affairs*, vol. 84, no. 1.

Dowler, T. and Howard, J. (1991), 'Countering the Well Armed Tyrant: a Modest Proposal for Small Nuclear Weapons', *Strategic Review*, vol. 19, no. 4.

Dowler, T. and Howard, J. (1995), 'Stability in a Proliferated World', *Strategic Review*, vol. 23, no. 2.

Dueck, C. (2004), 'Ideas and Alternatives in American Grand Strategy, 2000–2004', *Review of International Studies*, vol. 30, no. 4.

Dunbabin, J. P. D. (1994), *The Cold War: The Great Powers and Their Allies*, Longman, London.

Fetter, S. and Glaser, C. (2001), 'National Missile Defense and the Future of U.S. Nuclear Weapons Policy', *International Security*, vol. 26, no. 1.

Flournoy, M. and Murdock, C. (1998), *Revitalizing the U.S. Nuclear Deterrent*, Center for Strategic and International Studies, Washington, D.C.

Freedman, L. (1989), *The Evolution of Nuclear Strategy*, Macmillan Press, Basingstoke.

Gaddis, J. L. (1997), *We Now Know: Rethinking Cold War History*, Clarendon Press, Oxford.

Garrity, P. (1991), 'The Depreciation of Nuclear Weapons in International Politics', *Journal of Strategic Studies*, vol. 14, no. 4.

Glaser, C. (1992), 'Nuclear Policy Without an Adversary: U.S. Planning for the Post-Soviet Era', *International Security*, vol. 14, no. 4.

Glaser, C. (1998), 'The Flawed Case for Nuclear Disarmament', *Survival*, vol. 40, no. 1.

Glaser, C. and Fetter, S. (2005), 'Counterforce Revisited: Assessing the Nuclear Posture Review's New Missions', *International Security*, vol. 30, no. 2.

Goldfischer, D. (1998), 'Rethinking the Unthinkable After the Cold War: Toward Long-Term Nuclear Policy Planning', *Security Studies*, vol. 7, no. 4.

Goldman, E. (2001), 'New Threats, New Identities and New Ways of War: The Sources of Change in National Security Doctrine', *Journal of Strategic Studies*, vol. 24, no. 2 (June 2001).

Goldstein, J. and Keohane, R. O. (eds) (1993), *Ideas and Foreign Policy: Beliefs, Institutions and Political Change*, Cornell University Press, Ithaca.

Goodby, J. E. (1990), 'Can Arms Control Survive Peace?' *The Washington Quarterly*, vol. 13, no. 4.

Goodpaster Committee (1995), 'The Declining Utility of Nuclear Weapons', *The Washington Quarterly*, vol. 20, no. 3.

Gottemoeller, R. (1992), *Strategic Arms Control in the Post-START Era*, Brasseys for the IISS, London.

Gottemoeller, R. (2002), 'Arms Control in the New Era', *The Washington Quarterly*, vol. 25, no. 2.

Gray, C. (1992), *House of Cards: Why Arms Control Must Fail*, Cornell University Press, Ithaca.

Gray, C. (1999), *The Second Nuclear Age*, Lynne Rienner, London.

Gray, C. (2000), 'Deterrence in the 21st Century', *Comparative Strategy*, vol. 19, no. 3.

Habiger, E. E. (1997), 'Deterrence in a New Security Environment', *Strategic Forum*, no. 109.

Hall, G. M., Capello, J. T. and Lambert, S. R. (1998), *A Post-Cold War Nuclear Strategy Model*, Institute for National Security Studies, U.S. Air Force Academy, Colorado.

Halperin, M. H. and Clapp, P. A. (2006), *National Security Policy-Making*, Brookings Institution Press, Washington, D.C.

Hippel, F. v. and Fievesen, H. (1990), 'Beyond START: How to Make Much Deeper Cuts', *International Security*, vol. 15, no. 1.

Hopf, T. (1998), 'The Promise of Constructivism in International Relations Theory', *International Security*, vol. 23, no. 1.

Houghton, D. (2007), 'Reinvigorating the Study of Foreign Policy Decision Making: Toward a Constructivist Approach', *Foreign Policy Analysis*, vol. 3, no. 1.

Jervis, R. (1984), *The Illogic of American Nuclear Strategy*, Cornell University Press, Ithaca.

Jordan, A. A., Mazarr, M. J. and Taylor, W. J. (1999), *American National Security*, Johns Hopkins University Press, Baltimore.

Joseph, R. (1997), 'Nuclear Deterrence and Regional Proliferators', *The Washington Quarterly*, vol. 20, no. 3.

Joseph, R. and Lehman, R. (1998), *U.S. Nuclear Policy in the 21st Century: A Fresh Look at National Strategy and Requirements*, National Defense University and Lawrence Livermore National Laboratory, Washington, D.C.

Kaarbo, J. (2003), 'Foreign Policy Analysis in the Twenty-First Century: Back to Comparison, Forward to Identity and Ideas', *International Studies Review*, vol. 5, no. 2

Katzenstein, P. J. (ed.) (1996), *The Culture of National Security: Norms and Identity in World Politics*, Columbia University Press, New York.

Keysen, C., McNamara, R. S. and Rathjens, G. W. (1991), 'Nuclear Weapons after the Cold War', *Foreign Affairs*, vol. 70, no. 4.

Klare, M. (1995), *Rogue States and Nuclear Outlaws*, Hill and Wang, New York.

Kozak, D. C. and Keagle, J. M. (eds) (1988), *Bureaucratic Politics and National Security*, Lynne Rienner Publishers, Boulder.

Krepon, M. (2003), *Cooperative Threat Reduction, Missile Defense and the Nuclear Future*, Palgrave Macmillan, New York.

Kristensen, H. and Handler, J. (1996), 'The USA and Counter-Proliferation: a New and Dubious Role for U.S. Nuclear Weapons', *Security Dialogue*, vol. 27, no. 4.

Kull, S. (1988), *Minds at War: Nuclear Reality and the Inner Conflicts of Defense Policy-makers*, Basic Books, New York.

Lake, A. (1995), 'A Year of Decision: Arms Control and Nonproliferation in 1995', *Non-Proliferation Review*, vol. 2, no. 2.

Lebow, R. and Stein, J. (1994), *We all Lost the Cold War*, Princeton University Press, Princeton, NJ.

Lennon, A. (ed.) (2001), *Contemporary Nuclear Debates*, The MIT Press, Cambridge, MA.

Lepingwell, J. (1995), 'START II and the Politics of Arms Control in Russia', *International Security*, vol. 20, no. 2.

Lieber, K. and Press, D. (2006), 'The Rise of Nuclear Primacy', *Foreign Affairs*, vol. 85, no. 2.

Lindsay, J. M. (1991), *Congress and Nuclear Weapons*, The Johns Hopkins University Press, Baltimore.

Lodal, J. (2001), *The Price of Dominance: the New Weapons of Mass Destruction and Their Challenge to American Leadership*, Council on Foreign Relations Press, New York.

McCauley, M. (2004), *Russia, America and the Cold War*, Longman, London.

McGwire, M. (1994), 'Is There a Future for Nuclear Weapons?', *International Affairs*, vol. 70, no. 2.

Mandelbaum, M. (1979), *The Nuclear Question: the United States and Nuclear Weapons, 1946-1976*, Cambridge University Press, Cambridge.

Mazarr, M. (1992), 'Nuclear Weapons after the Cold War', *The Washington Quarterly*, vol. 15, no. 3.

Mehan, H., Nathanson, C. E. and Skelly, J. M. (1990), 'Nuclear Discourse in the 1980s: The Unravelling Conventions of the Cold War', *Discourse and Society*, vol. 1, no. 2.

Mendelsohn, J. (1997), 'The Current and Future US–Russian Nuclear Arms Control Agenda', *Disarmament Diplomacy*, no. 19.

Millot, M. D. (1994), 'Facing the Emerging Reality of Regional Nuclear Adversaries', *The Washington Quarterly*, vol. 17, no. 3.

Muckerman, J. and Powers, J. (1994), 'Rethink the Nuclear Threat', *Orbis*, vol. 38, no. 1.

Newmann, W. W. (2003), *Managing National Security Policy: The President and the Process*, University of Pittsburgh Press, Pittsburgh.

Nolan, J. (1999), *An Elusive Consensus: Nuclear Weapons and American Security after the Cold War*, Brookings Institution Press, Washington, D.C.

Paulsen, R. A. (1994), *The Role of Nuclear Weapons in the Post-Cold War Era*, Air University Press, Maxwell Air Force Base, Alabama.

Payne, K. (1996), *Deterrence in the Second Nuclear Age*, University of Kentucky Press, Kentucky.

Payne, K. (1998), 'The Case against Nuclear Abolition and for Nuclear Deterrence', *Comparative Strategy*, vol. 17, no. 1.

Payne, K. (2005), 'The Nuclear Posture Review: Setting the Record Straight', *The Washington Quarterly*, vol. 28, no. 3.

Perkovich, G. (2003), 'Bush's Nuclear Revolution: a Regime Change in Nonproliferation', *Foreign Affairs*, vol. 82, no. 2.

Powaski, R. E. (2000), *Return to Armageddon: The United States and the Nuclear Arms Race, 1981-1999*, Oxford University Press, New York.

Price, R. and Reus-Smit, C. (1998), 'Dangerous Liaisons? Critical International Theory and Constructivism', *European Journal of International Relations*, vol. 4, no. 3.

Quinlan, M. (1996), 'The Future of Nuclear Weapons in World Affairs', *The Washington Quarterly*, vol. 20, no. 3.

Robinson, C. P. and Bailey, K. C. (1997), 'To Zero or Not to Zero: a U.S. Perspective on Nuclear Disarmament', *Security Dialogue*, vol. 28, no. 2.

Rogers, P., Whitby, S. and Young, S. (1996), *Nuclear Futures: The Role of Nuclear Weapons in Security Policy*, British American Security Information Council, London.

Sarkesian, S. C. (1989), *U.S. National Security: Policymakers, Processes, and Politics*, Lynne Rienner Publishers, Boulder.

Sauer, T. (2005), *Nuclear Inertia: US Nuclear Weapons Policy after the Cold War*, I.B. Taurus, London.

Schell, J. (1998), *The Gift of Time*, Granta Books, London.

Schell, J. (2000), 'The Folly of Arms Control', *Foreign Affairs*, vol. 79, no. 5.

Schwartzman, D. (1988), *Games of Chicken: Four Decades of U.S. Nuclear Policy*, Praeger, London.

Slocombe, W. (2006), *Democratic Control of Nuclear Weapons*, Policy Paper No. 12, Geneva Centre for the Democratic Control of Armed Forces, Geneva.

Sloss, L. (1991), 'U.S. Strategic Forces after the Cold War: Policies and Strategies', *The Washington Quarterly*, vol. 14, no. 4.

Sloss, L. (2001), 'Deterrence, Defenses, Nuclear Weapons and Arms Control', *Comparative Strategy*, vol. 20, no. 5.

Sokolsky, R. (2002), 'Demystifying the U.S. Nuclear Posture Review', *Survival*, vol. 44, no. 3.

Sokov, N. (1996), 'Russia's Approach to Nuclear Weapons', *The Washington Quarterly*, vol. 23, no. 3.

Sorokin, K. (1994), 'Russia After the Crisis: the Nuclear Strategy Debate', *Orbis*, vol. 38, no. 1.

Stockton, P. (1991), 'The New Game on the Hill: The Politics of Arms Control and Strategic Force Modernization', *International Security*, vol. 16, no. 2.

Tannenwald, N. (1999), 'The Nuclear Taboo: The United States and the Normative Basis of Nuclear Non-Use', *International Organization*, vol. 53, no. 3.

Trubowitz, P., Rhodes, E. and Goldman, E. O. (eds), *The Politics of Strategic Adjustment: Ideas, Institutions and Interests*, Columbia University Press, New York.

Walker, R. (2000), 'What is to be Done About Nuclear Weapons? A Rejoinder', *Security Dialogue*, vol. 31, no. 2.

Wendt, A. (1992), 'Anarchy is What States Make of It: The Social Construction of Power Politics', *International Organization*, vol. 46, no. 2.

Wendt, A. (1995), 'Constructing International Politics', *International Security*, vol. 20, no. 1.

Wendt, A. (1999), *Social Theory of International Politics*, Cambridge University Press, Cambridge.

Wirtz, J. J. and Larsen, J. A. (eds) (2005), *Nuclear Transformation: The New U.S. Nuclear Doctrine*, Palgrave Macmillan, New York.

Wurst, J. and Burroughs, J. (2001), 'Ending the Nuclear Nightmare: a Strategy for the Bush Administration', *World Policy Journal*, vol. XVIII, no. 1.

Yee, A. S. (1996), 'The Causal Effects of Ideas on Policies', *International Organization*, vol. 50, no. 1.

Independent reports

(1996), Report of the Canberra Commission on the Elimination of Nuclear Weapons, Commonwealth of Australia, Canberra.

(1997), The Future of U.S. Nuclear Weapons Policy, National Academy Press, Washington, D.C.

(2003), Differentiation and Defense: An Agenda for the Nuclear Weapons Program, U.S. House of Representatives Republican Policy Committee, Washington, D.C.

Drell, S. D. and Goodby, J. E. (2005), What are Nuclear Weapons for? Recommendations for Restructuring U.S. Strategic Nuclear Forces, Arms Control Association, Washington, D.C.

Goodpaster, A. J. (1997), An American Legacy: Building a Nuclear-Weapon-Free World – Final Report of the Steering Committee Project on Eliminating Weapons of Mass Destruction, Henry L. Stimson Center, Washington, D.C.

Guthe, K. (2002), The Nuclear Posture Review: How is the 'New Triad' New?, Center for Strategic and Budgetary Assessments, Washington, D.C.

Hartung, W. D. and Reingold, J. (2002), About Face: The Role of the Arms Lobby In the Bush Administration's Radical Reversal of Two Decades of U.S. Nuclear Policy, World Policy Institute, New York.

Kristensen, H. (2000), U.S. Nuclear Strategy Reform in the 1990s, Nautilus Institute, Berkeley, CA.

Kristensen, H. (2001), The Matrix of Deterrence: U.S. Strategic Command Force Structure Studies, The Nautilus Institute, Berkeley, CA.

Kristensen, H. (2003), Changing Targets II: A Chronology of U.S. Nuclear Policy Against Weapons of Mass Destruction, Greenpeace, Washington, D.C.

Norris, R. S., Kristensen, H. M. and Paine, C. E. (2004), Nuclear Insecurity: A Critique of the Bush Administration's Nuclear Weapons Policies, National Resources Defense Council, Washington, D.C.

Oelrich, I. (2005), Missions for Nuclear Weapons After the Cold War, Federation of American Scientists, Washington, D.C.

Paine, C. (2004), Weaponeers of Waste, Natural Resources Defense Council, Washington, D.C.

Payne, K. (2001), Rationale and Requirements for U.S. Nuclear Forces and Arms Control, National Institute for Public Policy, Fairfax, VA.

Congressional Research Service reports

Medalia, J. (2004), *'Bunker Busters': Sources of Confusion in the Robust Nuclear Earth Penetrator Debate*, September 22, 2004, Congressional Research Service, Washington, D.C.

Medalia, J. (2004), *Nuclear Testing and Comprehensive Test Ban: Chronology Starting September 1992*, Congressional Research Service, Washington, D.C.

Medalia, J. (2004), *Nuclear Warhead 'Pit' Production: Background and Issues for Congress*, March 29, 2004, Congressional Research Service, Washington, D.C.

Medalia, J. (2004), *Nuclear Weapon Initiatives: Low-Yield R&D, Advanced Concepts, Earth Penetrators, Test Readiness*, Congressional Research Service, Washington, D.C.

Medalia, J. (2006), *Nuclear Weapons Complex Reconfiguration: Analysis of an Energy Department Task Force Report*, February 1, 2006, Congressional Research Service, Washington, D.C.

Medalia, J. (2007), *Nuclear Warheads: The Reliable Replacement Warhead Program and the Life Extension Program*, July 16, 2007, Congressional Research Service, Washington, D.C.

Woolf, A. (1996), *Nuclear Arms Control and Nuclear Threat Reduction: Issues and Agenda*, October 1996, CRS Issue Brief, Congressional Research Service, Washington, D.C.

Woolf, A. (2001), *Arms Control after START II: Next Steps on the US-Russian Agenda*, June 22, 2001, Congressional Research Service, Washington, D.C.

Woolf, A. (2001), *Missile Defense, Arms Control, and Deterrence: A New Strategic Framework*, October 31, 2001, Congressional Research Service, Washington, D.C.

Woolf, A. (2002), *The Nuclear Posture Review: Overview and Emerging Issues*, January 31, 2002, Congressional Research Service, Washington, D.C.

Woolf, A. (2003), *Nuclear Arms Control: the Strategic Offensive Reductions Treaty*, Congressional Research Service, Washington, D.C.

Woolf, A. (2003), *Nuclear Weapons and U.S. National Security: A Need for New Weapons Programs?* September 15, 2003, Congressional Research Service, Washington, D.C.

Woolf, A. (2006), *U.S. Nuclear Weapons: Changes in Policy and Force Structure*, January 2006, Congressional Research Service, Washington, D.C.

Woolf, A. (2007), *Conventional Warheads for Long-Range Ballistic Missiles: Background and Issues for Congress*, June 2007, Congressional Research Service, Washington, D.C.

Index

For Product Safety Concerns and Information please contact our EU representative GPSR@taylorandfrancis.com
Taylor & Francis Verlag GmbH, Kaufingerstraße 24, 80331 München, Germany

www.ingramcontent.com/pod-product-compliance
Lightning Source LLC
Chambersburg PA
CBHW050427280326
41932CB00013BA/2014